Democracy and Autocracy in Eurasia

Democracy and Autocracy in Eurasia

GEORGIA IN TRANSITION

Irakly Areshidze

Michigan State University Press • *East Lansing*

Michigan State University Press
East Lansing, Michigan 48823-5245
www.msupress.msu.edu

 1947· CELEBRATING 60 YEARS of SCHOLARLY PUBLISHING ·2007

Printed and bound in the United States of America.

13 12 11 10 09 08 07   1 2 3 4 5 6 7 8 9 10

LIBRARY OF CONGRESS CATALOGING-IN-PUBLICATION DATA
Areshidze, Irakly.
Democracy and autocracy in Eurasia : Georgia in transition / Irakly Areshidze.
p. cm.
Includes bibliographical references and index.
ISBN 978-0-87013-790-7 (pbk. : alk. paper)
1. Georgia (Republic)—Politics and government—1991- 2.
Democracy—Georgia (Republic) 3. Elections—Georgia (Republic) 4. Georgia
(Republic)—History—Rose Revolution, 2003. I. Title.
JQ1759.7.A95A74 2007
320.94758—dc22
2007015419

Cover design by Erin Kirk New
Cover photo by Goga Chanadiri
Book design by Sharp Des!gns, Inc., Lansing, MI

g green Michigan State University Press is a member of the Green Press
  press Initiative and is committed to developing and encouraging ecolog-
ically responsible publishing practices. For more information about the Green
Press Initiative and the use of recycled paper in book publishing, please visit
www.greenpressinitiative.com.

To my teachers

at Hebron Academy and at Middlebury College, and especially to Murray Dry, Paul Nelson, and the late Eve Adler. By teaching the great books, they helped me understand the philosophy of politics and gave me a grasp of the possibilities and the limits of human life in a political community. What I learned from them is the source of my devotion to individual liberty and a government founded on republican principles. To each one, I owe more than words can express.

Contents

Preface

D emocracy and Autocracy in Eurasia: Georgia in Transition is a book about politics and policymaking. However, the core of my argument does not build on an examination of theories of democratic development or nation-building. The book does not merely raise questions, present facts, and provide formalistic analysis, but combines analysis with stories from personal experiences in Georgian politics, and presents behind-the-scenes details that should help the reader better understand what happened in Georgia. As such, in many respects this book is a break from the norms of present-day political science, and is somewhat an autobiographical narrative. If the work models itself after any other, I would venture to suggest Alexis de Tocqueville's Democracy in America. Fully realizing my limitations, I do not mean to compare myself to Tocqueville as a political philosopher, but rather as an author of a book based on personal observations.

Because of its character, the book is intended for a wide variety of readers. It is my hope that representatives of different groups of readers will find varying elements of the work interesting and educational. I expect that scholars and students of Georgia and the former Soviet Union will find the book useful in assessing political developments in the region since the collapse of Communism. I trust that the book will not only provide these readers with new details and a unique outlook on the events, but also serve as a primary source for political scientists and historians who may one day consider anew the events that took place in Georgia between 1989 and 2006.

At the same time, I anticipate that Georgian citizens who are involved in public life will see in the book a vision for how to balance shorter-term personal goals with long-term strategic ends that can serve the good of the country.

Indeed, I very much hope that all Georgians will see the book as an inspiration to continue their quest to achieve real democracy.

Beyond these groups, I hope the book appeals to young people, increases their interest in politics, and drives them to get involved in shaping the process of democratic self-government. At the same time, I am optimistic that the book will attract the attention of Americans—both those who are involved in foreign policymaking, and also ordinary citizens who care about their country's foreign policy. I believe that the narrative presented in this book offers a unique case study of what America does right and what it does wrong in advancing its noble foreign-policy goals. As such, I hope the findings of this book can help improve the U.S. foreign policymaking process.

Because of my involvement with Georgian politics during part of the time covered in this book, I was fortunate to have first-hand knowledge of events and people that shaped developments in the country. In writing this book, I relied heavily on the notes I kept as part of a personal dairy about the political events in which I was playing a part over the last four years. In order to refresh my memory and gain access to information I did not have, I interviewed or held informal discussions with over one hundred politicians, NGO activists, journalists, academics and intellectuals, businessmen, and religious leaders. The list of the majority of those who were interviewed appears in the bibliography, though a number of individuals are purposefully left off the list because making it publicly known that they spoke with me could very well endanger their careers or even their lives. For that reason, I seldom cite primary sources by name. In the political environment that has developed in Georgia since the Rose Revolution, citizens have to resort to Communist-era tactics of living a double life—one in public and the other in private. My inability to cite those I interviewed is an example of this sad development.

Because my first-hand knowledge plays such a key part in my presentation, it is incumbent that I provide some details about myself. I was born in the Soviet Georgia, when Communism was still a great menace to freedom, and witnessed Ronald Reagan's victory over Soviet totalitarianism from the inside. It was Reagan who enchanted me with politics and its power to change lives for the better. I spent my formative years in the United States, where I moved to attend high school and college at the age of fourteen. Later, as a student at Middlebury College, I was exposed to Aristotelian political science, which does not underestimate the importance of regimes and political systems when considering the fundamental questions of politics. It does not merely try to describe facts, but is prescriptive about political events and speaks to the fundamental question of how men should live.

The influence of such a political science on my thinking is visible throughout these pages. It is evident, for example, in the particular focus that I place on the question of constitutionalism, and the character of the regime that the Constitution creates as the main issue in the democratic transition. Because of the aforementioned reasons, I do not retell facts without value judgments, nor do I stay neutral, since that is neither advisable nor possible. I have tried my very best to stay true to the realities that took place on the ground. While all of the information presented in this book is accurate to the best of my knowledge, some, especially those who might not like the conclusions I reach, may dispute my take on events—not because I am wrong, but because they might not like the picture reality paints.

In the summer of 2000, after graduation from Middlebury, I spent time in Georgia and looked at the nation's political challenges from a new perspective. Georgia was facing huge problems, particularly because its politics were dominated by a group of self-absorbed leaders, all of whom were united in the governing Citizens Union of Georgia (CUG) by nothing more than their desire for power. Furthermore, I saw that if democracy were to take hold, Georgia required significant revisions of its constitutional structure. Even though its Constitution was the best of any republic in the former USSR, it required a much clearer delineation of institutional checks and balances, and limitation on the powers of the president.

That summer, I also saw an opportunity. Notwithstanding the CUG's dominance, change for the better was possible, because Shevardnadze's era was ending (the president was in his last five-year term in office), and something new had to be born no matter what happened. Furthermore, that summer was the beginning of a political movement that ultimately ended the CUG. Though still in its infancy, this movement in the government ranks by businessmen-turned-politicians was extremely encouraging. At the same time, I had learned from Tocqueville that civil society components within the body politic are crucial to the success of republican government. In Georgia, unlike most of the former Soviet republics, you could see key elements of civil society, especially pluralistic media, free business, active citizenry, and a vibrant religious community.

All of this gave me a great deal of hope about the country's future and convinced me that I should play a small role in moving Georgia toward real democracy. As a result, against the advice of some in my family, in the fall of 2001, I became active in a two-pronged process that I hoped would allow me to play a role in advancing democracy in Georgia in the lead-up to the election of a new president in April 2005. The first involved policy work in Washington, focused on trying to advocate on behalf of the possibility of democratic change in Georgia, while the second involved engagement with Georgian politics directly. When in November 2001, I witnessed further expressions of democratic characteristics of the Georgian people—when tens of thousands of ordinary citizens marched to defend Rustavi 2 Television after the government raided its headquarters—I became even more certain that Georgia was worth the fight.

The pages that follow constitute a painful narrative for me, because they tell the story of how a nation was taken from the brink of free government to the reality of a closing society in which authoritarianism is very real. This happened because of the personal ambitions of a small group of politicians who put their own interests above those of the nation. This analysis leaves very little reason for a hopeful future for Georgia in the short term, but I hope that it describes a road forward that can allow the country to succeed in the long term. I also hope that friends of Georgian democracy, both inside and outside the country, will find in this book an avenue towards helping nurture the country's democratic future, and will see in my argument reasons for making an even stronger effort in support of the Georgian people.

I believe that the current Georgian government can avoid the deep political crisis that is becoming obvious to even its most ardent supporters by charting an utterly new political course that would try to redress past mistakes and intentional injustices against its citizens. Nevertheless, it would be wrong to propose concrete solutions without understanding what has happened thus far. As a result, first and foremost, this book aims to provide a comprehensive answer to the question of what went wrong in Georgia—to explain why the country was unable to transition to democracy when the possibility of such a transition was so real. This knowledge can help both Georgians and their foreign friends come up with a pathway toward democracy.

What I aim to do requires honesty. It is irresponsible and dangerous to pretend that everything is going well, in hopes that some imaginary reality will suddenly materialize. In the past, when I have been honest about less-than-exemplary developments in Georgia, some have accused me of wishing the government harm.[1] In reality, the opposite is true: analysts who wish the current government to fail would say nothing about its shortcomings, waiting for its downfall, while those who want to see it succeed are realistic about events unfolding in the country and are offering criticism in hopes of pushing the government to change its course. Therein lies one of the motives for writing this book: I hope that by presenting a real picture of what is happening in Georgia, I can assist others to stave off a disastrous political outcome for Georgia. Although this is not the only goal of the book, I hope to encourage a policy debate both in Georgia and among its friends abroad about the events unfolding in the country, so as to ensure that Georgia can get on the right political track and become a true democratic success story. It is with an eye to helping Georgia salvage its chance for democratic government that I undertook this analytical study of the events that led to the Rose Revolution, so as to ultimately supply policymakers both in Georgia and abroad with the political lessons that are necessary for successful democratization.

My other reason for writing this book has to do with my faith in the Georgian people, and my sincere hope that one day they will secure the truly just and democratic government that they so deserve. Today, many around the world are still under the illusion that the Rose Revolution was a wonderful development for Georgia. As a result, while heralding the revolution as a success story, they have a propensity to ignore the deep political challenges that it created. However, sooner or later, facts on the ground will become too obvious to ignore, and the problems of the new regime will become self-evident. Once this happens, some in the West, as well as most intellectuals in Georgia, will begin to blame these problems on the Georgian people.[2] We saw this once, when so many analysts faulted Georgian culture, history, the Orthodox Church, and first and foremost, the Georgian people, for the failures of the Shevardnadze regime. I hope that telling a full story of what happened before and after the Rose Revolution will prevent similar claims from being made again.

It is true that the public as a whole had a role in bringing about the revolution—the people bought into its rhetoric. That said, it would be greatly unfair, indeed wrong, to blame the Georgian culture, history, or people for the new government's failures, especially when the new postrevolutionary political system gives citizens even less real political authority than they had before. My goal, therefore, is to show that Georgians are a good people, and to point to the true origins of Georgia's problems. It is my hope that this account will explain why Georgians truly can live, and live well, under a real, representative democracy.

Finally, I wrote this book because I love America, the country that offered me opportunities I could have never experienced anywhere else in the world. I respect those U.S. leaders who, after the attacks of September 11, pressed for a morally clear foreign policy grounded on America's founding political principles. However, this foreign-policy vision has not always been implemented with full success. This narrative tells of certain collective truths about what works and what does not when it comes to building democracy and promoting freedom abroad. In other words, this is not only a story of what happened in Georgia, but is also an attempt to use Georgia as an example for understanding how to successfully secure free institutions through nation-building. I believe that this understanding has implications for the monumental American struggle to advance democracy in the Middle East and elsewhere around the world.

Failure in this effort is unacceptable, because liberty is the only antidote to the totalitarian ideology of radical Islam, the root cause of global terrorism. Because I believe that there are important lessons, applicable globally, that one can glean from the Georgian experience with regard to the development of democratic institutions, I hope that this book will contribute to the success of other U.S. efforts to promote democracy. Thus, while I criticize the U.S. administration's actions in Georgia, I strongly believe that America's morally clear foreign policy is fundamentally the only workable approach today. I want this criticism to help the policymakers in implementing this vision, which both is true to American founding principles and can provide for the security of all free peoples.

Much of my work on this manuscript was done while I was living in Tbilisi in 2005, though some parts of the book were updated in late 2006. When this book becomes available to the public, I will be away from Georgia, living in Washington, D.C., pursuing a career with no connection to Georgian politics. However, I leave behind in Georgia my father, other members of my family, and many colleagues and friends. I am full of concern for what my decision to publish this work will mean for them. If the claims I make about Mikheil Saakashvili's government are at all accurate, their well-being may be endangered. I hope that I am wrong in being concerned, but only time will tell.

Acknowledgments

I could never thank all the people who helped me bring this work to completion. First and foremost, I owe a huge debt of gratitude to numerous sources, both Georgians and foreigners. The list of many of my primary sources appears in the bibliography, but the identity of others must remain confidential to protect their well-being. These sources made this book possible because without them, I could have never gathered the information I needed for its completion.

This book also would not have been possible without the encouragement and support of my friends and colleagues at the Partnership for Social Initiatives (PSI), a think tank in Tbilisi I helped found in 2000. In particular, Devi Khechinashvili, Gia Areshidze, and the late Tina Danelia played a crucial role in framing my thinking. They read and reread various versions of my manuscript several times, listened to me complain about challenges of writing, and encouraged me to carry on when I thought that finishing was impossible. In many respects, this book is a product of our mutual thought and I am grateful for their support. In February 2007, Tina lost a courageous battle to cancer. With her passing, Georgia lost one of its most vigorous advocates of political and economic freedom. I do sincerely hope this work will contribute to moving Georgia toward the values of freedom and democracy, to which Tina devoted so much in her life.

Nino Lezhava, a research fellow at PSI, ably led a team that consisted of Levan Pachkoria, Lasha Bliadze, Nini Davitashvili, and Meri Machitidze, who helped me with my research. They contributed tireless hours to monitoring the media for news on political developments after the Rose Revolution, to checking historical data, and to conducting interviews. I also owe a word of thanks to Sergo Papashvili, the security officer at PSI's office, for spending many evenings waiting for me to finish writing, well past regular hours. Thanks are also due to the National Endowment for Democracy (NED), whose support to PSI made it possible to conduct key elements of the research that is used in Part Three of this book.

Many others friends and colleagues read the manuscript in full or in part, and their comments greatly helped improve this work. Charles H. Fairbanks's feedback, suggestions, and constructive criticism were invaluable in strengthening my arguments, even when he did not always agree with the case that I was making. At short notice, Matt Christ scrupulously edited the penultimate version of the book in its entirety. I never could have finished without his assistance. Matt and Elisabeth Brocking, who also read the entire manuscript and provided helpful and valued advice, served the United States exceptionally well in their time at the U.S. Embassy in Georgia. Pikria Chikhradze and David Gamkrelidze provided vital feedback on many chapters helped me understand the exact nature of certain crucial developments, and assisted me in remembering developments few in Georgia could recall. Thanks are also due to Miriam Lanskoy, Cory Welt, Thomas Pangle, Murray Dry, Maia Chuchulashvili, Marina Muskhelishvili, David Kochel, and Toby Dougherty for thoughtful comments on various parts of the book.

I thank Norman Graham and the anonymous reviewers of Michigan State University Press for accepting this book for publication. Their valuable comments greatly improved this work. I am also grateful to Julie Loehr, Kristine Blakeslee, and Annette Tanner for their support and assistance in preparing this manuscript for publication. I appreciate Bonnie Cobb's scrupulous copy editing of the manuscript, which significantly improved its quality.

Because this book completes a particular stage in my career, I wish to extend my appreciation to those individuals who contributed to my work on and in Georgia in a variety of ways. David Gamkrelidze afforded me amazing opportunities to experience politics from the inside. For his friendship and trust, I owe him greatly. For what he, Pikria Chikhradze and his other colleagues are trying to do for Georgia, they deserve great admiration. When I first arrived in Washington in 2000, Charles H. Fairbanks guided me through a city that seemed like a maze and helped me understand how to shape policy. He has been a wonderful mentor and friend ever since. In addition to the aforementioned, in Washington, Elena Suhir, Gary Schmit, Ellen Bork, Fiona Hill, Enders Wimbush, Dan McKivergan, Dan Twining, Mike Murphy, Jim Pitts, Brian Hook, Monty Brown, Michael Horowitz, Zeyno Baran, Miriam Lanskoy, Paul Joyal, Mamuka Tsereteli, and David Soumbadze have been valuable mentors and friends, and to each I express my gratitude.

Friendship, Aristotle teaches us, is one of the most important of human virtues and a vital element of the good life. Over ten years ago, Toby Dougherty helped me understand why Aristotle was right. His example is always an inspiration, and I can only hope to be as good of a friend to him as he has been to me. One of my great fortunes in life is that I have been blessed with an incredible group of friends from high school and college, as well as from years in politics and business. They have helped me be happy and stay sane, especially as I brought this work to conclusion. Each of them knows who they are, and to each I want to express my appreciation and love, for putting up with my bad habits and always encouraging me to pursue my dreams, even as I sometimes made career choices that seemed crazy to some.

My brother, Giorgi Areshidze, has been a part of this project from the start. He read every chapter of this book numerous times, helped research democratic theory, and pushed me to clarify my complicated arguments. I have been blessed to have a brother who shares my passion for politics, political philosophy, and a free way of life. His devotion to scholastic inquiry is worthy of great praise, and no one could ever ask for a better sibling.

My parents, Gia Areshidze and Nana Smith, did what was almost unthinkable in Georgia nine months after the collapse of the Soviet Union, when they sent me halfway around the world to pursue an education in America. My life would have been very different had they not pushed me in this direction throughout my early years, or had they hesitated to let me go. This was undoubtedly the hardest, yet the best decision they could have made. I would have never gotten to the United States, nor succeeded there, had it not been for Kathy and Jared Cadwell. By bringing me to the United States, they changed my life forever in ways that I could never express. Ever since then, Kathy, Jared, Celia, and Parker have been more than a second family to me for over half my life. I thank all of them, along with Ken Smith and the rest of my family in Georgia, for their many years of support and devotion.

None of the aforementioned individuals, or any others who contributed to my writing, are responsible for any results or conclusions. All faults are due to only my own limitations.

Introduction

On November 23, 2003, with tens of thousands of protesters in front of the nation's Parliament demanding his departure, Georgia's longtime president Eduard Shevardnadze resigned. He left office a year and a half before the end of his term and handed power to a young, charismatic, and erratic former protégé, Mikheil Saakashvili—who along with his allies Nino Burdjanadze and Zurab Zhvania had organized demonstrations against Shevardnadze, alleging fraud during the November 2 parliamentary elections. This change of power was dubbed the Rose Revolution, because of the roses that Saakashvili and his supporters carried with them when on November 22 they stormed the first session of the newly elected Parliament.

The protests that eventually brought down Shevardnadze in this extraconstitutional transition of power had been months, if not years, in the making. As early as the fall of 2002, activists at several nongovernmental organizations (NGOs) advocated using revolutionary tactics against President Shevardnadze. These groups wanted to emulate the example of Serbia, where the dictator Slobodan Milosevic was overthrown through public protests. In Serbia, the so-called NGO sector, with assistance from George Soros and other Western donors, played a very active role in mobilizing the Serbian public against Slobodan Milosevic. Initially, Georgian NGOs did not find support for their initiative from political leaders. Saakashvili began to lean their way only when he saw the revolutionary path as a way of gaining power, though he did not fully commit to the revolution even when he launched a wave of protests immediately after the November 2 elections. Indeed, the storming of Parliament was as much a spontaneous event as a planned exercise, as I discuss in detail later.

Nonetheless, when Shevardnadze finally resigned, an idea born in the wishful imagination of a small group of NGO activists had become reality. Furthermore, the international media, political analysts, and even political leaders warmly welcomed the outcome, and the opportunity to describe the Rose Revolution as a perfect way to promote democratic change and institute democracy in the former Soviet Union and elsewhere around the world, such as the broader Middle East.

When it happened in 2003, the Rose Revolution was quite possibly the single most important political event in the former Soviet space since the collapse of Communism in 1991. Up until that point, in virtually every republic in the Commonwealth of Independent States (CIS),[1] the succession from the Soviet-era apparatchik national leader to a younger-generation politician happened through what has been called "managed transition." This was the case in Russia in 1999 when President Boris Yeltsin handed over power to a chosen heir, the KGB-trained Vladimir Putin, and in Azerbaijan, when Ilham Aliev took over for his father, Gaidar, when the latter fell ill in 2003. In many other republics, transition of power had not taken place at all, with leaders managing to stay in office through dictatorial and neo-Communist tactics. The most glaring examples of this include Belarus and countries in Central Asia.

The Rose Revolution was perceived and heralded as a break from this pattern. Political change was spontaneous, bloodless, and popular with the people, which made it particularly appealing to the international community. It brought to power leaders who on the surface had democratic credentials and appeared to be the sort of individuals one wanted to see in power in transitional countries. However, it would have made sense to pay more attention to the background of those who led the protest movement, since their experiences in the government of the very man they had just removed raised serious questions about their democratic credentials.

Another reason why political leaders and intellectuals welcomed the Rose Revolution was that it gave them hope that the drift toward dictatorial rule could be broken in other post-Soviet countries as well. Supporters of the Rose Revolution claimed that their hopes had become reality when Ukrainians took to the streets in 2004 to ensure a free and fair presidential election, and when the opposition in Kyrgyzstan used mass protests to depose an unpopular president after fraudulent parliamentary elections, because in both countries opposition leaders and the public at large pointed to Georgia as their inspiration. For this reason, the evaluation of the Rose Revolution is of interest not only to those who care for Georgia, but to anyone who is concerned with democracy-building in transitional or authoritarian societies.

In Ukraine, protests were necessary to prevent President Leonid Kuchma from handing power to a chosen successor against the wishes of the majority of

Ukrainians. In Kyrgyzstan, democracy was merely a façade, much like in Serbia under Milosevic, and the only way of opening up political space even a little bit was to remove President Askar Akayev through whatever means were available.

In Georgia's case, however, questions remain as to whether democracy was truly under threat from Shevardnadze, and whether it was really necessary to remove him extraconstitutionally. It is not at all clear that Georgia was on its way to following the post-Soviet pattern of drifting toward dictatorial rule, which would have justified the use of any and all methods to prevent Shevard-nadze from either anointing a successor or staying in power for an extended period of time, or whether the country might not have broken with the Soviet pattern even if the constitutionally decreed transition process been followed.

In late 2003, Georgia was a semi-pluralistic and open democracy, albeit a chaotic and far from perfect one. It had a vibrant, free media, and a politically active business sector that helped nurture political pluralism. The newly elected legislature was going to be controlled by opposition parties even if the fraudulent official results had stayed in place.[2] President Shevardnadze was unpopular and was bound to leave office by April 2005, when his term was scheduled to end. The heads of the four opposition parties that had gained seats in Parliament were the most frequently mentioned potential successors, and it was unlikely that a pro-Shevardnadze candidate could have beaten any one of them in the race for president.[3]

As a result, the Georgian political environment was very different from other republics in the Newly Independent States (NIS), even before the Rose Revolution. I believe that Georgia could have stuck to the constitutional rules and procedures and still escaped the post-Soviet pattern, while simultaneously going through its first *legal* transfer of power in post-independence history.[4] This could have been an important step toward consolidation of the country's democratic institutions, promotion of the respect for the rule of law, and preservation of political pluralism that had become the hallmark of Georgian politics since 2001.

Instead, Saakashvili and his allies went outside of the constitutional frame-work and removed the president through a "revolution," and then imple-mented decisions that made democratic consolidation in Georgia nearly impossible at this stage. Unlike their Ukrainian counterparts, who ultimately achieved their end of free and fair elections through a court order, Georgian revolutionaries chose a route that benefited Saakashvili's personal interests and, though popular with the Georgian people at the time, greatly damaged the Georgian body politic in the long term. Given what has happened in Georgia since November 2003, my intention is to argue that the "revolutionary" change was actually a deterrent to freedom, because democracy is far less secure in Georgia today than it was before the revolution.

Considering the question of whether the revolution was necessary, and what it meant for the Georgian people and their statehood, was not the concern of the international media that converged on Tbilisi during the Rose Revolution. The media, driven by what Richard Carlson called "sixties-sentimentalit[ies],"[5] was simply enchanted with the idea of peaceful protests. It compared the uprising to "People Power" in the Philippines, and heralded Georgia's democratic "success story." The media provided Saakashvili with a powerful megaphone to present his achievement, and journalists from as far away as Japan and China were in Tbilisi to cover his ascent to power. The major exception to this was the *Wall Street Journal*, which called the revolution by its proper name—"popular coup."[6]

While one could excuse the media's reaction, given that it was consumed by the moment and lacked real knowledge of Georgian politics, political analysts who had worked on Georgia for years also ignored the realities. They praised Saakashvili, Burdjanadze, and Zhvania as if these three were incarnations of George Washington, James Madison, and Alexander Hamilton. It was striking that in their commentary, these analysts often suggested that Shevardnadze was some sort of bloody dictator who had ruled with an iron fist, even though only months before, many of them were correctly calling Shevardnadze the most democratic of the post-Soviet leaders.

Zeyno Baran of the Nixon Center declared that "the November 23 democratic revolution—not coup—in Georgia . . . is an historic moment. Demonstrators succeeded in peacefully enforcing their constitutional rights and refused to let the election be stolen. Georgia may now become a beachhead in U.S. efforts to promote democracy throughout the greater Middle East." She went on to argue that "Georgian opposition's methods of defending their democratic future should teach lessons to opposition groups across the region. . . . When democratic forces entered the Georgian parliament on November 22, their hands were in the air to show that they were not holding arms, but only roses."[7]

Baran was far from the only one. David Phillips of the Council on Foreign Relations wrote that "Georgia's Rose Revolution . . . represents a victory for liberal democracy over cynicism."[8] Stephen Blank, a professor at the U.S. Army War College, wrote that "the United States has achieved an opportunity to help promote a democracy that came to power peacefully and to use it as an example throughout the CIS."[9] Ariel Cohen of the Heritage Foundation agreed, writing that "the Georgian revolution may be a model to dissolve dictatorships in other parts of the former Soviet empire, where the surge of freedom, started in 1989 with the collapse of the Berlin Wall, has not been completed."[10]

Even those commentators who were cautious in their analysis because they thought the new government still had a great deal to prove nevertheless saw much that was positive in the revolution. Writing in the *Journal of Democracy*,

Charles Fairbanks called the developments in Georgia "inspiring," from which democracy activists around the world had much to learn.[11] Meanwhile, calling Shevardnadze's legacy "dismal," Charles King declared in *Foreign Affairs* that Georgia had an opportunity to become a "beacon of hope for a troubled region."[12]

This positive analysis often did not change even after the new Georgia began to show its true face. For example, testifying in front of the Subcommittee on European Affairs of the U.S. Senate Committee on Foreign Relations about a year and a half after the November 2003 events, Bruce Jackson stated: "Georgia's democratic revolution is only slightly less well-known than Ukraine's and is succeeding against even longer odds. Georgia, under the leadership of President Misha Saakashvili, has finished an extraordinary first year of reform, which saw the breakaway province of Adjaria reunited with the constitutional government in Tbilisi. By all indicators, such as its qualification for participation within the Millennium Challenge Account, Georgia is delivering on its commitments to economic reform and the democratic transformation of its society and government."[13]

World leaders were also full of praise for Saakashvili. At the G-8 Summit in June 2004, which was largely devoted to democracy promotion as part of President Bush's Broader Middle East Initiative, Georgia and the G-8 signed a "Compact to Promote Transparency and Combat Corruption," which praised the new Georgian government's alleged fight against corruption, and its steps to promote good governance. French President Jacques Chirac even permitted the appointment of his ambassador to Georgia—Salome Zurabishvili, who is of Georgian descent—as Saakashvili's foreign minister, while keeping her on the French payroll.[14] The greatest praise for the Rose Revolution, however, came from the U.S. government. Indeed, both in Georgia and abroad, conspiracy theories about the alleged U.S. role in bringing about the revolution have been abundant, though there is little evidence to support this allegation. That said, after November 2003 the Bush administration hailed the revolution as a successful example of its democracy-promotion strategy. President Bush and other officials have often cited Georgia, along with Iraq, Afghanistan, Ukraine, and Lebanon, among countries where the president's policies are helping bring about democratic change.[15] To back these declarations, the administration has poured hundreds of millions of dollars into aid to Georgia since the revolution (on top of over a billion in aid that went to Georgia under Shevardnadze). What is more troubling is that it has often ignored the facts on the ground and tried to present a far prettier picture of Georgia under Saakashvili than reality permits.

Less than a month after his inauguration as president in January 2004, Saakashvili traveled to the United States, where Bush declared that he was "impressed by this leader . . . by his vision . . . by his courage [and] heartened by the fact that we have such a strong friend, a friend with whom we share values."[16] Then, a little over a year later, in May of 2005, Bush visited Georgia himself. In a speech in Tbilisi attended by tens of thousands of Georgians, it seemed that he built on the praise for the Rose Revolution originally offered by Zeyno Baran. Speaking of Georgia's fight against Communism, and of April 9, 1991, when the country declared its independence from the Soviet Union, the president said: "On that historic day, you reclaimed your sovereignty, but the hopeful start you made was not fulfilled. So 18 months ago, Georgians returned to this square to complete the task you began in 1989. You gathered here armed with nothing but roses and the power of your convictions, and you claimed your liberty. And because you acted, Georgia is today both sovereign and free, and a beacon of liberty for this region and the world."[17]

The key problem with this remark was that it was based on a wholly inaccurate understanding of Georgia's recent history. Georgians won their freedom from Communism in 1989–1991, and the republic was internationally recognized in 1992. Meanwhile, Georgian sovereignty was secured, with tremendous assistance from the United States, in the years that followed. If any one year can be seen as particularly crucial, it would be 1995, when the Georgian Constitution was ratified. The Rose Revolution had nothing to do with the Georgian struggle for freedom or the country's sovereignty. The leaders of the Rose Revolution were never a part of the pro-independence movement, and the spirit of that struggle was not an inspiration for their actions in November 2003. Saying otherwise was a huge disservice to those who had fought and in some cases died for Georgia's independence in the late 1980s and early 1990s.

The inaccurate remark about the Rose Revolution securing Georgian sovereignty and freedom was a perfect example of how the Bush administration has used, or misused, Georgia in building a case for the success of the president's foreign policy—misrepresenting reality in order to make its argument about success and democracy in the aftermath of the Rose Revolution more plausible. Unfortunately, this sort of misrepresentation gives the president's detractors, many of whom do not believe in the democracy-promotion agenda, ammunition to question the sincerity of the president's claims about spreading democracy and freedom.

In his speech, the president also endorsed the view that Georgia is a model for others to follow: "Your most important contribution is your example. In recent months, the world has marveled at the hopeful changes taking place from Baghdad to Beirut to Bishkek. But before there was a Purple Revolution in Iraq, or an Orange Revolution in Ukraine, or a Cedar Revolution in Lebanon, there was the Rose Revolution in Georgia. Your courage is inspiring democratic reformers and sending a message that echoes across the world: Freedom will be the future of every nation and every people on Earth." Later on in the speech, speaking on the same subject, he told Georgians that people around the world "have been inspired by your example and they take hope in your success."

With these remarks, by making developments in Georgia comparable to Iraq (and presumably Afghanistan as well), President Bush tied the Rose Revolution and its aftermath to what is arguably the most important part of his legacy—his courageous project to promote democracy abroad. The president in effect declared that the success of his democracy agenda should be judged at least in part on whether Georgia is able to consolidate its democratic institutions under Saakashvili. That was a very risky and unnecessary thing to do, in light of what the Rose Revolution meant for Georgia's democracy and what has happened in the country since Saakashvili came to power.

There are two things that those who praised the Rose Revolution, including President Bush, ignored—that the revolution was not democratic by any measure, and that free and fair elections were by no means the central concern of the protest leaders.

Revolutions in general, from demonstrations to violence, are carried out by extraconstitutional means, and for this reason they do not register majority and minority opinions. In most cases, there is no way of knowing how much support there is for a revolution or for its leaders. However, in the case of Georgia's Rose Revolution, individuals leading the demonstrations did not have the right to speak for even a majority of those who voted in the elections, let alone all Georgians. According to the U.S.-funded parallel vote tabulations (PVT) of the November election results, which were universally acknowledged as being more accurate than the official results, parties led by Saakashvili, Burdjanadze, and Zhvania received only about 37 percent of the popular vote. By contrast, four other parties (two opposition and two governmental) that had enough votes to gain seats in Parliament strongly opposed the revolution, and together received over 50 percent. Thus, the leaders of the revolution were speaking for only a little more than one-third of the Georgian voters, while its opponents spoke for a majority.[18]

By removing Shevardnadze through extraconstitutional means, revolutionaries were able to grab 100 percent of power and authority, even though the majority of the country's voters had just voted for parties that opposed Saakashvili and his allies. This reality should have raised serious questions about how democratic the Rose Revolution actually was, since democracy, at its core, is based not on street protests but on majority rule through the ballot box. The best measurement available of the opinion of the Georgian people—an honest count of the election results, which gave the two revolutionary parties 37 percent—shows that the leaders of the protests had nothing near a mandate from the majority.[19]

Lack of majority support was one crucial element that made Georgia's Rose Revolution very different from the Philippines' "People Power," which the revolutionary leaders and their supporters abroad most often cited to justify their actions. In the Philippines, popular protests were a vehicle for Corazon Aquino, the overwhelming winner of the *presidential* elections, to take control of the office that was rightly hers. By contrast in Georgia, protests were used to give executive power, through illegitimate means, to individuals who had failed to win a majority in *parliamentary* elections. Thus, in Georgia the revolution was a power grab, albeit a somewhat popular one, whereas in the Philippines people went into the streets to actually defend the real election outcome. The media, along with those officials and analysts in Washington and elsewhere who became enchanted with the Georgian version of "People Power," ignored this vital difference. In contrast, the situation in Ukraine in 2004 paralleled the Philippines much more than Georgia in 2003.

Meanwhile, had revolutionary leaders been truly concerned with fraud and not with the political power they had just failed to win at the ballot box, they could have accepted one of a number of solutions, short of Shevardnadze's removal, that were presented to them. After several days of protests, Shevardnadze consented to a proposal that called for new elections to be held by late spring of 2004. This would have made the newly elected Parliament a lame-duck legislature for a brief six-month period. This idea was floated by opposition leaders who had refused to join the revolutionaries. The proposal entailed waiting for several months before holding new elections in order to solve systemic problems that had made the elections so problematic, especially the inaccurate electoral lists that prevented tens of thousands of eligible citizens from voting. After Saakashvili rejected this proposal, Shevardnadze accepted a more radical alternative, which involved his own resignation immediately after new parliamentary elections.

Either one of these compromises would have had several benefits, especially solving the problem of fraudulent November 2 elections—a very real problem that hurt all opposition parties, not just those supporting the revolution. However, a compromise would have simultaneously protected the rights of those citizens who did not vote for Saakashvili, Burdjanadze, and Zhvania, and who did not wish to see them gain all political power in Georgia through extralegal means. These citizens had the option of voting for parties led by these individuals, but they had refused to do so. It seems that to those who praised the "democratic revolution," these voters really did not matter. This is particularly striking given that by any measure, those who did not vote for the revolutionary leaders far outnumbered those voters who were disenfranchised by fraud. It is true that electoral fraud diminished every real vote, but the issue is that the voters who supported those parties that opposed the protests were simply ignored. A compromise would have protected both the revolutionary voters and their opponents.

At the same time, a compromise would have ensured transition from She-vardnadze to a younger leader in accordance with the constitutional process, rather than the extraconstitutional means that were used as a result of Shevard-nadze's "popular" removal. Having a succession happen through the Constitu-tion was crucial for Georgia's hopes of consolidating its democratic institutions.

The greatest benefit of either compromise was that it would have prevented the country's rapid collapse into a state of one-man rule under a revolutionary government. Ultimately, that may be the most important issue in judging the revolution, because events in Georgia after November 2003 developed in an extremely undemocratic manner. Almost immediately after winning the spe-cial presidential election in January 2004, Saakashvili amended the Constitu-tion to create a Russian-style, hyper-presidential system of government, in which his powers became unlimited while those of the legislative and judiciary branches were greatly weakened. His administration has governed with com-plete disregard for the rule of law, jailing dozens of individuals without ever charging them with a crime, and equal disregard for the sanctity of private property, extorting over a quarter-billion U.S. dollars from businessmen and former government officials in exchange for their freedom. Meanwhile, politi-cal pluralism in Georgia has diminished greatly since the revolution, while free media is under constant threat. And these are just a few problems that have arisen, though they were all very predictable.

Thinking about Georgia and its transition to democracy is not only impor-tant because of the attention paid to the Rose Revolution by international polit-ical analysts or the Bush administration. The question of consolidation of Georgian democracy is of great geopolitical importance as well. Georgia is the place where Europe meets Asia, and because of this, for centuries the country has been of interest to various powers who wished to advance their empires either from Europe into Asia or vice versa. This is true even today, with four countries—Russia, Iran, Turkey, and the United States—vying for influence in Georgia. Each has a stake in the success or failure of the democratic consolida-tion process there, making Georgia into a key battleground in the war to make the world safer for freedom.

Immediately after the collapse of the Soviet Union, U.S. interest in Geor-gia was largely connected to the energy resources found in the Caspian Sea and Central Asia. The Caspian Energy Strategy, as envisioned by the Clinton administration, proposed oil and gas routes through Georgia as the only viable means for bringing these energy resources to the European market. The suc-cess of this project was crucial in allowing the West to take advantage of the most significant untapped energy reserves in the world. To bring this about, both the Clinton and the Bush administrations devoted disproportionate political and financial resources to allow Georgia to develop into a stable and democratic nation.

In 2004, with the completion of the BTC oil pipeline, which originates at the Caspian Sea and transports oil through Georgia to the Turkish seaport of Ceyhan, the initial component of this strategy was finally realized. However after September 11, Georgia's strategic importance moved far beyond energy. Washington began to see the Caucasus as an indispensable gateway to Central Asia and Afghanistan, and an important corridor to the broader Middle East. To quote Charles King, "A stable and democratic Georgia is the linchpin of U.S. policy in the Caucasus, and the Caucasus, in turn, is a critical part of the strategic future of Eurasia and the greater Middle East."[20] As a result, the U.S. stake in the success of Georgia's statehood and democracy grew disproportionately.

Whereas the United States and Turkey are both keenly interested in a free Georgia that could join NATO and become the outpost of democracy in this region, totalitarian mullahs in Iran and especially the KGB thugs in Russia hope that Georgia will fail in consolidating its democracy and statehood, so as to hinder the spread of democracy in the Caucasus and Central Asia. For this reason, the question of Georgian democracy has vast geopolitical and strategic implications, and this should matter even to those who do not subscribe to President Bush's democracy-advancement agenda.

In the account that follows, I aim to show how fifteen years of failed political leadership three times destroyed conditions that were very favorable for complete transition to democratic rule. In telling this story, I have divided the narrative into three parts.

Part One—Three Openings for Democracy in Georgia—is a historical account of Georgia's three separate opportunities to consolidate its democracy between 1989 and 2001. The first opportunity arose in the period between 1989 and 1992, at the height of the movement for independence. Georgians failed to take advantage of it because of the failed policies of the country's first post-Soviet president, Zviad Gamsakhurdia. The second democratic opening was brought about by Eduard Shevardnadze in 1995, with the ratification of a new Constitution. By 2000 this opening had closed, largely because of the rise of the so-called "young reformers," who gained power under Shevardnadze. The third opening came with the collapse of the Citizens Union of Georgia (CUG), the party of Shevardnadze and the "young reformers," in 2002. This gave rise to a level of political pluralism not seen anywhere in the former Soviet Union, and once again made transition to democracy possible in Georgia. Unfortunately, this opening was also not realized.

Part Two—Chaotic Pluralism on the Brink of a Consolidated Democracy—considers politics in Georgia during the period of this third democratic opening (2001–2003), the period that immediately preceded the Rose Revolution, and provides a detailed account of how Georgia failed to take advantage of it. To tell the story of this period, I analyze the 2002 local-government elections; preparations by parties for the November 2003 elections, as well as attempts to unite the opposition; active U.S. engagement in promoting free and fair elections; and planning undertaken by the NGOs toward a revolution. This section also includes a chapter about the final stretch of the campaign prior to the November 2 vote, and a chapter with a detailed narrative of the revolutionary events of November 2–23, 2003. I hope that a detailed account of this period will show how unique and real the third democratic opening was, and how close Georgia came to consolidating its democracy.

Part Three—Dangers of New Authoritarianism—examines Georgian political developments after the Rose Revolution. Whereas the first two parts are largely chronological narratives, this one is thematic, with a particular eye toward those actions of the government that have had an impact on the level and the quality of democratic governance, pluralism, and political liberty. This section offers a blunt but fair analysis of what the revolution did to political freedom in Georgia, and provides evidence in defense of my proposition that the country has moved dramatically backward, rather than forward, since Shevardnadze's resignation.

In the Conclusion, I discuss what Georgia's experiences following the collapse of the Soviet Union in general, and the events surrounding the Rose Revolution in particular, have to teach us about democratic change. My contention is that this revolution was the worst possible outcome for Georgia because it inevitably closed the country's third democratic opening, while Saakashvili's constitutional changes set Georgia's political developments back by at least a decade.

There will undoubtedly be readers who will disagree with the facts, analytical observations, and conclusions presented in this book. For them, the work should spark a debate about what is happening in Georgia and what is the best course for the country's development. If there is a different argument to be made about events unfolding in Georgia, it would be best for the country for this case to be presented.

There will also be other readers who will agree with the facts and analysis of this work, but disagree with the conclusions as to what this means for Georgia and its future. Many of these readers may point to the fact that in 2006, Georgia still compares quite well to most other countries in the CIS. They may argue that the democratic process in Georgia is still in far better shape than in other parts of the former USSR.

This would certainly be an accurate assessment, because Georgia in 2006 is nothing like Uzbekistan and Belarus, or even Moldova and Armenia. Indeed, by most criteria that matter, Georgia looks much more democratic than any of these countries and most others in the CIS. However, the idea of judging democracy in Georgia in a comparative context vis-à-vis other former Soviet republics simply misses the point. The argument presented in the pages that follow is based on the notion that in November 2003 Georgia was on the verge of real democracy, and as such it was fundamentally different from almost all other states in the CIS.[21] As a result, the decisive question should not be whether Georgia in 2006 looks better or worse than other post-Soviet states, but instead how it looks when compared to Georgia in 2003.

The Rose Revolution should be judged based on whether it moved Georgia closer to or further from real democracy. The evidence presented in this work shows convincingly that democracy in Georgia is much further away at this time than it was before Shevardnadze's removal. If I am right, then the question of where Georgia stands when compared to other countries in the former USSR is really beside the point as far as assessing the effects of the revolution are concerned. Instead, we should analyze Georgia and the Rose Revolution on its own terms, as this work tries to do.

Cast of Characters

ASLAN ABASHIDZE, autocratic leader of the Autonomous Republic of Adjara (1992–2004)

GIA BARAMIDZE, minister of defense (2004), minister of interior (2003–2004), member of Parliament of Georgia (1995–2003)

GIGA BOKERIA, co-head of the Liberty Institute, member of Parliament (2004–present)

MATTHEW J. BRYZA, director, Caucasus and Central Asia, U.S. National Security Council (2001–2005), deputy assistant secretary of state (2005–present)

NINO BURDJANADZE, speaker of Parliament (2001–present), served as acting president (2003–2004)

GIA CHANTURIA, chairman of the National Democratic Party, senior figure in the Georgian independence movement; assassinated on December 3, 1994

ZURAB CHIABERASHVILI, chairman of the Central Election Commission (2004), head of the organization Free Elections (2003)

PIKRIA CHIKHRADZE, senior figure in the opposition New Rights Party (2001–present), member of Parliament of Georgia (1995–present), leader of the student pro-independence movement

KOBA DAVITASHVILI, general secretary of National Movement (2001–2004), member of Parliament of Georgia (1999–present), leader of left-wing Conservative Party (2004–present)

NANA DEVDARIANI, chairman of the Central Election Commission (2003), public defender of Georgia (2000–2003)

DAVID GAMKRELIDZE, leader of the opposition New Rights Party (2001–present); leader of the rebellion against Zhvania in Parliament (2000–2001);

member of Parliament of Georgia (1999–present); founder, chairman, and chief executive officer, Aldagi Insurance Company (1990–1999)

ZVIAD GAMSAKHURDIA, first president of Georgia (1990–1992); killed himself on December 31, 1993

INGA GRIGOLIA, leading Georgian journalist (Mze TV, 2003–2004, and Imedi TV, 2004–present)

IRAKLI IMNAISHVILI, Georgian journalist (Mze TV)

AVTANDIL JORBENADZE, state minister of Georgia (2001–2003)

TINATIN KHIDASHELI, former head of Georgian Young Lawyers' Association (GYLA), senior figure in the left-wing Republican Party (2005–present)

EKA KHOPERIA, leading Georgian journalist (Rustavi 2 TV)

EROSI KITSMARISHVILI, owner of Rustavi 2 TV (until 2004)

KAKHA LOMAIA, executive director, Open Society Georgia Foundation (Soros Foundation) (2002–2003), minister of education of Georgia (2003–present)

VANO MERABISHVILI, minister of interior and security (2004–present), minister of security (2004, prior to merger of two ministries), member of Parliament of Georgia (1999–2003)

RICHARD MILES, U.S. ambassador to Georgia (2002–2005)

SHALVA NATELASHVILI, founder and leader of the opposition Labor Party (1995–present)

GHIA NODIA, founder and chairman, Caucasus Institute for Peace, Democracy, and Development (founded in August 1992)

IRAKLI OKRUASHVILI, minister of defense (2004–2006), minister of interior (2004), prosecutor general (2003–2004), prominent attorney and lobbyist (1995–2003)

LEVAN RAMISHVILI, co-head of the Liberty Institute

MIKHEIL SAAKASHVILI, third president of Georgia (2004–present), leader of the opposition National Movement (2001–2004), justice minister (2000–2001), senior figure in the governmental Citizens Union of Georgia (1995–2000)

EDUARD SHEVARDNADZE, second president of Georgia (1992–2003), Soviet foreign minister (1985–1990), chairman of the Communist Party of Georgia (1972–1985)

DAVID USUPASHVILI, prominent lawyer, chairman, Republican Party of Georgia (2005–present) (Note: Khidasheli and Usupashvili are married)

ZURAB ZHVANIA, prime minister of Georgia (2004–2005), leader of the opposition United Democrats (2002–2004), speaker of Parliament and leader of Citizens Union of Georgia (1995–2001); died under mysterious circumstances in 2005

PART 1

Three Openings for Democracy in Georgia

1

Independence and the Failure
of Gamsakhurdia's Rule

G eorgia is an ancient country with a history that dates back millennia. However, its current experiment with statehood began on April 9, 1991, when Georgia became the second republic in the former Soviet Union to declare its independence. This was the great achievement of the student-led movement against Soviet tyranny that dominated Georgian society starting in February 1987.

Independence and Gamsakhurdia's Presidency

During the so-called era of Glasnost and Perestroika, Georgia was a hotbed of protests and demonstrations, driven by a combination of factors, the most pronounced of which was liberal nationalism—a belief that Georgians were first and foremost Georgian and not Soviet, and that its people were "Western" and had the right to live in an independent country. This liberal nationalism was most heavily influenced by the Georgian Orthodox Church, which in the late 1970s and early 1980s, under the leadership of Patriarch Ilia II, pressed for recognition of its independence from the Russian Orthodox Church and achieved it in 1989.[1]

Almost all the leaders of the pro-independence movement were very strong believers and practicing Orthodox Christians. Several were patriarch's "strkarosani," the name for lay individuals who are authorized to assist him in conducting mass. Thus, the center of the anti-Soviet movement in Georgia was the Orthodox Church. Its role in anti-Communist activities of the 1980s is somewhat akin to that of the Catholic Church in Poland, while Patriarch Ilia

II's role in mobilizing the Georgian people against the Soviet Union can be compared to the role of Pope John Paul II in his homeland. For this reason, it is not surprising that Georgia has experienced a tremendous revival of religiosity since independence.

Georgians first expressed their liberal nationalism viewpoint in 1956, when in an unprecedented event in the USSR, students in Tbilisi went into the streets to protest the perceived anti-Georgian spirit in the Soviet Communist leadership that followed Stalin's death. In dispersing this demonstration, Soviet troops killed dozens of the protestors. In 1978, students went into the streets again in opposition to a proposal for a new Georgian Constitution that eliminated the privileges afforded to the Georgian language, limited its teaching in schools, and forced the government to use Russian, rather than Georgian, for official purposes. This Constitution was produced in Moscow and was being imposed on the local Georgian leadership from there. Bloodshed was avoided because then Georgian Communist Party leader Eduard Shevardnadze successfully used the protests to persuade then Soviet leader Leonid Breznev to alter Moscow's constitutional proposal. By protecting their national language through a minor "rebellion," for the first time the Georgian public saw and experienced the power of their free action against Soviet totalitarianism.[2]

Given this history of unprecedented public anti-Soviet activities that had taken place in Georgia in the past, few were surprised when pro-independence demonstrations began to take hold under the perceived openness of Mikheil Gorbachev's policies. In addition to liberal nationalism, the protests were successful thanks to a group of young, charismatic leaders who were viewed as dissidents and who spoke directly to the pro-independence beliefs of the large majority of the Georgian people. Zviad Gamsakhurdia, who would later become the first Georgian president, came to be known as the most prominent of these individuals, though there were several others who were just as important. Merab Kostava and Zurab Chavchavadze were close in age to Gamsakhurdia, but they died tragically and under mysterious circumstances in a car accident in 1989. Gia Chanturia, Mamuka Giorgadze, Irakli Tsereteli, and several others were younger leaders who also played a crucial role. In addition, student activists were the key to mobilizing the core support for pro-independence demonstrations.

At the same time, Ronald Reagan's call for people oppressed by Communism to demand freedom influenced Georgians just as it touched Eastern Europeans, giving people a sense that the United States was getting serious about ending Soviet totalitarianism. Indeed, most leaders of the Georgian pro-independence movement believed that Gorbachev's dubious "reform" process was largely the byproduct of America's political, economic, and rhetorical pressure on the USSR and its tyrannical rule.

By 1988, protests in Georgia, including mass demonstrations and hunger strikes demanding free legislative elections and the declaration of independence from the Soviet Union, became systematic and exposed the illegitimacy of Soviet rule. This, coupled with the fact that much of the Georgian "nomenklatura" did not actually believe in Communism, made the Communist Party's grip on power very tenuous. By the spring of 1989, the Soviet leadership was so concerned with the unraveling of events in Georgia that President Mikheil Gorbachev authorized the use of Soviet troops to crush the protests and put an end to this open rebellion against Communist rule. Soviet troops marched into Tbilisi on April 9 to disperse a demonstration in the center of Tbilisi, on Rustaveli Avenue. The troops used poisonous gas and killed at least twenty-one people, including students and women, one of whom was pregnant.

This tragedy became a symbol for Georgian freedom fighters. In its aftermath, nationalistic and pro-independence feelings increased dramatically, while the Communist Party lost what little legitimacy it had with the public. However, it also helped bring about a final split in the pro-independence movement that had been brewing for years. The majority wing went with Gamsakhurdia, who rode the wave of emotion following the April 9 tragedy to extreme popularity across the country, especially his native region of Samegrelo. A minority wing went with Chanturia, the leader of the National Democratic Party (NDP), who accused Gamsakhurdia of cooperation with the Soviet authorities and not fighting for independence hard enough. The latter group, which included most of the luminaries of the Georgian pro-independence struggle, was far less mobilized, while the Soviet leadership (especially in Moscow) favored Gamsakhurdia because he was not psychologically balanced and, although popular, was not a strong and principled leader, whereas Chanturia presented a real threat.

Discredited by the April 9 tragedy, the "state" in Georgia began to weaken dramatically, to the extent that Georgian Communist leaders were no longer capable of governing.[3] On October 9, 1990, in some respects against the wishes of their bosses in Moscow, leaders of the Georgian Communist government held the first free elections for the Supreme Soviet in any republic in the USSR. While the Chanturia-led pro-independence groups did not compete in the elections, Gamsakhurdia's Round Table did. It won an overwhelming majority of seats in the legislative body (155 of 246 seats). Smaller pro-independence groups elected 18 legislators, while the Communists elected 64. After the elections, Gamsakhurdia became the head of the Georgian Supreme Soviet, and as such, the effective ruler. This was the first peaceful and legal transition of power from the Communists to their opposition in the Soviet Union. Incidentally, Georgia has not had a change of government that respected constitutional forms and legal procedures since then.

The 1990 election presented Georgia with its first post-Soviet democratic opening—indeed, only the second opportunity to move toward modern, liberal democratic government ever (the first being in 1918–1921, when Georgia became briefly independent after the fall of the Russian tsar). The election of a nationalistic pro-independence leader allowed Georgians to see the power that they possessed as citizens. They realized that their voice and their hunger for freedom were stronger than the awesome power of the Soviet army, which was not able to crush the pro-independence forces. People also witnessed the great democratic opportunity—the ability of citizens to break chains of tyranny, if and when citizens chose to exercise their natural right to self-government. Through the 1990 election, Georgians replaced a government that oppressed them with a government that was one of their own and that spoke to their interest. People also probably hoped that a democratically elected government would move the country toward more sustainable democratic practices. Unfortunately, this never happened.

GAMSAKHURDIA'S RULE AND HIS FAILURE

Gamsakhurdia, along with a number of other leaders of the pro-independence movement, played a crucial role in bringing about this moment of democratic opportunity. His historic achievement as a leader of the movement can never be disputed. However, he had a number of serious character flaws, making him quite possibly the worst leader any country could have during a troublesome period of such monumental change. Indeed, he turned out to be a leader who brought the country to its first democratic opening, but also the leader who made it impossible for Georgia to take advantage of the opportunity that he helped create.

One of Gamsakhurdia's alleged strong suits was his dissident past. Yet unlike Vaclav Havel and Lech Walesa, or some of the Soviet dissidents like Elena Bonner, Gamsakhurdia's background was always questionable, since he allegedly had a history of cooperation with the KGB in the 1970s and early 1980s. Most of the real Georgian dissidents were in the other wing of the pro-independence movement, while the leading dissident who could have challenged Gamsakhurdia in a personality contest, Zviad Kostava, had died in 1989.

In addition to his past, those who worked with Gamsakhurdia point to serious mental problems that undermined his ability to govern. While overwhelmingly popular and a master of public relations, Gamsakhurdia was a show horse rather than a workhorse. His experiences failed to prepare him for a position of executive authority, especially in a time of transition. As a child, he was raised in a great deal of loneliness. This had a huge impact on him as an adult and may be one reason he constantly craved attention. Furthermore, his father was a beloved novelist, and Gamsakhurdia always felt the need to live up to his achievements. Gamsakhurdia was also paranoid about everyone around him, and within a year of coming to power, he began to isolate himself from all other political leaders, refusing to hear or acknowledge the existence of a point of view different from his own. As a result, he also became very dependent on his wife, who suddenly became the most powerful person in Georgia.

Not only did Gamsakhurdia not know *how* to govern, but he lacked a political team that could help him. He was unwilling to place strong personalities in positions of authority, and rejected anyone who had any connection to the Soviet rule, including professionals who knew something about managing affairs of the state and who were "Communists" in name only. He accused them of being "occupiers," even though many privately favored independence.

Instead of seeking strong managers, Gamsakhurdia appointed to positions of great responsibility inexperienced and incompetent men who had failed in their own careers. A metallurgical scientist of no distinction, Tengiz Sigua, was made prime minister and put in charge of the day-to-day running of the government. Guram Absandze, a man whose profession or educational background I was not able to determine, notwithstanding countless queries of people who participated in politics during that time, was made minister of finance, even though he had absolutely no knowledge of the budgetary process. A mediocre artist, Tengiz Kitovani, became the head of the National Guard, Georgia's ragtag army. Gamsakhurdia's other advisors were not much different. Some called this the rise of a new political class, but in reality it was a colossal failure of governance.

These men not only did not know what they were supposed to do in their respective positions, but most of them were not even prominent individuals within the pro-independence movement. As a result, they lacked the respect of both the population at large and the political class. Their political authority was completely tied to Gamsakhurdia's good will. Accordingly, they never challenged his actions, nor did they ever give him a dissenting piece of advice. Not surprisingly, such a group had no capacity to deal with the monumental economic problems facing Georgia, which became even more acute as relations with Moscow deteriorated. With their actions, Gamsakhurdia and his team destroyed the unique chance that was afforded to Georgia by its first post-Soviet democratic election.

Gamsakhurdia's biggest political blunder was to fall into a trap that Moscow set up for him in the north-central Georgian region of South Ossetia. Under Soviet rule, this region—historically known as Samachablo—had seen an influx of ethnic Ossetians from the bordering Russian region of Northern Ossetia. As a result, following their common practice, Soviet authorities granted the area autonomous status and called the region "South Ossetia."[4]

This system of ethnic autonomies was ostensibly a means of protecting national minorities, but in reality it was a time bomb that Moscow could blow up at its leisure by pushing the "protected" minorities toward separatism.[5] Thus, this situation gave Moscow a means to weaken and destabilize republics where nationalistic feelings ran high, such as Georgia (through Ossetia and Abkhazia), Moldova (through Transnistia), and Ukraine (through Crimea).

In 1989, Moscow began to encourage ethnic leaders in South Ossetia to demand secession from Georgia. Gamsakhurdia, then the pro-independence opposition leader, responded to this with strong nationalist, anti-Ossetian rhetoric, creating an unnecessary feeling of fear among ethnic Ossetians who had lived in various parts of the country for centuries. Many began to flee to Russia. In August 1990, two months before Gamsakhurdia's election victory, South Ossetians followed Moscow's advice and declared their region sovereign from Georgia. Moscow's goal in pressing for and supporting the South Ossetian "independence" movement was to create a weapon against what inevitably would be a pro-independence legislative majority in Georgia after the October elections.

After gaining power, Gamsakhurdia failed to act calmly and rationally to resolve the problem with South Ossetia peacefully. Instead, one of the new legislature's first moves was to annul the autonomous status of South Ossetia in December 1990. While probably a good decision on public-policy grounds, it was a huge strategic and political blunder. Gamsakhurdia then ordered Georgia's new, untrained, and inexperienced military forces (called the National Guard) into Tskhinvali, the region's administrative capital, resulting in fighting during which the Ossetians were openly supported by Soviet troops. Ultimately hundreds, possibly thousands, died, and 25,000–40,000 people were forced to flee the region.

This contrasts sharply with how Gamsakhurdia handled Abkhazia, Georgia's other ethnic autonomous republic. Even though there were separatist tendencies there as well—which would come to the surface eventually —Gamsakhurdia was able to work with the Abkhaz because he apparently believed in a romantic ethnic theory that the Abkhaz, along with the Chechens, were "real" Caucasians, just like the Georgians. By contrast, he did not hold this view about the Ossetians and the Armenians.[7]

Because the Georgians did not have a strong enough military with which to fight the Ossetians and the Russians, Gamsakhurdia authorized Jaba Ioseliani, a poet and a criminal figure,[8] to organize a private militia—called Mkhedrioni—to support the government in Ossetia. The Soviet troops based in Georgia were all too happy to supply both the National Guard and Mkhedrioni with weaponry, since this gave them not only a means to earn extra income but also an instrument to weaken the Georgian leader, given that Gamsakhurdia did not have any real authority over these armed formations. As a result, to Moscow's delight, by giving rise to paramilitary groups, the Ossetian conflict crippled Gamsakhurdia's ability to govern the rest of the country.

Charles H. Fairbanks advanced a persuasive view that the rise of these paramilitary groups was not connected just to the conflict in Ossetia, but was an unfortunate byproduct of Gamsakhurdia's background of not being part of the Communist ruling elite. "Because he was not, unlike Boris Yeltsin, Nursultan Nazarbayev [and other rulers of the USSR successor states], of Communist background, the need for a Georgian defensive force was filled by undisciplined forces and by private militias not organized by the state. Thus, the new Georgian state lost control of the means of coercion, so important for modern statehood, from the very beginning."[9]

Because of the Ossetian conflict, Gamsakhurdia started to lose popularity. He also wanted to become "president," rather than the chairman of the Supreme Soviet. To this end, in order to regain popular support, he proposed a referendum on whether Georgia should become independent and whether it should be a "presidential republic." Both proposals were overwhelmingly approved in a popular vote on March 31, 1991, Gamsakhurdia's birth date.[10] A week later, on the second anniversary of the April 9 massacre, the legislature declared Georgia an independent country. In practical terms this declaration did not mean very much, because internationally no country was willing to recognize Georgia's sovereignty. However, Gamsakhurdia rode a wave of popularity, stemming from the declaration of independence, to victory in a race for the new post of president in an election that took place on May 26, 1991, winning 86 percent of the vote.[11] This election was the first in a series of national votes for a Georgian leader in which the winner was predetermined, either because one individual dominated the political scene or because other political figures refused to participate in the contest.

THE COUP AGAINST GAMSAKHURDIA

The newly elected president took his overwhelming victory as a sign that any and all of his actions were legitimate, and that he could not be constrained by anyone. This, coupled with his paranoia, led Gamsakhurdia to take further steps that undermined his own authority. In the summer of 1991, his leadership style became more erratic and authoritarian, while his rhetoric against anyone who had a different opinion was vicious. For example, the president went after some of the most prominent professors at Tbilisi State University, the cradle of the pro-independence movement, accusing them of being Communists and disloyal to the Georgian fight for independence. Gamsakhurdia would regularly appear on television and, in a language reminiscent of the French and Russian revolutions, chastise the "enemies of the people," Russian "spies," and "agents of the Kremlin." Such charges reminded many Georgians of the Soviet propaganda during the purges of the 1930s and caused grave worry about the state of Gamsakhurdia's mental health.

In this environment, Gamsakhurdia's rule began to unravel in August 1991, when the president made a colossal mistake in refusing to condemn the attempted coup in Moscow against Gorbachev. Throughout 1991, Gorbachev was working relentlessly to develop a plan that could preserve the Soviet Union, probably as a loose federation of states, in light of growing pro-independence demands in the Baltic republics and Georgia. Gamsakhurdia rightly refused to cooperate with Gorbachev in these efforts. The coup was organized by the so-called "conservative" Communists, who felt that the Soviet Union would fall apart (and they would lose power) unless Gorbachev's alleged "reforms" were stopped. Thus, it seemed logical that Gamsakhurdia would oppose them even more than he opposed Gorbachev.

When the coup was launched on August 19, Gamsakhurdia reversed course and told his ministers that the coup would probably succeed. Short of using the Georgian State TV, which he controlled, to spread the usual anti-Moscow, pro-Georgian independence message, Gamsakhurdia directed the media to cover the coup in a favorable manner. Most importantly, to show the coup plotters that he was willing to be obedient, Gamsakhurdia ordered the National Guard to disband, turn in its weapons, and become part of the Ministry of Interior police force. In response to what was perceived as a position of capitulation, Tengiz Kitovani, the head of the Guard, led his troops into a rebellion against Gamsakhurdia by refusing to disarm and removing them to the outskirts of Tbilisi.

Gamsakhurdia's moves were incomprehensible to almost everyone in Georgia, since the coup plotters in Moscow included all those Communist leaders who were seen as the biggest opponents of Georgian independence and who justified the coup on the grounds that it was the only means to preserve the Soviet Union. Gamsakhurdia, who at this point had clearly lost touch with reality, was probably scared that he would lose power. At the same time, it is likely that he wanted to avoid being on the same side as Eduard Shevardnadze, who had warned of the coming dictatorship when he resigned as Soviet foreign minister several months earlier, and who was widely perceived as one of the leading figures fighting the coup in Moscow. Gamsakhurdia's opponents also saw his statements and actions as appeasement. Critics accused Gamsakhurdia of caring more for his power than for Georgian independence, and Prime Minister Sigua resigned in protest.

For Gamsakhurdia's opposition, the coup was an impetus to start an active campaign against Gamsakhurdia.[12] They demanded that the president resign and call new legislative elections. The opposition found significant public support for its stance, because Gamsakhurdia was rapidly losing popularity in Tbilisi and other urban areas. However, the opposition was ignoring the less active popular majority, which still supported and trusted the president. Initially, the opposition resorted to the tried and true method of public protests, but Gamsakhurdia refused to compromise, forcibly broke up a large demonstration in Tbilisi in September 1991, and arrested the leading opposition figures, including Gia Chanturia, his most prominent critic.

On September 16, Gamsakhurdia ordered Georgia State TV off the air and shut off the transmission of the national television frequency. In response, journalists went on strike in front of the station's headquarters. They were soon joined by much of the Tbilisi elite, including leading academics from Tbilisi Sate University and other higher-education institutions, as well as other members of the Soviet-era "intelligentsia" (the group of people who were supposed to set the public mood in the republics), students, and leading figures of the other wing of the pro-independence movement. Meanwhile, Gamsakhurdia brought supporters from outside of Tbilisi, largely from Samegrelo, to back him through public protests.

On December 22, the government once again broke up an opposition demonstration, whose organizers called on Kitovani to defend them. In response, Kitovani's National Guard and Ioseliani's Mkhedrioni moved on Tbilisi and isolated Gamsakhurdia in the legislature's building on Rustaveli Avenue. Two weeks of bloody fighting followed. Russian military officials followed their traditional mantra of "divide and rule" and supported both sides. They encouraged Gamsakhurdia to fight on, while they also supplied weapons to the coup leaders. Russian military commanders hoped that fighting between these two armed bands would continue for a long time, helping destroy any possibility of the creation of a sovereign Georgian state and instead making "Georgia" fully dependent on Russia.

Eventually Gamsakhurdia realized that he was trapped and unable to maintain his defenses. On January 6, 1992, he fled to Grozny—the capital of the Russian republic of Chechnya, where pro-independence sentiments were also running high—hoping that he could launch a counteroffensive from there. During the period of the fighting, both Georgian and Russian television channels were largely off the air in the country, and the people missed that on December 25, the Soviet Union officially broke up and Georgia finally regained its formal independence.

Some who read my manuscript or know my views about the Gamsakhurdia era have argued that I am overly harsh on Georgia's first president. For example, should Gamsakhurdia be blamed for being unprepared? While my interlocutors admit that he was a bad president, they suggest that any anti-Communist leader in Georgia would have had a difficult time running the country. Others have suggested that the West, enchanted with Gorbachev and largely opposed to any kind of nationalism, did not give him any help.

These arguments, and several others that point to a less harsh assessment of Gamsakhurdia's rule, are real and should be given some weight. For example, the West's refusal to support him and recognize Georgian independence complicated his situation significantly. However, Gamsakhurdia's problems started from his inability to keep the pro-independence movement together because he was too interested in gaining power for himself. Only Gamsakhurdia had the capacity to forestall the split in this movement. Had his patriotism not given way to his personal ambition, he could have followed the example of his fellow freedom fighters in the Baltic republics of the USSR. There, individuals of differing political views worked together in order to ensure their freedom, and became opponents only after they had won. Georgian history would have developed very differently had its independence movement similarly avoided infighting. My judgment of Gamsakhurdia's rule at least partially originates from his role in this split. That said, one factor for which I cannot account is the role of the Soviet security services, especially the KGB, in pushing Gamsakhurdia toward splitting the pro-independence movement.

LOSING ABKHAZIA AND SHEVARDNADZE'S ROLE IN SAVING THE GEORGIAN STATE

While the coup leaders gained control of the government in Tbilisi, they lacked both the legitimacy and the political savvy necessary to maintain control of the country. Georgia was on the verge of becoming a failed, criminal state akin to Somalia. This was exactly what the Russian military leadership had hoped would happen as a result of the coup, and this was why they had supplied both sides with weapons. Only one living Georgian, Eduard Shevardnadze, had the stature and the authority both domestically and internationally to prevent the country's complete meltdown. Under pressure from all the leading elements of Georgian society, Kitovani and Ioseliani invited him to return to Georgia to take over the reins of power. Transfer of authority to a respected civilian was probably the best decision Kitovani and Ioseliani could have made.

On March 7, 1992, Shevardnadze flew from Moscow to a triumphant welcome in Tbilisi and was made chairman of the temporary State Council, which consisted of prominent politicians and citizens and was "empowered" to run the country. Real power, however, was with Kitovani and Ioseliani. Conventional wisdom in Georgia characterized Shevardnadze's return as engineered by Russia, because at that time he was living there. However, his return was probably Moscow's least preferred outcome, because Shevardnadze's international stature brought Georgia Western recognition and secured support from his friends abroad, who universally credited him with a crucial role in ending the Cold War.

Immediately after Shevardnadze's return, Germany became the first country to post an ambassador in Georgia, in part because its foreign minister, Hans-Dietrich Genscher, had urged Shevardnadze to return. On May 25–26, against the advice of his aides, U.S. Secretary of State James Baker made a special visit to Tbilisi to shore up his friend's authority.[13] Both Germany and the United States pledged political and financial assistance, which was crucial to securing Shevardnadze's tenuous grip on power. Thus, the mere personality of Shevardnadze was important enough to ensure Western interest in Georgia, something that did not suit Russian interests. No other post-Soviet republic received this sort of direct Western help so quickly after the collapse of the USSR.[14] Meanwhile, for Moscow, the best outcome would have been a chaotic Georgia in which no one but Russia would take an interest.

One of Shevardnadze's first orders of business was to end the fighting in Ossetia. In June 1992, Georgia signed a cease-fire agreement with the Ossetians and the Russians. However, the new Georgian leader was unable to avoid a similar trap that Moscow helped set up for him in Abkhazia—a beautiful Black Sea province that, under Soviet rule, also had autonomy within Georgia. Unlike South Ossetia, where ethnic Ossetians constituted a majority of the population, ethnic Georgians were a plurality in Abkhazia.[15] Beginning in 1978, Soviet authorities had created a system that afforded the Abkhazians 67 percent of government and party positions, even though many more ethnic Georgians than Abkhazians lived in the region. Urged on by Moscow, the regional Abkhaz leaders declared independence from Georgia on July 23, 1992, just weeks after Shevardnadze arranged for a cease-fire with the Ossetians. In response, Kitovani, who was serving as defense minister at the time, marched Georgian forces into Abkhazia on August 14, 1992, claiming that he had received a pledge that Russian troops would not support the separatists.

Fighting in Abkhazia lasted for over a year. The proclaimed pledge of neutrality notwithstanding, Russian forces openly fought on behalf of the separatists, as they had in Ossetia. Abkhazians also received help from mercenaries from the Northern Caucasus, including those Chechen fighters whom Russia would brand as terrorists in the future. Ultimately, Georgians lost control of Sukhumi, Abkhazia's capital, on September 28, 1993, and Shevardnadze's security detail forced him to flee the city at the last minute.

With Abkhaz and Russian forces advancing at Georgian positions further south and east, closer to the Georgian-Abkhaz administrative border, over two hundred thousand Georgians living in Abkhazia were forced to flee in the most gruesome act of ethnic cleansing in the former Soviet Union.[16] Indeed, this was the only case of a plurality nationality being ethnically cleansed by a small

minority. It would have never happened had the Abkhazians not received support from Moscow, which engaged in the conflict as part of its dramatic effort
to control Georgia.

With no hope of support from the West, Shevardnadze was forced to call
on Moscow to broker an end to hostilities. In return, Russian soldiers, who had
fought on the side of Abkhazia during the war, were dispatched to the region
to keep the "peace," giving Moscow a powerful leverage against the Georgian
government.[17]

As the conflict of Abkhazia was turning against the Georgians in September 1993, Gamsakhurdia returned to Georgia from Grozny to launch an uprising against Shevardnadze. The uprising started in Samegrelo, home to the
Mingrelian ethnic subgroup to which Gamsakhurdia belonged. Many Georgian analysts of that time period whom I spoke with while researching these
events believe that Gamsakhurdia's rebellion played an important role in the
ultimate defeat of the Georgian side in Abkhazia, both because fighters from
Samegrelo refused to fight on Georgia's behalf, and because the Georgian
authorities became distracted by the rebellion in Samegrelo.

There is some evidence that Gamsakhurdia returned to Georgia after he
received a pledge of support from Russian authorities. While it is unclear what
Moscow promised the former president, at a minimum they pledged and actually supplied weapons to his supporters. Samegrelo and surrounding regions
in Western Georgia inevitably became the center of the fighting. Weeks of
bloodshed ensued between Gamsakhurdia's supporters and Georgia's military
forces. Having just lost Sukhumi, Shevardnadze's supporters could not defeat
the rebellion on their own, and by mid-October, the Georgian leader had to
turn to Russia for assistance. Moscow was once again given a chance to play
both sides against each other while advancing its own interest. With Russian
weapons and troops helping Shevardnadze's forces, the Gamsakhurdia insurgency eventually collapsed.

It is unclear whether Shevardnadze knew of Kitovani's plans to invade Abkhazia, and if he did, whether he authorized them. I discussed this with a number of individuals in senior positions at the time, and no clear picture emerged.
Some alleged that the decision was fully Shevardnadze's, while most claimed
that at this point he was not anywhere near in full control of the government
and could not direct Kitovani's actions.[18] It is hard for me to imagine Shevardnadze authorizing this invasion if he knew about it, simply because Moscow's
tactics were not new to him. Without too much difficulty, he should have been
able to anticipate that Russian troops would never honor their pledge of neutrality and would ultimately side against the Georgians in order to try to destabilize the country. In other words, I can envision Kitovani falling for the

Russian promise, but not Shevardnadze, though I am not basing this observation on any specific evidence related to this incident.

That said, had Shevardnadze known about the invasion and been opposed to it, he was probably not in a position to stop Kitovani. He was extremely dependent on Kitovani's National Guard and Ioseliani's Mkhedrioni to safeguard his position. As a result, Kitovani may very well have moved on Abkhazia without Shevardnadze's approval, maybe with the hope that victory there would endear him to the population and position him as an alternative figure to Shevardnadze. Either way, in the years that followed, Shevardnadze always took full responsibility for the mistake of the war in Abkhazia, while the scars from the conflict often shaped his actions in ways that were detrimental to Georgia's future.

The Meaning of Gamsakhurdia's Removal

I belonged to that group of Georgians who never liked Gamsakhurdia and thought him unworthy of being the father of Georgian independence. This group strongly cheered the coup on, not realizing the havoc it would wreak on Georgia for years to come and the difficulties it would cause to Georgia's democratic development. It was obvious to many then, and it is obvious to many more now, that Gamsakhurdia could never have been a successful president—he did not have the character, the skills, or the mental strength necessary for the job. However, even his most ardent opponents acknowledge that his violent removal caused grave problems for Georgia, both in the short and the long term. There are five key reasons for this.[19]

First, the coup was plainly illegal and took place with complete disregard of the rule of law and of the political process. As a result, it undermined the rule of law and furthered the notion, which had existed in Georgia throughout the Soviet period, that lawbreaking was justifiable. At times, revolutions are not only justifiable, but they are indeed necessary. Whether such a revolution would have been justifiable in Georgia in 1991 remains an open question. However, the coup was not a revolution, since it was not a popular uprising, but an action of a small group of military men who took control of the government. It was a wise move on their part to give the power to a civilian soon after the coup, but that does not change the fact that their actions violated the peaceful and legitimate political process. Throughout Shevardnadze's rule, in the eyes of some he was an illegitimate leader because of his association with the coup. The country was finally going to have a chance to go beyond this question of the illegitimacy of Shevardnadze's rule by achieving a constitutional transition of power in 2005, when his term was scheduled to end; but instead, Georgia furthered the precedent of the extraconstitutional transition by forcing him to leave through another coup, albeit this time a popular one.

Second, the coup led to the near collapse of the Georgian state. After Gamsakhurdia fled, the new government nominally controlled Tbilisi and eastern Georgia, while the situation in the rest of the country (especially in the western regions) was quite chaotic. Because everyone expected Gamsakhurdia to launch a bid to return to power, Shevardnadze's grip on authority was dependent on the armed gangs that had brought down the former president—the National Guard and Mkhedrioni. These groups engaged in racketeering and terrorized the population at large all over the country. This made life very difficult for ordinary citizens, for businessmen, for farmers, and for all others whose contribution to the economy was crucial for the country's development. Political instability also took a huge toll on Shevardnadze—he had to use his first years of rule not on promoting political change and moving Georgia closer to the West (his ultimate goal), but on strengthening his own authority inside the country. It would take Shevardnadze two years to bring a semblance of stability to Georgia, at great cost to both the citizens and the state.

Third, the coup helped foster an environment in which Russia gained a great deal of power over the independent Georgia. Moscow would have been far more successful had it not been for Shevardnadze's leadership and personal standing with Western leaders who supported him during those difficult years. However, Russia was very successful at playing various groups of Georgians against each other to advance its interests and to maintain a strong influence in Georgia, notwithstanding the country's independence. Ultimately, in return for shoring up Shevardnadze's authority against Gamsakhurdia's rebellion in 1993, Russia forced Georgia to join the CIS, in which Tbilisi had initially refused to participate, and to keep Russian bases and forces in Georgia.[20] It took over a decade of negotiations for an agreement to be signed in 2005 that stipulates withdrawal of these bases in 2008.

Fourth, the civil war that followed Gamsakhurdia's attempt to return to power in 1993 left very destructive wounds on residents of his home province of Samegrelo. During the last battle in Samegrelo, Mkhedrioni militia marched into the province and indiscriminately killed dozens of their fellow citizens and raped numerous women and children. Georgians had never attacked each other in this way before, and many in the country were in shock that this could happen at the end of the twentieth century. This incident increased hatred toward Shevardnadze among Mingrelians and created a great schism in the body politic that has not yet healed. Incidentally, it was the Mingrelians who would become the principal supporters of the Rose Revolution in 2003.

Finally and most importantly, the coup against Gamsakhurdia took away a very important sense of hope from a large group of common people—those regular citizens whose role is crucial to the success of democracy, but who never had a say under Communism. For many citizens, Gamsakhurdia had become an icon of freedom from tyranny and of national independence. Probably a majority of Georgians had placed (albeit mistakenly) their hopes and aspirations in this man. For them, he was the embodiment of their belief in the possibility of democracy and in their ability to control their destiny and their future. This was true not only for those who supported Gamsakhurdia to the end, but even for some who had problems with his rule but who were encouraged by the possibility that people could participate in self-government as exemplified by the Georgian fight for independence. This was not obvious to those of us who were happy to see Gamsakhurdia gone in 1992,[21] but thinking about the event now, it is clear that the overthrow was a great blow for all these citizens.

The result was devastating because it gave birth to political apathy in Georgian society that continued to exist perhaps until the Rose Revolution in 2003, with most people thinking that their role in governance did not really matter, since some amorphous "they" (i.e., those who are in power) would make all the decisions for them anyway. This was far from a predominant view in 1990–92, when ordinary citizens saw how their own actions could bring about change—first, when peaceful protests forced Georgia's Communist masters to agree to free elections, and afterwards, when people overwhelmingly voted for Georgian independence.

It is very difficult, it not impossible, to build a democracy in an environment of apathy. Because of this, many of the challenges of transition that developed during the 1990s can be traced to this feeling of indifference. Unfortunately, some of the actions of the Shevardnadze government in the years that followed only helped strengthen this view among the majority of the Georgian population. Without understanding the origins of the disgust that many Georgians felt with the political process as a result of Gamsakhurdia's overthrow, one cannot fully appreciate the problems that the country would face during the 1990s. This is the main reason why I started my analysis with Gamsakhurdia's rule and his overthrow, rather than with a consideration of Shevardnadze's rule.

Gamsakhurdia committed suicide on December 31, 1993, ending the most devastating and damaging year of Georgia's independence. At this point, Georgia was an internationally recognized state (six countries had opened embassies in Tbilisi); but the central government had lost control over two provinces, while civil strife had divided the people and armed gangs and militia were roaming the country, even on the streets of the capital. Furthermore, Russia engineered an environment in which Georgia could not become too independent and would remain within its sphere of influence. Having given up so much to Moscow, it would take Shevardnadze years of maneuvering to move Georgia out of the Russian orbit and reorient it toward the West.

2

Shevardnadze's Constitutional Founding and the Rise of Zhvania's "Young Reformers"

hevardnadze's great achievement in the 1990s was to bring a semblance of stability and peace to Georgia by increasing the authority of the state, dramatically reducing crime and disbanding the military gangs, establishing an environment in which basic economic development could take place, creating a framework necessary for a just constitutional regime, and moving slowly, but deliberately, to build a strategic partnership with the United States. These achievements of Shevardnadze's rule gave birth to Georgia's second democratic opening. Unfortunately, yet again, while Shevardnadze helped secure this democratic opening, his willingness to give significant power to people who had no interest in real democracy, and his own methods of rule, made it impossible for Georgia to take advantage of this opening.

Putting Together the Georgian State

The first step in stabilizing Georgia after the coup was to give the governing authorities a certain level of legitimacy. Parliamentary elections on October 11, 1992, just six months after Shevardnadze's return to Georgia, accomplished this. The elections took place in the context of the 1921 Constitution—a document that was approved during Georgia's brief period of independence after the Russian Revolution in 1917, and that the State Council reestablished on August 4, 1992. The council also established the post of a popularly elected speaker of Parliament, with the effective powers of a president. Thus, in the October 11 elections, Georgians voted not only for a new legislature, but cast direct ballots for a national leader as well.

The vote was by and large free and fair. Because Shevardnadze did not support a particular political party but controlled the electoral administration, state resources were not used to support one group or another. However, the vote did not take place in certain parts of the country, like Abkhazia, which accounted for about one-tenth of all eligible voters. Furthermore, the vote was taking place in a semi-warlike environment. In Tbilisi, for example, ordinary citizens who had nothing to do with the rebellion against Gamsakhurdia, and who were not politically active, were defending polling stations with automatic rifles from possible disturbances and attacks by Gamsakhurdia's supporters. People went to vote not so much because they supported Shevardnadze, but because many still had hope that there was a chance for something better. This was not true of the hundreds of thousands of Gamsakhurdia's supporters who stayed away completely.

Shevardnadze was the only candidate to run for the position of speaker, and received over 96 percent of the vote—he got more votes than any Georgian leader in any election before or since. Unfortunately, much like with Gamsakhurdia's election in 1991, people did not have a choice of candidates; many were voting for Shevardnadze not necessarily because they favored him, but because no one else was running. This pattern of having only one viable candidate on the ballot for national office has continued in Georgia to this day, and is a serious problem in the process of transitioning to true democracy.

The legislature was elected through a mixed system of majoritarian districts, in which people voted directly for candidates, and of proportional lists that were submitted by coalitions and parties. However, because the parties had to file separate lists for each of Georgia's ten historic provinces, even the proportional elections were arranged in such a manner as to promote a direct connection between local representatives and their electors. This helped to ensure that local concerns were not ignored. This system, which was unfortunately abandoned in later years, not only promoted a stronger relationship between elected officials and the people they ostensibly represented, but also encouraged greater cohesion of the country by catering to, rather than trying to change, the provincial divisions that have existed in Georgia for centuries.

The legislative elections were very competitive, with forty-two parties and four coalitions running, and gave citizens a wide choice between younger leaders who were part of the pro-independence movement and older, Soviet nomenklatura representatives. No one party received a majority, allowing Shevardnadze to exercise a great deal of influence over the political process after the elections because he was the only individual who commanded the respect of the various groups. Initially, Shevardnadze commanded the support of both the so-called nationalist, younger parliamentarians and the older generation. However, after he agreed to join the CIS in December 1993, many of these younger leaders went into the opposition. On the one hand, this was a positive development because it created greater political pluralism and gave a clear platform to Gia Chanturia, the leader of the National Democratic Party, who was widely perceived as the only politician other than Shevardnadze with national stature. Unfortunately, this also made Shevardnadze more dependent on the nomenklatura and other individuals and groups in Parliament who were less interested in democracy and political progress, but rather engaged in politics for power and financial gain.

After convening, the Parliament appointed Shevardnadze to the amorphous position of "head of state" (not wanting to call him "president" because it reminded people of Gamsakhurdia). Because he had also been elected as speaker of Parliament, both legislative and executive powers were united in the hands of one individual.

As part of the effort to strengthen his grip on power, in 1993 Shevardnadze helped launch a new political party, the Citizens Union of Georgia (CUG).[1] This was a strange combination of political forces—nomenklatura and regional Communist leaders, the academic intelligentsia, and the Green Party—that came together only because the CUG was Shevardnadze's party and was seen as the foundation of his political base for the future. Among those who joined the CUG, the Green Party is of particular note. It had little to no national support, but its "leadership" was a close-knit group led by Zurab Zhvania, a biologist who would become Shevardnadze's best political student and would help engineer Shevardnadze's eventual downfall. This group had steadfastly stood aside during the pro-independence movement during the late 1980s, and in the eyes of many of the more nationalist leaders was willing to cooperate with the Communist authorities far too much.

Shevardnadze spent much of 1994 and 1995 trying to strengthen his authority and to rein in gangs and militias that had been roaming the country ever since the middle of Gamsakhurdia's term. The biggest problem was Mkhedrioni, the private militia led by Jaba Ioseliani that played an important role in the coup against Gamsakhurdia. Meanwhile, in return for protecting enterprises from the mafia, Ioseliani's deputies took stakes in many of the private businesses that got started in Georgia in 1993 and 1994. In 1994, Shevardnadze legalized Mkhedrioni, renaming the group "Mashvelta Korpusi" (Corps of Helpers). However, with the Georgian state becoming stronger and Shevardnadze's authority growing, an eventual collision with Mkhedrioni was inevitable.

During the same period, Shevardnadze began to develop closer ties between Georgia and the United States. He visited Washington for the first time as Georgian leader in March 1994. Coming on the heels of his acceptance of Russian hegemony over Georgia in February, the visit put Georgia on a very long road toward a strong relationship with the United States, which would ultimately blossom into a close friendship. Shevardnadze met with President Clinton, and the two leaders held a news conference together at the White House, with the United States pledging over $70 million in aid. More importantly, the visit got Georgia involved in the massive project to develop the energy resources of the Caspian Sea, which in turn increased American interest in the country. While many have criticized the Clinton administration for not doing enough,[2] given the political environment in Washington, the reception Shevardnadze received was far more than could have been expected. With President Clinton's team generally failing to keep Russia away from getting involved in the so-called "near abroad,"[3] it was only Shevardnadze's personal star power that got Georgia even the limited attention that it received from the administration.[4]

Dramatic changes between 1994 and 1995 were noticeable domestically as well, even during my brief visits to Georgia in the summers. During my trip in the summer of 1994, it was dangerous to go outside at night even in the center of Tbilisi (and in many places even during the day). The country was using a temporary currency called the "coupon," which was so hyperinflated that the economy actually operated in dollars, and my mother had to carry a whole suitcase of "coupons" in order to do regular shopping at the market. By contrast, when I returned in the summer of 1995, it was clear that Georgia had turned a corner. The economy was clearly growing: a number of private banks had organized, and parts of the country's industry, such as wine factories, had also begun to reopen. Young students were finally planning on returning to school on a regular basis the next fall, after almost four years in which middle- and high-school students had spent very little to no time learning. In short, evidence of stability was visible everywhere.

Georgia's Constitutional Founding

It was during my stay in Georgia in the summer of 1995 that I had a chance to witness a monumental event in Georgian history—the Parliament's deliberations over a new Constitution. The founding of the United States has long been a favorite period in my studies of U.S. history, and watching Georgian political leaders discuss the drafting of their Constitution inevitably led me to compare their work to that of the American Founders. Unfortunately, the Georgian lawgivers were not even coming close to doing their job right. No one wanted to begin the discussion from the most crucial question—how to create a government that would be simultaneously effective at governing, yet also dependent on and respectful of the will of the people and protective of the citizens' fundamental rights and liberties. No consideration was being given to Georgian mores, history, and traditions, nor was there any serious discussion of other nations' experiences with liberal constitutionalism.

Instead of discussing how Georgia should secure a balanced regime, the entire debate was about whether Georgia should have a "parliamentary" or a "presidential" system, with various groups favoring the alternatives not based on strong arguments of why one system was better than the other, but based on which system would benefit their own interests most. Shevardnadze first proposed a hyper-presidential system. It would have granted him (the certain future president) near absolute powers, akin to the current Russian president's, including the right to disband the Parliament virtually at will and to fire the prime minister, whose powers were so weak that he was going to be nothing but a servant of the president. By contrast, a group of opposition-oriented parliamentarians wanted a purely continental European system of a weak president and a powerful prime minister, who would receive his authority from the Parliament. These groups had no hope of success in an election unless they were part of a broad coalition. While Shevardnadze's initial proposal was simply dangerous for democracy, the alternative European model failed to account for the needs and political realities of the Georgian state, such as the problems that would inevitably arise if Georgia were to go through the yearly government transitions that Italy and Japan have experienced under a similar system.[5]

To my great surprise, the constitutional debate was completely removed from the people. I knew all too well why the American Founders wrote the U.S. Constitution in secret, and realized that had the process been public, a very different document might have emerged. In Georgia, the process seemed very public, with live TV coverage of the debates and too much political pandering. However, the real decision-making took place behind the scenes and involved a very small group of people who cared little about the nature of the political system they were creating, and were much more concerned with maximizing their own powers under whatever arrangement emerged.

The role of the people as a supreme decision maker in a democracy was the last thing that these individuals wanted to consider. The Parliament was claiming to be devising a social contract to govern a nation and a people, yet Georgians would never be asked to consent to this contract. In some ways, the Soviets used to pay more attention to the people, and used to try to get people more involved in the political process, than the authors of the 1995 Constitution. In the Soviet Union, constitutional changes were usually approved in a "referendum," albeit one that had a predetermined outcome; the Georgian government in 1995 did not even bother to do something as symbolic as this. By contrast, hours during the parliamentary debate were devoted to the discussion of whether parliamentarians should have absolute, partial, or no immunity from prosecution.

In my discussion of this issue with those who were involved in the process of drafting the Constitution in 1995, many usually answered my criticism of lack of ratification by telling me that Georgia was on the verge of civil war—so how was it possible to have a referendum or some other form of ratification? I never quite bought into this argument—especially at the time of this writing, with the Iraqi people getting ready for a constitutional referendum in the middle of a bloody insurgency that is far worse than anything Georgia was facing in 1995. In my personal view, a referendum was not the best way to proceed with ratification. Rather, a U.S.-style set of ratification conventions by elected officials within Georgia's historic provinces would have promoted a more educational and serious debate about the Constitution and its importance.

For all the problems during the drafting process, either by chance or because no single group had a majority in Parliament and thus compromise was essential, the debates in Parliament produced the most balanced constitutional system of government in the former Soviet Union. As a result, the constitutional process was to an extent a product of active democratic governance and give-and-take. One reason for this may have been that after several weeks of debate, Shevardnadze himself took his old draconian proposal off the table and pushed for a compromise that would have kept the "presidential" system envisioned by his original draft but weakened presidential powers significantly.[6] Indeed, some have suggested that he had proposed a hyper-presidential system in order to make acceptance of a more balanced, but nonetheless presidential, system plausible.

The Constitution was unique because it created a fundamentally just, albeit flawed, political regime. This is not to say it was perfect—it certainly left much to be desired. Two-thirds of deputies were elected using a national proportional ballot: citizens voted for a national party list, and seats were awarded to each party based on the percentage of total votes that it received.[7] By opting for this system rather than constituency- (or district-) based elections (like the systems in the U.S. House of Representatives and the UK House of Commons), the Constitution failed to provide for a truly representative system. Under this system, two-thirds of members of Parliament would not represent the people directly, nor would they be speaking on behalf of their constituents.[8]

At the same time, the Constitution's conception of "human rights" was wholly postmodern, with a much greater emphasis placed on social (what are often described as "positive") rights than natural (what are often mistakenly called "negative") liberties. The section on rights was also flawed, because it was written from the perspective that the government grants people rights, rather than vice versa.

Nonetheless, the new system had a number of strengths. The Parliament, though much weaker than it should have been in a good regime, had real powers. Most significantly, it was an *independent* and *coequal* branch of government, and as such, it could confront the executive branch without fear of retribution from the president in the form of dissolution and early legislative elections. (Elections in Georgia were held only at specified times.)

The legislature had the power to confirm each ministerial appointment separately. It was also charged with appropriating and overseeing government spending. Significantly, while the legislature could not amend the budget proposed by the president, it could reject it without triggering a power found in many post-Soviet constitutions that allows the president to disband Parliament if the budget is not approved. As a result, the Parliament could force a compromise on tax-and-spend matters. While the president, as head of the executive branch, could both propose legislation and veto laws, he had no constitutional power to force the legislature to accept his proposals, whereas the Parliament could override a presidential veto. Thus, in a number of areas, real checks and balances between the legislature and the executive, and to a lesser degree between these two branches and the judiciary, were feasible.

It is true that the balance between the three branches of government under the 1995 Constitution was nowhere near sufficient to truly secure liberty and provide for proper checks on the potential abuse of power by the executive. I was at the forefront of the argument that executive powers were greater than they should have been, and serious reform was necessary in order to strengthen the legislative and the judiciary branches. Indeed, Georgia had tendencies of a semi-authoritarian state after 1995, first and foremost because of this constitutional imbalance. However, because the system was fundamentally just, it had the potential to serve as a basis for the consolidation of democratic government. This was also true because the Constitution contained within it the means for forcing a compromise in governance, because of the aforementioned checks and balances.

Unlike what transpired in Russia and Central Asia, Shevardnadze could never become a truly authoritarian, autocratic ruler, even if he wanted to do so, because the Georgian president's powers were constrained by the constitutional framework. The judiciary, though the weakest of Georgia's constitutional institutions, was independent enough to serve as a check on both the legislature and the executive. Meanwhile, with a Parliament possessing real powers, opposition within the legislature (even when in the minority) had the ability to influence the political process.

For this reason, while during Shevardnadze's presidency Georgia had some features of so-called "competitive authoritarianism" (for example, elections were not free and fair), it was not a regime in which all political decision-making was ultimately traceable to the president.[9] Rather, the Georgian legislature was one of the two centers of power in the country. It had the capacity to be the engine of public policy, and it positioned itself regularly at the forefront of policy initiatives. As I examine below, throughout the 1990s a very large share of public policy changes originated in the legislature. The difference between the Georgia regime and "competitive authoritarianism" was particularly true during the period of Georgia's third democratic opening, when the president's governing majority collapsed in Parliament. At that point, the center of political gravity shifted to the pluralist legislature, and only compromise and debate could advance public policy.

Most fundamentally, the Constitution was also unique because it made possible transition of power from one leader to another. Because Georgia did not have a prime minister, Shevardnadze could not hand powers to a chosen successor and then resign, elevating his replacement to the presidency—as Boris Yeltsin did in Russia.

These structural limitations on executive power in the Constitution empowered the opposition and made it more difficult for the president to try to pressure the media, political parties, business, and the NGO community, allowing these extraconstitutional democratic institutions to grow and strengthen. This is not to suggest that the institutional constraints on presidential powers were fully sufficient to prevent soft authoritarianism and fully protect democratic rule—far from it. However, limits were good enough to create an environment of chaotic pluralism in 2001–2003, from which movement toward real democratic consolidation was possible.

The Constitution was ratified on August 24, 1995. As he was heading to a ceremonial signing of the new Constitution on August 29, Shevardnadze suffered an assassination attempt. It was never proven who exactly was responsible for the attack. Shevardnadze, and most Georgians, blamed an alliance between Igor Giorgadze, the former minister for national security, and Mkhedrioni leaders. Giorgadze, who along with former Defense Minister Vardiko Nadibaidze was given a cabinet post at the insistence of Moscow in 1994—as part of a deal between Shevardnadze and Yeltsin made after Russia helped quell the Gamsakhurdia insurgency—fled to Moscow and has lived there ever since. To this day, in my conversations with leading politicians and analysts from this period, I have encountered a near universal agreement that this attack was engineered by Giorgadze on Moscow's behalf, since Russian officials wanted to prevent Georgia from achieving constitutional consolidation.

While much evidence pointed to Giorgadze, the Ministry of Interior forces, which were not controlled by Russian-appointed officials and had become Shevardnadze's key base of support, used the terrorist act as an excuse to go after Mkhedrioni (although it was quite possible that key elements within Mkhedrioni had cooperated with Giorgadze and others in implementing the terrorist plot). The police arrested Mkhedrioni's leadership, including Ioseliani and many of his associates.[10] The government's tactics were clearly questionable from the legal and human-rights points of view, but crushing Mkhedrioni and removing its stranglehold on the country was a very important move in the process of strengthening the Georgian state.

Elections of 1995 and the Rise of the "Young Reformers"

While the formal signing of the Constitution was delayed because of the terrorist attack, Georgia went ahead with presidential and parliamentary elections on November 5, 1995. Shevardnadze won the presidency overwhelmingly, while his Citizens Union of Georgia (CUG) triumphed in the legislative elections. Zurab Zhvania, the former Green who had become Shevardnadze's closest ally, assumed the post of speaker of Parliament. With a comfortable parliamentary majority, Zhvania and his allies came to dominate the legislative process. It was through this process that a number of individuals closely associated with Shevardnadze and Zhvania—including future president Mikheil Saakashvili and future speaker of Parliament and (immediately after the Rose Revolution acting president) Nino Burdjanadze—gained a foothold in Georgian politics.[11] While they created for themselves an image of Zhvania-led "young reformers" committed to democracy, their rule sadly destroyed Georgia's second democratic opening, which the new Constitution had created.

The center-right National Democratic Party (NDP) led a marginalized opposition. The NDP might have had some potential to become a more significant anti-government force were it not for the 1994 assassination of its popular leader, Gia Chanturia. By the 1995 parliamentary elections, a new force, the Revival Party, had emerged in the autonomous republic of Adjaria in southwestern Georgia. Its support was built around the region's authoritarian leader, Aslan Abashidze. In the 1995 elections, Revival was allied with Shevardnadze and Zhvania, though after the elections it moved somewhat mildly into the opposition. Revival's true intention on the national political scene was always to preserve Abashidze's Adjarian fiefdom (in which he wielded nearly absolute power), rather than to lay claim to a national political role.

After his election as speaker of Parliament, Zhvania became the key player in Georgian domestic politics, largely because Shevardnadze left him alone and seldom intervened in the running of Parliament or of the CUG. All of this allowed Zhvania to increase his powers tremendously, at the expense of political pluralism, since he used his power to undermine those who opposed him or the CUG inside or outside the Parliament. Because of his vast influence, Zhvania was able to promote or destroy the careers of ambitious young politicians, many of whom were forever grateful if and when he helped them. Over time, Zhvania gained control over the economic policy of the country and had Shevardnadze appoint his protégés to powerful positions within the cabinet, such as several successive finance ministers and the second-to-last state minister to serve under Shevardnadze.

Zhvania also increased his powers outside of the immediate political arena, especially within the so-called civil society (i.e., foreign donor-supported nongovernmental organizations) and the media. He spearheaded the process of building the NGOs by encouraging the formation of new organizations and by directing funds from USAID, the Soros Foundation, and other donor groups to those NGO leaders that were willing to support him and other so-called reformers. In some respects, Zhvania had virtually complete veto power over who would get foreign donor support and who would not. This way, not only did the groups that he favored benefit greatly, such as the Georgian Young Lawyers' Association (GYLA), Caucasus Institute for Peace, Democracy, and Development (CIPDD), Liberty Institute, UN Association of Georgia, etc., but groups that wanted to promote a more pluralistic reform view, especially NGOs that advanced a pro-business or pro-faith agenda, were blocked from receiving funds.

Once the NGO community became influential, Zhvania directed it to attack Shevardnadze as standing in the way of "reforms." Even though almost everything Zhvania wanted could and would pass in Parliament, Shevardnadze was made into the scapegoat for the alleged failure of reforms. This weakened him—especially in the eyes of foreigners. Meanwhile, Zhvania's position vis-à-vis the president was strengthened, since Shevardnadze was becoming more and more dependent on the speaker of Parliament.

During the same period, Zhvania also gained a foothold in controlling the media, particularly the private TV station Rustavi 2, which by the late 1990s was watched by almost everyone in the country as their main source of news. The story of Zhvania's relationship with the network is very important, because this channel would play a crucial role in many of the political events that would take place in Georgia in the years ahead.

Rustavi 2 was established in 1993 by Erosi Kitsmarishvili in the city of Rustavi, the provincial municipality of the region of Kvemo Kartli, as an alternative to the local government station there, which was controlled by the governor, Levan Mamaladze, a Shevardnadze and Zhvania ally.[12] Mamaladze could not stand the negativity that was coming from Rustavi 2 and tried to get it shut down several times, with full backing from Zhvania.

Around the same time, a private TV station called Tamarioni was being developed in Tbilisi. To operate, Tamarioni needed a television frequency, which was hard to come by but which it secured from Shevardnadze. Zhvania, then a senior member of the newly formed CUG, had tried to get control of the same frequency that was given to Tamarioni, but ultimately lost that particular battle to Pikria Chikhradze, who was a leading pro-independence student leader in the 1980s and who, in the 1992–1994 period (when Shevardnadze was attacked by nationalists for signing a deal with Yeltsin) supported Shevard-nadze and lent her nationalist credentials to him. In 1994, though not in public office, Chikhradze used her influence to provide political cover for Tamarioni, and succeeded in getting the president to grant the station a Tbilisi-based television frequency.

Realizing that Mamaladze would never let him succeed in Rustavi, Kitsmarishvili approached Tamarioni's leaders, who were very inexperienced in business dealings, about forming a joint venture. Ultimately, Tamarioni's television frequency was transferred to this new venture, which was formally controlled by Kitsmarishvili.

In 1995, at Shevardnadze's request, Chikhradze accepted a top position on the CUG electoral list and was elected to Parliament, giving up any formal association with the Tamarioni-Rustavi 2 joint venture. In the new Parliament, Chikhradze and Zhvania soon became leading opponents. One of their fights was over this TV station, which Zhvania still hoped to control. Through tactics unknown to me, Zhvania got Kitsmarishvili to break with his partners, and the two started a partnership of their own. Given that Kitsmarishvili controlled the company that was given the frequency that was meant for Tamarioni, he in effect left Tamarioni's original leadership out in the cold. It was never clear to me what exact role Zhvania had in Rustavi 2—whether he actually owned the station (off the books, of course), or whether he simply had some sort of arrangement with Kitsmarishvili to secure positive coverage. However, a close relationship certainly existed, as was evident through numerous developments in the years that followed. In subsequent years, Zhvania directed a great deal of foreign donor assistance to the channel, helping it become the dominant station in the country by 1999.

FAILURE OF "REFORMS"

There is no doubt that the Parliament elected in 1995 passed some important reforms, and Georgia began to develop real political institutions. Because it was constitutionally independent, the Parliament itself gained a great deal of prestige and influence over the political process. Georgia moved away from being the totally lawless country that it had been after the coup against Gamsakhurdia. Notwithstanding the fact that the legal and regulatory framework that was implemented was far from a real free-market system, the control of lawlessness was sufficient to help bring about massive economic growth. For example, after falling 22 percent in 1991, 45 percent in 1992, and 29 percent in 1993, the economy stayed static in 1994 and then grew at a rate of only 3.1

percent in 1995. However, in 1996 the economy grew by a staggering 11.2 percent, and in 1997 by 10.5 percent.[13] There was also significant job creation, though most of it in the informal sector.

While legislative changes were an important success, they were a far cry from the awesome achievement Zhvania painted during his travels abroad, when he often spoke of the seven hundred new laws passed by the Parliament.[14] The fact is that these laws were often mutually contradictory. They also greatly expanded the scope and the power of government at the expense of political and economic freedom. Most importantly, they created a regulatory system in which extralegality and corruption were unavoidable, because operating by the laws was simply not possible if one wanted to succeed in an enterprise or lead a seminormal lifestyle.

Indeed, while Zhvania believed that "corruption and irregularities in the rule of law present the greatest obstacles to implementing new laws and regulations,"[15] in reality the new laws and regulations that Zhvania and his allies had pushed through the legislature were actually primarily responsible for much of the corruption. Nothing demonstrates this better than the value-added tax (VAT), which was introduced in 1997 as part of a new tax law, adopted as part of "European integration."

Zhvania and the "young reformers" were the great cheerleaders for this new law, which imposed a 20 percent VAT on all businesses with turnover of over 24,000 Georgian lari (about $12,000 in 1997). Georgia chose an "income/credit" form of VAT, requiring the tax to be charged on the full price at each stage of the sale. Such a system presupposes an economy in which every transaction is documented—which is often true in fully developed modern states, but certainly was not true in Georgia. As a result, the tax was very easy to avoid, because it did not have to be reported when a receipt was not issued. Given that Georgia was largely a cash economy, receipts were issued infrequently anyway, and so most people simply avoided the VAT, thus reducing the cost of doing business. In other words, the VAT became like a 20 percent sales tax on all products—because it had to be added to the price, but the government virtually never reimbursed it.[16]

Most of Georgia's so-called civil society (i.e., the majority of the foreign-funded NGOs) and the government (especially Zhvania and other "young reformers," such as Saakashvili and Zurab Nogaideli, who was finance minister under Shevardnadze) called this "corruption" and "law-breaking." They never bothered to consider the fact that a 20 percent VAT was too high in a transitional, weak, underdeveloped economy like that of Georgia. Indeed, most economists outside of continental Europe would agree that any VAT would probably have been detrimental for the Georgian economy, period. However, adding 20 percent to the costs of goods would make those goods simply too expensive for anyone to be able to afford them. Thus, people avoided the VAT not because they were "corrupt," but because it increased the cost of doing business so much that the only solution for those who wanted to survive in the market was to ignore it. Furthermore, the low rate of collection was not simply the fault of those who avoided the tax, but also of the government, which did not take into account Georgian realities (such as the cash economy, which does not require receipts) when it created the VAT system.

If the tax law, which imposed the VAT, accomplished anything at all, it was to slow down economic growth and push even more of the economy into the shadow market. In 1998 economic growth fell to 3.1 percent (three times less than the year before), while in 1999 growth was at 2.9 percent.[17] The social tax was another significant problem because it required employers to pay a 33 percent add-on for all salaried employees. Neither the worker nor the employer saw any benefit from this tax, since Georgia did not have a social-security system that guaranteed a decent retirement pension. Instead, the social tax was used to pay a monthly 14 lari (approximately US $7) "pension" to all retirees. Most of the time, these pensions were late anyway. Thus, neither businesses nor workers had any incentive to actually pay the tax. Furthermore, because it was so high, paying the social tax would have made it impossible for most businesses to employ workers—that is, creating jobs became far too expensive. As a result, businesses simply kept most employees off the books or reported a very small wage, while paying a much higher real wage off the books.

The introduction of the new tax law was an excellent example of how the "young reformers" saw progress as a carbon-copy imitation of Western laws, without considering the real political, social, and economic context in which they were operating. Additionally, the "young reformers" and the NGOs enchantment with a tax scheme in which the VAT played such a prominent role was a clear indication that these groups saw continental Europe's "welfare state" as the best model for Georgia, rather than America's and Britain's more libertarian, free-market system.[18]

The tax law was far from the only example of how lawmaking by "young reformers" failed to take into account local needs or national political and economic realities, and how it simply tried to impose from the top "reforms" that actually moved Georgia backwards on the road to good governance. However, it is probably the most tangible example, and the one that had the most detrimental impact on the country's economy. It is also a very real demonstration of the fact that the "young reformers" were, more often than not, creating a Potemkin village in Georgia—an image that looked a lot better than the reality. They were creating a system that could never survive in the long term, but that appeared good on the outside, at least for a while.

A good summary of the results of the reform process undertaken by Zhvania and the "young reformers" was made by the USAID. In a request for applications for its "Citizens Advocate!" program in early 2002, it provided a surprisingly honest picture of what had gone on in Georgia during the 1990s, precisely at the time when USAID was also spending a tremendous amount of money supporting the "reform process" and portraying policymakers in Georgia as a success of democratic development. It was true that this real picture of Georgia was hidden amid praise for alleged reforms, but in true USAID fashion, the document often classified the very same developments as both successes and failures. Nonetheless, the level of honesty in the presentation was hard to miss:

> After about a decade of large-scale corruption, largely failed and unimplemented reforms and, most importantly, a sharp decline in the quality of life for the vast majority of Georgians, euphoria and optimism have given way to cynicism and defeatism. Recent opinion polls show that indifference, apathy, and cynicism are at an all-time high in Georgia since independence from the Soviet Union. "Georgians' confidence in their government has declined across the board," with the number of people who believe that Georgia is not a democracy exceeding the number of people who believe it is. Citizens in a recent focus group analysis said that they feel forgotten by government, do not know who their local government representatives are, and do not believe that they (the officials) can accomplish anything. Not only does the public have little faith that the government can solve any of their problems, the government is often seen as the source of many problems.
>
> Corruption remains at an all-time high in Georgia, pervading all sectors of society. Favorable judgments are often for sale or depend on connections. Full and equitable access to justice does not exist. Many people have no faith in being able to obtain a fair judgment and avoid courts altogether. Even when corruption is uncovered and widely publicized, perpetrators are not brought to justice.[19]

Foreign policy was probably an area of greater success during the tenure of the 1995 Parliament.[20] At that time, the U.S. energy strategy for the Caspian began to take hold; a consortium led by British Petroleum agreed to build a pipeline through Georgia and Turkey to deliver Caspian oil to the world.[21]

More broadly, Georgia's relationship with the West in general, and the United States in particular, grew much stronger. On April 22, 1998, Georgia was accepted into the Council of Europe. Shevardnadze and Zhvania presented this as a great testament to their "reforms," and proof of Georgia's "Europeanisms."

Zhvania believed that Georgia's inclusion in the Council was his great achievement. During the acceptance ceremony, he gave a passionate speech, declaring that "I am Georgian and therefore I am European."

Membership in the Council required Georgia to accept certain obligations. The implementation of these obligations—such as protecting freedom of speech, establishing a framework for an independent judiciary, reforming the police and criminal justice system, and delineating powers between the central authority in Tbilisi and the local authorities in the regions—could help protect democracy and pluralism in the country. However, there were other obligations that carried a great price.

By the mid-1990s, postmodern views about human rights and the nature and purpose of government had largely become the norm in continental Europe, and these views had a prominent role in the treaties and other commitments that Georgia had to sign in order to be allowed to call itself "European." Among other things, Georgia was required to abolish the death penalty, because Europeans believe that the death penalty is unjust. In addition, Tbilisi had to sign the European Social Charter, which made the "right to strike" a fundamental right, and as such severely limits the ability of entrepreneurs and business to engage in the free market.

The obligation that created the most tension in Georgia was the government's acquiescence to the demand that the ethnic Turks from the region of Meskheti, who number over 100,000, be permitted to return to Georgia. These Meskhetian Turks were deported to Uzbekistan by the Soviet authorities in 1940–1944. Their return is staunchly opposed by almost all Georgians, who view them with suspicion because they originally moved to Georgia during the Turkish occupation. Because permitting their return would cause an upheaval in Meskheti and surrounding regions, the Georgian government has steadfastly declined to fulfill this obligation since 1995. Indeed, while Shevardnadze's government was successful in implementing some of the charter's measures (such as the abolition of the death penalty), most others (including those that would have helped Georgia's democratic transition) have been delayed.

Elections of 1999 and 2000, and the Closure of Georgia's Second Democratic Opening

After three years of "reforms" that failed to move Georgia toward the consolidation of democracy made possible by the adoption of the new Constitution in 1995, Georgia once again moved into an electoral period. In these elections, Zhvania served as the campaign manager for both the CUG in legislative elections in October 1999, and Shevardnadze's reelection effort in April 2000. The legislative race proved far more complicated for him than the presidential one. While the CUG was still quite popular, victory was by no means guaranteed, because people were upset by the lack of real reforms and by slow economic progress. In response, the CUG campaigned on the promise "From Stability to Prosperity."

Zhvania also brought to Georgia several Russian political consultants, who designed a strategy of turning the Revival Party—CUG's former ally, which was controlled by the local dictator in Adjaria, Aslan Abashidze—into the main "enemy" of the sitting government. The idea was to give citizens a simple choice between the CUG and Revival. This, the consultants reasoned correctly, would lead most people to vote for the CUG, notwithstanding their misgivings about it, because an overwhelming majority of Georgians despised Abashidze and disapproved of his methods of governance in Adjaria. The strategy ultimately proved very successful and helped marginalize other opposition political parties.

As part of his strategy, Zhvania used the NGO community and the media very effectively. At the height of the 1999 legislative campaign, Zhvania unleashed Rustavi 2 and the NGO sector against Revival and its leader, Aslan Abashidze—who was justifiably painted as a brutal dictator, thus further reducing the number of real votes that he may have received across the country.

Ultimately, however, electoral fraud and manipulation were the most important part of Zhvania's path to victory. These efforts were coordinated for him by Khatuna Gogorishvili, who was both his chief of staff and CUG's main representative to the Central Election Commission (CEC), where the party had a controlling majority. Prior to the actual vote, the CEC dramatically expanded voter rolls, putting about 10 percent more people on them than were actually residing in Georgia.[22] These voters then "went to vote" on election day and "cast" their ballots for CUG. In other words, expanding voter rolls and reporting unreal voters was a more clever way of ballot stuffing and a novel technique of electoral fraud. Furthermore, instead of adding ballots during the vote count, precinct electoral protocols were simply changed at the district and national level, increasing the total turnout figure and the CUG tally. Since CUG controlled the electoral commissions, demands for recounts, which may have shown discrepancies, were never honored. Manipulations were particularly flagrant in Kvemo Kartli and Javakheti, two regions that are populated by ethnic Azeris and Armenians, respectively.

By increasing the total turnout through these manipulations, Zhvania was in a position to increase the number of votes opposition parties needed to receive in order to reach 7 percent, the threshold for entering the legislature through proportional elections. This way, he could keep parties outside of

Parliament without ever touching the ballots cast for these parties. In all likelihood, at least two groups—Shalva Natelashvili's Labor Party and Irina Sarishvili-Chanturia's National Democratic Party—surpassed the 7 percent barrier among real voters, but were kept out of Parliament through padded turnout figures.

Incidentally, the 7 percent barrier had been introduced in Parliament just prior to the 1999 elections by the National Democratic Party's leader, Irina Sarishvili-Chanturia, widow of the late Gia Chanturia. The 1995 Constitution had originally set the barrier at 5 percent, which was far easier to overcome. Sarishvili-Chanturia made this proposal at the urging of Zhvania, who had promised to use the government's administrative resources to support NDP at the expense of other opposition parties. This way, NDP would "overcome" the new 7 percent barrier while other parties would not. Sarisvhili-Chanturia's proposal would have never passed without the CUG's vote in favor of it in Parliament. Ultimately, the NDP probably got just barely over 7 percent without government support, but Zhvania broke his promise and kept the party out of Parliament anyway.

The CEC's final vote total was reported at about two million, probably at least 30 percent more than the actual turnout. The CUG allegedly received 894,850 votes (42.07 percent, or 85 proportional seats in Parliament), while Revival allegedly received 540,389 votes (24.41 percent, or 51 seats). Abashidze did not have the capacity to manipulate votes across the country, but in Adjaria he reported 100 percent turnout, with a near unanimous vote for Revival. Protocols from Adjaria were so "perfect" that they were reminiscent of Soviet days. In addition to CUG and Revival, the only other party to overcome the 7 percent barrier was Industry Will Save Georgia, which was founded by beer magnate Gogi Topadze. According to sources both inside the CUG and Industry, Zhvania tried hard to keep this party out of the legislature as well by proposing to increase the total turnout even more. However, this move was vetoed by Shevardnadze.[23]

In the wake of the parliamentary election, in April 2000, Shevardnadze easily won reelection as president. Former Communist leader Jumber Patiashvili provided token opposition in the race. He garnered little support due to the fact that he was one of the most despised politicians in Georgia after his role in authorizing the April 9 massacre of pro-independence demonstrators in 1989. However, it remains unclear whether the turnout actually reached 50 percent (the minimum necessary to validate the vote), or whether techniques similar to those used in the legislative elections were also applied during the presidential vote.

These two elections, especially the one in 1999, were characterized by greater and more serious electoral violations than anything ever seen in Georgia before or since. As a result, they ended Georgia's second democratic opening.

Another magnificent opportunity to consolidate democratic institutions and to create a truly just and representative political regime was destroyed. In 2000, Georgia was undoubtedly in better shape than at the end of its first democratic opening in 1992. The country had made significant progress, from near complete collapse to a political regime that was just at its core, but had failed to fulfill the hopes and aspirations of the Georgian people and was quickly becoming politically bankrupt, having to resort to fraud in order to win an election in an environment in which it faced limited opposition.

Unfortunately, the West stood by while Zhvania and Shevardnadze manipulated elections. While there were hundreds of monitors in Georgia for the 1999 parliamentary election, their reporting failed to account for the government's most shameful actions. Unfortunately, the West preferred Shevardnadze and Zhvania to the principles of democracy. Sadly, experience suggests that this has been the case before and since in far too many transitional democracies.

Shevardnadze had played an indispensable role in Georgia between 1992 and 1996. He stabilized the country and secured its independence and sovereignty, engineered its international recognition, and brought about the founding of the Constitution. In effect, he secured and protected from collapse a country that was on the verge of becoming a completely failed state dominated by warlords and criminals. If Georgia remains an independent country well into the twenty-first century, which is likely, this will largely be because of the indispensable role Shevardnadze played in the 1992–1995 period.

Nonetheless, he is also responsible for many of the failures that followed 1995. Blame should not be placed solely on Shevardnadze, of course. The so-called "young reformers" were probably as responsible, if not more so, for discrediting the idea of democracy, for electoral manipulations, and for failures of governance. Seemingly pro-Western, with good English skills and knowledge of "democratic terminology," they were able to deceive much of the West into believing that they were pushing successful reforms (and, starting in 2001, that Shevardnadze was the main force resisting them). In reality, these "reforms" were the main problem for Georgia—especially in the area of economic development, an area in which "reformers" controlled all governmental posts.[24]

While the spring of 2000 marked the "official" end to Georgia's "second democratic opening," the Georgian political system and the people's natural democratic instincts soon gave birth to another opportunity for democratic change. This time around, it was the business community that helped usher in the democratic opening that I consider next.

3

Gamkrelidze and the Collapse of the CUG

n 2001–2002, in advance of the 2003 legislative elections and Shevardnadze's planned retirement in 2005, a new democratic opening presented
itself. It was largely brought about by Georgian businessmen, and their
decision to challenge Shevardnadze and the "young reformers." In this
chapter, I examine the factors that led to this opening and discuss the extent to
which this development changed politics in Georgia. This change was the
beginning of my direct involvement in Georgian politics, and I therefore give
a personal as well as a factual assessment.

Challenge to CUG's Dominance

In order to win the 1999 elections, the CUG relied on the financial support of
the Georgian business community, and in return included on its electoral list
a number of prominent businessmen. Having these individuals on the list was
a means for Zhvania to expand his influence into a part of civil society where
his power was weakest. More immediately, he could argue that the CUG was
seeking a new mandate with "new faces" to help tackle the nation's problems.
Indeed, the "new" or "fresh" faces campaign was the second key component of
Zhvania's strategy.

Many of these businessmen were less interested in politics than in using
the parliamentary platform to benefit their business interests. Otherwise,
it would be hard to explain the hundreds of thousands of dollars that some
spent on supporting the CUG. However, some of the entrepreneurs were amateurs politically, and it appears that they honestly believed the promises from

Shevardnadze, Zhvania, and the rest of the CUG's leadership that the party intended to change its ways and to press for real free-market reforms, and that it wanted representatives of the business community involved in this process.

Understanding the character of the Georgian business community is crucial. It was pluralistic and diversified. The state never controlled it. While businessmen did avoid taxes, because paying them all would have resulted in bankruptcy (especially after 1998), unlike their Russian counterparts, entrepreneurs in Georgia had not built their companies at the expense of the government or cheap privatization of high-value state property. Rather, most of the large businessmen had started out as small entrepreneurs in the early 1990s and succeeded in developing a private sector *despite* the government's policies and actions that hurt the free market. As a result, unlike much of the NGO community, which was dependent on Zhvania, the business community owed little to Shevardnadze or Zhvania. Furthermore, the business sector was very different from its counterparts in other post-Soviet states.

Some of these businessmen, though complete political "amateurs," came into office in 1999 truly intending to change things. After the elections, two of the most prominent business leaders in this group were given important leadership positions. Levan Gachechiladze, the country's most dominant wine magnate, became head of the Economic Policy and Reform Committee. Meanwhile, David Gamkrelidze became the head of the Parliament's Health and Social Issues Committee. Gamkrelidze, a pediatrician, was the founder of the largest insurance company Aldagi, a firm he started in 1990 that eventually grew to dominate the Georgian insurance market. Under the leadership of these two, entrepreneurs pushed for the reforms they had been promised, and soon discovered how naive they had been about the intentions of CUG's leadership.

Immediately after the legislative elections, in late 1999 and early 2000, Zhvania, Saakashvili (who had become head of the CUG's faction in the new Parliament),[1] and other leaders rejected calls for free-market reforms, claiming that they were "delaying" these initiatives until after the April 2000 presidential elections. They wanted to focus on Shevardnadze's reelection, and claimed that immediately thereafter, the real reform movement, with which they enticed a number of prominent businessmen to join their camp, would start.

Nothing changed, however, after Shevardnadze was reelected on April 9, 2000. Instead, Zhvania arranged for his close ally Giorgi Arsenishvili to be appointed as state minister. This was the senior government position charged with coordinating the work of the economic ministries (such as Finance, Economic Development, Transport, Energy, etc.). Zhvania pushed this appointment, even though he had promised Gamkrelidze and Gachechiladze to push for the appointment of a truly competent individual who could lead the government in tackling the country's economic problems. That was something no one expected Arsenishvili to do, because he was not a figure of sufficient stature.

Gamkrelidze, Gachechiladze, and several other businessmen-parliamentarians who had been listening to Zhvania's unfulfilled promises since November 1999 were furious. This led to an open conflict. Immediately after the announcement of Arsenishvili's appointment, Zhvania and Saakashvili left for Strasbourg to attend a meeting of the Parliamentary Assembly of the Council of Europe. In Tbilisi, meanwhile, Gamkrelidze and Gachechiladze got over 118 deputies (more than the parliamentary majority) to sign a letter demanding an investigation of the budget deficit, and calling for criminal charges to be filed against those in the government who were responsible for the failure to meet the budgetary guidelines. The letter was a response to the official budget report, announced several days before Shevardnadze's reelection, which detailed an unplanned budget deficit of 300 million lari.

The deficit was largely caused by Zhvania's election maneuvers in 1999 and 2000 (such as using state funds to pay for a constant supply of electricity, road repair work, etc.). This was the largest deficit Georgia had seen since at least 1995 and was largely the responsibility of David Onoprishvili, a member of Zhvania's team whom Shevardnadze had appointed as finance minister at the insistence of the "young reformers." Because an investigation was going to create huge problems for the "young reformers," Zhvania and Saakashvili opposed the idea. Nonetheless, many leading CUG parliamentarians, including several committee chairmen, signed the letter demanding one.

From Strasbourg, Zhvania demanded that signatories in leadership positions either take back their signatures or resign, while threatening with reprisal all other deputies who dared to support the letter. Many CUG members did withdraw their support, including Nino Burdjanadze, who would later become speaker of Parliament. Meanwhile, according to Gamkrelidze, in several phone conversations both Zhvania and Saakashvili made it clear that they were not willing to cooperate on this issue. As a result, the two rebels decided to meet Zhvania (with TV cameras in tow) in front of his office the first day he returned to Tbilisi, and hand in their letters of resignation. This was partially a publicity stunt, but the media loved the move because no one had done anything like this since Zhvania had become speaker—the notion of giving up power by choice was not a principle many in the CUG followed. This was the beginning of the end of the CUG and its one-party dominance of Georgian politics.

Several weeks later, in mid-May, with popular and media support growing for a budgetary investigation, Zhvania gave in, agreed to form a committee for this purpose, and proposed that Gamkrelidze become its chairman. Meanwhile, as this investigation proceeded throughout the summer, the debate between the rebellious parliamentarians and the young reformers raged on. It soon became clear that the businessmen who dared to challenge Zhvania-Saakashvili's team were becoming very popular.[2] The response was understandably vicious and immediate. Zhvania's team called the businessmen traitors and declared that they were endangering Georgia's stability and democracy, which they claimed only Shevardnadze and the CUG could provide.

The "young reformers" also claimed that the businessmen were corrupt. This argument was somewhat convoluted, given that a year ago they had taken a great deal of pride in including these same individuals on the CUG electoral list. However, calling these businessmen corrupt was the beginning of a three-year campaign to discredit the entire Georgian business sector, and to convince the people that it was full of Russian-style oligarchs. The problem with this argument was that Georgian businessmen were fundamentally different—unlike their Russian counterparts, most of the Georgian entrepreneurs were not under the power of the state. They had not made their money through the abuse of state resources and privatization.[3] For this reason, most did not qualify for the term "oligarch," which in the post-Soviet space usually has been used to refer to "entrepreneurs" who made their wealth by taking over property that used to be state-owned at minimal or no cost. This tirade against the businessmen was supported by key elements within the NGO community—representatives from organizations such as the Liberty Institute, CIPDD, and GYLA—whose political ideology was heavily influenced by their leftist counterparts in continental Europe and was thus strongly anti-business.

Initially, inexperienced in political debates, Gamkrelidze and Gachechiladze often lost joint live TV appearances to Zhvania, Saakashvili, and other young reformers, who were very well versed in using populist propaganda to advance their message. The big break for Gamkrelidze came when he had an opportunity to present the findings of his budgetary investigative committee to Parliament. This became one of the most dramatic scenes ever in Parliament.

The expectation was that Gamkrelidze would outline the massive problems related to the management of the budget and then place blame on Shevardnadze. This was a perfect scenario for Zhvania because citizens would hear a powerful critique of Shevardnadze (something that would weaken the president even more and make him more dependent on Zhvania), while the speaker, by engineering a defense, would be able to show Shevardnadze how useful he was. However, while Shevardnadze deserved a great deal of the blame, the young reformers were most at fault: it was their alleged "reforms" and "enlightened" legislation and governance style that had created an environment in which corruption thrived. In fact, Zhvania's team members had controlled the economic positions in the government at least since 1998, and most of the serious financial problems started after they had gained these positions.

Gamkrelidze presented his findings to a chamber full of dumbfounded legislators and an even more confused Zhvania, who was not expecting such treatment and had no ready answer. This debate moved Gamkrelidze to a much higher standing as a politician.

One of Gamkrelidze's problems throughout his debates with the young reformers was that he and his allies lacked the political infrastructure necessary to take on their opponents on an equal footing. For a while, Gamkrelidze's entire staff consisted of just two people—a press secretary, and an economist who was helping him with research into budgetary corruption. By contrast, the young reformers had the extensive party machine of the CUG behind them, along with the entire state apparatus. Gamkrelidze began to counter this in November 2000, when he announced the formation of the New Faction. Ten other parliamentarians withstood a great deal of pressure from the young reformers and decided to join. By forming a unit in Parliament, the rebels received a seat on the Parliament's Bureau, which in Georgia functions like the House of Representatives' Rules Committee. Six months later, in June 2001, Gamkrelidze and his allies formed the New Rights Party (NRP), which they presented as a philosophically driven alternative to the CUG.[4]

Whatever one might think of the Georgian business community and its leaders, one thing was clear: for whatever reason, these individuals were willing to put their own financial interests and well-being at risk, seemingly for the sake of some noble ideas. Such actions on the part of the most well-off individuals in the country suggested that Georgia could indeed have a favorable future.[5] The conflict between those who joined the New Faction and the CUG (especially the so-called "young reformers" wing of the majority party) was a crucial development for Georgian democracy. For the first time since the CUG had become the dominant force in Georgia at the time of the 1995 parliamentary elections, a real political alternative was born—one that was not perceived by a majority of the people as being worse than Shevardnadze, Zhvania, Saakashvili, and the rest of the CUG.[6] In other words, a force emerged that a large share of the population perceived favorably.[7] At the same time, people took the new opponents of the governing party seriously because they had a proven track record of success. It seems that citizens were particularly impressed by the fact that this group offered something more than petty bickering. Even though the majority of those who formed the New Faction did not quite understand the difference between center-right and center-left (or conservative and liberal) ideologies, by instinct they were what in America are called free-market conservatives. As such, they offered a critique of the Shevardnadze-Zhvania government that was founded on this ideological point of view. For many Georgians, especially those under the age of thirty, this perspective was very refreshing.

When I had a chance to speak to Gamkrelidze about this period more than two years later, he had a very simple but satisfying answer for why he had begun to attack Zhvania and Saakashvili. According to him, it was impossible to have political pluralism in Georgia as long as the country was dominated by the CUG. As a result, he felt that breaking with the CUG was the only way to make real democratic change possible. Given the small number of his allies that were in Parliament, he felt that his only choice was to pit the two factions within the CUG—Zhvania-Saakashvili's "young reformers" and Shevard-nadze's traditional nomenklatura supporters—against each other, so that ulti-mately they could no longer coexist in the same party. This, he believed accurately, would help open Georgian political space. He also felt that given Zhvania-Saakashvili's control of the Parliament and the legislative process, it was logical for him to direct his fire against them, as a representative of the leg-islative opposition, rather than Shevardnadze, who was not involved in the run-ning of the legislature. Moreover, given that Shevardnadze was going to be retiring soon anyway, he did not represent a real challenge on the political stage—unlike Zhvania and Saakashvili, who were the future of the CUG.

By mid-2001, it was clear to the young reformers that there was a huge risk for their long-term success in being associated with Shevardnadze, even if this association came with the benefit of a great deal of power. Additionally, it became apparent that the rebellion and the relentless attacks on the two wings of the CUG—Shevardnadze's group and Zhvania-Saakashvili's group—was particularly taxing for the latter team, since unlike the unpopular president, the "young reformers" actually had public support that they could lose if they were tied to Shevardnadze's team in the minds of the people. This had the effect of pitting the two CUG camps against each other, since the young reformers had no choice but to go after the Shevardnadze wing if they wanted to keep faith with the public. As a result, the confrontation between the two sides became inevitable.

War inside the CUG

Initially, neither the speaker of Parliament nor his young but restless protégé was prepared to break with the president. In October 2000, Saakashvili had accepted the position of justice minister, and from there tried to position him-self against the more unpopular members of Shevardnadze's administration. His goal was to present himself to the people as a crusader against corruption. Though it was not quite clear what actions he was actually taking against cor-ruption (if he was taking any at all), Saakashvili was a master showman who did an excellent job at selling himself to the public.

It was for exactly these reasons that on August 9, 2001, during a cabinet meeting, Saakashvili angrily challenged various ministers and declared that they were corrupt. He pulled out photos of fancy buildings that were under construction in Tbilisi and claimed that they were owned by these ministers. This scandal was the sort of sensationalist, albeit effective, incident that one came to expect from Saakashvili. He had little proof for the allegations that he was making, which were based on charges that most Georgians already believed were true. Meanwhile, the solution Saakashvili offered against these alleged offenders—to confiscate property from those government officials who could not prove the origin of their property—was also quite typical of him, and of the neo-Bolshevik ideas that many in the NGO community were spreading. Instead of treating the individuals in question as innocent until proven guilty, making it incumbent upon the government to prove whatever charges it might have against these officials and show some respect for the fundamental right of private property, Saakashvili pandered to the angry masses by demanding that it be up to the accused to prove their innocence.

Less than a month after this incident, Saakashvili resigned as justice minister, declaring, "I consider it immoral for me to remain as a member of Shevardnadze's government."[8] To many, this claim sounded very disingenuous, given that Saakashvili's entire career had been tied to Shevardnadze, on whose team he had served for seven years. Shevardnadze in 2001 was not much different than he had been half a decade earlier, when Saakashvili joined his team, while many of the problems of Shevardnadze's governance actually originated with the "young reformers" whom Zhvania and Saakashvili led. However, Saakashvili's anti-Shevardnadze rhetoric was powerful and influenced the public. In September, Saakashvili won his old legislative seat in the Vake district of Tbilisi in a race against Irina Sarishvili-Chanturia, the leader of the National Democratic Party. Compared to 1999, Saakashvili did not owe this victory to ballot stuffing and fraud. On September 22, Saakashvili registered his own political party—United National Movement. Publicly, he aligned it with a small group of supporters of the late President Zviad Gamsakhurdia, led by Zviad Dzidziguri, and the Republican Party, an NGO-led group of "intellectuals," and several nonprofit organizations (such as the Georgian Young Lawyers' Association) that were supporting them.

Saakashvili's decision to go on his own weakened Zhvania, particularly in the "civil society," because many of the speaker's old allies (who had benefited greatly from their association with him through the 1990s) now backed his younger protégé. Nonetheless, as the more senior individual, Zhvania had far more to lose than Saakashvili by breaking with Shevardnadze. As a result, he took a more moderate route.

There are reports that in early 2001 Zhvania tried to convince Shevardnadze to resign, so that he could take the reins of power as acting president and
run for the office of president as a semi-incumbent.[9] While I have not been
able to confirm this, I have one report that during the height of the winter 2001
electricity crisis, when Tbilisi saw regular demonstrations and street closures
by the people who were demanding electrical power, Zhvania actually convinced Shevardnadze to resign. There are allegations that these protests were
in fact engineered and manipulated by Zhvania from behind the scenes.
Allegedly, the president was so overwhelmed by the problems of the winter that
he was about to sign the resignation letter when Interior Minister Kakha
Targmadze (a powerful Zhvania opponent) stormed into Shevardnadze's office
and stopped him. If this incident is indeed true, as I have some reason to suspect that it is, then this was probably the beginning of the souring of the relationship between Shevardnadze and Zhvania.

Also in that winter, Zhvania convinced Shevardnadze that Georgia needed
a more powerful president and a prime minister, in a system akin to Russia.
He had the president submitted a set of constitutional amendments that would
have created this post and turned Georgia into a hyper-presidential system.
However, unlike the European prime minister, the Georgian one would derive
his powers not from the legislature, but from the president. This was the
model Shevardnadze had initially backed in 1995, when the Constitution was
being written. The amendments were never acted upon, because soon a large
number of CUG parliamentarians, many of whom were beginning to turn
against Zhvania by this time, perceived the amendments as a ploy by the
speaker to engineer for himself an executive-branch position.

Zhvania's first public break with the president happened in the spring of
2001, when he sent an open letter to Shevardnadze complaining about corruption in Georgia. This was a direct response to Gamkrelidze's attacks and rising
popularity. However throughout the summer, he continued to serve as speaker
of Parliament and controlled the legislative process on Shevardnadze's behalf.
Indeed, at a government meeting several days after sending the letter, Zhvania
gave an impassioned speech, praising Shevardnadze and even crying while
apologizing for his corruption letter.

During that same period in 2001, Zhvania and Saakashvili, while still formally allied with Shevardnadze inside the country, began to undermine his
standing internationally. Over the years, Shevardnadze had successfully used
his international prestige to solve domestic political problems. As a result, the
young reformers realized that their political hopes could not advance unless
the West, especially Washington, became convinced that Shevardnadze was a
problem. In April 2001, Peter Baker of the *Washington Post* wrote an article

titled "A Hero to the West, a Villain at Home: Shevardnadze Leads Georgians to Hardship."[10] The article included a quote from a Saakashvili ally, Vano Merabishvili, who stated that it is "impossible to do serious business in Georgia if you do not have a relation with the president." "He is tired now," Merabishvili went on. "He does not want to hear the word reform now."

This was vintage "young reformers": while inside the country they were defending Shevardnadze and CUG against attacks from Gamkrelidze and his allies, internationally they were criticizing the president, using the very same arguments, and accusing him of being fully responsible for problems that they had helped create.

Later in 2001, Georgetown professor Charles King published an article in *The National Interest* entitled "Potemkin Georgia: Four Myths about Post-Soviet Georgia."[11] The article was the most one-sided narrative of events in Georgia that one could imagine, and parts of it could have been written by Zhvania himself. While King had a few excellent points, including a semicritical description of the "young reformers" and a very accurate presentation of the problem of American foreign aid to Georgia, Zhvania received the most glowing treatment. King called him "the most powerful genuine democrat on the Georgian scene," even though Zhvania himself was responsible for spreading in the West the very same myths about Georgian democracy that King was trying to debunk.

King had never really studied Georgian politics with much care and had based his piece on a very brief stay in the country, during which he primarily met with English-speaking "analysts" who shaped his outlook.[12] This probably explains why he failed to account for some very obvious realities. For example, while he correctly criticized the 1999 and 2000 elections for fraud, he made no mention of the fact that the "genuine democrat" Zhvania, who was the CUG's campaign manager, was the one who was responsible for that fraud. In addition, King correctly assessed that the CUG had become "a mechanism for capture of the state rather than transforming it," yet he failed to mention that it was the so-called democrats that he was praising and not Shevardnadze, who had spearheaded this process of capturing the state apparatus. Furthermore, for all his criticism of Georgian democracy, he did not account for the most important developments that were taking place in Georgian politics at the time of his writing, which involved the challenge to the CUG presented by the businessmen turned politicians.

Nonetheless, while these and other publications about Georgia in 2001 often failed to tell the full story, they were successfully undermining Shevardnadze's standing abroad and the support that Washington and other foreign capitals were willing to give him.

Protests in October–November 2001

Domestically, by the mid-fall of 2001, with Saakashvili now openly breaking with Shevardnadze in order to maintain his popularity, it was clear that Gamkrelidze's strategy of pitting the two sides of the CUG against each other was working, and was leading to the collapse of the dominant party. It was in this environment that on October 30, 2001, officers from the Security Ministry entered Rustavi 2 television, allegedly to conduct an investigation of whether the station was paying all of its taxes properly. However, it was not clear why the Security Ministry was investigating this issue. Meanwhile, thousands of Georgians were outraged. Earlier, on July 25, Rustavi 2's star anchorman, Irakli Sanaia, had been found dead in what many in Georgia regarded as a government-engineered crime, and after Security Ministry stormed Rustavi, many people became convinced that the government was after the only television station that was reporting independent news.

Rustavi 2 was quite likely guilty of some of the allegations that were being made against it by the financial police—as any other prominent business in Georgia would be, since most did not pay all of the taxes that were required of them. Meanwhile, Sanaia's death probably had little to do with politics; evidence suggests that a private dispute was the real reason behind his murder. However, the station went into overdrive in an attempt to protect itself, calling on the people to come into the streets to defend freedom of speech. Tbilisi residents responded by the thousands and gathered in front of Parliament as they had in years past during the pro-independence protests. The demonstrations soon turned into an airing of general grievances against Shevardnadze and the government, whom most people associated with the crushing economic hardship and the failure of reforms.

The generally known story of how the situation was resolved goes something like this: Zhvania decided to sacrifice his position of speaker and made a deal with the president—he would resign as long as Shevardnadze fired the government. In reality, the picture was far more complicated.

Throughout the late summer and the fall, David Gamkrelidze had been circulating a petition in Parliament which called for a no-confidence vote on Zhvania's leadership. The petition needed majority support to succeed. It had garnered the support of most deputies who opposed Zhvania, but not of those CUG deputies who were beholden to Shevardnadze rather than Zhvania. Without these CUG members, the petition could not get majority support. Once the protests started, by the morning of November 1, enough CUG parliamentarians broke from his legislative majority and signed the petition to guarantee Zhvania's removal.

That morning, the demonstrators were demanding that Shevardnadze fire all "power ministers."[13] However, with enough signatures to remove Zhvania, Gamkrelidze suggested to Shevardnadze that the president fire the whole government, and that Zhvania resign. Shevardnadze agreed, and so did Zhvania.[14] However, the speaker upped the ante by publicly announcing that he would resign if Shevardnadze pledged to not return Interior Minister Targamadze to the government. Zhvania's calculation was that Shevardnadze and Targamadze would never agree to this. By expressing his willingness to resign, Zhvania hoped to take the wind out of the petition demanding his removal. The surprise came when Targamadze announced his readiness to go if Zhvania were to resign, and Gamkrelidze got Shevardnadze to agree to this as well. Thus, Zhvania's resignation was more of a forced development, rather than a sacrifice he was willing to make to restore peace.

I was on my way to Tbilisi from Washington when the incident happened, but had stopped over in Serbia for a couple of days to attend a conference on education. Because of this, I was quite short on news regarding the developments, but from afar, the people's willingness to go into the streets seemed to me yet another expression of the intrinsic democratic nature of the Georgian nation, and a confirmation of my view that democracy could indeed take hold in the country. Because of this, I approved of the protests, though I was disappointed to learn later about the extent to which students who first went into the streets had been choreographed from above and paid for by a variety of interested parties—including Rustavi 2's owner, who would later play a vital role in the Rose Revolution.

Personal Observations on Political Players in the Post-CUG, Pluralistic Georgia

On the level of political personalities, the incident had two big losers and three big winners. Zhvania and Shevardnadze were the clear losers: the former lost the position from which he hoped to become president, while the latter lost many of his key advisors (on whom he could depend to protect his authority) and was forced to acknowledge the extent to which his regime had become politically bankrupt and unpopular.

The winners, meanwhile, were Saakashvili, Gamkrelidze, and Nino Burdjanadze, who was elected to succeed Zhvania as speaker.[15] From this position, Burdjanadze suddenly was placed in the middle of Georgian politics, even though she had very little independent political standing. Saakashvili won, because Zhvania's downfall gave him an opportunity to finally emerge from his mentor's long shadow and take on the "reformer" mantle.

Finally, Gamkrelidze won, because he was able to break the CUG into three pieces (Shevardnadze's team, Saakashvili's team, and Zhvania's team) and get a place for himself at the table of "grownups" in Georgian politics. Dismissed just six months earlier as an amateur (a businessman who was merely dabbling in politics), he was suddenly thrust into the position of being quite possibly the most important single legislator, because he not only possessed the mantle of the opposition (indeed, the first opposition to Shevardnadze and Zhvania in the eyes of most), but was simultaneously able to talk to Shevardnadze.

The biggest winner, though, was not any particular politician, but rather the Georgian people. November's upheaval can be seen as the event that ultimately ended the CUG's dominance of Georgian politics. This process had started when a few courageous and naive businessmen who had come to politics in late 1999 decided to take on Zhvania's control of the legislature, and as a result created an opportunity for the opening of Georgia's political space. Thus Georgians were given a unique new opportunity for democratic consolidation—what I have termed the third democratic opening.

Starting in 1995, as I have examined in the previous chapter, the second democratic opening in Georgia was destroyed by two main factors—Shevardnadze's inability to bring about real change, and dominance of the so-called "reform" by a group of self-styled young democrats who had very little in common with proponents of real democracy. As a result, democracy was squeezed between Shevardnadze's nomenklatura allies and Zhvania's "young reformers," as was confirmed by the extremely corrupt 1999 legislative elections in which these "reformers" oversaw more fraud than ever observed in Georgia. These elections were the clearest sign of the closure of Georgia's political space between 1995 and 1999.

With Zhvania's resignation as speaker of Parliament, and the end of the CUG's dominance of the legislative process, political pluralism once again became possible, as was apparent during the elections in 2002 and 2003. Given that none of this likely would have happened without the rebellion of the businessmen-turned-politicians, Gamkrelidze and his New Rights Party can be credited with playing an indispensable role in helping to usher in two years of political pluralism in Georgia, between November 2001 and November 2003. No matter how one may judge Gamkrelidze's future actions, his achievement in bringing down the CUG cannot be underestimated.

I first met Gamkrelidze professionally in the immediate aftermath of the November protests and the dramatic change that Zhvania's resignation brought about. At that point, I had given up my job as a business consultant in Washington and had accepted a fellowship at the Central Asia-Caucasus Institute at the Johns Hopkins University School for Advanced International Studies (SAIS), where I was going to research and write on Georgian politics. In the late fall, I had returned to Georgia for a month to gain a better understanding of the political situation there.[16]

After spending a few weeks closely observing Gamkrelidze in November and December 2001, I became convinced that I could indeed strongly support him and his cause, and that I could play my small part in helping him advance the cause of democracy in Georgia. I was particularly impressed by the passion with which he spoke about the issues facing Georgia during his meetings with U.S. officials. It seemed to me that there was something genuine in him— something that I had not noticed in almost any other Georgian politician. In the months and years that followed, I had a chance to experience this genuineness many times, and to see the morally clear choices that he was so often willing to make, even if they contradicted political expediency.

A few months later, in April 2002, Gamkrelidze came to Washington on his first trip to the United States as a politician. He was joined by his deputy Pikria Chikhradze during this visit, which I helped organize. Gamkrelidze was not known in Washington at all, and those few "Georgia watchers" that had heard of him had a bad impression, thanks to the constant barrage of negative comments against the Georgian business community that were coming from Zhvania, Saakashvili, and most Georgian NGO leaders and political analysts. I joined Gamkrelidze at many meetings with senior U.S. officials and opinion makers, and was greatly impressed by his ability to charm his American hosts. Given his somewhat "removed" public image in Georgia, which made it difficult for Gamkrelidze to connect with ordinary voters, I thought that transferring his one-on-one style to the broader community could greatly improve his standing with the public.

While the trip was only the first step in placing Gamkrelidze on the American radar screen, it was clear that many Americans found it difficult to appreciate a political leader who had a very different set of principles and ideas than most other politicians from Georgia that they had met. Most "Georgia watchers" had never seen a prominent political visitor who was genuinely driven by political values. Instead, most were looking for Gamkrelidze's "hidden agenda"—one that in reality did not exist. By contrast, some so-called "ideological" Washington opinion makers, especially the conservative ones, saw something very refreshing in Gamkrelidze—a politician who was pushing an agenda that was very similar to their own, and that was very difficult to sell in a post-Soviet political environment.

Unlike Gamkrelidze, Zhvania and Saakashvili had been making such trips for years, and were thus well known to the Washington policymaking community. Indeed, the two had made a joint trip to Washington in February 2002. That visit was organized by the National Democratic Institute (NDI). This is a nonprofit organization that is affiliated with the Democratic Party, but in its international efforts it is supposed to work on a nonpartisan basis with all "democratic" parties—though in Georgia, at least, it usually sided with the "young reformers," all the while complaining about the unwillingness of other parties to work with it.[17] The visit was an amusing event to watch. Here were two politicians whose entire career had been built by and around Eduard Shevardnadze, who owed their standing in Georgian society entirely to him, and who had ruled the country alongside him for at least half a decade—yet who were now alleging that Shevardnadze was leading the country on a "downward spiral."[18] Having politicians change their minds is certainly not unusual. Yet when this happens, one also expects them to acknowledge the past mistakes that led them to change their positions, especially when the new position is 180 degrees opposite from what it had been for as long as anyone could remember.

It was during a lecture at the NDI at the start of his visit that Zhvania first publicly broached the idea that the opposition parties had to unite into a broad coalition in order to challenge Shevardnadze and promote reforms. Creating this coalition would become the focus of Zhvania's activities in the summer of 2002 and throughout 2003. In his talk, Zhvania stated that "we should not allow people to have unfair alternatives" in the forthcoming parliamentary elections. Presumably he meant that it would be "unfair" for people to have to choose between political parties representing different points of view and varying solutions to Georgia's problems. Instead, he pushed a much narrower set of political choices. He argued that the election had to become a choice between the "civil society," represented by the broad coalition, and the "elite," represented by Shevardnadze. In other words, Zhvania was proposing a reconstruction of the CUG, minus Shevardnadze, now called "civil society."

I was at this lecture and was struck by Zhvania's statement that giving people a wide choice was like giving them "unfair alternatives," since I believed that having such a wide choice was precisely what democratic pluralism was all about. I therefore asked him about whether it made sense for Georgia to have yet another amorphous political union akin to the CUG without any real political principles or ideas, or whether it would be better to try to build two or three political parties organized around political ideologies. I found in Zhvania's response yet another confirmation of why I so strongly opposed his tactics and why he was clearly not a democrat—all his talk of democracy notwithstanding. Zhvania told me, and Saakashvili did not disagree, that Georgia was "far away from the state of democratic and political party life similar to ways that are in Western Europe or America," and for that reason, party-building was impossible. I was left to wonder how one could ever get to the condition of real democracy in Georgia without trying to establish the institutions that are necessary for it—including political parties, which Zhvania hoped to undermine by creating a large coalition. Zhvania spoke about his commitment to democracy, but he did not believe in pluralism. Fortunately, it seemed that Georgia was moving in a very different direction.

In early 2002, Georgia had entered its third democratic opening. This was a period that would be characterized by an unparalleled level of pluralism and political competitiveness, but all of this in a very disorganized and messy environment. In some respects, this was probably the best opportunity Georgia ever had for creating a system of government in which rule of law was respected, and in which the people, through their elected representatives, were sovereign.

This transition was going to be a long process. If it were to succeed, the transition process was bound to continue until April 2005, when Shevardnadze's term was scheduled to end. However, the weakness of Shevardnadze's authority and of the state in general, the collapse of the CUG, the loss of power by Zhvania and the young reformers, the rise of an active business community willing to risk things in order to advance change, and the presence of a powerful independent media (which was bound to get even stronger in the months ahead) created fertile soil for consolidation of democracy. Georgia had become a state of chaotic pluralism, and as such, it was unique among all former Soviet republics. This was not real liberal democracy yet, but it had a foundation for it. The key question was whether Georgia would be able to move from chaotic pluralism to institutionalized pluralism based on the respect for the Constitution, its procedures, and the rule of law.

PART 2

Chaotic Pluralism on the Brink of a Consolidated Democracy

4

2002 Local-Government Elections and Zhvania's Political Rebirth

The first big test of strength for the various political parties in the newly semi-pluralistic Georgia that arose after the collapse of the CUG was the local-government elections in June 2002. The vote was rightly seen as a dress rehearsal for the November 2003 parliamentary contest. This local elections were the first vote since 1992 that took place in an environment of political pluralism, with a variety of parties—with differing ideologies—competing with each other. Furthermore, the level of fraud in the elections was minimal, and the real voice of the people was heard through the voting.

Highlights of the Campaign

Shevardnadze and the government apparatus refrained from supporting anyone in the local-government elections because the CUG was not running candidates in most districts. While the upheaval in October and November 2001 heralded the end of the CUG's dominance of Georgian politics, the party continued to exist in its old form until the next spring. For six months, Georgia witnessed a nasty fight between the pro-Shevardnadze and pro-Zhvania wings of the CUG for control of whatever was left of the party. Both groups wanted to control the CUG, notwithstanding the negativity associated with its name, because it had a vast national network and property in every district of the country.

Initially after Zhvania's resignation, the two sides reached a truce, but in May 2002, just weeks before the elections, the pro-Shevardnadze wing filed a suit against Zhvania's wing, which wanted to control the nomination of candidates. A Tbilisi-based court ruled against Zhvania and granted the pro-Shevardnadze wing, which had a majority in the party's national committee, control. This decision was later upheld by the Supreme Court, even though the Court was stacked with Zhvania's allies.

As a result, Zhvania was forced to compete in the local elections with a borrowed party name. However, this setback was actually a godsend to Zhvania, and indeed, some have suggested that he engineered a loss because he knew that it would benefit him. This public battle for control of the CUG lasted weeks and pitted Zhvania and his team against the only people in Georgian politics who were more unpopular than the former speaker and his allies—the president and his cronies. As a result, the struggle allowed Zhvania to gain the status of a "victim" in the eyes of many, and claim the mantle of an opposition leader—even though only months before, he had been the second most powerful man in Georgia and a key CUG leader.

The conduct of the elections was actually quite chaotic. The International Society for Fair Elections and Democracy (ISFED) identified two important problems with the vote. First, the "disastrous state of voter registration lists," which were so inaccurate that one of the most prominent politicians in Georgia, beer magnate and leader of the Industry Will Save Georgia party Gogi Topadze, could not find himself or the rest of his family on the voter list in his Vake precinct (Vake is the wealthiest part of Tbilisi). Second, violence, largely in the regions, and especially in Zugdidi. Two deputy governors of Samegrelo region, of which Zugdidi is the capital, resigned because of the violence. Violations were also reported in the fairly large and politically significant town of Rustavi, where elections were cancelled completely after armed men stole the ballots, which were belatedly (at 8:00 A.M. on Sunday) on their way to the city.

While electoral violations were numerous, few, if any, observers suggested that President Eduard Shevardnadze's government engaged in a conspiracy to engineer false results. ISFED, for example, reported that "parallel turnout tabulation[s] . . . revealed that there was not likely to have been massive and centrally organized fraud."

Even though administratively the elections were abysmal, the fact that Georgia held largely fraud-free elections for the local-government bodies, especially in such a pluralistic environment, was an achievement. While not perfect, the vote was an excellent opportunity for people to engage in self-government. At 46 percent, the turnout in Tbilisi was 10 percent higher than anticipated by pollsters. According to ISFED estimates, regionally the turnout was over 60 percent, which suggests that citizens at large took seriously the opportunity to elect individuals who could impact their lives directly. The fact that the government did not actively engage in voter fraud was also encouraging for the future, especially given the history of the 1999 legislative vote.

In some respects, there were two elections—one in Tbilisi, which was the focus of all attention, and one in the rest of the country, which mattered just as much if not more, but was largely ignored. In Tbilisi the election was fought over both political issues and political personalities. The Labor Party and National Movement received about the same number of votes in the race for seats in the Tbilisi Sakrebulo (City Council)—71,145 votes or 24.5 percent, and 66,256 votes or 23.8 percent, respectively. They were followed by the New Rights Party (33,695 votes/11.4 percent), Zhvania's team (20,284/ 7.3), Industry Will Save Georgia (19,898/7.13), and Revival (17,682/6.34).

While they attracted far less attention, the regional results were actually just as important, if not more so, as those in Tbilisi, as far as the upcoming 2003 parliamentary election was concerned. Here, the New Rights Party won 851 seats from 4,787 available.[1] This total was only exceeded by over 2,500 "independent deputies," about 600 of which were pro-Shevardnadze CUG candidates who had to run independently because their party ballot had been in dispute. New Rights' closest competitor was Industry Will Save Georgia, which elected 484 individuals, and was followed by Revival Party (203), Socialist Party (183), Labor Party (164). Meanwhile, notwithstanding his success in Tbilisi, Saakashvili had a very limited showing nationally with 25 seats, while Zhvania had none at all.

The Meaning of the Election

Most Georgian analysts and representatives of the NGO community ignored the reality of the results and declared that Saakashvili and Labor Party leader Shalva Natelashvili had won the local-government elections, even though that was true only in Tbilisi. In many respects, this sort of commentary stems from the elitism of the Georgian political establishment and civil-society leaders, in whose view politics in Georgia only take place in the Tbilisi center, and the views of the people at large really do not matter. This view indicates a great deal about the "democratic commitment" of the Georgian political elite as compared to the people.

Another thing that most Georgian analysts failed to discuss was the political message around which the various campaigns in Tbilisi were built, and the impact that this had on voters. Instead, almost everyone focused merely on the political personalities involved. While there are no exit polls to back this up, in all likelihood about two-thirds of Saakashvili's and Natelashvili's vote was driven by the very populist, demagogic message presented by the National Movement and the Labor Party. Whether Saakashvili and Natelashvili actually believed in their message was unclear, but Natelashvili openly presented himself as a neo-Communist who was willing to steal from the rich in order to "give to the poor," while Saakashvili claimed to be an anti-corruption crusader who was willing to use any and all means to punish allegedly crooked officials. Saakashvili also peppered his message with appeals to nationalism.

By contrast, the New Rights Party actually did build its campaign around a personality, rather than an ideological message. This was particularly ironic given that in reality it was the one Georgian party that was founded on real political values rather than around a political leader. However, it was running wine magnate Levan Gachechiladze as its main candidate in Tbilisi, and he wanted to present himself as the "good guy next door." Unfortunately, it was unclear what this "good guy" was going to do for the voters. While this image might have been helpful in selling a message, without a message it was not really worth much at all.

The New Rights Party also suffered from Gachechiladze's unwillingness to consult others before making public announcements of grave importance. For example, while Gamkrelidze was on his U.S. visit, Tbilisi suffered a serious earthquake. Without telling anyone, Gachechiladze went on TV and declared that his campaign would set aside all of its funds to support those who had lost their homes in the quake rather than buy advertisements. Initially, this decision had a very favorable reception from the public. However, the election was still six weeks away, and this favorable view quickly vanished. Additionally, numerous individuals who applied for support but were turned down (because their losses were judged to have not been as great as others') became very upset with Gachechiladze and the party.

Meanwhile, Saakashvili was running very populist and negative advertisements in which he presented himself as the only real challenger to Shevardnadze, taking away the platform that the New Rights Party had built for itself from the very beginning of its existence. Given its promise to spend all campaign cash on the quake victims, the NRP could not even buy advertisements with *new* campaign funds, since its opponents would immediately allege that it was turning back on its promise.

Thus, Gachechiladze's decision to make his campaign about the "good guy" who was supporting the victims of the earthquake—rather than about his party's message of job creation, low taxes, and moral values—backfired dramatically, and is one reason why the party did not have a better showing. This is important for understanding not only the party's problems in 2002 but also the New Rights' failure to fully implement its parliamentary election strategy in 2003.

The other reason for the New Rights Party's underperformance (and National Movement's and Labor's success) in Tbilisi had to with the fact that the free-market vote was split between two parties—New Rights, and Industry Will Save Georgia. Gamkrelidze had actually offered Gogi Topadze, the leader of Industry, a chance to form a preelection alliance, which would have allowed pro-business voters to support just one party. Simply adding the results of the two parties in Tbilisi would have brought them much closer to Labor and the National Movement, but in reality, this would have been an alliance in which one plus one would have equaled three, rather than two, because many voters would have become convinced that business leaders were able to put their personal interests aside for the good of their country. This, in turn, would have given the two parties a strong chance to come in first in Tbilisi.[2] Their joint result nationally, meanwhile, would have been even stronger, since they came in first and second separately.

The 2002 local-government vote was the first independent electoral test for two political leaders who largely shaped Georgian politics after 1999—Saakashvili and Gamkrelidze. In addition to their different message, the two parties they led followed a very different strategy of where to seek votes, with the National Movement focusing almost entirely on Tbilisi, and the New Rights Party spreading its resources across the country. Results were mixed for both. While the National Movement came in second in Tbilisi, New Rights came in third, but far behind. The "young reformers" called this a loss. However, given New Rights' mistakes in message and strategy, this election result should actually have been seen as a success. Meanwhile, in light of New Rights' strength in the regions, where the turnout was 15 percent higher than in Tbilisi, voters outside of Tbilisi were clearly going to be the battleground for the 2003 legislative vote. In that situation, the NRP was in stronger shape. It appeared, based on these results, that Saakashvili's and Gamkrelidze's future was to be determined by the extent to which each could find common ground with his most logical partner—respectively, Zhvania and Topadze (of Industry Will Save Georgia). This was particularly true of Gamkrelidze.

The pluralism of the 2002 local-government elections can be seen as the formal confirmation of the existence of Georgia's third democratic opening, which was brought about by the rebellion of the Georgian businessmen-turned-politicians against Zhvania and the CUG, an act that ultimately led to the collapse of the CUG. The result confirmed the possibility that in light of Shevardnadze's planned departure in 2005, one could see in Georgia a real possibility of democratic consolidation through two future elections (for Parliament in 2003, and president in 2005). The country had diverse political parties with very clear differences, giving people a chance to have an informed choice in the elections rather than having to choose between black and white alternatives, as was the case in 1999. Georgia had a media environment that was not fully controlled by the government, a civil society (broadly understood to include the NGO sector and the business community) that was interested in playing an active role in the political process, and most importantly, citizens who wanted to control their own lives and futures. All of this was a cause for great hope and optimism, though many challenges still lay ahead.

After the Local-Government Elections: The Summer and Fall of Discontent

While many hoped there would be a brief period of calm in Georgian politics after the local-government elections, the political class simply shifted gears and immediately started planning for the 2003 parliamentary vote. The real pre-election period would not start until early 2003, but the rest of 2002 was an opportunity for parties to reposition themselves for the forthcoming race. Though almost a year and a half away, everyone understood that these elections would determine Georgia's political future, since they were seen as the precursor to the 2005 presidential vote during which Shevardnadze could no longer run, and hence a new national political leader was bound to emerge. No one needed to reposition himself more than Zhvania, and for this reason, he was the first to start maneuvering.

PUSH TOWARD AN "OPPOSITION ALLIANCE"

Given that Zhvania was left without a party by the court decision that awarded the control of the CUG to a rival faction beholden to Shevardnadze, his first task after the elections was to organize his experienced but small political team into an official party. This happened in July 2002, when Zhvania launched the United Democrats. During the first party convention, Zhvania announced that his team planned to field a presidential candidate in 2005. Everyone in Georgian politics always assumed that Zhvania was planning on running for president, and thus few were surprised by this announcement. However, this was the first time any politician in Georgia publicly spoke of wanting to succeed Shevardnadze, and thus the announcement was a significant political novelty.

For all the pomp that surrounded the founding of the United Democrats, Zhvania knew that his team could not succeed in taking the reins of power alone. Indeed, Zhvania was the second most unpopular politician in Georgia after Shevardnadze, and unlike some of his rivals (like Gamkrelidze), he had almost 100 percent name recognition, with people having already made up their minds about him. Thus, simply reintroducing him to the public in a new way was not a solution to his woes.

Because of Zhvania's highly unfavorable ratings, it was assumed by many analysts that the United Democrats could not overcome the 7 percent barrier necessary to gain seats in Parliament without a political ally. Zhvania well understood this himself and knew that he needed to form an alliance with another party or group of parties in order to have any hope of revitalizing his political standing. Cleverly, after almost two years of having to function in a political environment that was defined for him by Gamkrelidze and the rebellious businessmen—an environment in which Zhvania was the villain, while his opponents were the good guys—the former speaker took the political initiative into his own hands by putting the issue of an opposition alliance at the top of the national agenda.

As discussed earlier, Zhvania had first mentioned this idea early in 2002 during his visit to Washington. However, after the local-government vote, he reintroduced this notion inside the country—by working directly with opposition leaders to convince them to join him; by convincing the media to focus almost all of its attention on the question "Will the opposition unite?"; by getting his allies at Rustavi 2 and in the Georgian and international NGO community to talk constantly about this issue; and by mentioning the issue of the alliance during every public appearance that he ever made. By contrast, Gamkrelidze, who at the time was opposed to an alliance, refused to spend too much time talking about why such a union was not in the best interests of Georgia. Thus Zhvania's calls were left unchallenged and had an even greater impact on the political class.

By late summer, once Zhvania's PR campaign had an opportunity to work through one full cycle, many in Georgia were convinced that a united opposition was simply necessary and inevitable, notwithstanding the fact that the parties that Zhvania wanted to bring together (his own, National Movement, and the New Rights Party) had very little in common. Furthermore, under Zhvania's influence, no one in the media or the political community even bothered to ask why an "opposition alliance" was not to include Labor, one of the more popular opposition parties. Labor clearly could bring a lot of voters to the table, but Zhvania excluded it from the proposed alliance. Thus, Zhvania succeeded in changing the political discourse in Georgia and reformulating it in a way that necessarily benefited him and his cause.

Indeed, Zhvania's campaign was so successful that by late summer, few could remember the huge defeat that his political team had suffered in late May 2002. At that point, with support from almost all groups in Parliament, Gamkrelidze engineered the removal of all parliamentary committee chairmen, virtually all of whom were allied with Zhvania. They were replaced by a diverse group representing each of the factions in Parliament, bringing far greater democracy to the legislature but further eroding Zhvania's influence over the political process.

With this move, Gamkrelidze had become the undisputed leader of the Parliament, because he was the only politician capable of working with all the different and opposing groups, none of which individually had anywhere near a majority, to get anything done. Thus, the summer and fall of 2002 should have been his shinning moment as a political figure. In some respects it was— for example, in September 2002 Gamkrelidze got the Parliament to declare NATO membership to be the principal foreign-policy priority for Georgia. However, with Zhvania's successful efforts to rehabilitate himself by putting the idea of an opposition alliance at the forefront of the political debate, Gamkrelidze's great achievement in the legislature was largely lost on most people.

ZHVANIA'S POLITICKING AND DÉMARCHE AGAINST SHEVARDNADZE

Zhvania's relationship with Saakashvili was quite strong, notwithstanding their differences on the surface. While the two were clearly different leaders, each with his own agenda, in the eyes of most Georgians the two were actually one and the same; indeed, the term "Zhvania-Saakashvili" was so commonly used in the media and by the public that many often joked that Saakashvili's first name was Zhvania. Because of this, Zhvania understood that an alliance with Saakashvili would not get him very far in terms of new electoral synergies. His main target, therefore, was Gamkrelidze and the New Rights Party.

Even though Gamkrelidze was responsible for Zhvania's downfall from the post of speaker and the two had been grave enemies, in the summer of 2002 Zhvania started to open lines of communication with Gamkrelidze. His willingness to do so and the tenacity with which he pursued his goal speak volumes about his temperament and his strong sense of how to find the right political path for himself under any circumstance (though at times at great cost to his country). As Gamkrelidze told me, Zhvania often "started from zero," but ultimately was able to reach his goal.

In his pursuit of Gamkrelidze, Zhvania convinced Gamkrelidze's biggest financial supporters of the wisdom of a union between the New Rights Party and the United Democrats, many of whom saw personal advantages in such an alliance because they could benefit from a broader base of political support when faced with possible government pressure. Many in the business community and some in the NGO community wanted an alliance because they did not want to have to make a choice between different groups and were looking for a short-term, easy solution, no matter what impact it might have in the long term. At the same time, many in the NGO community saw that the alliance would weaken the NRP, which they welcomed.

Accordingly, Zhvania dispatched his team members (some of whom were openly on his side and others who were not known publicly to be his allies) to convince members of Gamkrelidze's inner circle of the need for the two groups to work together. This strategy worked magnificently, and toward the end of the summer of 2002 some of Gamkrelidze's senior-most party members were pushing for a union.

In the meantime, Gamkrelidze himself was facing pressure inside his own party. The source of this pressure was a brewing dispute with Levan Gachechiladze, who had been the party's standard-bearer in the Tbilisi local-government elections. Though in the summer of 2002 this dispute was still new, over the next year and a half it would be a near constant annoyance for the party and the source of its greatest challenges. Gachechiladze tried to put all the blame about the results on Gamkrelidze. He argued that the party should have taken a far more populist and negative position vis-à-vis Shevardnadze (i.e., a position akin to Saakashvili's) and that Gamkrelidze had prevented him from doing this. Furthermore, he refused to notice the party's achievements outside of Tbilisi—something for which Gamkrelidze was actually responsible, unlike the strategy for the Tbilisi campaign—and claimed that the Tbilisi result would have been far better had he been in total control.

This infighting was taking a toll on Gamkrelidze, who did not want to see his friendship and partnership with Gachechiladze fall apart. As a result, he agreed to temporarily allow Gachechiladze to run the party operation. It turned out, ultimately, that Gachechiladze was a lot of talk and no action, because once empowered to do so, he took no interest in running the party machinery. The period during which he was in charge actually took a huge toll on the party, and there was a great loss of financial and human resources. However, in this deteriorating environment, it is not surprising that Gamkrelidze agreed to consider a hidden alliance with Zhvania. The first result of this was the end of public feuding between the United Democrats and the New Rights Party, which in itself was a great benefit to Zhvania since he was no longer under a barrage of attacks.

The one and only person in the NRP who saw through Zhvania's rhetoric and who strongly opposed the idea of any sort of alliance was Pikria Chikhradze. She had a long history with Zhvania and regarded him—quite accurately, in my opinion—as the greatest impediment to genuine democratic development in Georgia. However, her voice alone was not powerful enough to overcome the arguments Zhvania put forward.

Push came to shove several days before Shevardnadze was scheduled to give his State of the Nation address in October 2002. Gamkrelidze and Zhvania had asked the president to give a speech that would frankly address the problems facing the country and articulate a vision for what needed to be done. They hoped that this way it would be possible to respond constructively and not be totally overshadowed by the more radical response that was bound to come from Saakashvili.

In his parliamentary speech the president, unfortunately, gave an unrealistic view about how wonderful things were going in Georgia. In response,

Gamkrelidze went to the microphone and told the president that he had made a mockery of the situation in Georgia and that as a result, deputies from the New Rights Party, United Democrats, and National Movement, along with some other opposition parliamentarians, would be walking out of the session. This came to be known as the démarche against Shevardnadze and ushered in a new level of confrontation between the government and the opposition parties. That said, for the New Rights Party, participating in it was probably the biggest political mistake since the time of its founding (and maybe at any point since).

The démarche was Zhvania's great political recovery—his return to politics in full force, at the expense of Gamkrelidze and the New Rights Party. Ironically, it took place almost a year to the day after Gamkrelidze had succeeded in bringing Zhvania down from his position of speaker. However, by the fall of 2002, Zhvania had retaken control of the political process in Georgia. Now he was defining the terms of politics, and everyone was dancing to his tune. Certain that this would be the result, before the démarche Chikhradze had advised Gamkrelidze not to participate. Instead, she urged him to give an individual but forceful response to Shevardnadze and the failures of his administration, and to use the opportunity presented by the State of the Nation address to clearly differentiate the NRP from the government and from those opposition groups that had until recently been a vital part of the government.[3]

Sadly, Gamkrelidze did not follow this advice. Instead, he joined the "young reformers," in a way that contradicted everything that he had said about them in the past and strengthened their argument that it was Shevardnadze who was at fault for everything, including the failures of the "reformers" during the time when they were in power between 1995 and 2001. This way, without realizing it, Gamkrelidze lost a significant part of his independent political standing. Thus, after two years of very successful politicking that brought about Georgia's third democratic opening and helped make him a very serious player on the Georgian political scene, and after at least a partly successful first election campaign, Gamkrelidze committed his greatest political blunder, which helped lay the foundation of the Rose Revolution. While the démarche gave Zhvania what he wanted—people were identifying the NRP, United Democrats, and National Movement together—for him this was just the beginning, since his goal was to actually create an opposition alliance that he would lead.

SAAKASHVILI'S ELECTION AS CHAIR OF THE SAKREBULO

While all of this behind-the-scenes politicking was taking place between Zhvania and Gamkrelidze in the summer of 2002, Saakashvili took a different course and put almost all of his emphasis on public politics, trying to influence voters. His tactic was to allege that the Tbilisi local election had been rigged, even though there was little to no evidence of fraud; to challenge the results in court; and then to protest legal decisions by alleging that the courts were controlled by the government (even though one of his prized "achievements" as the CUG's leader had been the supposed reform of the court system).

Eventually Saakashvili got a court order for a recount of the Sakrebulo vote, which did not change the outcome one bit. However, the tactic of challenging the results allowed Saakashvili to stay on television continuously and to be the center of attention. He constantly tried to present National Movement as the main opposition to Shevardnadze and to allege that fraud was committed in order to prevent him from taking power, because the president's corrupt cronies were afraid of him. This helped his ratings tremendously, allowing Saakashvili to wash off whatever impressions of his connection with Shevardnadze and the CUG that the majority of the people might have retained.

The different ways in which Zhvania and Gamkrelidze on the one hand, and Saakashvili on the other, approached the period immediately after the local-government election points to a huge difference in their understanding of politics. The latter understood that to gain power, one had to go through the people—thus he focused on public politicking, though he used rhetoric that was unbecoming of a person who claimed to be a democrat. Meanwhile, the other two viewed the elite level of discussions as far more important and focused on behind-the-scenes politicking. Actually both are important, and the best politicians are able to combine the two. However, in an environment in which no one was challenging his claims, Saakashvili benefited greatly from his actions. He followed the same formula during the preelection period before the 2003 parliamentary elections to great success.

After over six months of delay caused by Saakashvili's lawsuits and the recount, the Sakrebulo eventually met on November 4, 2002. However, given the election results, no party had enough seats to single-handedly elect the chairman, the main prize of the election (the mayor of Tbilisi was appointed by the president). To gain the necessary votes, Saakashvili first persuaded Natelashvili to support him, even though the two were bitter enemies during the campaign. While Natelashvili never explained publicly why he backed Saakashvili, especially given that National Movement was taking away votes from Labor, he told me in private that he did this in order to show the people that Saakashvili was not capable of accomplishing anything, even from a position of great authority. (As my discussion in the next chapter will show, Natelashvili seriously misjudged Saakashvili and gave him a huge platform from which to run in the parliamentary elections. For Saakashvili, holding office was a lot more important than actually accomplishing something with the office, since being chairman of the Sakrebulo gave him an opportunity to engage in public politics like never before.)

With this deal, and with the support of Zhvania's members of the Sakrebulo, Saakashvili had enough voters to become chairman.[4] Yet when the chamber convened, it turned out that Saakashvili had a huge problem. The Law on Membership in Parliament clearly prohibited parliamentarians from membership in any other elected body in Georgia during the term of their service in Parliament. Two of the top people on Zhvania's Sakrebulo electoral lists were parliamentarians and thus could not vote in the elections for chairman, unless they resigned their parliamentary seats. Zhvania had placed a number of his famous team members on the top of the proportional list for the Tbilisi Sakrebulo, with the idea that they would later excuse themselves from the Sakrebulo and give their seats to individuals lower on the list. The problem was that this could only take place *after* the Sakrebulo convened and conducted what the Law on Local Government prescribed to be its first order of business—election of its chairman. As a result, legally those Sakrebulo members who were parliamentarians had to either abstain from voting for the chairman, or give up their seats in Parliament and then vote as members of the Sakrebulo. Zhvania's team members simple ignored this requirement and voted anyway, even though Zhvania had indicated to Gamkrelidze that they would not vote. Because Saakashvili did not have enough votes to win without their support, a deputy speaker of Parliament and the former chairman of the Committee on Human Rights cast their ballots for him illegally, giving him the victory.

While they were in power, Zhvania and Saakashvili had a long history of simply ignoring laws governing elections, especially ones that got in their way. This was particularly ironic, given that most of these laws were written either by them or by members of their "young reformers" team. The moral of the incident with Saakashvili's election of the Sakrebulo chairman was that Zhvania and Saakashvili had no intention of changing their tactics and following the rule of law now that they were in the opposition. For them, it was perfectly acceptable to use any and all possible means to achieve their ends, even if such tactics did not square with their pronouncements about democracy.

The lack of full appreciation of Zhvania's and Saakashvili's tactics among the population is partly the responsibility of other opposition groups, especially the New Rights Party, which failed to resolutely confront the "young reformers" once they were out of power. While Gamkrelidze was successful at removing the "young reformers" from power under Shevardnadze, he miscalculated when he chose to avoid a full debate with them once they claimed to be in the opposition side, alongside him. In the post-démarche environment, Zhvania may have very well succeeded in his efforts to create an opposition alliance.

However, in the aftermath of the Sakrebulo chairmanship election, Gamkre-lidze realized that being associated so closely with Zhvania was actually not such a good idea, simply because one could not trust this individual with anything. Unfortunately, in the months ahead, Zhvania would make sure that the question of an alliance would rear its ugly head once more.

5

Parties Prepare for the Parliamentary Elections While the NGO Community and Rustavi 2 Prepare for the Revolution

S aakashvili's election as the chairman of the Sakrebulo was the last political event of 2002 with important implications for the 2003 legislative
elections. From this moment on, parties entered a new stage of preelection planning that lasted all the way through early September 2003,
when the final stage of the long electoral marathon started. The period that
began in late 2002 is too large and involves too many events to be described
together. These events can be grouped into two parallel tracks. On the one track
are activities involving individual political parties trying to shape their image in
the eyes of the public and activities of the nongovernmental sector and the
business community. On the other track are multiparty events and international engagement that focused on the reform of the Electoral Code and negotiations between the New Rights Party, National Movement, and United
Democrats over a possible alliance. I have divided these two tracks into two
separate chapters. The present chapter focuses on the first track and takes us
into September of 2003, while the next chapter covers roughly the same time
period but focuses on the second track.

Enter Mike Murphy

In December 2002, when I was still at the Central Asia-Caucasus Institute at
Johns Hopkins SAIS, Gamkrelidze asked me if I would consider returning to
Georgia in order to play a role in the forthcoming campaign for the parliamentary elections.[1] While I was still contemplating my own choice, Gamkrelidze
and I had several long discussions about the possibility of hiring foreign

consultants who would help with the strategy for the election campaign. Zhvania had used Russian consultants in the past, and there was evidence that they would be in Georgia working on his behalf again in 2003. The NRP clearly did not want Russian consultants—the American alternative was far more appealing. With this in mind, I set out to look for possible Republican consultants who could not only help with the development of an electoral strategy, but also could promote Gamkrelidze's interests in Washington. Through friends, I had an opportunity to meet with two groups of consultants—one including Terry Nelson, who would later play a leading role in President Bush's reelection campaign in 2004, and the other led by Mike Murphy, who had played an instrumental role in Senator John McCain's presidential campaign in 2000 and was Florida Governor Jeb Bush's chief strategist. Both teams brought very strong points to the table, but after much discussion, ultimately the decision was made to work with Murphy.

Initially, Gamkrelidze was scheduled to travel to the United States to meet with Murphy and his two partners, Phil Anderson and Jim Pitts, in order to decide whether he indeed wanted to engage them.[2] However, political developments kept Gamkrelidze in Georgia, and instead, Murphy and Pitts came to Tbilisi in late April 2003. The idea was that during his visit, Murphy would study Georgian politics, launch an extensive field poll, and based on the results of the poll and his analysis, write an electoral strategy that the NRP could either implement on its own, or engage Murphy and his partners to help with implementation.

Murphy held extensive meetings with a wide variety of individuals—politicians, reporters and media executives, NGO community representatives, foreigners working on Georgian democracy and political issues, and so forth. Many yielded information that was most useful for campaign planning. One of the most intriguing meetings took place with the owner of Rustavi 2 television, Erosi Kitsmarishvili. Murphy saw through his façade right away, and it became apparent that Kitsmarishvili was trying to control the political process in Georgia and was using his station to blackmail different political leaders. However, for all his faults, Kitsmarishvili had also turned Rustavi 2 into a powerful television medium, and Murphy saw great benefits in using television to advance the New Rights Party's agenda.

Murphy's meeting with Marc Mullen and Lincoln Mitchell, representatives in Georgia for NDI, was also quite unique. It actually shed light on what would become in my opinion their (especially Mullen's) extremely negative role in the preelection period.[3] The two spent over an hour telling one of the most successful and accomplished political consultants in America that he did not have a place in Georgia, because he could never conceivably understand the country as well as they did. They argued that standard political rules did not apply to

Georgia, largely due to the fact that Georgians were not yet ready for real democratic politics. Mullen and Mitchell's problem was that Murphy was getting in their way, because their goal was to try to create a "democratic coalition" consisting of Gamkrelidze, Saakashvili, and Zhvania, and led by Nino Burdjanadze, the Parliament's speaker. Anyone that argued against it or who believed that New Rights had the potential to succeed in the elections on its own, especially someone from America, was not welcome.

After a week in Georgia, Murphy was able to articulate the condition of Georgian politics and what was wrong with it better and more clearly than anyone I had ever spoken with before (or since). Murphy's main conclusion was that in Georgia, the political class was out of touch with or disconnected from the people. The political class was focused on the intrigue of politics and on talking to each other about who was uniting with whom, who was making a deal with whom, and so forth, without addressing the needs of the people and the issues that concerned them most. In other words, Murphy was suggesting that it was not the people who were not ready for democratic politics (as many, like Mullen and Mitchell, argued), but that their leaders were not capable of engaging in democratic governance, because most did not know how to speak to the people. This was a crucial finding, if one may call it this. It seemed so simple, yet no one I had spoken with before had ever grasped it so well and in such simple terms.

Not only was Murphy's finding true of the politicians and the so-called civil society (i.e., the NGO community), but also of the media. The Georgian press focused its coverage on political intrigue, or the rumors and drama that surround day-to-day politics, but failed to pay attention to real policy issues that were on the minds of their viewers and readers. The media never wanted to examine, for example, what may have been in a given law that passed Parliament, and instead devoted a great deal of time to trying to decipher what sort of a deal the law's sponsor had to reach with other parliamentarians in order to get it passed.

During his trip, Murphy helped design a poll, which the NRP put into the field immediately with a quick turnaround. The poll asked not only the obvious questions about support for various political leaders, parties, and issues, but also tried to measure the ideological leanings of the Georgian voters through a variety of complicated questions designed to determine what would be the best way to influence citizens' decision-making before the election. The poll had a field of 5,000 people and provided results not only for the whole country but also for Tbilisi and almost all of the provinces. It was not fielded in Adjaria, Azeri-populated parts of Kvemo Kartli, and Armenian-populated parts of Javakheti, because the NRP assumed that either Abashidze or Shevardnadze would control the voting in these districts, as they had always in the past, and hence it did not make sense to focus on the realities there.

The poll asked several question about what policies voters favored—such as higher taxes and more government services versus lower taxes and less government services, a private pension plan or a public one, more or less business regulations, etc. The goal of these questions, which were neutral in nature, was to divide voters by ideology and to determine what percentage of the population could be sold on the NRP's message. It turned out that about 51 percent of the voters could be classified as being for a free market, while about 49 percent were anti–free market and wanted to go back to the old times. Those supporting the free market were the NRP's potential voters. Though the NRP could not get them all, having about a one-third vote for the party was realistic. Given that this was not a poll of the whole country, on a national level this translated to about 15 percent of the electorate. Getting such a high result depended, of course, on the NRP running a nearly perfect campaign on every level.

The following are some of the results of the poll:

▶ Voters in Georgia misunderstood the meaning of the terms "right," "center," and "left." When asked to categorize themselves, very few picked left, 30 percent chose center, and 24 percent chose right. However, just as many "right" voters favored big government and anti-free-market ideas as those who favored free-market policies. This did not mean that voters did not know what they wanted. Rather, voters did not understand the relationship between the policies that they generally supported and how those policies should be classified.

▶ Age was a clear delineating line in Georgian politics. Among voters under the age of thirty-five, 50 percent favored free-market policies, while 35 percent wanted to go back to old times. Among middle-aged voters (age thirty-six to fifty-five), 54 percent favored the free market, while 41 percent wanted to go back. However, among voters fifty-five and older, 32 percent wanted a free market, while 59 percent wanted to go back.

▶ Voters favored particular parties without always knowing what those parties stood for. For example, among Labor and National Movement voters, many did not support the policies of these parties. Among the former, 51 percent wanted to go back to the old times, while 44 wanted to move to a free market; among the latter, support was split evenly, 49–47 percent, even though both parties espoused anti-free market ideas. By contrast, among the NRP's voters, 65 percent favored free-market policies, while 28 percent wanted to go back to old times. (In my view, even that 28 percent was far too high.)

▶ Shevardnadze was extremely unpopular, and 83 percent of voters in Georgia felt that the country was on the wrong track. Anti-free-market, pro-old-times voters were more strongly opposed to Shevardnadze than those who

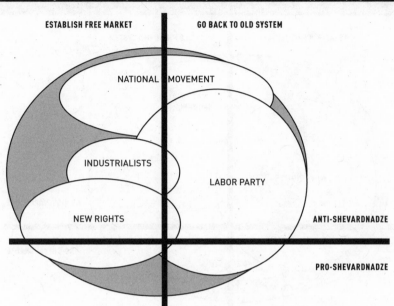

GRAPH 1 Georgian Political Parties by Comparative Popularity and Political Views of their Supporters, Spring 2003

favored the free market. This was probably because Shevardnadze was particularly unpopular among older pensioners.

► Jobs were by far the issue of greatest concern to Georgians. Seven in ten
picked it as one of the two principal issues they wanted addressed. Many
other issues that were of great concern to the political elite—Abkhazia, corruption, and even pensions, not to mention NATO and foreign affairs—did
not register with voters to any great extent.

Based on this poll and his own observations of Georgia, Murphy proposed a
detailed electoral strategy. His main piece of advice to the NRP was that
Gamkrelidze had to push through the chattering class and speak directly to the
people about issues that mattered to them, with solutions that could win him
their support. This piece of advice was far more complicated to implement than
one might initially think, because it went against everything the NRP had practiced before. However, toward the middle of 2003, it appeared that Saakashvili,
who never got Murphy's advice, heard it far better than Gamkrelidze.

Murphy believed that Georgian politics had two dividing lines: division over
pursuing free-market policies versus going back to old times, and division over
support for and opposition to Shevardnadze. He diagrammed a map based on
these dividing lines and placed political parties and their voters on it (graph 1).[4]

GRAPH 2 Mike Murphy's Vision for How New Rights Party Could Come to Dominate Free Market/ Anti-Shevardnadze Segment of the Population

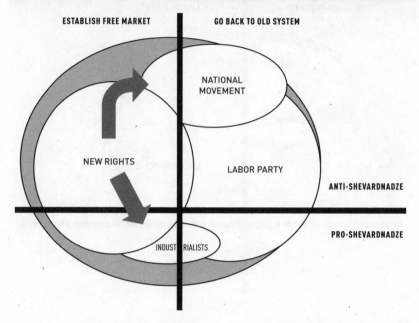

With the right campaign, Murphy believed that the NRP could grow to reposition itself (and other parties) (graph 2). To bring about this change, Murphy advocated a strategy of having the NRP step away from "insider politics" that focused on the interplay between political party leaders about the process and issues that were not of great concern to voters. Instead, he urged the NRP to use the mass media as an avenue to connect with ordinary voters in order to sell a message about change, jobs, and cleaning up corruption. Murphy believed that these three issues could turn the election in the NRP's favor. He also thought that the NRP was in a good position to sell this message, because this message was what the party really believed.

Murphy advocated a massive TV advertising campaign—far greater than anything Georgia had ever seen—starting in the summer. The first ads would introduce David Gamkrelidze and the NRP to the public, because a little under half of those who were polled said that they either did not know, or had no opinion of the party and its leader. Then, in September, Murphy's plan called on the NRP to focus on the subject of jobs. The message would be that no one could help create jobs better than the NRP. Finally, in mid-October, the focus would turn to commercials that could help bring people to vote.

In addition to heavy commercials, Murphy wanted party leaders to alter their language and their lifestyle. He wanted jobs and change to become the two most-used words in their vocabulary, so that they would talk about these two subjects in every TV appearance and public meeting. At the same time, he wanted the leaders to spend far more time with the people—in rallies with them, rather than in meetings at the party headquarters or the Parliament. He had many concrete ideas for how this should be done. The one that deserves particular mention is a national tour on a campaign bus, akin to Senator John McCain's Straight Talk Express from the 2000 presidential campaign. Murphy even suggested that the NRP buy a satellite phone to allow reporters to file stories from the bus from remote parts of the country. I had pushed the bus idea even before Murphy had recommended this, and was glad that he had included the bus among his initiatives.

Murphy believed that the NRP could implement his strategy on its own, but that it would be in a far stronger position if it were to unite with Industry Will Save Georgia (Industrialists). Not only did the NRP and Industry share many positions on domestic policy issues, but Industry had a positive image, which was rare in Georgian politics. Many voters, including those who were not going to vote for Industry, believed that it was a party that could help create jobs. This would strengthen the NRP's argument about job creation. Finally, voters from both parties favored an alliance. Thus Murphy urged the NRP and Industry to form an alliance, preferably one that would ultimately lead to one party being born from the two. He also believed that it was best to stay away from National Movement and United Democrats, since Zhvania was extremely unpopular among NRP voters.

In June, the NRP accepted Murphy's strategy, and he returned to Georgia with his own crew of filmmakers in order to tape extensive footage for advertisements.

IMPLEMENTING THE MURPHY STRATEGY

Initially, the NRP moved diligently to implement the strategy. In late spring, the NRP completed the party platform, which was not only a clear articulation of the party's positions and philosophic vision of government, but also included a number of ideas drawing on conservative public policy that could sell well to the people. I was particularly pleased with the "900 Days of Change, Renewal, and Jobs," as the platform was called, because I had a large role in writing it and believed that it formed a strong basis for an issue-driven campaign. Furthermore, no party leader could beat Gamkrelidze in a debate over the economic positions taken in the platform, and thus I felt that debates about the NRP's ideas could serve it well with the electorate.

The platform was presented to the public at a party convention in July. Working with Murphy and building on my own knowledge of American party conventions, we envisioned an event that would be specially designed for television coverage. In the end, the event was full of the sort of pomp and circumstance that was bound to include a lot of good footage and make the journalists happy. Gamkrelidze gave a powerful speech outlining the party's vision for the future, and presented himself as the one leader in Georgia with a clear plan for what should happen in the future. The journalists who attended the convention were largely stunned, and the coverage that evening was exceptional. All the NRP could wish for was that this pattern would continue in the future.

After the convention, the NRP was the first political party to launch TV advertisements. The party's decision to begin ads surprised its opponents and the rest of the political community in Tbilisi. Many talking heads criticized this decision, either because they favored other parties, or because they did not understand the idea behind it. These "experts" thought that ads were only useful in the last weeks of the campaign, since they had never experienced an effort to define the political discourse for the election way before Election Day—as was the case with Bill Clinton and Bob Dole in the 1996 U.S. election, when Clinton's early advertisements connected Dole to the unpopular Newt Gingrich and that was an impression the senator was never able to overcome. Some others, such as Gocha Tskitishvili, the owner of the Institute for Polling and Marketing (IPM), voiced negative comments about the ads because they resented not been consulted about the advertisement campaign.

When the NRP launched two advertisements about Gamkrelidze's biography in early August, talking heads became even more critical, since most felt that Gamkrelidze was too ambitious. One of the ads talked about Gamkrelidze's background as a doctor, entrepreneur, and political leader, and the other had him speaking directly into the camera about his experiences as a doctor and his compassion. The advertisements presented a side of Gamkrelidze that those who knew him closely saw in him, but that most people did not know.

On his last day in Tbilisi during the footage shoot in late June 2003, Murphy warned Gamkrelidze that he should prepare himself for a likely barrage of criticism from people around him and from the political class once the advertisements went on the air. This prediction came true, and while Gamkrelidze took the criticism in stride, others at the NRP did not. With nonstop criticism in Georgian papers, these NRP officials, activists, and financial backers began to question Murphy's strategy.[5] This was particularly true of those who were not intimately familiar with the strategy. "How can an American be so right and all these Georgians so wrong?" many asked.

While the NRP was successful in putting the advertisement campaign on the air, in August the NRP made one of its biggest mistakes of the campaign. Specifically, the NRP did not support the media buy with political activity— that is, the party did not campaign, hold press conferences, and participate in political debates. Thus, while the NRP was buying a great deal of television time, it was not competing for earned media. Indeed, many of the NRP leaders went on vacation for much for the month of August. Meanwhile, other parties, particularly the United Democrats, were extremely active during this time, and to a great extent their political activity had more impact than the NRP's advertising campaign. This was a mistake for which I am partly responsible, since I did not realize the impact that the decision to not be politically engaged could have.

When party leaders returned to Tbilisi in late August, the NRP shifted to behind-the-scenes negotiations with Industry Will Save Georgia over a possible alliance. These discussions caused a further delay in the launch of the party's public campaign, a development that Murphy strongly opposed; he could not understand how these discussions could continue for so many days, or how the party intended to do well in the election if it did not campaign. The alliance with Industry was of course very important, not only because it made electoral sense and simplified the implementation of the Murphy strategy, but because the NRP's financial backers were far more inclined to finance the full campaign if there was an alliance.

All of Industry's leaders were in favor of an alliance except for Gogi Topadze, who unfortunately was the party's chairman. Topadze did not want to become second fiddle to Gamkrelidze, even though the latter was offering him the first spot on the electoral list. After weeks of negotiations, Topadze rejected the alliance, just as he had in 2002, without giving a reason. I learned after the Rose Revolution that State Minister Avtandil Jorbenadze had an important role in convincing Topadze to reject the alliance. Jorbenadze apparently convinced Topadze that with the government's help, Industry could overcome the 7 percent barrier on its own.

The collapse of negotiations with Industry was a significant blow to the NRP, because it called into question the party's ability to raise the funds it needed to implement the Murphy strategy. This created a great deal of unease inside the party, where many people were already heavily influenced by the barrage of criticism that had been levied against the ads in Georgian newspapers. The problems only got worse several days later, when the NRP received results from a poll it had commissioned from a company called the Institute for Polling and Marketing (IPM) to measure the extent to which the advertisements in July and August were having an impact. In the poll, the party support was measured at 9 percent, which was 2 percent higher than in the poll taken in April. However, the poll in April had only covered 70 percent of the country, whereas the later poll included the whole country (including Javakheti, Kvemo Kartli, and Adjaria). When compared to a similar national poll also conducted by IPM in April, the party's support had nearly doubled. The poll also used a different methodology than NRP's poll in April, so comparing the two was not necessarily wise. Finally, in all likelihood, the NRP's popularity probably had fallen during the summer of 2003 (for reasons examined in chapter six), so the advertisements were clearly working, but had to change more minds than initially anticipated.

Nonetheless, everyone perceived the results as a 2 percent increase, and this took the wind out of the party's sails. Levan Gachechiladze used this opportunity to voice his many concerns. The party's financial backers in particular felt that it was difficult to move forward from this result and achieve a serious showing. I felt that it was dangerous to put so much stock in one poll, especially given that there were major discrepancies in the internal results. However, the poll results only added to the uncertainty of what the NRP would do, and many people inside began to question the whole party strategy and whether or not it made sense.

Electoral Strategies of the Main Parties

While other political parties did not have American consultants, they were also working actively on campaign planning, and in many respects did a better job at implementing their plans than the NRP.

SAAKASHVILI'S AND NATELASHVILI'S ELECTORAL STRATEGY

On the left side of the political spectrum, the campaign was quite rancorous. The Labor Party's Natelashvili was generally absent from the political scene, though somehow (quite amazingly) maintained a decent rating, ranging from 10–15 percent, in opinion polls. By contrast, during the first half of 2003, Saakashvili's National Movement was the noisiest group of all, and it turned out that it was developing the most successful electoral strategy of any party.

With Saakashvili in charge of the Tbilisi City Council, he was able to put into the city budget a number of spending initiatives that were conducive to excellent PR. Specifically, Saakashvili placed money in the budget to pay for repairs of elevators and roofs, construction of soccer stadiums, and an increase in the pensions for Tbilisi residents of three lari per month.

Most of these moves were purely symbolic, because the Tbilisi municipality budget did not have enough money to repair a substantial number of elevators and roofs, or to have a real impact on the lives of the citizens. A three-lari pension increase was, after all, merely the equivalent of six loaves of bread. However, Saakashvili was able to effectively use these initiatives to get regular positive photo opportunities on television. His message was very simple: "Look at what I am doing with the little authority I have, and just imagine what I will be able to do with real power." In this respect, Saakashvili accomplished what Natelashvili thought was impossible when he decided to support Saakashvili's bid to become chairman of the Sakrebulo. While Saakashvili was not changing anything serious in Tbilisi, he was able to build for himself a "workhorse" reputation.

The New Rights Party also had similar initiatives in the city budget, which purchased at least ten computers for each of Tbilisi's secondary schools and paid the salary of a special instructor in computer science. However, unlike Saakashvili, the NRP was unable to generate similar publicity for its initiatives, even though one of the three dominant private TV stations, Imedi, tried its best to provide the party with favorable coverage during the delivery of these computers to each of the schools. Whether this was simply the fault of the fact that Gamkrelidze was not as populist as Saakashvili, or that Gamkrelidze himself was not participating in the ribbon-cutting ceremonies while Saakashvili visited every single elevator and roof that was repaired with the city's money, is unclear. The end result is what really mattered: Saakashvili got huge mileage with the public from his actions, while the NRP did not.

Saakashvili's other big PR stunt in the spring involved a hunger strike by the leading parliamentarians from the National Movement over the issue of pensions. For years, Georgia had had a huge problem with pension arrears— that is, the government was late in paying pensions over periods of many months. These pensions were generally little more than symbolic—14 lari per person per month in most cases[6]—but the elderly regarded these arrears as a huge problem. Sensing an opportunity, Koba Davitashvili, Saakashvili's leading deputy, conceived a plan to have senior citizens sue the state over these unpaid pensions. The National Movement collected signatures from large groups of elderly citizens and filed lawsuits on their behalf in district courts all over the country. In most circumstances, the National Movement won these cases, because the government's failure to pay these pensions was a clear violation of the rule of law (these ruling suggested that the courts were less under Shevardnadze's control than many believed). However, the state had no money, so it ignored the court decisions and continued to not pay the pensions.

To force the government's hand, Davitashvili, Zviad Dzidziguri, Lado Chipashvili, and several other National Movement parliamentarians launched a hunger strike in front of the Ministry of Health, Labor, and Pensions. The hunger strike was televised on a daily basis and initially appeared ridiculous. However, as days went by, the parliamentarians lost weight, and the strike became a serious problem for the Shevardnadze government. Eventually, the only way of resolving the problem was to meet their demands, which the government did. The National Movement got a huge victory vis-à-vis the government as a result, and was once again viewed by the people, especially the poor and the elderly, as the one group that cared about its concerns. In short, thanks to this initiative and his actions as chairman of the Sakrebulo, Saakashvili was becoming more and more popular on the left end of the political spectrum.

Through such a populist campaign, Saakashvili started to win the hearts of the voters who had previously discounted him because of his past association with Shevardnadze. Most of his new support came at the expense of Nate-lashvili, who either failed to realize or did not appreciate the extent to which the National Movement had advanced into Labor's electoral space.[7] Saakashvili coupled his populist message with promises to summarily confiscate property, and inflammatory rhetoric that gave no regard to the due process of the law. His promises seemed extremely unrealistic and unsustainable, but they sold well because, rightly or wrongly, people blamed the government for everything and wanted to punish the alleged culprits. All in all, through the spring and summer of 2003, Saakashvili laid the groundwork for a huge popularity surge, which peaked in October. Many in Georgian politics, myself included, failed to notice this until it was too late.

FOR NEW GEORGIA

The only other group that was almost as active in the first half of the year as the National Movement was the governmental Citizens Union of Georgia, which in March launched the process of reforming itself into an electoral alliance called For New Georgia, under the leadership of State Minister Avtandil Jorbenadze. However, unlike the National Movement, its actions did nothing to improve the government's image with the public.

Throughout the spring and early summer, a number of "parties" joined the alliance; these were tiny entities, often referred to as "cabinet" parties, that had no political support and that joined FNG in hopes of securing one or two seats in Parliament. While FNG tried to spin this in a positive light, it remained extremely unpopular under the barrage of negative publicity.[8] This negativity in the media was engineered not by the opposition, but rather by the journal-ists themselves, most of whom could not stand the vast majority of individuals who were coming together under FNG's banners. What is most interesting in this regard is the extent to which journalists, especially reporters at private TV stations, were free to say almost anything they wanted about the government party, without any real fear of retribution from the state or from the owners of their stations.

FNG's cause was damaged even more when it appointed Irina Sarishvili-Chanturia, the head of the National Democratic Party, to serve as its principal spokesperson. She would regularly make the most outlandish claims about how Russia was funding the opposition, creating a great deal of political intrigue but also leading many to believe that the government party was full of paranoia. Thus, as the summer progressed, it became obvious that FNG would have a very difficult time garnering a serious result; one way or another, the opposition was going to come out on top. Indeed, it appeared at times that in order to go beyond 25 percent, the government would have to resort to levels of fraud that would exceed even 1999. This, most hoped, would be impossible with the procedures set forth in the new Electoral Code.

ZHVANIA'S DEMOCRATS AND BURDJANADZE, OR THE BURDJANADZE-DEMOCRATS

Zhvania's political team attempted to increase its popularity in the spring of 2003 with a proposal to require an increase in the minimal government salaries and pensions to equal the income necessary to live above the poverty line, which in early 2003 was 118 Georgian lari per month (in 2003 this was approximately $56).

Zhvania knew very well that the Georgian budget could never sustain such an increase in expenditures; it hardly had the funds to pay the salaries and pensions that the government was already obliged to cover. Yet he made a deal with deputies from Aslan Abashidze's Revival Party, and in return for supporting a move to grant Adjaria tax-free status, the United Democrats received Revival's support for the minimum salary/pension proposal. Zhvania made similar deals with other legislative groups and ultimately gained enough votes in the Parliament to pass his bill, which Shevardnadze then vetoed because of the country's fiscal realities.

This incident was illustrative of Zhvania's style. He did not care that giving Adjaria tax-free status would do nothing but damage the Georgian economy and political stability by simply giving Abashidze legislative cover for his refusals to transfer taxes collected in Adjaria into the national treasury. In other words, for Zhvania, personal interests and power were far more important than national interests. However, either because citizens were aware of his dealings with Abashidze or because his public image was so damaged that he could not even sell to the people what should have been a very popular idea, the minimal salary/pensions proposal did nothing to help the United Democrats in the polls, where they languished below 5 percent.

As the summer progressed and Zhvania's efforts to unite the opposition failed, in August he decided to make a splash with the announcement of an "alliance" with Nino Burdjanadze, the speaker of Parliament. Since her election as speaker in 2001, Burdjanadze had managed to gain a very favorable opinion from the public. As one of the three leading public officials—alongside Shevardnadze and State Minister Avtandil Jorbenadze—she was constantly in the news, often taking part in "stately" events. She used the parliamentary platform to challenge, albeit very mildly, the government's policies. As chairman of the legislature, she made numerous visits abroad, most of which got favorable coverage in the media. In short, when compared to the other two national officials of similar stature (Shevardnadze and Jorbenadze), Burdjanadze looked far superior. However, she did not have a political base of her own and was under a great deal of influence from Zhvania's key allies—indeed, she actually retained Zhvania's longtime ally Khatuna Gogorishvili as chief of staff when she became speaker.

During the first half of 2003, Burdjanadze hoped to join a united opposition alliance as a leading personality. However, when negotiations failed, she was left with just two choices—to officially join with United Democrats, or to accept an offer from Gamkrelidze to abandon Zhvania altogether and join the NRP as number one on the party's electoral list. Gamkrelidze was far less generous with Burdjanadze than Zhvania because he wanted her to become a member of the NRP while he remained as its leader. Burdjanadze would become the NRP's legislative leader, but Gamkrelidze would stay as the party's national leader. For Burdjanadze, such power-sharing was not enough. She wanted to be seen as an *equal* to the party, and preferred to form an "alliance" between her and the party. Alternatively, she wanted to displace Gamkrelidze as leader of the NRP and in effect take over the party. Because of these differences, the two could not reach an agreement.

For Zhvania, by contrast, creating an "alliance" with Burdjanadze was ideal, because this would allow him to argue that a "union" he had spent so much time talking about had actually finally happened. Furthermore, he could hide himself behind Burdjanadze in hopes of riding to victory on her personal popularity. When negotiations between Gamkrelidze and Burdjanadze broke down, Zhvania helped the speaker engineer an announcement of the "Burdjanadze team," which was full of old Zhvania allies but was successfully sold to the public as a new entity in Georgian politics. This was followed by an announcement of a "union" between the Burdjanadze team and United Democrats into an alliance called "Burdjanadze-Democrats."

The announcement was made in mid-August, when most other political leaders (including Gamkrelidze and Saakashvili) were on vacation. Thus, the media was hungry for political news, and the announcement received extensive and glowing coverage on all national networks for several days. Suddenly, Burdjanadze was at the center of everyone's attention, posters with her face were plastered all over the country, and she traveled around in an extremely well-organized campaign in which she said little but appeared with ordinary voters who seemed to love her. The popularity ratings for Burdjanadze-Democrats soared, and in late August ranged between 15 and 20 percent, ahead of all other parties.

Burdjanadze's rise came at a very inopportune time for the NRP, because it was still in the early stages of introducing Gamkrelidze to voters. She pressed heavily into its electoral space; her supporters, like those of the NRP, were voters who opposed Shevardnadze but did not like the National Movement's and Labor's populism and radicalism. While her voters were more heavily female and in their mid-forties and mid-fifties, and the NRP's were more male and in their mid-twenties and mid-thirties, the Burdjanadze-Democrats nonetheless took away votes from the NRP at a time when the NRP's numbers were bound to be on the increase because of the heavy advertising campaign. This was a development the NRP had not anticipated, and for which it did not have a quick response.

NGOs Prepare for the Revolution

While the parties prepared for the election, so did the NGO community—under the umbrella of the Open Society Foundation, a grant-making organization that was part of George Soros's network of foundations. Soros had invested millions in Georgia over the years, allegedly promoting democracy and civil society, though his funds were largely supporting a small group of partisan NGOs that constantly attacked the business community, the Georgian Orthodox Church, and the country's history and traditions. As I have already examined, over the years, many of these NGOs—either openly or behind the scenes—supported the "young reformers." As the election approached, they too were getting ready to play a key role on their behalf.

FROM A DEMOCRACY COALITION TO A REVOLUTIONARY COALITION

The Open Society Foundation's planning for a potential revolution actually started in September 2002, when its executive director, Kakha Lomaia, invited six NGOs to join what he called a Democracy Coalition. These six were Liberty Institute; Georgian Young Lawyers' Association (GYLA); Caucasus Institute for Peace, Democracy, and Development (CIPDD); Center for Social Research (CSR); Former Political Prisoners for Human Rights (FPPHR); and Partnership for Social Initiatives (PSI), an organization that I had helped start in 2000.

This coalition was surprisingly diverse and included groups that were, at least below the surface, quite hostile to each other ideologically, and were politically aligned with different groups. For example, Liberty, GYLA, and CIPDD had been great beneficiaries of Soros's funds and had been supporting the "young reformers" for years, though in 2002 their preference slowly shifted from Zhvania toward Saakashvili. Meanwhile, CSR and FPPHR, even though they had far less resources, had been opposing the "young reformers" for just as long. NGOs close to the "young reformers" accused CSR and FPPHR of developing ties with Jorbenadze in late 2002. Meanwhile, PSI, which was the only organization in the group with ties to the business community, was the youngest of these six and was politically most neutral—though I believe, because of my involvement with the NRP and ideological similarities, that its alignment was never in doubt.

According to Lomaia, the Democracy Coalition's mission was to help promote free and fair elections in 2003. Because it was so broad, it seemed for a while that the coalition could actually succeed in this goal, since it appeared that all organizations shared this one objective. However, as the fall progressed, it turned out that free and fair elections were not the real intent of some of the members of the coalition. Rather, the idea was to use the coalition to lay the groundwork for the removal of Eduard Shevardnadze after the November elections. Some members, especially Liberty's Giga Bokeria and Levan Ramishvili, and GYLA's Tinatin Khidasheli, did not hide that their intention was to not wait until 2005 when the president's term was up. Rather, they wanted to engineer a change in the position of president early, through extraconstitutional means if necessary.

The issue of whether the goal should be to work toward free and fair elections or to nurture an environment necessary for revolutionary change at the earliest possible moment divided the coalition. Liberty, GYLA, CIPDD, and Fair Elections (which became a coalition member later) supported the revolutionary model, though to varying degrees. (Ghia Nodia, CIPDD's chairman, was less vocal in supporting this course than others.) Meanwhile, PSI, CSR, and FPPHR refused to go along with the revolutionary strategy. As this split developed, Lomaia slowly disbanded the coalition, declaring that the higher authorities in the Soros Foundation network had decided not to finance its activities. In reality, however, this broad coalition was replaced with a narrow group of NGOs, all of whom shared the vision of revolutionary. They secured very large funds from the Soros Foundation for their work. Led by the Liberty Institute, and to a lesser extent by GYLA, and with active participation from CIPDD and Fair Elections, along with several other groups, this new "revolutionary coalition" quickly set to work to try to emulate the Serbian example, where an alliance of NGO groups and political parties had toppled Slobodan Milosevic in 2001.

As one of its first moves in this process, early in 2003 the Liberty Institute launched Kmara, the Georgian version of the Serb Otpor Movement. Kmara consisted of a small group of students at Tbilisi State University and other institutions, and saw as its mission nothing less than to undermine the government and its control over the country. With funds from Soros, Liberty brought trainers from Serbia to teach Kmara activists and other NGO leaders how to engage in anti-governmental activities. Many, myself included, believed that Georgian politics did not require guerrilla tactics and that these activities made little sense, but from Liberty's perspective, this was a key part of the revolutionary process.

It is not clear how much impact Kmara actually had, because unlike the movement for independence, it was never a real student movement with active participation from a large group of people. Rather, it consisted of a very small group of activists in Tbilisi, and the organization's regional representatives in several important towns. That said, it helped create an aura that the society was revolting against an authoritarian government that was limiting civil space and liberties in the country, even though this really was not the case. In particular, Kmara constantly plastered the city with posters derogating Shevardnadze and his allies, or simply posters saying "kmara," Georgian for "enough." Its activists would also graffiti the word "kmara" on buildings and walls. In April 2003, the organization's leaders painted "kmara" all over the steps of the Ministry of Interior, resulting in their arrest.[9] This brought out opposition leaders who demanded their release, even though the activists had clearly violated the law. This was a good example of the sort of tactics Liberty Institute and its NGO allies were willing to use in order to advance their agenda. It did not matter if their actions were legal or illegal; as long as they were in the service of their cause, they were acceptable to them.

At the same time, this revolutionary coalition went to work internationally, spreading the message—through interviews with the press, and visits to foreign capitals by NGO activists—that Georgia was becoming a dictatorship. The idea was to try to create a new image of Shevardnadze—that he was some kind of a Milosevic-like tyrant, rather than a weak leader who was presiding over a largely pluralistic political society (especially in late 2002 and early 2003). This strategy was extremely effective, especially in Washington, where opinion makers listened to what these NGO activists had to say because they viewed them as "democrats."

Part of the strategy was to discredit not only Shevardnadze, but also the business community. For example, in a talk at Radio Free Europe/Radio Liberty in Washington in October 2002, Ghia Nodia spent a great deal of time describing the entire business community as being full of "oligarchs" who were ready to use "violence" in order to gain power.[10]

THE NDI'S AND GEORGE SOROS'S ROLES

While the NGOs in the revolutionary coalition had close ties to Saakashvili and Zhvania, the Tbilisi office of the National Democratic Institute (NDI) was their conduit to other political parties. The NDI's activities in Georgia were largely funded by USAID, though some money apparently came from the Soros Foundation and other private donors. In emulating Serbia, the NDI and the NGOs wanted to engineer an alliance of opposition parties. In this, the revolutionary

NGOs were preaching the same mantra as Zhvania. To help push the alliance process along, the NDI invited Gamkrelidze, Saakashvili, and Zhvania to go on a trip to Serbia in January 2003, where they could learn from the politicians how Milosevic had been toppled.

Deciding whether to go on this trip was not easy for Gamkrelidze, but Soros was one factor that pushed him toward going. In December 2002, Gamkrelidze made his second trip to the United States. In addition to Washington, he traveled to New York, where he gave a lecture at Soros's Open Society Institute. Given Soros's role in funding the aforementioned NGOs, both Gamkrelidze and I were surprised that the Institute not only approached Gamkrelidze with an invitation to give a lecture there, but also arranged for him to meet with Soros himself. For a variety of reasons, both Gamkrelidze and I viewed this meeting with a great deal of concern, thinking that Soros would put pressure on Gamkrelidze to join Zhvania and Saakashvili in forming an opposition alliance, and that this was all part of an elaborate plan to get the NRP involved in a process the party did not support. Soros, however, appeared to put our fears to rest, because he approached the situation quite differently from what either Gamkrelidze or I had expected.

Soros told Gamkrelidze that he fully understood and appreciated the need for ideological differences in the political spectrum, and that in the context of Georgian politics, the NRP was akin to the American Republican Party, while Zhvania-Saakashvili were like American Democratic Party. Soros also claimed that his intention was not to push for a creation of a large opposition alliance that would compete in the election as one ticket, or to help create a revolutionary environment in Georgia. Rather, Soros alleged that he wanted the three groups to coordinate in ensuring that the elections were free and fair by working together to amend the Election Code and to implement other methods of preventing governmental fraud.

As part of this coordinating effort, Soros asked the New Rights Party to participate in a coordinating council that Soros hoped would be run by David Usupashvili, a prominent lawyer and a leading member of the Georgian Republican Party (a group of intellectuals without a serious basis of public support who had joined Saakashvili's National Movement in 2001). Accordingly, he strongly urged Gamkrelidze to go on the NDI-sponsored trip to Belgrade, because he thought that this sort of cooperation was crucial.

While we left the meeting hoping that this sort of rhetoric would signal a dramatic shift in Soros Foundation's strategy in Georgia, our hopes never materialized. Specifically, we hoped that the Foundation would become less one-sided, as would those NGOs that it funded, especially on the issue of opposition unity or revolutionary change. In reality, the Soros-funded NGOs and the NDI continued to act as they had in the past, though with more intensity. Many have suggested to me that this was because the Georgian branch of the Soros Foundation operated largely independently, with limited oversight from its headquarters in New York. Whether this was true remains an open question.

The NDI was so active in pressing for an opposition alliance that it often seemed that the NDI was working from a strategy prepared by Zhvania himself. (It is my view that in these activities, the NDI's representatives in Georgia were acting on their own, without any clear instructions or control from its headquarters in Washington.) The organization constantly presented Georgian political parties with coalition-building ideas, training sessions to teach various party staff members how to work together efficiently, and so forth. Marc Mullen and Lincoln Mitchell, the NDI representatives in Tbilisi, regularly lectured party leaders that creating such an alliance was essential if they hoped to receive American support.

Whether Zhvania took the idea of a coalition from the NDI and ran with it (coalition-building has been part of the NDI's strategy in other countries around the world), or the NDI liked Zhvania's idea and supported it through its own efforts—or there was some sort of a combination of these two alternatives—remains unclear. However, one way or another, instead of working to help build the capacity of the various political parties on behalf of democratic principles, as its mandate dictates, the NDI in Tbilisi became a partisan vehicle on behalf of the causes being advanced (for different reasons) by Zhvania and the revolutionary NGOs, and was using all of its resources in the service of this goal.[11]

This is the context in which one must understand the NDI's push for a trip to Serbia by opposition leaders in January 2003. Had the NDI truly wanted to help Georgian political parties learn how to consolidate a democracy from a semi-democratic state, using Taiwan, the Philippines, or maybe even Slovakia as instructive examples, would have made sense. Serbia offered a very different lesson, given that the opposition there had been dealing with a nationalist tyrant who had been responsible for killing hundreds of thousands of people; who had ruled Serbia with an iron fist, controlling the media, business, and almost all other aspects of life; and who even at the time of his removal had a strong base of support. By contrast, Georgia in 2002–3 was at a minimum a semi-pluralistic democracy, with a weak and unpopular president who had no capacity to control the media and the business community, and who was all but certain to leave office in 2005.

It is true that everyone in Georgia feared that there would be electoral fraud, and hoped to minimize it through American pressure on Shevardnadze and changes to the electoral legislation. However, this did not require modeling one's activities on a revolution that had taken place in Serbia.

Unfortunately, it turned out that a revolution was exactly what the NDI and its Georgian allies had in mind.

While the NDI was a catalyst behind a push for the opposition alliance in Georgia, in general, pressing parties in transitional democracies to form grand alliances across ideological and philosophic differences is in some respects a mistake that is often made in American foreign policy. For example, in the fall of 2004, the U.S. State Department advocated for the creation of such an alliance in Iraq, in order to strengthen the allegedly secular Sh'ia and weaken the allegedly Islamist ones. From afar, especially among those who do not have experience with practical politics, this policy seems to make sense—after all, does not America work very well with two large political parties? Is having two (or at most three) main political parties not the defining element of almost all successful democracies? Indeed, it is. However, the Republican and Democratic parties in the United States (or the Conservative and Labour parties in the United Kingdom) came together naturally, based on different interest groups and factions finding enough in common to moderate their passions and unite into political groupings that can actually win elections. As a result, both the Republican and Democratic parties, while not purely ideological, have a set of core philosophic ideas on which they base their political proposals and unified party agendas.

In this respect, the Republican and Democratic parties are what Madison suggested would happen in America in Federalist Papers 10 and 51, where he argued that the best way to prevent a faction from oppressing the minority was to force factions to come together into groups that united more than one single interest in order to gain political success.[12] However, the NDI and others who were pushing for an opposition alliance in Georgia, and who push for similar unnatural alliances elsewhere in transitional democracies, have something very different in mind.

Unlike Madison, who argued in *The Federalist Papers* that ambition should be pitted against ambition in order to protect liberty, present-day opposition coalition advocates have a postmodern belief that ambition is bad for politics. As a result, their goal is to force politicians into an environment in which they will have to set their ambition aside, instead of creating an environment in which ambition can be directed toward securing the common good. In a way, this is the fault of having people with no, or very little, practical political experience design and try to implement policies that have a dramatic impact on the practical politics of a given transitional democracy. This results in a policy that fails to appreciate that citizens want political parties to reflect their diversity (especially philosophic diversity).

Consolidation of the various political parties was certainly in order in Georgia, but in such a manner that would have enabled people to make informed choices and strengthened the democratic elements within the society. For example, it made sense for the New Rights Party and Industry Will Save Georgia to merge, because their commonalities were far greater than their differences, or for United Democrats and National Movement to merge, because fundamentally these parties had much in common. However, this did not mean that Georgia needed to create an alliance of the NRP, United Democrats, and National Movement, since this was more like mixing water and oil. Incidentally, the mergers that made sense but failed to take place before the November 2, 2003 election (unions of NRP and Industry, and of National Movement and United Democrats) took place quickly after the Rose Revolution in preparation for the March 2004 parliamentary revote.

Most who pressed for the creation of an opposition alliance clearly did not believe in giving citizens an opportunity to have a democratic, informed choice in an election (just like Zhvania had himself said during his appearance at NDI in 2002 in Washington). Though they never said this openly, in my view their reason for wanting an opposition alliance was fundamentally based on the notion that the Georgian people did not have the capacity either to make judgments about political issues or to rule themselves.

This view, of course, contradicted their alleged desire to promote a democracy in Georgia and elsewhere in the world, but many who have this view also oppose the push for democracy in the broader Middle East, based on the notion that the Arabs are simply not ready for free government. Instead, they wanted to give Georgians a very simple black and white choice, because in their view this was easy. But Georgians already had had a black and white choice in 1999—and it had not worked out very well for either democracy or good governance. The situation was not much different now, except that instead of Shevardnadze-Zhvania-Saakashvili being white and Aslan Abashidze and his Revival Party being black, the goal was to make Shevardnadze black and Zhvania-Saakashvili-Gamkrelidze-Burdjanadze white.

While such an election choice would have certainly simplified things on Election Day for many people, or even made the revolution easier to bring about, this was not a way to build a democracy. Everyone who pushed for a grand opposition coalition, especially the folks at the NDI office in Tbilisi, agreed that such an alliance would not last very long after the election. Thus, the promises made by the alliance to the people would never be fulfilled. The end result would be disenchantment of Georgian citizens with politics and politicians, who would once again be responsible for disappointing the people. As a result, at its core, demanding a united opposition was simply anti-democratic, because democracy is not possible when people feel disenchanted and apathetic.

There was, however, another view in support of an alliance that was more practical in its reasoning. Gamkrelidze and I heard its clearest articulation

during a dinner in Washington in July 2003 from Matthew J. Bryza, the director of Caucasus and Central Asia at the National Security Council. Bryza had
done yeoman's work on Georgia's behalf over the years. He appeared motivated
by nothing but Georgia's hopeful future (something you could not say about all
of the NDI's representatives in Georgia). Because of this, Gamkrelidze and I
both took his views seriously, since unlike those in Tbilisi (both Georgians and
foreigners alike) who were pushing for this alliance in order to advance their
personal interests, we knew that Bryza pressed this issue because he felt that
it was in the best interests of the country.

Bryza believed, with some merit, that some form of united opposition was
better positioned to take on Shevardnadze and the government resources that
were working on behalf of the For New Georgia alliance. Whether this was
because he simply did not believe that an electoral strategy based on a philosophic point of view could succeed in Georgia or he overestimated the capabilities of the Shevardnadze government, I do not know. However, he thought
that an alliance would strengthen the opposition against possible pressure,
intimidation, and fraud that the government could engineer. Addressing that
problem, Bryza felt, was paramount.

Unlike the NDI and Georgian NGOs, however, Bryza understood the problems that voters had with Zhvania, his ties to Shevardnadze, and his massive
unpopularity, especially with those who supported the New Rights Party. For
this reason, he argued simply that "if you have to dump Zhvania, that is fine,
just do an alliance with Misha [Saakashvili]."[13] His basic point (another reason
why he was pushing for an alliance) was that he would have a much easier time
convincing senior-level decision makers inside the administration of the
benefits associated with supporting a group that included two opposition leaders, and ideally three, rather than just one. In other words, Bryza did not care
which two of the three parties would unite, so long as at least two did. At the
time, I did not quite appreciate the extent to which this mattered to Bryza, and
the level at which it would influence his actions after the November elections,
during the Rose Revolution.

Business's and the Media's Roles

Unlike the NGO community, the business sector was much less organized in
protecting and advancing its interests in the forthcoming electoral struggle.
However, because the business community was the only self-sustaining element of Georgian civil society, it had two crucial roles to play, without which
neither the opposition parties nor the NGOs could have gotten very far.

First, the business sector financed opposition parties—actually quite extravagantly, given the nature of the campaigns that most were running. By my own rough estimation, about $15–20 million went into the election campaigns from Georgian businessmen. While this included money from those entrepreneurs whose financial dealings were largely abroad, nonetheless this is a very large amount for a small, economically weak country like Georgia.

Business's second big role was to nurture and help sustain the open and pluralistic media environment that allowed opposition politicians and NGO leaders to garner public support. For years, businesses' willingness to pay fairly large sums to purchase commercials on Rustavi 2 had been an essential element in allowing the channel to function more or less independently. While the commercials never fully covered the costs of its operations (with Rustavi 2 also needing foreign support from USAID, Soros Foundation, and others), money from the business community was the core of its financial base.

Unfortunately, most observers of Georgian politics abroad, just like NGO activists and analysts in Tbilisi, never gave business its due in nurturing the free media. The view was that the free media simply existed, without giving any thought to where the money that paid the reporters' salaries and other bills came from.

When in the first half of 2003 two new private stations—Imedi, owned by billionaire Badri Patarkatsishvili, and Mze, owned by banking magnate Vano Chkhartishvili—were launched, business's role in creating a pluralistic media environment grew disproportionately. Of the two new stations, Mze was smaller and had fewer resources, but it employed a number of famous anchors, including Inga Grigolia, probably the most popular and best-known TV personality in Georgia. Mze quickly became a strong backer of the opposition and constantly challenged the government, especially Shevardnadze. Its goal was to rival Rustavi 2, but it put less of a pro-Zhvania and pro-Saakashvili spin on events. While Mze did not surpass Rustavi 2 in its overall popularity and reach until after the Rose Revolution, Grigolia's nighttime debate talk show became extremely popular and influential.

Unlike Mze, Imedi had what seemed like unlimited resources. Patarkatsishvili, a Georgian citizen who had made almost all of his money in Russia, was forced to live in Georgia because Putin's regime had issued a warrant for his arrest as part of a crackdown on independent businessmen. Most of his business interests in Georgia, including Imedi, were more philanthropic than money-making.

In its political coverage, Imedi generally stayed above the fray and soon gained a reputation as the most neutral, fair, and accurate station, at least on the surface. Patarkatsishvili invested over $20 million installing television-frequency amplifiers that allowed Imedi to transmit into every corner of the country without having to rely on local affiliates. Thus, unlike Rustavi 2, which was only available nationally for two to three hours a day (when local stations turned on news coverage), Imedi was available everywhere, all the time. Its national coverage actually rivaled that of State Channel One, whose amplifier network dated back to the Soviet days.

Rustavi 2's Kitsmarishvili, who according to two reporters at the station had refused Patarkatsishvili's offer of over $25 million to sell the channel, was greatly threatened by these two stations. Kitsmarishvili was afraid not only of the inevitable loss of revenue, but also of the possibility that Rustavi 2 would lose its supremacy as the principal source of news for most citizens. While Mze was a problem in the short term, Imedi was a threat to him in the long term because it was bound to become the dominant station in the country, due to its national availability and Patarkatsishvili's willingness to pay higher wages to his employees and to spare no expense in buying foreign shows and rights to international sporting events.

This threat was one of the reasons why Kitsmarishvili started to press his case with Shevardnadze to be awarded the so-called "ORT frequency"—an unused frequency that used to belong to Soviet Channel One and that already had a national network of amplifiers left over from the days of the USSR. Kitsmarishvili was willing to use any means necessary to gain this frequency. He initially sought a deal with State Minister Avtantin Jorbenadze, offering to limit criticism of the government in return for a favorable outcome of his application to buy this "ORT frequency."[14]

When this deal failed, Kitsmarishvili resorted to more confrontational tactics. The change in Rustavi 2's tone in coverage of the government in late August was noticeable. Throughout the summer, when Kitsmarishvili was negotiating with the government over the ORT frequency, Rustavi 2 criticized the government, but not Shevardnadze himself, and limited the amount of opposition criticism that went on the air. However, in late August the rhetoric quickly became far more scathing. The anti-government message was ratcheted up until Election Day, and ultimately Rustavi 2 became the driving force in bringing the people into the streets to support the revolution.

Based on conversations that I have had over the years with reporters at Rustavi 2 and others involved in these discussions, I believe that Kitsmarishvili joined the revolutionary cause largely because his request for the "ORT frequency" was denied. Had Shevardnadze consented to Kitsmarishvili's demands for the frequency, Rustavi 2 would have been far more supportive of the government in the lead-up to the election and afterwards. Thus, Kitsmarishvili's desire to gain this frequency was the driving factor in the outcome of the Rose Revolution.

At the same time, as I have already mentioned, Kitsmarishvili needed new advertising revenue in light of greater competition. The Soros-sponsored revolutionary coalition, which had a great deal of money for anti-Shevardnadze advertisements, presented a unique opportunity. It decided to make a deal with Kitsmarishvili: through the Kmara Movement, it would buy advertisements exclusively on Rustavi 2, while in return, the channel would support the revolutionary NGOs. Since Shevardnadze had rejected Kitsmarishvili's demands for the ORT frequency, this deal was perfect for Kitsmarishvili, who needed money to support Rustavi 2's operations. As a result, throughout the fall, Rustavi 2 played commercials criticizing the president in unbecoming terms. They usually would end with a declaration: "Shevardnadze, you are the disease, get out."[15] Ultimately, the deal between Kitsmarishvili and the NGOs was crucial not because of the commercials, but because it swung Rustavi 2 toward supporting Saakashvili and his campaign in the last weeks of the race, as I examine in chapters 7 and 8.

6

Failure of the United Opposition
and Failure of the Baker Formula

On a parallel track with events discussed in the previous chapter, Georgian politicians were dealing with the issue that would eventually define the elections and shape all political decision-making in the country. This was the question of how the Electoral Code would be amended, especially in the area of the composition of the electoral commissions at the national and local level.

Starting in the early winter of 2003, a group of parliamentarians representing almost all serious political parties had been working on rewriting the Election Code, which Zhvania had authored while serving as speaker of Parliament and the CUG's campaign manager. It was designed solely to enable Zhvania to manipulate the election results. The opposition's goal was to implement mechanisms to prevent fraud in 2003. Almost everyone supported some of the new initiatives, such as requiring that all ballot boxes be made of clear plastic; that every voter be required to have his hand marked after voting; that so-called "additional lists" (i.e., lists on which individuals were added to voter rolls on Election Day) be banned; and that the Ministry of Interior be mandated to create a full nationwide voter registry, which had to be posted in precinct electoral-commission headquarters a full sixty days before the election in order to enable citizens to check whether they were actually on the voter lists.

The sticking point in the negotiations over the new Electoral Code became the question of who would get to appoint members to the Central Election Commission (CEC), as well as district- and precinct-level commissions, and how many members each party would have. The battle over the commissions' composition was the most important part of the negotiations over the Electoral

Code, because it would be nearly impossible to prevent fraud if the government party were to dominate the commissions as it had in years past.

The debate over the commissions was taking place at the same time as the Georgian president was under intense pressure from the United States and its allies to support a democratic electoral process and ensure a fair vote count in November. U.S. President George W. Bush had sent repeated letters to Shevardnadze calling for democratic elections. Similar messages were delivered by American and other Western representatives, including then NATO Secretary-General Lord George Robertson, right before the deadlock over the electoral commissions became a matter of huge public controversy.

Initially, the opposition proposed total party parity on the commissions— that is, that every political party with serious national standing be given one seat each on the election commission. Specifically, the opposition wanted one seat for the three parties that had overcome the 7 percent barrier necessary to enter Parliament in 1999 (the CUG, as represented by For New Georgia, Revival Party, and Industry Will Save Georgia), as well as one seat for those parties not included in the first list that had overcome the 4 percent barrier necessary to gain seats in the Sakrebulo during the Tbilisi local-government elections in 2002 (Labor, National Movement, New Rights Party, and Unity).

For New Georgia flatly rejected this idea, claiming that the government deserved more than one seat. After weeks of intense but fruitless discussions, on May 30 the Parliament rejected the opposition's call for the old commission to be disbanded and drew up a plan that would have dramatically limited the opposition's representation. Under their scenario, For New Georgia and Aslan Abashidze's Revival Party (which was technically in opposition to Shevardnadze, but when it came to electoral manipulation was a governmental entity just like the For New Georgia alliance) had a two-thirds majority and effectively controlled the commissions.

In response, speaking on behalf of the entire opposition, Gamkrelidze announced that the opposition would hold a mass protest on June 3 to demand parity in the composition of the electoral commissions. The call for protests was a somewhat spontaneous decision on part of the opposition, but it ultimately turned out to be Gamkrelidze's second great political mistake after the démarche against Shevardnadze the year earlier.

The day before the protest, leaders of the five major opposition parties met with Avtandil Jorbenadze, the state minister who was the head of the For New Georgia alliance, for over six hours to try to reach a compromise. The opposition offered a plan that would have given the president and For New Georgia alliance about one-third of the seats on commissions at all levels—either 6 out of 16, or 5 out of 15—with the other seats divided based on parity between the various opposition parties. Eventually Jorbenadze agreed to a formula of the government appointing 8 of 22 members at the CEC level, but rejected the opposition's call for similar composition at the precinct level. This led to a breakdown in talks, and the opposition leaders pressed ahead with plans for the protests.

On June 3, a crowd estimated at up to five thousand people gathered outside the Parliament building in Tbilisi, and demonstrations were reported in many of the country's other major cities and towns. Intensive coverage by independent television channels, including Rustavi 2, Imedi, and Mze (which had gone on the air just two days before), helped swell the ranks of the protesters throughout the day. However, Shevardnadze and Jorbenadze, especially the latter, were not willing to budge, while the opposition forces did not yet have the capacity or the organizational plan to continue with the protests for more than a day. Instead, opposition leaders were forced to disband the demonstration by first marching hand-in-hand to the State Chancellery (where Shevardnadze's office was located) and then calling on their supporters to go home.

The pictures of Gamkrelidze, Zhvania, Saakashvili, and other opposition leaders together leading a large crowd in Tbilisi with their arms crossed was probably the most depressing thing I had seen in my entire period of involvement in Georgian public life. This moment totally diluted, far more than the démarche, Gamkrelidze's standing with many of his own supporters, because he was forced to join together with the very people who were responsible for all the electoral problems that the opposition was now fighting. Because of this, many did not believe that the fight was actually about free and fair elections, since Georgians could not stomach the idea of Zhvania talking about ways to prevent fraud. In the minds of most, Zhvania was the mastermind who had actually invented and implemented the means to perpetuate massive fraud.

Having nothing else to tell the protesters at the end of the rally, the three leaders declared that they were launching a joint "movement" to prevent fraud in the forthcoming elections. As the first joint event of this movement, a couple of days after the Tbilisi demonstration, Gamkrelidze, Saakashvili, and Zhvania traveled together to Kutaisi, Georgia's second largest city, where they held a forum in the Opera building. This event was a means of compensating for their lack of capacity to organize another large protest in Tbilisi, since it was much easier to arrange for a meeting in a closed space. After the event, Zhvania suggested that they travel to the tomb of David the Builder—the greatest of Georgian kings, who was buried in Kutaisi—in order to make a promise that they would not violate their "union." Saakashvili and Gamkrelidze agreed, and that evening Georgian television was full of images of the three leaders jointly kneeling at King David's tomb promising to stick together, to my great disgust.

The protest and the visit to Kutaisi had a very negative impact on the image of the New Rights Party. It made all of the opposition parties look the same and reduced the NRP to the lowest-common-denominator level of United Democrats and National Movement. From then on, winning over voters' minds became far more difficult, because if they had to choose from among parties that were similar, then why not choose one that was far more radical in its opposition to Shevardnadze than the one that was more moderate? In other words, by joining forces with Zhvania and Saakashvili, Gamkrelidze lost even more of the unique credibility that he had presented to voters who wanted neither Shevardnadze nor those who had been responsible for rule alongside Shevardnadze throughout the 1990s.

This observation is based on my conversations with members of the political class in Tbilisi who supported the NRP and Gamkrelidze (such as journalists and opinion makers), and reports that the NRP's headquarters received from party representatives in the countryside. I had to spend hours explaining to relatives, friends, neighbors, and acquaintances—as well as members of the political establishment, some of whom had come to support Gamkrelidze because of his opposition to the "young reformers"—why the demonstration and subsequent joint appearances were necessary (even though I myself did not believe in these explanations).

Additionally, polling that the NRP had conducted in April made it clear that the party's voters had an extremely unfavorable view of Zhvania. Specifically, of those who had said they would vote for the NRP, 22 percent had a very favorable (5 percent) or somewhat favorable (17 percent) impression of Zhvania, while 50 percent had a somewhat unfavorable (23 percent) or very unfavorable (27 percent) impression. In the general population, Zhvania had a 34 percent favorable and 45 percent unfavorable rating. This was less of a problem with Saakashvili. Thirty-eight percent of the NRP's voters had a positive impression of Saakashvili (10 percent very favorable, and 28 percent somewhat favorable), while 37 percent had a negative impression (16 percent somewhat unfavorable, and 21 percent very unfavorable). His general population numbers were 43 favorable and 32 unfavorable. Thus, the question for me was not whether in the short term (i.e., by the November 2003 elections) an alliance would benefit the NRP, but whether by associating with Zhvania (and less so with Saakashvili), Gamkrelidze was hurting his image as a *real* reformer in the minds of those who understood what Zhvania's "young reformers" were really all about.

The Failed Attempt to Unite the Opposition

The protests themselves were a total failure since they did not achieve their goal of getting Shevardnadze and Jorbenadze to change their position on the question of the composition of the electoral commissions. The opposition, however, was not willing to admit to this failure. Zhvania, meanwhile, took advantage of this situation and pressed the case for an alliance. In the post-demonstration environment, having gained no concessions from the government, the idea of an alliance sounded pretty good to both Saakashvili and Gamkrelidze.

While there were some at the NRP, Pikria Chikhradze and myself included, who were strongly against such an alliance, Gamkrelidze was insistent. After the Kutaisi visit, trying to change his mind was hopeless. Indeed, I vividly remember a phone conversation with Gamkrelidze as he was returning from Kutaisi to Tbilisi, telling me to immediately get in touch with Murphy and have him start planning for a new strategy, tailored to the three parties running together. At this point, suggesting that maybe it was best to first consider whether such an alliance was actually beneficial was useless. Thus, the NRP was plunged into a deep discussion of forming a union with its former bitter enemies, not through a strategic choice, but by what appeared to be a necessity caused by others' successful political maneuvers. That is never a good place to be in politics.

Much of the rest of June was consumed by discussions between Zhvania, Saakashvili, and Gamkrelidze, and at times Nino Burdjanadze, about the sort of alliance they should form. Most of the negotiations took place at the NRP's office, and I had an opportunity to be present at some of the meetings or to receive a first-hand account of those meetings I did not attend. At the meetings, Zhvania was the biggest advocate of forming an alliance quickly since he had the most to gain from it, though Gamkrelidze also was quite open and, unlike Zhvania, willing to compromise in order to make the alliance happen.

Initially, the focus was on establishing a short-term electoral block. Zhvania was proposing dividing the electoral list into four parts, with each of the three parties getting 30 percent and Burdjanadze and other minor parties getting the rest. Saakashvili was unwilling to accept this deal. He argued, quite accurately, that the NRP and National Movement had a similar standing with the electorate. His party had a higher rating, he argued, but the NRP was better organized and had already engaged very prominent foreign consultants. As a result, Saakashvili wanted the NRP and National Movement to have an equal share of the electoral list, either 35 or 40 percent, while Zhvania, Burdjanadze, and all other parties had to be satisfied with the other 30, or maybe even 20, percent.

While I agreed with Saakashvili's analysis of the political situation in the country, this idea was clearly not going to go anywhere. Zhvania actually found such a proposal offensive, and at one point he and Saakashvili almost got into a fistfight, with the latter screaming that the opposition's only problem was

Zhvania's unpopularity, while the former reminded Saakashvili that he would not be anywhere today had it not been for Zhvania's willingness to mentor Saakashvili over the years. As a result, the discussion of how the parties should divide the list ended inconclusively.

The other big question during these discussions was who would head the list. Zhvania proposed Burdjanadze, as a "neutral" person, though everyone knew that she was quite close to him and his team. Meanwhile, Zhvania also wanted Gamkrelidze to be the head of the election campaign, the same role that Zhvania had played in 1999 for the Citizens Union of Georgia. On this issue there seemed to be more of an agreement, because Gamkrelidze was willing to accept Zhvania's offer, while Saakashvili was persuaded to seek the position of mayor of Tbilisi, with the alliance making the introduction of an elected city mayor a key priority after the elections.

After a few discussions that focused on these issues, with the sides still unable to agree on how to move forward, I wrote a memorandum for Gamkrelidze suggesting an alternative—that he propose a full party union, with the three parties uniting into one large party, rather than a short-term preelection alliance. I argued that this could be a way to overcome the issue of how to divide the list, because once the party was formed, its three leaders could sit down and together write an electoral list by assessing the merits of each of the individual candidates separately, without the consideration of whether a given candidate was from the NRP, United Democrats, or National Movement.

My intention was partly to break the deadlock, since the opposition's inability to agree on what to do looked very bad in the domestic and international press, and partly to make sure that Gamkrelidze would appear at the negotiating table as the most reasonable of the three leaders. After all, given that the NRP was the most organized of the three parties, he had the most to give up if a full party alliance were formed. I also believed that such an idea could sound particularly credible coming from the person who had been most opposed to an alliance earlier. Finally, I believed that a party-based union would at least partially allay my concerns about the short-term opposition alliance. At the minimum, if an alliance were to become a party, it was unlikely to fall apart immediately after the elections. This way it would be in a position to at least fulfill some of the promises it would made to the people. That said, in the back of my mind I felt that it was best for the NRP to appear in the elections independently, and I somewhat hoped that Zhvania and Saakashvili would reject such a party alliance, thus admit that they only wanted an alliance for short-term political gain rather than to promote real political change.

After a couple of weeks of negotiations, it became clear that Zhvania and Saakashvili could not agree. Zhvania wanted to be an equal partner with Saakashvili and Gamkrelidze, while Saakashvili wanted him to be a junior partner. For Zhvania, such a role was tantamount to humiliation, since he saw himself as the most experienced and deserving of the three due to his previous position in Georgian politics. As a result, the deal between the three parties fizzled. However, these weeks of discussion did even more damage to the NRP. They took away valuable time from working on implementing the Murphy strategy, and as I have already discussed, damaged the NRP's standing as an independent party.

All this talk and constant pressure toward an alliance probably severely damaged the NRP's standing with the public, especially its own supporters, and hurt Gamkrelidze's chances of presenting himself as an honest broker between the opposition and Shevardnadze, as he had been during the upheaval over Rustavi 2 in October–November 2001. At the same time, the talk of an alliance—especially the January trip to Serbia—scared Shevardnadze and got him to take steps to resurrect his own political base. Shevardnadze may very well have felt that he was being railroaded by the opposition, which appeared to want to hand him Milosevic's fate. This was probably the impetus for him to agree to demands from some of his allies in the government—especially State Minister Avtandil Jorbenadze—to start rebuilding the Citizens Union of Georgia as the For New Georgia alliance. This was not formalized until March–April 2003, when Shevardnadze announced the formation of the alliance, but this process clearly started in January, on the heels of the opposition leaders' trip to Serbia.

Pressure on Shevardnadze from Washington

Throughout the period of these opposition negotiations, a variety of influences in Washington also tried to put pressure on Shevardnadze to ensure that he would agree to an acceptable compromise on the issue of elections, and specifically election commissions. For example, Mike Murphy advised Senator John McCain on this issue in order to seek his involvement. McCain, who had been a longtime friend of Georgia, decided to press Shevardnadze, and in July sent a strongly worded letter urging him to agree to changes in the electoral administration.

McCain's letter read in part:

> I write out of respect for the leadership you have shown in securing Georgia's independence and fostering a strategic partnership between our nations. . . .
>
> As a friend of Georgia, I am deeply concerned about the pre-election environment as your country approaches parliamentary elections in November. . . .
>
> I do not believe the composition of Georgia's electoral commission as currently

constructed will enable the Georgian people and the international community to have the necessary confidence in the outcome of the upcoming elections. An electoral commission composed primarily of known supporters of the government, if allowed to stand, will be a grave setback to the progress of democracy in Georgia. It will tilt the pre-election environment in favor of parties associated with the current government and will cause political debate to focus on real or imagined efforts to undercut free elections, rather than allowing politicians to speak to the Georgian people about the issues themselves.

An electoral commission that is not truly independent . . . will call the outcome of the election itself into doubt, with consequences both for the people of Georgia and for U.S. assistance to your country. Should parties associated with the government win a free and fair election, the result will be tainted and the new government's legitimacy questioned through certification by what will widely be seen as a subjective body. This could make an already difficult country to govern even more ungovernable as increasing numbers of Georgians feel they lack a stake and a voice in a government that does not represent them.[1]

The letter made it into the Georgian media and immediately became a huge topic. Shevardnadze's office initially denied that such a letter existed, then tried to twist its meaning to suggest that McCain did not really mean that the electoral commissions had to be changed. The opposition, by contrast, jumped all over the letter, and suggested that Washington was finally beginning to lose patience with Shevardnadze's government and its unwillingness to guarantee an opportunity for democratic elections. While the letter did not influence Shevardnadze to the extent that one had hoped, it had a clear impact on the public at large—it was yet another confirmation that the United States was supporting Georgia rather than Shevardnadze (as the president too often tried to suggest).

Enter Jim Baker

When Gamkrelidze was in Washington in December 2002, he had pressed officials there to consider sending someone to Tbilisi to deliver a very strict message to Shevardnadze about the need to have free elections. The idea was well received, because the Bush administration was already thinking about doing this. In the spring, Matthew Bryza of the National Security Council wrote a memo making a case for such a visit by a senior U.S. representative. This proposal was eventually approved by the Deputies Committee (consisting of Deputy Secretary of State Richard Armitage, Deputy Secretary of Defense Paul Wolfowitz, and Deputy National Security Advisor Steve Hadley), which recommended sending former Secretary of State James Baker because of his long-standing relationship with Shevardnadze. Baker came to Georgia over the July 4th weekend, accompanied by Assistant Secretary of State for European Affairs Elizabeth Jones and Bryza.

At this point, the U.S. government (through the Department of State and USAID) was already spending a tremendous amount of money on promoting free and fair elections in Georgia. The funds were being spent on preparing real voter rolls and on ensuring honest reporting. In addition, a great deal of money was appropriated for monitoring of the elections.

Baker's visit was very unexpected in Georgia—it came with no warning and was a surprise to many people, including some officials at the U.S. Embassy. I first learned about it when Gamkrelidze received a phone call from the embassy a day or two before the visit, asking if he could attend a meeting with the secretary in the early evening of July 4, prior to Baker's meeting with Shevardnadze. Only afterwards did I visit the White House website and find this brief announcement:

> Former Secretary of State James Baker will visit Tbilisi, Georgia on July 4 and 5 on behalf of President Bush. The mission's primary objective will be to discuss with Georgian President Eduard Shevardnadze ways to advance political and economic reform in Georgia through free and fair Parliamentary elections this fall. Mr. Baker will also discuss U.S.–Georgian cooperation on counterterrorism and other security matters. The Baker mission reflects the United States' readiness to work with all Georgian citizens who are committed to advancing reform and fighting corruption in pursuit of a democratic, prosperous, and stable Georgia.[2]

While his trip was unexpected, Baker came to Tbilisi with a clear agenda. He had a ten-point plan about how to secure free and fair elections, including a proposal for parallel vote tabulations (PVT), which the United States would finance. The most important part of Baker's proposals was a formula for the appointment of the electoral commissions at all levels. According to the Baker formula, Shevardnadze would appoint five members; opposition parties would appoint eight members, one per party; and the Organization for Security and Cooperation in Europe (OSCE) would select the chairman at the national level. This chairman would then appoint chairs at district and precinct levels. Decisions were to be made by a two-thirds majority, ensuring that most parties would have to agree on a decision in order to get it passed.

Upon arriving in Tbilisi, Baker first met with the opposition leaders, including Gamkrelidze, Zhvania, Saakashvili, Natelashvili, Gemal Gogitidze of the Revival Party, and Akaki Asatiani of the Traditionalist Party. The opposition was delighted with Baker's formula since it gave them what they had always wanted.³ Later, Baker went to see Shevardnadze, who after tense negotiations agreed to all the points Baker presented.

The next morning, Baker once again met with the opposition to tell them about the agreement that he had reached with Shevardnadze. According to several Georgian participants, Baker made it crystal-clear that the eight opposition seats had to be divided on the basis of parity, with one seat per party. To underscore this point, he pointed to each of the leaders, asking, "You have a party, right? If so, one member for you."

Baker also told the leaders that he was asking Assistant Secretary Jones to stay in Tbilisi for an additional day to coordinate a meeting between the opposition and Shevardnadze. Finally, he emphasized that the U.S. Embassy would be extensively involved in making sure that the agreement was put into effect through proper legislation. It appears that Bryza realized that this last issue could become a problem in the future. Because of this, he whispered into Gamkrelidze's ear, asking him to point out to Baker why the embassy's involvement was so important. When Gamkrelidze raised this point, according to Georgian attendees Baker turned to U.S. Ambassador Richard Miles and emphasized that his direct involvement was indeed vital.

Following this meeting, Baker left Georgia, but Jones stayed and, after some uncertainty caused by Shevardnadze's saber-rattling, arranged for a meeting between the president and the opposition leaders. The meeting was nothing but smiles, with everyone pledging to follow through on the agreement. Thus, the Americans were satisfied by what appeared to be the overwhelming success of the mission. Unfortunately, things did not end that simply.

Observing this process was a magnificent experience. While I had been a supporter of the idea of sending someone to speak to Shevardnadze about free and fair elections for many months, I could have never imagined that it would be Baker, nor did I think that the Bush administration would come with such a concrete plan for what needed to happen. It was all but certain that if the Baker agreement were followed, it would have made electoral fraud very difficult, if not impossible. Having Jones stay in Georgia for an extra day was like icing on the cake—here was one of the busiest U.S. diplomats spending so much time and energy trying to arrange a meeting between the opposition and the president in a small, economically desperate country. This was probably the best example of the extent to which things had changed for Georgia since the days when it had declared its independence from the USSR, yet was dependent on Russia for its survival. Most missed the irony of the fact that the only reason Washington was devoting so much time to promoting free elections in Georgia was because of the success of Shevardnadze's leadership in the early- and mid-1990s, and of his policies that had enabled Georgia to develop a strategic partnership with the United States. Yet his policies also had failed to bring about the development of a real democratic state, and for this reason, American engagement in pressing for democracy was essential.

In a way, Baker's visit represented the Bush foreign policy at its finest. After September 11, the U.S. president had set forth a national-security strategy that rightly placed democracy at the center of the American international agenda. The Bush administration declared its willingness to use Washington's resources to advance the cause of free societies. In the years since, there has been a great deal of resistance to actually applying President Bush's doctrine to specific circumstances—especially in the lower-profile countries, which are handled by the government's foreign-policy bureaucracy rather than by political appointees. Furthermore, the administration has often strayed off course from following through on its own rhetoric. The Baker mission was a clear illustration of how the Bush foreign policy was supposed to work, and how American power could be used nobly on behalf of democracy.

Many administration officials deserve credit for this, but in particular, praise must go to Matt Bryza for conceiving this mission and for being willing to make the case for why American should help advance democracy in Georgia. Unfortunately, what happened during the course of the summer after the Baker mission is a far more negative testament about the problems associated with U.S. foreign policy under President George W. Bush, especially in the lack of necessary follow-up in the process of implementation of excellent foreign-policy initiatives. On that front, Bryza, as the most active official responsible for Georgia in the administration, is at least partly to blame. However, given that Bryza was relatively junior and the Department of State is always the senior agency in the process of implementing the president's foreign policy, the greatest blame lies with the principal officials in the Bureau of European Affairs.

For several weeks after the Baker visit, it seemed that everything had changed in Georgia. A week or two later, Gamkrelidze and I traveled to the United States, and it appeared that there, too, officials were far more positive about Georgia than they had been in the past. The mission dramatically raised Georgia's profile in the American foreign-policy agenda, as became clear when the subject of the Baker visit came up even during Gamkrelidze's meeting with Florida Governor Jeb Bush. In Washington, everyone had the feeling that the Baker agreement was finally giving Georgia a chance to realize its just future and move toward the consolidation of democratic governance. Officials were particularly struck by Shevardnadze's apparent willingness to listen to Baker and work with the opposition. The notion that the Georgian president was always willing to work with you if and when you pushed him hard enough was apparently true. This had been the American experience with the Pankisi Gorge, and the same formula once again worked with the Electoral Code—or so it seemed.

Rejection of the Baker Agreement

When Gamkrelidze and I returned to Tbilisi from Washington, the main focus of all politicians was on the impending vote to implement the Baker agreement in the Electoral Code. At first, everything went according to plan, and all of the key elements of the agreement were included in the draft legislation that was being debated in Parliament. While some members from the Shevardnadze camp resisted, on the first reading opposition parliamentarians and the president's most loyal supporters mustered a majority necessary to pass a formula for the composition of the electoral commissions that mirrored Baker's proposal. However, something changed between the first and second readings, because when it came to voting on the proposal again, the votes were no longer there. (Georgian parliament is required to vote for legislation three times before it can be sent to the president for his signature.)

It became apparent later that Jorbenadze, the state minister and the head of the For New Georgia election campaign, convinced Shevardnadze to backtrack and renege on the agreement. The process allegedly went something like this. First, a week or two after Baker's visit, Shevardnadze met with Richard Miles, the U.S. ambassador, to test him on the level of American commitment to the exact framework of the Baker formula. According to several Shevardnadze advisors, Miles was far less definitive and demanding than Baker about the need to follow the agreement strictly. This, in turn, opened the way for Shevardnadze to walk away from the Baker formula.

As another test for the Americans, the president gave a radio interview in which he spoke about how the Baker formula was merely a framework rather than an agreement on the specific details, which could be changed if necessary. When this remark was left unanswered by the U.S. Embassy, Jorbenadze and his teammates were emboldened. They cooked up a plan which allegedly followed the letter of the Baker agreement, but not its spirit and most important detail—parity of the opposition representation in order to prevent a faction-based two-thirds majority. Working with deputies from Revival, the party controlled by the Adjarian leader Aslan Abashidze that was officially in "opposition" but was simultaneously "governmental," and Industry Will Save Georgia, whom the NRP was trying to convince of the wisdom of an alliance but whose leadership was far more comfortable in making a deal with Jorbenadze, FNG leaders proposed a new way of dividing the eight opposition representatives. They said that Revival should get three, as the second-place finisher in the 1999 elections; Industry should get two, as the third-place finisher; while the top four finishers in the 2002 local-government elections in Tbilisi (Labor, National Movement, NRP, and United Democrats) should get one each. Jorbenadze then got Shevardnadze to agree to this proposal, and its supporters quickly pushed it to a vote in Parliament.

Opposition parties cried foul and argued that this proposal did not reflect the Baker agreement. However, they did not have the votes to prevent its passage. Instead, they used every procedural tactic available to delay the vote and kept the Parliament in session all night.

During the nighttime session, Senator McCain tried to aid the opposition's efforts with this statement: "I strongly support the efforts of the Georgian Parliament to pass a new election code modeled on the Baker Elections Scorecard, as proposed by former U.S. Secretary of State James Baker during his mission to Georgia as a presidential envoy earlier this month. Last week, the new election code passed its first reading in the Parliament, but is in danger of failing or being altered in such a way as to weaken the provisions for parity among opposition parties in representation on the electoral commission, as put forth in Secretary Baker's proposal. I strongly support passage of an election law that mirrors the Baker proposal. Any effort by political parties or the government to gain advantage at the expense of parity on the electoral commission could gravely threaten the fairness of parliamentary elections in November."[4] However, by that point, Shevardnadze's allies had gone so far in rejecting the American position that they really did not care about what anyone might be urging them to do.

What was probably even more striking than the action of Shevardnadze's allies was the refusal by the U.S. Embassy to get involved. All opposition leaders pleaded with the embassy to issue a statement about the need to follow the true Baker formula, or at least to have the ambassador speak to Shevardnadze, but nothing happened. While officials in the embassy's political section were sympathetic, they were powerless, because Ambassador Miles simply refused to get involved. This was an excellent example of an endemic problem when senior nonpolitical foreign service officials are unwilling to act in order to not rock the boat. Some in Washington have argued that this happens because they seek to protect their careers. I by no means intend to suggest that all officials suffer from this problem, but sadly, some do.

Zhvania spoke with Ambassador Miles himself and pleaded with him to get directly involved, but he flatly refused to do so, claiming that it was not the business of the United States to engage in the process so directly. Thus I learned where this "policy" of silence originated: with Miles. The excuse made no sense at all, given that the boldness and the direct involvement of the U.S. administration was the only reason why the composition of the commissions was an issue of such magnitude at all. In other words, had it not been for the Baker visit, the government would have long ago passed its own version of the law for the composition of the commissions. Meanwhile, what was in question now was whether the agreement reached by the former secretary of state was going to hold. Furthermore, no matter what the excuse, by refusing to get involved Miles appeared to be contradicting instructions that Baker had personally given him, and thus not following policy set for by the president's personal envoy.

While Shevardnadze deserves the most blame for the collapse of the Baker agreement—after all, he failed to keep his own word—Miles, and by extension his superiors in Washington, were also partly at fault but not trying to force the Georgian president's hand. For better or worse, the Bush administration had put American prestige and the president's foreign policy, in which disrespect for the fundamental rights of man has real consequences, on the line in Georgia by having an individual of the stature of Jim Baker go there to secure an agreement that would provide for free and fair elections. By not getting involved to protect the agreement, Ambassador Miles was thus hurting both the administration's policy and American prestige and interests.

With numerous other far more immediate problems requiring their attention, senior individuals in the administration had little time and interest to once again focus on Georgia. As a result, dealing with Georgia was left to lower-ranked officials in Washington, some of whom (like Miles) appeared to not believe in what the president rhetoric about democracy required them to do, not only in Georgia but all over the world. Indeed, some would have preferred it if the United States had stayed out of the business of "advancing democracy" in general. As a result, when it became necessary for them to act in order to advance the president's agenda in Georgia, an agenda that had been made crystal-clear by Baker during his visit, they failed to do so. Instead, they argued that what was approved by the Parliament was no different from the formula that Baker had recommended—even though the two formulas were poles apart.

A couple of weeks before the November vote, I had an opportunity to discuss this incident with a senior embassy official during a visit to Georgia by Senator McCain. Without giving away anything confidential, this person told me that defending the real Baker formula meant going "further than this embassy was willing to go." In other words, the ambassador simply did not care about following the instructions that he had received from Baker.[5] However, he also knew that he could never publicly admit to the fact that the Baker formula had been rejected. Instead, he continued to insist that what was approved was actually the Baker plan. Incidentally, he did so during an appearance in Tbilisi with McCain, even though the senator had said the opposite before, having called for the adoption of parity-based composition during the parliamentary vote. The fact that his insistence on something that was simply not true made the U.S. administration that he represented look foolish apparently never occurred to the ambassador.

One additional piece of behind-the-scenes information (something that to my knowledge has never yet been discussed publicly) about the debate over the Baker formula is quite interesting. Even after Jorbenadze had convinced Shevardnadze to ignore the Baker agreement and pass an alternative with Revival and Industry Will Save Georgia, the latter group's parliamentary leader, Zurab Tkemaladze, approached Gamkrelidze with yet another proposal. This one *would* have followed the parity principle (thus Industry and Revival would have only had one seat each), but instead of one seat each being given to the four top finishers in the Tbilisi Sakrebulo elections in 2002, they would have gone to those four parties that had the most victories in the local-government races across the country. This would have had an impact only on one party—Zhvania's United Democrats would have been left without a seat and another, minor opposition party would have received a seat—while all other opposition parties with real chances in the parliamentary elections (National Movement, Labor and New Rights) would have gained one seat. Most importantly, the government and its allies would not have had a two-thirds majority.

Industry despised Zhvania so much that it was willing to sacrifice an additional seat for itself in return for getting him out of the picture—and its proposal was strong on policy grounds, because national results were probably a better barometer of party strengths than the Tbilisi vote. However, Gamkrelidze rejected this proposal because he did not want to stab Zhvania in the back, and because he felt that Baker had been very clear about how the seats should be allotted. In short, from Gamkrelidze's perspective, accepting Industry's proposal would have been a dishonorable thing to do.

This decision may have been ill-conceived for two reasons. First, in politics, honor can and should be a guiding principle, but it is hard to be honorable when your alleged partner is totally dishonorable in his own actions and is responsible for the most poisonous elements within the body politic. Second, from the practical point of view, even if Industry's proposal hurt Zhvania, it would have helped the greater, nobler cause of democracy, because parity in the opposition representation was critical for preventing fraud. Sacrificing Zhvania was not too high a price to pay for the sake of Georgian democracy and the country's national interests. In his actions, Gamkrelidze showed the great extent to which he has been influenced by his Christian morality and sense of decency—values that he could put to great use on behalf of Georgia someday, and which are sadly missing from the center of Georgian public life today.

The failure of the Baker proposal was a defining moment for Georgian politics, both in the immediate sense and in the long term. As the forthcoming analysis demonstrates, the single biggest factor contributing to the Rose Revolution was electoral fraud, which would have been far less prevalent, if not impossible, had the real Baker agreement been approved. While in early

August, few outside the NGO community were thinking about a possible revolution, opposition parties understood that the makeup of the electoral administration made fraud much more likely.

This became even more true when the OSCE refused to nominate one candidate for the position of chairman of the CEC, instead proposing a short list of
three, from which the president could pick.[6] The list included pro-governmental Nana Devdariani, and the far more neutral Vakhtang Khmaladze and David
Usupashvili.[7] This method gave Shevardnadze the final say in the selection
process, allowing him to pick the one candidate who would do FNG's bidding
while creating the appearance that the president had picked a "neutral" person.
Devdariani was probably a far better choice than the one Shevardnadze would
have appointed without the OSCE's involvement, but she was not the sort of
fighter for free and fair elections that the opposition would have preferred.

Either way, with these developments, the likelihood of free and fair elections decreased dramatically. Everyone realized that the election battle would
be bloodier than anyone had envisioned just a few weeks earlier.

A United Opposition After All?

Along with the failure of the Baker proposal, the opposition was facing problems from other sides as well. In late August, For New Georgia placed a great
deal of pressure on a number of the most prominent business supporters of
the opposition to stop funding these parties. In particular, pressure was put on
Badri Patarkatsishvili and Vano Chkhartishvili, respectively the owners of
Imedi and Mze television networks, with the government demanding that
these stations stop advancing the opposition's cause. Finally, the CEC reached
a number of decisions that were damaging to the opposition because they
opened the way for fraud—for example, the CEC decided that it would not
announce the total turnout until several days after the vote, giving the government time to manipulate and increase the turnout as Zhvania had done on
behalf of Citizens Union of Georgia in 1999.

These developments coincided with demands from Erosi Kitsmarishvili, the
owner of Rustavi 2 television, that Gamkrelidze, Zhvania, and Saakashvili come
together into an alliance. Kitsmarishvili was partly operating out of personal
interest, given that he would face a significant financial crisis soon after the election. Additionally, he was unable to reach an agreement with Jorbenadze over
his desire to acquire a national television frequency, for which he had been bidding for several years. That said, it is likely that at this point, Kitsmarishvili was
at least partly under the influence of the Soros-supported NGOs, which had
promised to buy a great deal of advertisement time for the Kmara Movement

exclusively on Rustavi 2. These NGOs wanted to see an opposition union because they felt that it would advance their revolutionary process, and were probably using Kitsmarishvili to try to achieve their desired end.

With Kitsmarishvili telling opposition leaders that if they formed an alliance he would direct his media resources to advance their cause, and with support from other stations likely to be greater if they united, in late August and early September, Zhvania, Gamkrelidze, and Saakashvili, joined by Burdjanadze and Kitsmarishvili, held several meetings at the Metekhi Palace Hotel to discuss a possible alliance. Zhvania was now speaking from a position of strength because the meetings were taking place on the heels of his "alliance" with Burdjanadze, and the Democrats were riding high in the polls, at least in the short term. By contrast, Gamkrelidze was speaking from a position of weakness. Not only was he uncertain about whether he would have the money to finance his campaign during the final stretch, but internal disagreements about the party's electoral strategy appeared to increase the need for an alliance.

Much as in the initial discussions of a possible alliance in June, the biggest sticking points became how to divide the electoral list and who would head it. Zhvania argued (again) that Burdjanadze should be considered a separate entity, and thus a list should be divided in four parts. Saakashvili, not surprisingly, objected to this. Zhvania also argued that Burdjanadze should be the first on the list, in light of her great popularity. This position was more acceptable to Saakashvili, but he wanted a greater share of the list if Burdjanadze got this position.

Eventually the leaders settled on discussing two alternatives for how to resolve these two issues. According to one option, Saakashvili was willing to accept a very low share of the list (maybe 20 percent), but in return, he would be first on the list. According to the other, Burdjanadze would head the list and together with Zhvania share 30 percent of it, while Saakashvili and Gamkrelidze would divide the rest. Under the latter circumstance, Saakashvili argued that Burdjanadze would be positioning herself for the position of president, and in return he wanted the alliance to make the passage of legislation to have an elected mayor in Tbilisi a top priority, and was demanding a promise that all of the leaders would support his candidacy for this position.

It seemed that the latter proposal would form the basis of an agreement, but on the following day, Zhvania came into the meeting and once again demanded 50 percent of the list. With this, the negotiations broke off, since Saakashvili and Gamkrelidze interpreted Zhvania's demand as his indication that he no longer favored an alliance. This was somewhat ironic, since the entire notion of an opposition alliance was initially Zhvania's idea, and he had been advocating it with great vigor for much of the year.

Thus, the final attempt to unite the opposition failed, and the political parties turned to the final stretch of the campaign. Few expected this period to be as unpredictable as it turned out to be, and no one expected that the revolutionary NGOs' dream of an extraconstitutional change of power would actually become possible. Yet this is exactly what happened, as I describe in the next two chapters.

7

The Fall Campaign

arties competed almost nonstop during the months of September and October. For me, as the principal strategist of the NRP, this period is somewhat of a blur, since I was working eighteen to twenty hours a day and hardly ever slept. Maybe because of this ungodly schedule and continuing problems with the party's campaign, I failed to fully notice and understand all of the successes and failures of the other campaigns until after things were over. However, after November 2003, I have had a chance to analyze and reflect on that period and have come to appreciate in particular Saakashvili's brilliant campaign.

In this chapter, I analyze the final campaign stretch, trying to present as comprehensive a picture as possible. When speaking about results, I generally refer to the parallel vote tabulations (PVT), a count of protocols from select precincts conducted by NDI and their Georgian partner, an NGO called Fair Elections. While there were significant problems with the PVT that raise concerns about its accuracy and point to the likely overestimation of the results for National Movement and Burdjanadze-Democrats, these numbers are nonetheless closer to telling us how people actually voted than the official count released by the CEC. The official count was corrupted both by fraud engineered by For New Georgia and, to a far greater extent, by the utterly fake results the Revival Party allegedly got in Adjaria.

The Fall Sprint to the Finish

As my analysis in chapters 5 and 6 suggests, the Burdjanadze-Democrats entered the final stretch of the campaign on a very high note. Indeed, the cautious

Zhvania felt so confident that he rejected a deal to form the very same opposition alliance that he had been trying to create for over two years. Burdjanadze was riding a wave of popularity, traveling the country, meeting large groups of citizens, and receiving favorable coverage in the media. It seemed that she was the unchallenged new darling of Georgian politics. For many, she even overcame the most important psychological barrier caused by the general inability of the population to answer the question "If not Shevardnadze, then who?" With her rise in August, the answer for many, including some supporters of the New Rights, was "Nino Burdjanadze."

From the very beginning, I was wary about these extremely favorable assessments. While she had a very positive favorability number, it was not clear from the polls that this would necessarily translate to a high ballot result. Furthermore, her poll numbers were at their height in the middle of September, five to seven weeks before the election. It was all but certain that something would happen during that time to change the situation—Georgian politics moved too fast to remain static for that long.

At the same time, even as he hid in the background behind Burdjanadze, Zhvania remained extremely unpopular, and in the eyes of most citizens he was still the real force behind the Burdjanadze-Democrats. This perception was only strengthened by the fact that Burdjanadze did not bring a single fresh face with her into the "alliance" of the Burdjanadze-Democrats; everyone who surrounded her, who spoke on her behalf on television, and who was perceived as a potential member of her inner circle was usually a well-known Zhvania ally. Burdjanadze's face may have been plastered on posters all over the country, but she did not appear to have any real influence in the "alliance's" decision-making.

Nonetheless, in early- and mid-September, Burdjanadze and Zhvania were clearly doing very well—certainly much better than United Democrats would have done had they not engineered the myth of an alliance with Burdjanadze. For whatever it was worth, the rebranding had an impact. However, as the campaign progressed, Burdjanadze's chances fizzled. Zhvania's strategy never went beyond the advertisement of Burdjanadze's name—it never offered the public a message, or a set of ideas, aimed at addressing the people's problems and concerns.

In a way, the campaign mirrored the strategy that Levant Gachechiladze of the New Rights Party had pressed for during the 2002 Tbilisi Sakrebulo elections, of presenting a "good guy" image who unfortunately had nothing particularly important to say. In a similar way, though well liked by almost everyone, Burdjanadze never had anything to say. The Burdjanadze-Democrats campaign probably spent more money on advertisements than any other party, but these advertisements were merely testimonials about what a good person

Burdjanadze was, and how people from all walks of life were supporting her—they never went beyond her personality. Yet people in Georgia did not want a simple focus on personalities; they wanted to hear how the politicians planned on changing their lives for the better.

For all these reasons, the Burdjanadze-Democrats were unable to attract a serious following, while Burdjanadze's support remained soft and very prone to attack. When two or three weeks before the vote, Saakashvili challenged certain members of the Democrats' electoral list on charges of corruption and suggested that Burdjanadze and Zhvania were using Shevardnadze-like tactics, the impact was quick and devastating. It was as if someone had finally said that the emperor had no clothes. While no one in the press realized this then, Saakashvili's attacks were nearly flawless. Saakashvili was able to not only once again present himself as Shevardnadze's main opponent, but also distinguish himself from the group that was rivaling him in the "reformer" electoral space.

Watching Saakashvili gain huge points from these attacks was devastating, given that the NRP had thought about using negative campaign tactics against Burdjanadze weeks earlier, when her popularity first challenged the NRP's election strategy. Murphy had a number of brilliant advertisement ideas that would have simultaneously linked Burdjanadze, Zhvania, and Saakashvili with Shevardnadze, while reminding people of their connection to the Citizens Union of Georgia (CUG) and their role in governing the country for a decade. Those sorts of ads would have killed three birds with one shot. However, the NRP was unable to use any of these ideas, because many of its financial backers were also backing Zhvania and Burdjanadze and did not want to see the two parties fighting each other.

Zhvania went into the November 2 elections expecting to do very well. He predicted to his supporters in confidence that the Burdjanadze-Democrats would win over 20 to 25 percent of the vote (coming in first overall, and far ahead of all opposition parties), placing Burdjanadze in an ideal position to serve as speaker for another term and transforming her into the leading candidate to succeed Shevardnadze. Indeed, Zhvania was already planning on introducing constitutional amendments to dramatically reduce presidential powers, converting the Georgian system into something like Poland's, so that Burdjanadze could serve as a quasi-ceremonial president while he could take over as prime minister in charge of the daily affairs of the country once Shevardnadze left office. Yet as the results came in, it became apparent that Zhvania had severely miscalculated, and under the best of circumstances—if we take the results of the PVT as being closest to the actual vote—Burdjanadze-Democrats received just over 10 percent of the vote.

NATIONAL MOVEMENT: SAAKASHVILI'S SUCCESSFUL ATTACK FROM THE LEFT

Unlike Burdjanadze, Saakashvili ran a nearly flawless campaign, though I only was able to grasp its full impact months after the voting was over. He was able to tap into the anti-governmental mood of the electorate, and by doing so, he propelled the National Movement to victory. Saakashvili had two goals—to maximize his voters on the center-left of the electoral spectrum, without losing his image of a reformer and a corruption fighter who cared for the small entrepreneurs and traders. Either by accident or through excellent analysis of the political situation, Saakashvili accomplished his goals through a campaign that managed to appeal to both sides simultaneously.

On the one hand, he ran a very populist, radically leftist campaign to appeal to the pensioners, the poor, and the disadvantaged in order to take votes away from Shalva Natelashvili's Labor Party. If we assume that Murphy was generally accurate in dividing the population roughly evenly between the center-left and the center-right, Saakashvili's populist appeal was aimed at the core voters on the left. To this end, Saakashvili advocated the doubling of pensions, the elimination of land taxation, free and better health care, and radical efforts to steal money from the rich and give it to the poor. He also constantly criticized businessmen, calling them oligarchs and declaring that they were eating the country's wealth, while depending on financial flows from millionaires and even a billionaire (albeit one who had made his wealth abroad).

Yet Saakashvili's proposals went beyond mere populism. He continued his efforts to cultivate a "reformist" image of a fighter against corruption who wanted to punish criminals in the government. He also appealed to small one- or two-person businesses, calling for the elimination of taxes for everyone working for himself or employing only a few people. While this reformist image did not quite square with his more populist, and at times near-Bolshevik message, Saakashvili managed to keep both of the story lines going at once (because no one challenged him on the internal contradictions of his message).

For the last five weeks of the campaign, Saakashvili ran a barrage of advertisements about his proposals. The ads were very long by traditional standards—far longer than the thirty-second political ads usually found in America. They were more like two- to three-minute infomercials. But they ran very often and clearly reached enough viewers to have the desired effect. This advertisement campaign was supported by tactics many, myself included, dubbed "crazy" at the time, but which clearly appealed to the masses. One thing that Saakashvili either realized or simply guessed accurately was that on the center-left of the electorate, the opposition to the Georgian president was far greater than on the center-right, and as a result, tactics used to challenge the Shevardnadze government that seemed unacceptable to many were actually right on target with the voters that he wanted to attract.

As a result, Saakashvili ratcheted up his anti-Shevardnadze rhetoric, taking his campaign to Kvemo Kartli, a region populated by ethnic Azeris whose governor, Levan Mamaladze, often acted as a spokesman for Shevardnadze's For New Georgia and was extremely disliked by the population at large. In Kvemo Kartli, Saakashvili's supporters provoked a bloody fistfight with the local police and other authorities. This was followed by the National Movement leaders (not including Saakashvili) going to Batumi, the capital of the autonomous province of Adjaria, to hold a large rally. Police forces loyal to the local authoritarian leader of Adjaria, Aslan Abashidze, severely beat Saakashvili's allies and kicked them out of the region. In response, Saakashvili tied Abashidze's actions to Shevardnadze, blaming the latter for his inability to keep a local dictatorial leader in check.

Both of these fights could have been expected. Indeed, other opposition parties did not spend much time campaigning in these provinces, because they did not want to disturb civil peace in the country. Saakashvili also must have realized that such conflicts were unavoidable before he decided to campaign in Kvemo Kartli and Adjaria, but it appears in hindsight that he wanted to see fighting and bloodshed. These events were inevitably covered by all TV stations, focusing attention on Saakashvili as the principal opponent of the Shevardnadze regime. The most unhappy, anti-Shevardnadze voters (who were also most center-left voters out there) wanted precisely this kind of candidate.

On top of this, Saakashvili remarkably always stayed on message during his television appearances. Even when interviewed or invited to talk about the bloody fights in Adjaria or Kvemo Kartli, he would instead talk about his achievements of fighting corruption, building stadiums, fixing roofs and elevators, and about his proposals for the future.

Finally, even though he was the most anti-Shevardnadze candidate in terms of his rhetoric, it became apparent later that Saakashvili was able to open a back channel to Avtandil Jorbenadze, the state minister and the head of the For New Georgia campaign. According to several sources with close proximity to Jorbenadze, the state minister was willing to deal with Saakashvili (and also Natelashvili) because he did not think that these two radicals could pose a threat to him in the long term. By contrast, he believed that Gamkrelidze and Burdjanadze, more moderate politicians, were a greater threat, because they could always find a way to speak to Shevardnadze and push him toward a soft-landing scenario of happy retirement in 2005. Jorbenadze did not want this to happen, because he wanted to be the successor to Shevardnadze. He thought that if the opposition were dominated by two radicals, he would become more appealing to both Shevardnadze and foreigners as a possible successor.

The state minister was helping Saakashvili to such an extent that he allowed National Movement to take credit at the local level for the repayment of some of the old pension arrears. These pensions were repaid just days before the election, mostly only in those districts where National Movement had helped pensioners file suits against the government. With the public clearly remembering a hunger strike by Saakashvili's key allies over these pensions, the National Movement got a lot of mileage from these payments, especially because they were often made by the local authorities in coordination with National Movement district activists. Indeed, Saakashvili's link with Jorbenadze was so strong that when local authorities objected to the involvement of local National Movement leaders, they were forced to comply by orders from Jorbenadze.

These tactics and message discipline, along with his well-placed attacks on Burdjanadze and Zhvania, had their desired effect, and toward the end of October, Saakashvili surged in the polls. On Election Day, Saakashvili ended up coming in first, with 26.6 percent of the vote, according to the more accurate PVT results.

LABOR PARTY: NATELASHVILI'S QUIET SUCCESS

Unlike Saakashvili, the other leftist candidate, Shalva Natelashvili, ran a minimalist campaign, with very limited public appearances and almost no TV advertisements until the very end. He attributed the lack of commercials to his party's allegedly meager financial resources, though it was well known that Natelashvili was accepting significant sums to include on his electoral list associates and relatives of a variety of wealthy businessmen or government officials who were not expected to stay with Labor once in Parliament. During the campaign, Natelashvili either did not notice that Saakashvili was successfully attacking him from the left, or did not know how to respond, because in many cases he let the attacks slide by him without a response. On a certain level, Natelashvili was also very confident of his own popularity and thought that Saakashvili could never surpass him, especially among the poor.

Given his lack of campaigning or serious get-out-the-vote strategy, it is actually quite surprising that Natelashvili did as well as he did. According to the PVT, he got 17.3 percent of the vote—just a point and a half below For New Georgia and third overall. However, Natelashvili himself was shocked and upset by the result. This was probably best expressed by his actions on the night of November 2, when he went on television and repeatedly called Georgians "stupid" for voting for National Movement in such large numbers.[1]

FOR NEW GEORGIA AND REVIVAL: RELYING ON FRAUD

The two parties that had support of the administrative resources—For New Georgia nationally and Revival Party in Adjaria—also ran very quiet campaigns. This contrasts sharply with the flamboyant and very activist campaigns ran by both Revival and the CUG, For New Georgia's predecessor, in 1999, when the two were the main competitors against each other. In a way, the fact that the two governmental parties were pushed to the side and the political debate was dominated by the opposition parties was actually a great testament to the level of political pluralism in Georgia in 2003, and the extent to which the parliamentary election presented a unique chance to move forward on the road of democratic consolidation.

For New Georgia's campaigning was limited to four main areas: (1) infrequent appearances by Shevardnadze and Jorbenadze at campaign rallies; (2) use of State Television to advance its cause; (3) utterly baseless and at times paranoid pronouncements by Irina Sarishvili-Chanturia, the spokeswoman for the government alliance, about Nino Burdjanadze's Russian ties (which actually did nothing but help Burdjanadze's cause); and (4) implementation of plans to increase its total result through "made-up" voting in districts populated by ethnic minorities—especially Javakheti, where Armenians form a large share of the population, and Kvemo Kartli, where Azeris are in the majority.

This last point was particularly disturbing because some government representatives did not have enough sense to not talk about the fact that For New Georgia was planning on doing this. Instead, during virtually every television appearance, Vakhtang Rcheulishvili, the leader of a very weak Socialist Party who had aligned himself with Abashidze in 1999 but now was on Shevardnadze's side, declared that the state possessed a "special resource" that it would deploy during the election, in effect admitting that fraud would be involved.

The campaigning done on For New Georgia's behalf by State Television was extensive, but only mildly so compared to what the same channel has done since the Rose Revolution on behalf of the new government. The station used public money to create advertisements for the various ministries in which senior officials were asked to speak about the achievements of the government. All of these "public-service announcements" ended with the announcer declaring that now it was time to move to new challenges "for the future of the new Georgia"—a not-too-subtle hint about what the goal of these announcements really was.

State Television advanced the government's agenda through its news programming as well. During the 8:00 P.M. news shows, the first fifteen to thirty minutes were always devoted to the government and its leaders, especially Shevardnadze and Jorbenadze, each of whom was discussed in the most glowing terms. The opposition parties and their political activity were discussed only later—in either neutral, or more often negative, ways.

At night, State TV ran a program hosted by the popular anchorman Koka Kandiashvili to counter the extremely popular evening political-debate shows on Rustavi 2 and Mze. Kandiashvili tried his best to stay neutral, both because he hoped to preserve his reputation and because he probably did not want to totally side with the government. However, appearances on his show by leading opposition figures were infrequent, because he was usually forced to present just two sides, For New Georgia and some part of the opposition (usually a lesser-known second-tier leader of an opposition party).

Revival actually did not have a campaign in much of the country. Either its leader, Aslan Abashidze, figured (correctly) that few were going to vote for him outside of Adjaria anyway, so it did not make sense to spend money on advertising and campaigning, or his deputies lied to him and did not use the money he gave them for campaign purposes. Either way, it was clear that Revival's showing was going to be totally dependent on the "result" Abashidze would "write" for himself in Adjaria.

No political party expected to be allowed to receive any real votes in Adjaria—that is, even if citizens were to vote for another party, Abashidze's control of the electoral commissions in Adjaria was so great that the real count would in no way matter as far as the official protocols were concerned. However, most politicians were willing to live with this because they were afraid that Abashidze would resort to secessionist tactics if he were pressured. In other words, Shevardnadze and Abashidze had a deal: the former would back For New Georgia in the rest of the country with his three seats on the electoral commissions, while the latter would accept whatever result Revival "received" in Adjaria.

Ultimately, For New Georgia's real result (18.92 percent, according to the PVT) was actually somewhat surprising; most expected something around 15 percent, which would then be "increased" to about 20 percent through manipulations in Kvemo Kartli and Javakheti. However, it turned out that its real result was actually much closer to what the For New Georgia leaders hoped to get. This showed that Shevardnadze still had significant, though far from majority, support. By contrast, the PVT result for Revival (8.13 percent) was around what everyone expected. But things went beyond anyone's wildest expectations when Abashidze decided to almost triple his showing through the made-up "results" in Adjaria.

NEW RIGHTS PARTY: A FAILED ATTEMPT TO IMPLEMENT A BRILLIANT PLAN

In the early summer, when parties were first gearing up for the fall campaign, it seemed for a while that the NRP would have the best-planned and best-executed campaign strategy.[2] On paper, the party's plans indeed looked very impressive. To this day, I believe that Mike Murphy designed a campaign plan that, although not flawless, would have yielded a very strong result had it been implemented fully and properly. However, this did not happen. The NRP implemented its strategy haphazardly, with key elements missing. As a result, not only did it not receive the full benefit that the strategy was originally envisioned to produce, but this partial campaigning may very well have hurt its chances in the end. I bear as much responsibility for what happened as anyone, but the party's problems were so deep that no one person ever could have fixed them.

The key problem was a significant internal difference between party leaders that went far beyond disagreements on specific elements of the electoral strategy and how one should campaign (though this too was an issue). Rather, the prevalent disagreement was over who should be the leader and the public face of the campaign. Ultimately, it became clear that this was an issue all along, starting in June 2003, but it did not reach the boiling point until the Gamkrelidze ads were placed on the air in August. Using the aforementioned August poll (which tried to measure the impact of the first month of advertising but failed to do so), alleged complaints from "friends and supporters" about the heavy advertisements featuring Gamkrelidze (complaints that Murphy had told Gamkrelidze to expect), Burdjanadze's rising popularity, and uncertainty about the availability of campaign funds in early September, Levan Gachechiladze started to question everything, with the goal of putting himself up front as a replacement for Gamkrelidze. The problems got even worse after the collapse of the negotiations about an alliance—first between the NRP and Industry Will Save Georgia, and later with the National Movement and Burdjanadze-Democrats.

Those who pushed for this idea were demanding that the NRP get rid of Murphy; cancel ads featuring Gamkrelidze (because they were said not to be authentic and natural); stop talking about jobs, taxes, and compassion; and revert to the tactics of the campaign for the Tbilisi Sakrebulo from 2002.

To many at the NRP, the issue of who was the leader had been decided long ago—after all, there was a reason why Murphy had recommended spending hundreds of thousands of dollars promoting Gamkrelidze's name. Furthermore, these were elections for serious office, precursors to the presidential election. While Gachechiladze was a good person with a good heart and popular with many rural voters, few took him seriously as a leading national politician who could compete with Saakashvili, Zhvania, or Burdjanadze, let alone Shevardnadze. Even I, notwithstanding all of my commitment to the NRP, would have had trouble voting for it if I were told that voting for the NRP meant voting primarily for Gachechiladze. On top of this, Gachechiladze was lazy and often failed to follow through on his promises to attend campaign events and rallies, which made him an even less attractive leading personality.

To his great credit, Gamkrelidze initially withstood pressure from many different quarters about ending the Murphy-engineered campaign. He wanted to stay the course, and constantly repeated the advice given to him not only by Murphy but also by Audrius Butkyevichus, the former Latvian defense minister who had served as an advisor to the NRP when the party was first getting off the ground, that it was wrong to abandon a strategy only a quarter of the way through. While Gamkrelidze acknowledged that course corrections were clearly necessary at times, and that this was probably the case with the NRP's strategy, he opposed abandoning the whole plan. However, pressure got to him when it became clear toward the end of the second week of September that the NRP simply could not raise all the money that would be necessary to implement the full strategy that Murphy had designed, plus pay for all other campaign-related activities, such as the "get out the vote" effort and the expenses of the NRP's candidates in the first-past-the-post districts.

Yet Gamkrelidze might have stuck with Murphy even under these difficult circumstances had it not been for what he perceived as Murphy's absence from the picture during the most crucial period. The problem was that in August, Murphy had been asked to take charge of Arnold Schwarzenegger's fledgling effort to become governor of California and was understandably very busy during late August and early September. Murphy was also very frustrated with the indecision in Tbilisi about party strategy, which was wasting valuable time and preventing the campaign from moving forward. While Murphy's representative in Tbilisi, David Kochel, tried his best to step in, Gamkrelidze wanted Murphy involved in the day-to-day management of the strategy, something that was not going to happen until after the California vote.

In many respects, Murphy also felt that he was in a bind, because the NRP was simply not willing to follow key parts of his advice. While it was true that the NRP had placed the advertisements as he had recommended, in other key parts of the strategy, party leaders did not think that they could follow most of his recommendations. For example, Murphy correctly believed that Gamkrelidze, Gachechiladze, and all other decision makers at the NRP were spending too much time discussing what the political elite was thinking about them, rather than getting out into the country to speak to the people. An additional problem was that the party leaders were unable to follow Murphy's advice to constantly stay on message and understand that saying something once did not amount to everyone understanding this position. The NRP also refused to challenge the party's opponents to a series of debates about policy issues and was unable to mount a negative attack against those who were eating into the party's electoral space, including the Burdjanadze-Democrats, National Movement, For New Georgia, and Industry. This was all on top of everyone wanting to play the role of a TV critic in making recommendations on how one of the most successful political-ad makers in the world should film images that he was using in the commercials.

Murphy's most straightforward proposal, and the party's most unjustified rejection, was to organize a national bus tour, akin to John McCain's Straight

Talk Express. Murphy hoped that by getting the candidate and the journalists on a bus together, traveling the country and attending small rallies, the press and the public would be mobilized to pay attention to the campaign. Murphy also wanted to buy a videophone and make it available to all the TV reporters so that they could file live reports from far-flung places. I thought that this was a brilliant idea—indeed, I myself had thought that a bus should be used long before the NRP had engaged Murphy. However, everyone in the NRP flatly refused, saying that Georgia was too small for such an endeavor. My argument that during every presidential primary season several bus campaigns simultaneously go through New Hampshire, a state with a population one-fourth of Georgia's, never got much traction.

Thus, while the advertisements were running in August and early September, all the other things that were necessary to support the ads and get the campaign going were simply not happening, and were not going to happen. In this environment, after almost three weeks lost on debating strategy rather than actually getting out there to get the public to vote for the party, Gamkrelidze, facing financial pressure and internal dissent, decided to let Murphy go on September 26, just six weeks before the vote. However, he also wanted to stick with the campaign strategy and some of its tactics. Unfortunately, from that moment on the campaign went further downhill. Murphy himself had asked just four days before if it made sense to continue in this environment. Incidentally, this decision was never made public, because of a feared backlash from the political class.

The internal debate about what sort of ads the NRP should run continued, now without Murphy involved. Gachechiladze did not want ads that included a message, and instead pressed for party-sponsored music videos of his brother, a prominent Georgian singer who uses the pseudonym Utsnobi ("unknown") and who was allegedly popular but probably did not move a single vote. By contrast, Gamkrelidze argued that the NRP needed message advertisements, but never came up with any that were really good enough—nor were they shown frequently enough to have a significant impact. To satisfy Gachechiladze, the NRP also organized an extensive concert series around the country; lots of people came, but no one ever told them why they should vote for the NRP. In addition, Gamkrelidze traveled to almost every district, although these travels were nowhere near as publicized as Saakashvili's, whose radical message attracted a great deal of interest from the press. Burdjanadze's travels were also more likely to get attention, and her campaign was also supported by extensive, though completely message-less advertisements.

As if internal differences had not crippled the party enough, the party leaders' inability to stay on message was another huge problem. Whenever thinking about this issue, or talking to Gamkrelidze about it, I always thought back to a remark on this subject by the late Texas Governor Ann Richards during a forum I attended in Washington in 1999. Richards was asked about differences between the two men who seemed likely to face each other in the 2000 presidential election—George Bush, who had beaten her, and Al Gore. Richards commented that Gore was very smart, but at times he came off as too smart. If you were to ask him, "What time is it?" she said, he would likely go into a long discussion of how a watch works and never actually tell you the time. Meanwhile, while Bush might not be as smart, according to Richards he knew how to stay on message. If you were to ask him the same question, he could very well respond by saying, "We have to teach every child in America how to tell time," as a means of emphasizing his education agenda.

The contrast between Gamkrelidze and Saakashvili was similar, albeit taken to the extreme. While the former would give long-winded answers that few could grasp, the latter would give very simple responses that focused on his message, even when the answer had nothing to do with the question. A perfect example of this was when in early September, Burdjanadze, Gamkrelidze, and Saakashvili were each asked, separately, about whether the opposition would unite. Burdjanadze gave an answer that said nothing and satisfied no one, especially the press. Gamkrelidze also had a long answer, which explained all the intimate details that were being discussed during the negotiations and the problems that the opposition was facing in reaching an agreement. His answer was very interesting to the media, the chattering class, and the roughly 5 percent of the population deeply interested in politics, but did not speak to the ordinary voters. Finally, Saakashvili gave a simple answer: "If the other parties agree to my policies on health care, then we will unite," he said.[3] Incidentally, he gave that answer in the courtyard of a Tbilisi hospital where he was inspecting ambulances that the city council had just purchased. This way, Saakashvili turned a question that had nothing to do with his campaign message into an opportunity to further promote it.[4] Murphy, Kochel, and I, along with several others at the NRP, were constantly pushing Gamkrelidze to do the same, but he was not this kind of campaigner.

Even with all these problems, in the days before the election the NRP still expected to get about 170,000 votes—what I thought would be 9–10 percent, depending on the turnout. For the NRP, this would have been a strong result in light of all the difficulties that had developed throughout the campaign, though much less than the 15 percent Murphy had thought possible in the spring. However, on Election Day these estimates proved to be wrong. According to the PVT, the NRP received almost 8 percent, which translated to about 140,259 in the final results.

Thinking about this two years later, I do not want to come off as suggesting that I was not responsible for some of the problems. Indeed, I take full responsibility for many things. Some, Gamkrelidze among them, think to this day that the party's ad buy in August was too heavy, and that this created a backlash as a result. If this is true, it is significantly my fault, since I was ultimately the one who designed the schedule. That said, I do not think the party oversaturated the airwaves, and if it did, it was only in a minimal way, judging by the frequency of the ads run by Burdjanadze-Democrats and National Movement later in the campaign. I should also probably be faulted for the polling errors— or rather for not raising more flags about pollsters and polling in Georgia. This was a matter of experience, since I did not know as much about this area of campaigning in Georgia until after the election.

More than anything else, I should be faulted for overestimating the NRP's capacity in early 2003, and for thinking that the NRP could implement a strategy for which the party was simply not ready. This is not a problem attributable to Gamkrelidze, who although not a perfect candidate has the makings of a statesman, and whose campaign skills (especially staying on message) could have improved dramatically if he had been in a position to concentrate on his campaign style. However, beyond Gamkrelidze and a few loyal lieutenants,[5] personal rivalries were too strong in the party's political leadership. Meanwhile, outside of Tbilisi, the NRP's field of candidates was quite weak. Many associated themselves with the NRP because it was seen as the party with money. At headquarters, only about half of the staff was devoted to the cause, while the rest simply did nothing at all, even during the most active months of the campaign. Few of the committed ones were capable of serious political thinking, though the press secretary, Maia Chuchulashvili, was one clear exception. I should have realized all, or at least some, of this and been less confident about the NRP's capacity to implement an excellent, well-planned, but very complex strategy— and maybe have been less opposed to an opposition alliance with Zhvania and Saakashvili in the summer of 2003. For all its faults, that was probably a preferable choice to what happened in Georgia in November 2003.

The Media and the NGO Community

Part of the problem for all of the campaigns, and particularly for the NRP, was the media, which did not serve the electorate well. While the media was free from government pressure and could report almost anything, Georgian reporters, unlike American journalists, did not care at all about what the various politicians were promising the people. Indeed, most did not even bother to familiarize themselves with the platforms of the various parties. Things were so bad that Saakashvili managed to introduce a "National Movement Economic Program," allegedly written by a Georgian-American economist, Gia Maisashvili

—even though such a program did not actually exist.[6] Nor did the journalists care about how Saakashvili and Natelashvili planned on paying for free health care or the pension increases that they promised, or what concrete steps Gamkrelidze was proposing to take in order to create more jobs, or why Burdjanadze did not have a single concrete proposal.

Lack of any interest in issues was probably partly the fault of the politicians themselves, since they never challenged each other on issues. For example, the NRP failed to challenge Saakashvili and Natelashvili on their claims that they would confiscate allegedly dishonest assets, without any regard for property rights or the due process of the law, nor did it raise questions about the lack of ideas in the Burdjanadze camp. I believed that an issue-based campaign would have benefited the NRP and been of great interest to the public, since this would have been something novel that went beyond the traditional petty bickering and intrigue. However, such a debate never got off the ground—though the Georgian people, and their democratic aspirations, would have been far better served had the politicians and the media made *policy* the focus of the campaign.

Some journalists did try to focus on real issues, but when this happened, it was an exception to the rule. Nonetheless, the likes of Rezo Sakevarashvili deserve great credit for realizing the importance of party proposals. Sakevarashvili had a weekly analysis of the economic proposals of each of the parties on the Saturday news show on Rustavi 2. He would spend about ten minutes analyzing the proposals and discussing what impact they would have on the economy. Because no one had any real economic proposals other than the NRP, I was extremely happy with how these stories turned out, while every other party was disgruntled with Sakevarashvili.

Another problem with the Georgian media had to do with the established practice of refusing to keep a story alive for more than one, or at most two, days. Television journalists also refused to do stories on topics that may have initially been raised at a different station. As a result, political parties constantly needed to find new topics and were fighting journalists over their refusal to build on stories that may have originated elsewhere. To address this problem, politicians inevitably had to resort to pressuring journalists through their owners, so Zhvania and Saakashvili would often demand that Erosi Kitsmarishvili, the owner of Rustavi 2, force his journalists to cover a particular topic, while Zhvania and Gamkrelidze had to make similar requests to Vano Chkhartishvili, owner of Mze, and Badri Patarkatsishvili, owner of Imedi.

This reality points to the fundamental problem of media in the former Soviet space. Even in Georgia, where in 2003 the media environment was extremely competitive and very free, the media market was far too easy to manipulate. I myself participated in more than one discussion with a station owner or news director about removing a particular story or including a particular sound bite, based on what would best serve the NRP's interests. While the NRP often got its way, depending on the party's relationship with each owner, the NRP's use of these tactics and ability to influence coverage was far more limited than the extent to which Zhvania, and later Saakashvili, manipulated news at Rustavi 2. Nonetheless, the idea of using owners to control news was taken to a totally new level after the revolution, when the government was able to impose massive censorship by following these same tactics.

MANIPULATION OF POLLING

Probably the most troubling area of media manipulation was the way polling data was presented on Rustavi 2—not with the goal of keeping the citizens informed, but rather to influence how they would vote on Election Day. Every Monday during the final eight weeks of the campaign, Rustavi 2 presented polling done by Gocha Tskitishvili, the owner of the Institute of Polling and Marketing (IPM), Georgia's largest and most prominent polling firm. This was the pollster who was responsible for the flawed poll for the NRP in August, which unfortunately forced a complete reevaluation of the party's strategy and greatly damaged the ultimate result.

In September and October, Tskitishvili would put on the air at Rustavi 2 a new poll that usually showed the Burdjanadze-Democrats in first place, followed by Labor and National Movement, with very low ratings for the NRP, Revival, and For New Georgia. Other TV stations were either not able to counter Rustavi 2 because they did not have the infrastructure necessary to even paint the illusion of polls, or refused to participate in this game. The poll had little to do with the real picture, but played a huge role in influencing the political establishment and its views of the political situation. In the view of the establishment, the poll also greatly influenced the positions of the citizens at large.

While in the early weeks of this public polling, Burdjanadze was still enjoying an upswing with the electorate, it was clear from the data that I was collecting for the NRP that Tskitishvili was inflating her numbers far beyond where they really were. Meanwhile, he was constantly depressing the numbers for the NRP. The latter was particularly important since Tskitishvili's goal was to suggest that the NRP would not surpass the 7 percent barrier. While ultimately the NRP did manage to surpass 7 percent, my own analysis suggests that the party lost support throughout September and October (because the party advertised less and did not campaign sufficiently to respond to other parties), and therefore the low numbers presented by Tskitishvili in September were particularly suspect.

I am not certain that Tskitishvili was purposefully dishonest and that he actually changed the numbers in the polls before putting them on the air. The truth is that he knows a great deal about polling and has done impressive work in the past. Furthermore, when some of the NRP's supporters tried to use both a carrot and a stick to get him to change his tune after he first came out with these dismal numbers, he refused to budge under a great deal of pressure, declaring that his numbers were real. On the other side of the coin, the poll that he conducted for the NRP in August was clearly suspect, as I have already examined, and in the past, I have heard of credible reports of his interviewers filling out polling questionnaires instead of the people they were allegedly polling, including once during a poll that he conducted for the NRP during the 2002 local-government elections.

The reality is that polls anywhere can be designed to get a particular result, so changing numbers was not necessarily needed in order to manipulate them. A poll is nothing more than a sample—true only for a particular moment in time. That is the reason why in the West, polls are done over two or three nights at most. In Georgia, because polling is done door-to-door, most take at least a week, if not longer, and thus political conditions may very well change while the poll is being conducted. In addition, polls are not always accurate. The German election in 2005, when the polls predicted a strong victory by Angela Merkel, is but the most recent example of pollsters failing to accurately gauge the mood of the electorate (in reality, Merkel barely won, without gaining a majority).

Furthermore, almost all polls have an error of at least plus or minus three points. This matters less when one is looking at trends, or when the spread is more than six points. However, with small numbers, such as party ratings that are in single or low double digits, this matters a great deal. The difference between 9 percent and 6 percent, for example, may not be that great in mathematical terms, but in September 20003 the difference mattered a great deal in Georgia—for the NRP, 9 percent would be a good result, while 6 percent would be a total disaster.

In addition to these general problems, there were a couple of issues that affected the NRP in particular. Even in the most developed Western democracies, polls have shown a pattern of having a bias against particular parties. For example, in the UK in 1997 and 2001, almost all polls depressed the results of the Conservative Party by one to five points.[7] This could have been caused by the samples, or by the unwillingness of some to say that they were going to vote for the Conservatives. In the 2005 election, some pollsters were able to use experiences from the past two elections to correct the bias against the Conservatives, though even then they overestimated Labour's margin of victory.[8] Unfortunately, in 2003 there was not enough evidence in Georgia to suggest that such a bias even existed in the country, let alone to find a way to correct it.

Understandably, given the problems of crime and lack of electricity at night, polling was done during the day, since most interviewers did not want to go door-to-door at night, especially outside of Tbilisi. This in itself was a bias against the NRP, since employed men and women, students, farmers, and other professionals were least likely to be at home during the day. The likelihood was far greater that the interviewer would encounter a homemaker (who was likely to vote for Burdjanadze), an old pensioner (who was likely to vote for either Natelashvili or Saakashvili), or an unemployed, disgruntled voter (who was also likely to vote for either Natelashvili or Saakashvili) in a given home during the day than a student or a working family man in his mid-twenties or thirties (members of the two groups that were most likely to support the NRP). Yet not only did Georgian pollsters, including Tskitishvili, not want to try to take steps to correct this problem, but they actually did not want to admit that such problems even existed.

In short, even without intentional dishonesty, which may or may not have been present in Tskitishvili's polling for Rustavi 2, realities in Georgia dictated that polls had to be taken with a grain of salt. Strategists and politicians needed polls to provide a general political picture and allow them to understand trends in the way people were thinking about politics. However, when it came to specific party ratings necessary to predict election results, especially when it came to parties with less than 10–12 percent of the vote, polls simply could not be trusted with any certainty.

For all these reasons, Rustavi 2's decision to put these polls on the air on a weekly basis without any warnings or explanations about problems that might be associated with them, and its refusal to give other polling data similar publicity until the last two weeks, was extremely questionable in terms of journalistic ethics. In a way, this was a clear effort to try to shape the minds of voters in order to suggest to them that they should not vote for given parties (the NRP and For New Georgia in particular) since they were hopeless, and instead to encourage support for the Burdjanadze-Democrats.

Even if the impact of this polling data on ordinary voters was small, the conventional wisdom in the political class and the business elite was that Tskitishvili's polls were helping determine how citizens would vote. That, in turn, had a huge impact on the level of support these groups were willing to give the NRP—especially in September, when it was not yet clear that the party would have the needed financial resources to pay for the full campaign. It also had an international impact, by making observers believe that Burdjanadze had more support than she really did.

SOROS, THE NGOS, AND SAAKASHVILI'S RESPONSE TO THE POLLS

While there was recognition on the part of most analysts of the dangers these Rustavi 2 polls created, only Saakashvili was in a position to do something about them, especially toward the latter part of October. Some at the NRP tried to exert pressure on Tskitishvili, with some of its supporters threatening him while others trying to bribe him, but ultimately this did not work. Saakashvili, by contrast, basically managed to buy off Rustavi 2's owner and to use polls favorable to him to actually gain a huge electoral advantage.

By late September, revolutionary NGOs, which had pressed, without success, for an opposition alliance in order to limit the choices anti-Shevardnadze voters would have on Election Day, turned to the National Movement as the vehicle to push forward the revolutionary process. This partly happened because it became apparent that Burdjanadze was losing steam, and partly because Saakashvili was most open to the possibility of a revolution. These NGOs had a number of ways to help National Movement, including with Rustavi 2.

During the final stretch, the Open Society Foundation, through the student group Kmara, was buying hundreds of thousands of dollars of ads on Rustavi 2 (and not on any other station) aimed at deepening the anti-Shevardnadze atmosphere (their slogan was "Shevardnadze, you are the illness, go away"), and was financing an exit poll that Rustavi 2 and the polling firm BCG planned on conducting on Election Day. This gave the Open Society Institute a great deal of leverage over Kitsmarishvili and the decision about whom the station would favor during the last weeks of its coverage.

Beholden to the pro–National Movement NGOs, not only did Rustavi 2 give Saakashvili extremely favorable coverage during the last weeks, but toward the end of October, BCG's preelection polling was put front and center, even ahead of Tskitishvili's numbers. BCG showed Saakashvili with almost 30 percent (actually quite close to his ultimate real result), but depressed the showings of the NRP dramatically to less than 5 percent. Meanwhile, at that point Tskitishvili was also showing Saakashvili with high numbers, but he still gave Burdjanadze first place. This was the first time that Rustavi 2 moved away from Zhvania and favored the National Movement over the Burdjanadze-Democrats.

Electoral Lists and the Crisis on Election Day

If there was one issue that could rival the makeup of the electoral commissions in importance in terms of securing a free and fair election, it was the lack of accurate voters lists. One reason for many of the inaccuracies in the lists used in the past was that Georgia had seen a massive wave of emigration in the mid- to late-1990s, yet many of the voters who were no longer living in Georgia were still listed on the rolls. In 1999, Zhvania used these inaccuracies to "cast" ballots in favor of the CUG, even though many of the actual voters listed never showed up to vote. When the Parliament began debating ways to reform the

Electoral Code in early 2003, creating new voters rolls and banning same-day registration were top priorities.

As part of this effort, the Parliament mandated the Ministry of Interior to prepare from scratch a list of all voting-age Georgian citizens living inside the country.9 The CEC was mandated to type up the list and post it in the precinct electoral commissions sixty days before the vote. Citizens would be asked to check if they were on the list, and could be added if they were not. Parties could also file paperwork on behalf of citizens requesting that they be added. The hope was that starting from scratch would help create an accurate list, while Georgians living abroad were asked to register at foreign embassies and consulates.

While in theory this sounded like a wonderful idea, everyone knew that there would be problems—Georgia was a very weak state, after all, and it was not clear that its government institutions had the capacity to create an accurate new list of the electorate. Even before the Parliament passed this new set of procedures, anticipating the need to have an accurate list, in the fall of 2002 the NRP launched a campaign called "protect your vote," which entailed party activists going door-to-door to create a national registry of all voters. Furthermore, because its list also specified its potential supporters, the NRP hoped to use it for get-out-the-vote purposes and to ensure that all of its voters were actually included on the government list.

The Ministry of Interior did actually send its employees from home to home across Georgia and created the first version of a national voter directory, which was sent to the CEC after Nana Devdariani was appointed chairman in August. The U.S. government had promised to help the CEC in typing the lists, and USAID hired IFES as a contractor to implement the project. IFES had done a great deal of other work in Georgia in the past, and by and large had been very helpful to the CEC, especially during the 2002 local-government election period. Unfortunately, in this particular project, IFES failed miserably.

When these typed lists were made public in September, it turned out that something had gone terribly wrong: the lists were extremely inaccurate, with numerous individuals appearing repetitively (often more than once in the same precinct), while many other voters were absent from the lists completely. NRP compared these typed lists to its own registry of voters, which it believed was largely accurate, and found a 30 to 40 percent discrepancy. Using these lists was simply impossible—so much so that even some For New Georgia officials began to contemplate the need to postpone the election if the problem was not somehow resolved. Devdariani tried to fix the problem and ordered precinct commissions to go door-to-door to clean up the lists. This worked to an extent; in many districts, the commissions turned to the NRP list to clean up the government ones.

While CEC went about its work, the inaccuracy of the lists became a serious political topic. The opposition party that paid the most attention to this issue was the NRP. The Burdjanadze-Democrats would voice similar concerns, but generally Zhvania tried to stay away from talking about the subject, given his history with electoral fraud. By contrast, the NRP was more than happy to talk about this issue, not only because the NRP felt that good lists were essential if it were to have any hope of success, but also because the party needed topics with which to get leaders on television, and this seemed like the only issue on which there was no difference of opinion inside the party.

Surprisingly, the NGO community was very quiet about this issue and generally said and did nothing to improve the situation. Once, in early October, Gamkrelidze invited leading activists from most of the leading NGOs (mostly these were the revolutionary ones) to the NRP headquarters to get their support for a letter Gamkrelidze wanted to send to all the members of the electoral commissions at the district and precinct level, telling them that they could face criminal charges if the lists were not prepared properly. While these groups were willing to sign the letter, once the discussion turned to what role they could play in helping with the process of making the lists more accurate, none of them wanted to be involved. Rather, they declared that the worse the lists, the better. Few could understand this. Only after the election did it become clear what they meant by hoping that everything would be blamed on Shevardnadze: if elections were bad, the government would then have to pay for this. It turned out that many of the participants actually wanted the lists to be bad so that this could be used as an excuse to bring people into the streets.

After this meeting was over, I had a chance to speak to Giga Bokeria, one of the key activists from the Liberty Institute. It was interesting to understand what his real goal was, since Bokeria was one of the leaders of the revolutionary process, which at that point still seemed more imaginary than real. Bokeria admitted that his mission was to turn the parliamentary election into a presidential race, with the goal of ultimately using it as a means of forcing Shevardnadze out. I did not quite digest the full meaning of what he was saying at the time, but I asked about whether he and his colleagues were willing to use unconstitutional means to achieve their end. The answer was an emphatic "yes." In Bokeria's mind, any and all tactics were acceptable to get rid of the "Shevardnadze regime," even if those tactics actually were counter to the rule of law that Bokeria allegedly wanted to help foster in Georgia.

Initially, opposition parties, NGO activists, and analysts all blamed the Ministry of Interior for failing to produce a good list. Indeed, I did a brief presentation for Senator McCain about the problems associated with the lists during his visit to Georgia that fall, as an example of how the government was playing around with the planning for the elections. However, it ultimately turned out that the problem had to do with a mistake in the computer program in which the lists were typed. Thus, the responsibility for the mistakes lay with IFES. From several American officials who were in Georgia at the time, I learned over a year after the election that IFES knew about the problem with its computer program even before it started to type the Ministry of Interior list. More problematically, apparently even USAID's Tbilisi office knew about the program flaw. However, neither IFES nor USAID did anything either to fix the problem or to let the Georgian politicians and CEC officials involved in this process know about what was wrong. Instead, they stood by while the opposition party leaders—Gamkrelidze the most vocal among them—blamed the government for something that really was not its fault.

As October progressed, it appeared that the precinct electoral commissions were being successful at cleaning up the lists. However, on Election Day it turned out that the lists were not as ready as CEC officials had hoped. How massive the problem actually was is unclear. According to the Rustavi 2 exit poll of election results, whose accuracy raises a great deal of skepticism, 4 percent of voters polled reported that they were not on the list. Clearly some districts had greater problems than others, and undoubtedly there were numerous citizens who were not on the list. This created a great deal of confusion at polling stations, making lines move slowly. This was a particular problem for the NRP because district chairmen feared accurately that many of their voters would leave, since they were busier and not able to stay in line all day—unlike the pensioners and the unemployed who were likely to vote for Saakashvili and Natelashvili.

Reports about problems with electoral lists also reached the media—as did other problems, such as the inability to open the polls on time in Kutaisi, Georgia's second-largest city. The media publicized these problems extensively, making it seem that the election was turning into uncontrollable chaos, just as many had feared, with the state institutions unable to provide for the most basic of citizens' rights. Saakashvili, for his part, did everything to help this perception along by declaring that "I was not on the voter list, thus I could not vote."[10] In reality, it was not clear that he actually double-checked whether his name was on the list, but his statement only made the perception of chaos seem even more real.[11]

After a barrage of calls from political leaders and nonstop TV reports complaining about what was happening, at around 11:00 A.M. Devdariani held an emergency briefing to announce that the CEC had decided to extend voting by two hours and to allow those who were not on electoral lists to cast ballots anyway, so long as they had an ID showing their residential address in a given precinct where they wanted to vote. This latter decision was contrary to the plain language of the Electoral Code, but at that point, the commission was most concerned about somehow getting through the day. The announcement added even more confusion to the chaos, and it was clear that no matter what happened during the counting, in the eyes of many, the election had already lost its legitimacy. The OSCE later declared that the election was full of "spectacular fraud."[12] There was indeed fraud, though by Georgian standards, given the experience of 1999, it was far from "spectacular." A far better description would have been to say that there was "fraud and spectacular chaos and disarray." In other words, there was a perfect environment for those who wanted to bring down Shevardnadze to achieve their goal.

8

The Rose Revolution

A
s Election Day ended, no one but the most irresponsible members of the Shevardnadze administration even tried to claim that the vote was fully democratic. As U.S. Ambassador to Georgia Richard Miles told one of the Western papers a few days later, the vote was a "mess from start to finish." The reality was that in at least a fourth of the country—Adjaria, a Black Sea region run by a pro-Russian strongman, Aslan Abashidze; Kvemo Kartli, a region densely populated by the ethnic Azeris on the Azerbaijan border; and Javakheti, a region densely populated by the ethnic Armenians on the Armenian border—voting was almost completely controlled, and the turnout was reported to be far higher than it actually was. While a majority of the people in these areas actually voted for the two parties with governmental support (Revival in Adjaria, and For New Georgia in Kvemo Kartli and Javakheti), this support was not as overwhelming as claimed in the official protocols later.

Extreme irregularities marred the voting in other parts of the country. For example, Georgia's police forces were put on special alert for Election Day, giving them an opportunity to vote not only in their home constituencies, but at their places of deployment. This resulted in policemen often voting more than once, usually for the For New Georgia block. In utter disregard of the Electoral Code, deployed policemen were also given a right to vote for the majoritarian candidates outside of their home districts, to the significant detriment of opposition candidates.

Nonetheless, no matter how serious and troubling, the voter fraud and irregularities that took place could not even be compared to the fraud that had characterized Georgian elections in years past. If in 2003 government officials controlled the electoral process in Kvemo Kartli, Javakheti, and Adjaria, in 1999 they had exercised similar, if not greater, control in *all* precincts and districts throughout Georgia. To put it bluntly, while elections were rigged in about a fourth of the country in 2003, in 1999 they had been rigged in *every* part of the country to a far greater extent. However, the chaos of the elections and the media's justified focus on reporting violations and fraud created a perfect environment for people to lose faith in the electoral process and whatever final results the CEC might issue. Creating this impression was the goal of the revolutionary NGO groups and, to a lesser degree, Saakashvili and the National Movement. Putting a proper spin on events on Election Night was a key part of this process.

Exit Polling as a Precursor to the Revolution

Weeks before the election, Rustavi 2 announced that on Election Night it would announce results of an exit poll which would be prepared by the polling firm BCG, with assistance from a pollster from the United States. Privately, almost everyone acknowledged that these exit polls were going to be manipulated in order to help Saakashvili and hurt the government, as well as other opposition parties.[1] While on November 2, Saakashvili had not yet fully embraced a revolutionary process, he was clearly leaning in this direction. Because of this, supporting Saakashvili was Rustavi 2's and the NGO community's goal. To counter the BCG/Rustavi 2 exit poll, at the last minute Badri Patarkatsishvili's Imedi brought its own team of foreign pollsters to design another exit poll, which was going to be tinkered with as well. The hope at Imedi was that people would be confused by all this additional polling data and come to believe that neither of the polls deserved to be trusted.

Ever since the summer, Zhvania had been the principal advocate for having an exit poll on Rustavi 2. At that point, his alliance with Erosi Kitsmarishvili was still strong, and he hoped to tinker with numbers to benefit himself. However, as Kitsmarishvili moved toward the revolutionary NGO coalition in October, Zhvania realized that the exit-poll numbers could actually do a lot of damage to the Burdjanadze-Democrats. As a result, in late October he began to oppose having an exit poll at all. On November 1, Zhvania and Gamkrelidze held meetings with Patarkatsishvili and Kitsmarishvili in hopes of reaching an agreement to not announce the results of either exit poll, and to put all of the emphasis on the parallel voter tabulations (PVT), which was bound to be more accurate, since manipulation of it was more difficult.

Patarkatsishvili was willing to not release Imedi's numbers so long as Kitsmarishvili did the same, but the latter was adamantly opposed. He had become incensed by Shevardnadze's and Jorbenadze's decision to deny him the "ORT frequency" and was planning on using the exit poll to make life difficult for the government. While Kitsmarishvili did not openly talk about a revolution, he was planning on using Rustavi 2 as a means of calling on people to come into the streets to protest the fraud, in order to create a crisis akin to the one in November 2001. His hope was that this way, he could force the government's hand on the frequency.[2]

The problem with the exit polls went far beyond manipulation by pollsters and station owners. Rather, methodologically it was very difficult to conduct such a poll—so even the real numbers had to be taken with a grain of salt.[3] Nearly 22 percent of voters in Rustavi 2's poll, and a little over 10 percent in Imedi's, refused to answer the question about how they voted—this was a large enough percentage to significantly impact the result. Furthermore, both polls were tilted toward big cities, where the Burdjanadze-Democrats and National Movement strongly outpolled other parties.[4] Thus, even the real results were bound to have strong bias toward these groups.

Rustavi 2 was the first out of the blocks in announcing its results. In violation of the CEC rule prohibiting the release of exit-polling data prior to the end of all voting in the country, at 8:00 P.M., while polls were still open in Kutaisi because of an extension, Rustavi 2's anchors announced the following results:[5]

National Movement . . . . .20.8 percent
For New Georgia 12.9
Labor Party 12.8
Burdjanadze-Democrats .7.6
Revival Party 6.2
New Rights Party 6.0
Industry Will Save Georgia Party 2.8

Rustavi 2 knew very well that these results were completely inaccurate, but it presented the polls as wholly accurate anyway. It is true that once the poll numbers were presented, the channel interviewed the American pollster who had assisted in designing the poll, and he explained that these were very early numbers and were bound to change. However, some of the key points that the pollster made about the tentative nature of the results in English were never translated into Georgian on the air. Rather than highlighting the tentative nature of the results, Rustavi 2's anchors emphasized three simple messages—that Saakashvili had won the election overwhelmingly, that the NRP had failed to overcome the 7 percent barrier, and that Burdjanadze-Democrats were not doing as well as originally planned. Ultimately, it turned out that the exit poll underreported the results of every political party to some degree.

Because Imedi was withholding its exit-poll results until after the voting ended everywhere, for about two hours the only "results" available to the people were from Rustavi 2's poll. As a result, a large part of the population became quite convinced that these numbers represented the actual results, especially given that most Georgians did not understand what the words "exit polebi" (as the exit polls were described) referred to anyway. All they saw on TV were numbers announced by a channel they trusted, and these numbers certainly appeared, and were presented, like real election results.

The impression that Rustavi 2's numbers were real was furthered by Saakashvili, who appeared on the station immediately after they were made public to declare that he had won, that the government was bound to steal his victory, and that it was very "unfortunate" that NRP and possibly the Burdjanadze-Democrats had failed to overcome the 7 percent barrier. He repeated this message so many times that people were bound to believe it to be true. As the night progressed, Imedi announced its exit-poll results as well, which confused the situation and made it more difficult for Saakashvili to continue with his pronouncements.[6] However, the initial impression left by the Rustavi 2 polling data was too powerful to counteract.

The problem at the NRP was that no one at the party was certain of its showing, and thus the party was not in position to respond. While the leaders knew that the party had the votes to get into Parliament so long as the government did not hike the total turnout to an extraordinary degree, the showing was still lower than had been expected, and party leaders did not feel comfortable appearing on television and responding to charges that the NRP had overcome the threshold. Whereas the NRP was simply concerned about the results, the Burdjanadze-Democrats were in real shock, given that just days before, Zhvania had predicted confidently that the party would come out on top with over 20 percent of the vote—yet on Election Night, it was not even clear that they had gotten into Parliament.

As the night progressed, there was no indication that the revolutionary process would move forward. Later, however, it became obvious that exit polls were a key part of creating a false euphoria in the country that could turn revolutionary. In practice, things got off the ground only over the next two days. What developed from then on were two stages of the Rose Revolution. The first stage, between November 3 and 14, consisted of street demonstrations and culminated in a large protest that failed to bring down President Shevardnadze. The second, between November 15 and 23, actually succeeded, and brought Saakashvili and his allies to power. In what follows, I will give a detailed account of each of the stages of the revolution.

The Unsuccessful Stage of the Rose Revolution

The first day after the elections—Monday, November 3—started with the NDI and its Georgian partner, Fair Elections, announcing the PVT results:

National Movement . . . . .26.26 percent

For New Georgia 18.92

Labor Party 17.36

Burdjanadze-Democrats .10.15

Revival Party 8.13

New Rights Party 7.99

Industry Will Save Georgia Party 5.20

These results differed significantly from the exit polls, especially for the NRP, because they confirmed the NRP's own view that the party had made it into Parliament. They also demonstrated that Saakashvili's declarations from the night before were quite inaccurate. The results confirmed that Saakashvili had indeed won, but that For New Georgia's results were also quite strong, along with those of Natelashvili's Labor Party. Analyzing the PVT, I could not help but think about how differently things might have turned out had the attempted alliance between the NRP and Industry gone through: the alliance would have gotten at least 13 percent, putting the business community in a much stronger position.

Incidentally, immediately after the announcement of the PVT results, BCG and Rustavi 2 announced new, allegedly final, exit-poll results, which were "adjusted" to approximate the PVT results. BCG declared that this was an ordinary correction based on more information, but the irony of its actions was hard to miss.

Saakashvili used the announcement of the PVT to ratchet up his rhetoric against Shevardnadze, and for the first time began to sound like a revolutionary. "Just like a car thief, the president is stealing the votes of those who have participated in the elections," he declared in a press briefing.[7] "According to our data, those currently in power got about 18 percent of the votes, and 9 percent of those from Armenians and Azerjanians who are closely concentrated in Samtkhe-Javakheti and Kvemo Kartli. The government lost! The time of Shevardnadze has passed! According to our data, the current powers lost by a landslide. This election is an historic opportunity to remove Shevardnadze."[8] Thus, Saakashvili pointed toward a revolutionary course, even though at this time the revolutionary NGOs were far more supportive of this idea than Saakashvili, whose goal at this stage was to strengthen his hand in possible negotiations with Shevardnadze.

There were other motives to Saakashvili's rhetoric as well. By putting an emphasis on his victory, Saakashvili positioned himself as the leader of the opposition, in preparation for the presidential elections in 2005. Furthermore, he was preparing to make the argument, which would be relevant once the final numbers were released, that the government "stole his votes" during the vote count. This was a ready-made explanation for why the National Movement would not be in a position to accomplish all of its promises. "We could not accomplish as much as we wanted," Saakashvili was bound to argue, "because our votes were stolen."

Comments about the results from the Burdjanadze-Democrats were far milder. On November 3, they simply declared that they "will not cooperate with the government," in the words of Nino Burdjanadze.[9] Internally, the situation was far more confused and uncertain. I heard about the Burdjanadze-Democrats' internal debates from David Gamkrelidze, whom Zhvania asked to attend a meeting at his headquarters on November 3. Though they differed on many things, the Burdjanadze-Democrats and the NRP shared one thing on November 3—both Saakashvili and State Minister Jorbenadze were trying to keep the two parties out of Parliament. Jorbenadze had worked against both during the campaign, while assisting the National Movement and Labor. After the election, Saakashvili wanted the parties out as well, since this would make him the only pro-Western opposition leader on the political scene. The reason behind the meeting was to see if there was a way in which the two parties could respond to this Jorbenadze-Saakashvili challenge in a joint manner.

Gamkrelidze first met with just Burdjanadze and Zhvania. The former was advocating street protests, while the latter sounded extremely depressed and said several times that he was "leaving politics." Burdjanadze's particular concern was that she would lose the parliamentary speakership even if official results reflected the PVT, complicating her presidential prospects. Meanwhile, Zhvania could not believe that Saakashvili had gotten the better of him.

Later in the evening, Zhvania's two deputies, Koka Gabashvili and Mikheil Machavariani, joined the meeting—along with Daniel Kunin, a longtime Zhvania advisor, who had flown in from Moscow where he was working for the NDI. Kunin was the son of former Vermont Governor Madeline Kunin and had been the first head of the NDI's office in Georgia. According to Gamkrelidze, Kunin spent a great deal of time making the case for revolutionary protests and arguing that things were bound to succeed if the National Movement, Burdjanadze-Democrats, and the NRP went into the streets together.

Toward the end of the meeting, Gamkrelidze told his hosts that he would not go into the streets. He made this choice because he knew that at the very least, revolutionary NGO leaders wanted to use street protests to bring about a change of government.[10] By contrast, Gamkrelidze told Burdjanadze and Zhvania that while he would aim to use all possible legal and constitutional tactics to protect his party's results, he was unwilling to pursue an extraconstitutional, revolutionary course, which streets protests almost inevitably entailed. It appears that after the meeting, Zhvania and Burdjanadze decided to pursue a different course—to join Saakashvili and protect their position in Georgian politics by riding his victory wave.

That evening, Gamkrelidze also spoke by phone with Saakashvili, who claimed that his comment the night before about the NRP's failure to get sufficient votes to enter Parliament had been misunderstood. Yet minutes later, he went on television and called on all opposition leaders to meet at his office in the Tbilisi City Council to plan their response to fraud, even though he had made no mention of this meeting during the phone conversation with Gamkrelidze. The following afternoon, Burdjanadze and Eldar Shengelaia, a leading Zhvania deputy, appeared at the meeting on behalf of the Burdjanadze-Democrats, while Gamkrelidze told the media that he would not be going because he had no intention of participating in revolutionary activities. However, Levan Gachechiladze's brother Giorgi (also known as "Utsnobi" in his singing career), whose concerts across the country the NRP had sponsored during the campaign, went to the meeting. This created press speculations that there was a split in the NRP. At the meeting, Saakashvili and Burdjanadze agreed to hold a rally that evening.

At around 5:00 P.M., supporters of the Burdjanadze-Democrats gathered in the Philharmonics Concert Hall, which is located on the north end of Rustaveli Avenue. After brief speeches by party leaders, Burdjanadze, Zhvania, and others led their supporters on foot across Rustaveli Avenue toward the Tbilisi City Hall, which is located past the south end of Rustaveli Avenue on Freedom Square, to join a National Movement rally that was starting there. Saakashvili had a simple message at the rally: "If Shevardnadze wants a revolution he will get one. He should not think that we plan on eating 'papa.'"[11]

Overall, the protest in Freedom Square was quite small—maybe even smaller than the demonstration on June 3, 2003, when the National Movement, the United Democrats, and the NRP jointly pressed for parity in the electoral commissions. The most interesting aspect was the radical difference in the positions taken by speakers from the National Movement and the Burdjanadze-Democrats. While Saakashvili and his allies declared that their goal was to force Shevardnadze to recognize the National Movement's victory in the elections, both Burdjanadze and Zhvania called for the election results to be annulled, and for a revote in 2004. The two parties apparently did not care that these two demands could not be reconciled, since recognizing the National

Movement's victory (that is, making the official results look like the PVT) meant that the Burdjanadze-Democrats would only get 10 or 11 percent. Neither Burdjanadze nor Zhvania were willing to recognize this result as reflective of what they should have gotten.

Another focus of the rally was an attempt to convince the NRP to come out and join the protests. David Berdzenishvili, a leading Saakashvili ally, declared that "instead of waiting for bloody votes [from Adjaria], it will be better for the NRP if they come here and stand next to us, and if they do not come and stand here, they will prove that they are with the government."[12] This message was repeated by other leaders from the National Movement and the Burdjanadze-Democrats. In discussions that I had after the Rose Revolution with representatives from both of the parties holding the rally, as well as from the government, I became convinced that had the NRP joined the rally, the revolution might very well have taken place that night. Many in the government in particular believed that while alone the two parties could not tip the balance, had the NRP joined them, a critical mass might have been reached quickly—not only among the public, but more crucially among the political and media elite—leading to the toppling of the Shevardnadze government.[13]

Revolutionary rhetoric notwithstanding, the protest ended peacefully. A far milder demonstration took place the next day, on November 5. At this one, Saakashvili made another derogatory statement, declaring that "on the one side is police and the society, and on the other side the President and 400 four-legged dogs," using the Georgian term for "cop."[14] He also said that if the votes turned out to be falsified, the National Movement and the Burdjanadze-Democrats would call for the peaceful mobilization of Georgia. Separately, the Burdjanadze-Democrats and several smaller opposition parties formed a "Resistance Front," which was supposedly going to be organized all across the country. The idea behind this move was to allow the Democrats to differentiate themselves from the National Movement in the days to come.

Also on November 5, the U.S. Embassy finally began to play a role, with Richard Miles meeting Shevardnadze to urge him to regain the voters' trust. However, at this stage, Washington was not yet certain about what policy to pursue vis-à-vis Georgia in light of the unfolding events, though certain individuals inside the Bush administration (especially Matt Bryza of the National Security Council) were pushing for a more public stance in favor of the National Movement's position, while most decision makers preferred to take a wait-and-see approach.

It also became apparent toward the end of the day that notwithstanding his rhetoric, Saakashvili had started intense negotiations with Jorbenadze to reach a deal. Initially, he demanded that the NRP and the Burdjanadze-Democrats be kept out of Parliament, though he amended this demand when the latter group joined him in the streets. Additionally, he wanted his first-place position to be protected, even if this meant adding votes to his own total in order to make it possible for votes to be added to Revival's and For New Georgia's showing (since both of these parties were bound to have votes added to their total). Later, Saakashvili expanded his demands, asking that he be given the freedom to appoint two of the four "power ministers."

Partly because of these negotiations between Jorbenadze and Saakashvili, a division began to emerge inside the For New Georgia alliance. Some in the government wanted to find a compromise with the opposition parties, while others were unwilling to discuss anything at all. Koba Narchemashvili, the interior minister, went so far as to start an investigation against Saakashvili, Zhvania, and Burdjanadze for organizing allegedly unauthorized demonstrations. November 5 ended with the CEC announcing partial results. For New Georgia was holding a three-point lead over National Movement, 26.3 to 23 percent.

THE FIRST TURNING POINT: SHEVARDNADZE'S ACQUIESCENCE
TO ABASHIDZE'S MADE-UP RESULTS

The next day, November 6, saw one of the most important developments of the revolutionary period, which was one of the two crucial turning points in the process of bringing down Eduard Shevardnadze's government. This was the announcement of election "results" from Adjaria. The numbers that were sent to the CEC from Adjaria were basically written in Aslan Abashidze's office and had nothing to do with either the way people actually voted, or the real number of Georgian citizens living in Adjaria. Abashidze wrote that his party, Revival, had received 269,000 votes out of an alleged 284,000 votes cast. This total was probably at least a third more than all of Adjaria's residents, including those under the age of eighteen. At 11:00 P.M., the CEC announced that with this result, Revival was first in the country. This moved For New Georgia into second place and the National Movement into third place, but not all votes had come in yet (especially in Kvemo Kartli and Javakheti, which would increase the FNG's total).

With Abashidze choosing to report blatantly false results, Shevardnadze was faced with a very difficult choice—either to accept these false results, thus guaranteeing that the final CEC results would include massively fraudulent numbers and give the revolutionary opposition an excuse to continue with the protests, or to reject these results and give Abashidze an impetus to secede from Georgia, as he had threatened to do in the past. Whether Abashidze was truly capable of seceding was questionable; he probably was not. However, Shevardnadze clearly felt that this was a real possibility and was very concerned about it, especially in light of his experiences with Abkhazia a decade earlier.

Dealing with this dilemma became the focus of Shevardnadze's actions, and in the days that followed, Abashidze would flex his muscles regularly in the face of Shevardnadze's perceived vulnerability. On November 7, Abashidze got the Adjarian Parliament to amend the region's constitution in order to change his title to president and to permit the local government to maintain armed military units. He also went on television and declared that if Shevardnadze could not bring order to Georgia, then Adjarian police and paramilitary forces would be happy to assist him. Abashidze also had Revival's Tbilisi-based leadership hold a rally in front of the CEC, declaring that they too could hold protests if necessary to protect their votes. This event greatly incensed ordinary Tbilisi residents who could not stand Abashidze and Revival. In the face of these actions, Shevardnadze did nothing and allowed the public's negative perception of Abashidze to simply transfer onto him and his inaction.

Another stunning announcement on November 7 came from the Burdjanadze-Democrats, who held a hastily arranged news conference and declared that they would not take their seats in Parliament, no matter what the final results were going to be. This appeared to be an attempt to pressure Saakashvili, whose public demands differed significantly: all he wanted was allegedly to protect his first place in the final CEC count, while the Burdjanadze-Democrats were refusing to recognize the results. This vital difference between the two groups notwithstanding, they continued to plan together for protests. There was one scheduled in front of Parliament on Rustaveli Avenue for November 7, but it was delayed by a day because of logistical reasons.

When the rally finally took place on November 8, it was not very large, but it continued into the night and became a sit-in, with a few hundred party activists present in front of Parliament at all times. There was a widespread assumption in Tbilisi that those spending the night were being paid to do so, though there is no official proof of this other than testimony from those protesters who received the money. Early on the morning of November 9, on his way to the State Chancellery, Shevardnadze had his motorcade drive by the Parliament and stop at the protest site. The president went out and walked among the protesters. Things happened so quickly that the television crews did not have a chance to record the whole period during which he was there. As a result, two different versions of how events unfolded after his arrival have emerged.

One version is presented in a book called *"Enough!"*. It claims that as the news passed through the crowd that "Shevardnadze is here . . . the more deafening grew the whistling. . . . He encountered Burdjanadze in the crowd and invited her to engage in a dialogue, . . . and Burdjanadze agreed. . . . Just as Shevardnadze was getting into his car, Saakashvili appeared and refused to take a step back, but the presidential guard managed to push him aside. Afterwards, Shevardnadze would say that he had not seen Saakashvili and had not understood why there was a momentary delay in driving away. But Saakashvili would accuse the President of cowardice. . . . And the crowd continued to whistle."[15]

The other version was presented on television on November 9. I have tried to reconstruct this version by speaking to several journalists who were covering the protests. According to this version of events, Shevardnadze seemed successful at charming many of the protesters by speaking to them in small groups, while many others were simply in shock because they did not expect the president to walk into enemy territory. According to my sources, initially there was no whistling at all. Rather, it appeared that the president was repeating the daring move from 1978, when during much larger student-led protests in opposition to Russian becoming the official language in the Georgian republic, Shevardnadze, then the Communist leader, charmed the students by joining their rally. He did talk to Burdjanadze, and the two agreed to hold a meeting with Zhvania and Saakashvili that night. With that, Shevardnadze prepared to leave, at which moment Saakashvili appeared with a small group of bodyguards. A scuffle developed between Saakashvili's guards and Shevardnadze's security forces, and then Saakashvili swore at Shevardnadze as he was getting into his car and began to scream, "Resign, resign!" With this, National Movement activists in the crowd picked up this chant as Shevardnadze drove off.

Thus, without Saakashvili's appearance, Shevardnadze would have walked away without an incident and succeeded in demonstrating to Georgians and the international community that he was trying to be responsive to the protesters. However, Saakashvili's sudden but well-timed appearance resulted in Shevardnadze leaving to chants demanding his resignation. This way, the crowd appeared far more confrontational than it actually was. Nonetheless, in the days that followed, among ordinary citizens Shevardnadze received a great deal of credit for going to the protesters, whereas Saakashvili's actions were seen as too offensive to some, especially vis-à-vis an old man like Shevardnadze, albeit an unpopular one.

That evening, Saakashvili, Burdjanadze, and Zhvania went to a meeting with the president at his residence in Krtsanisi, located on the outskirts of Tbilisi. The meeting went very badly, though there are conflicting accounts of what happened. Both sides agree that the opposition leaders presented Shevardnadze with their grievances, to which he responded by proposing that a commission be set up to investigate the allegations of fraud and electoral corruption. At this point, it appears that Saakashvili walked out of the meeting. Shevardnadze privately claimed later that Saakashvili swore at him before leaving, though publicly he merely said that Saakashvili "offended" him; Saakashvili himself rejected these claims.[16] Addressing the media outside the meeting, Saakashvili declared that he had walked out because the president had "decided to create a pro-Russian regime in Georgia."[17]

Burdjanadze and Zhvania stayed longer, but upon departing, defiantly declared that they were sticking with Saakashvili, and any attempt to split the opposition would not work. However in reality, unlike Saakashvili, who preferred to deal with Jorbenadze, Burdjanadze and Zhvania very much wanted to negotiate with Shevardnadze directly. This became even more obvious several days later when, in a meeting with Gamkrelidze, Burdjanadze spent a great deal of time complaining that Shevardnadze was not answering her calls, and asked Gamkrelidze to arrange for a discussion with Shevardnadze—something that he was not able to do.

After this failed meeting, Shevardnadze left Tbilisi for western Georgia. He traveled first to Guria, his home province, and the next day to Adjaria, for a meeting with Abashidze. The reason for this visit was undoubtedly the dilemma created by Abashidze's inflated and made-up results in Adjaria. Shevardnadze had to travel to Adjaria to meet with Abashidze because the latter refused to leave his regional enclave out of paranoid fear that he was going to be assassinated. Abashidze used Shevardnadze's catch-22 to his greatest advantage. He arranged for the president to attend a large rally at the football stadium in Batumi, where the two spoke about how they would not allow instability to develop in Georgia. Shevardnadze appeared quite helpless as he stood next to Abashidze, addressing people who were being forced to come out by Abashidze's police services and had no interest in actually cheering on the two leaders.

During the meeting, Shevardnadze apparently agreed to accept the Revival results in return for a promise from Abashidze that his party's deputies would support For New Georgia in key decisions.[18] This was not the first time Revival had promised to support Shevardnadze's government, though such agreements had fallen apart in the past. Nonetheless, from Shevardnadze's perspective he had no choice but to toe Abashidze's line, because of his fear that Adjaria (that is, Abashidze) would secede from Georgia. In reality, Abashidze was bluffing and secession was not a real danger, since Adjaria's residents were ethnic Georgians—unlike residents in South Ossetia and Abkhazia. Furthermore, neither Turkey nor the United States, nor even Russia, would have tolerated Abashidze going that far. However, Shevardnadze was paranoid about losing another territory on his watch, and he was willing to accept Abashidze's demands in hopes of neutralizing his threats in the short term.[19]

In addition to agreeing to accept the results, Shevardnadze also dispatched Abashidze to travel to Armenia, Azerbaijan, and Russia on his behalf. Some have argued that Shevardnadze was serious in making Abashidze his emissary, but I believe this view is extremely ill-informed, because the president would not have left his future in the hands of a lunatic (albeit a canny one) no matter how desperate he was. Abashidze did have business dealings with Moscow's Mayor Yuri Luzhkov, whose business circles (along with important elements of the KGB) had vastly profitable ties with Abashidze.[20] However, Shevardnadze never could have thought that Abashidze would be willing or able to use these ties to advance the president's cause in Moscow.

There is also a view that Shevardnadze simply enjoyed the "warm" welcome that he received in Adjaria, because this allowed him to retreat to the memories of the time when he was loved and cheered by all Georgians. According to this view, the visit allowed him to forget about the unpleasant facts and realities facing him back in Tbilisi, and his willingness to dispatch Abashidze as his emissary to Moscow was connected to this.

Whatever Shevardnadze's reasoning, his dealings with Abashidze and acquiescence to Revival's false results from Adjaria sent a horrible message across Georgia. First, the visit seemed like a confirmation of Saakashvili's claims from the night before that Shevardnadze was trying to create a pro-Russian regime in Georgia, since Abashidze was closely associated with Russia. Second, people could not believe that the president would sink to this level and treat Abashidze almost like his boss, rather than an authoritarian tyrant who was despised by almost all Georgians. Shevardnadze's actions made many believe that he was simply too removed from reality to be able to resolve the crisis confronting him. Even among my Georgian relatives and friends, most of whom were strongly against the opposition protests and disliked Saakashvili greatly, Shevardnadze's actions were incomprehensible.

Georgians were also taken aback by a declaration made during Shevardnadze's visit by Jemal Gogitidze, Revival's principal leader in Parliament, that "Revival will go to Tbilisi to help you," if this became necessary.[21] For most Georgians, Revival was associated with dictatorship, and having them in Tbilisi countering National Movement protesters was the last thing anyone wanted to see. The situation became even more awkward when the Revival, Industry Will Save Georgia, and Labor parties formed an "alternative opposition" as a counterweight to the National Movement–Democrats front in the streets.[22]

Shevardnadze himself never realized how badly his visit to Adjaria damaged him in the eyes of the people. According to a former government official who spoke with him upon his return, Shevardnadze thought that much of his dilemma had been solved. However in reality, his dealings with Abashidze energized the opposition, especially after Abashidze's trip to Yerevan, Baku, and Moscow received extensive coverage on television. The new friendship between Shevardnadze and Abashidze also damaged the president in Washington, where administration officials and opinion makers who specialized in Georgia did not take the threat of possible secession by Adjaria seriously. Indeed, most believed that this threat was simply a bluff, since Ankara would never let it happen, and Abashidze could never survive on his own if he were to close the border with Georgia without support from Turkey (which borders

Adjara on the south). Thus, they thought that Shevardnadze was simply using Abashidze's threats as an excuse to ignore the opposition's grievances and not address the core problem of the differences between the official results and the PVT. Because this view began to predominate in Washington's political circles, it helped contribute to Shevardnadze's loss of support in D.C. in the days that followed.

THE LULL BEFORE THE STORM

For the next three days (November 11–13), protests continued in front of Parliament with little fanfare. Probably the most notable development was on November 13, when Jumber Patiashvili, who had succeeded Shevardnadze as the head of the Georgian Communist Party in 1985 (when the latter became Soviet foreign minister) and in this capacity presided over the use of force against the pro-independence demonstrations on April 9, 1989, gave a rancorous address and accused Shevardnadze of being responsible for this tragedy. This account was an outrageous insult to Georgia and its history, yet Saakashvili, Burdjanadze, and Zhvania did nothing to correct it, even though they were standing next to him when he made these claims.

Numerous independent probes, including one generally trusted by most people in Georgia, had shown that Shevardnadze was largely unaware of what the Soviet authorities were planning on doing in Tbilisi that April. When the incident took place he was abroad, and after the incident he handed in his resignation to Soviet leader Mikheil Gorbachev, who refused it. By contrast, it was never clear if Patiashvili had actually asked for the Soviet troops to be brought into the city center during the protests, or had simply consented to a proposal made by the Russian general in charge of the troops in the Caucasus and approved by officials above Patiashvili in Moscow. Either way, there is absolutely no doubt that Patiashvili knew that the troops would be used at least one day before they terrorized the protesters, yet he did nothing to stop them; at the very least, he could have resigned in protest, and that way warned the public about the plans.

Because of this background, I have long referred to Patiashvili as the "Butcher of Tbilisi," because to me he was no different than the Chinese Communists who have often been called "butchers of Beijing" after the Tiananmen incident. Watching the most morally bankrupt of Georgian politicians from the Communist period make these outrageous claims was truly surreal, especially with Saakashvili, Burdjanadze, and Zhvania standing by and allowing Patiashvili to wash himself of his great responsibility. To me, this spoke volumes about how removed and different these three opposition leaders were from those members of their generation that had led the fight for Georgia's independence in the late 1980s.

With the exception of this incident, the protests did not make much news, though they received near constant coverage on TV. Meanwhile, behind the scenes, there was a great deal of activity. Saakashvili, Burdjanadze, Zhvania, and their leading allies were preparing for the mass rally that was called for Friday, November 14, 2005. The NGO activists and Erosi Kitsmarishvili, Rustavi 2's owner, hoped to use this mass demonstration to storm government buildings and take control of the affairs of state. Saakashvili, still in secret negotiations with Jorbenadze, was uncertain whether he favored this course—though he was leaning toward it—while at this stage in the process, Burdjanadze and Zhvania opposed this course. To his credit, Zhvania in particular did not favor a revolution and wanted to find a solution.

Part of Burdjanadze's and Zhvania's challenge was that after the leaders walked out from the discussion on November 9, Shevardnadze refused to answer phone calls from them. Possibly because Zhvania could not find a way out of the deadlock, it appears that on Wednesday, November 12, he decided to drop out of the process altogether. He called a U.S. Embassy official to say that he was afraid that the protests on Friday were going to become violent, that he did not want to be a part of this, and that he hoped to prevent this outcome by withdrawing his support for the demonstrations. Before reaching his decision, however, Zhvania wanted to talk to Ambassador Miles. This conversation took place just minutes before the ambassador was scheduled to meet with President Shevardnadze, and Zhvania probably knew about this meeting, given that he had a network of allies inside Shevardnadze's inner circle. Knowing Zhvania's way of thinking, probably part of his plan behind the phone call was to have Ambassador Miles pass this information to the president in hopes that this would be an impetus to restart a dialogue with Shevardnadze. However, Zhvania never got a chance to speak to Miles, the message was never delivered, and Zhvania never dropped out.[23]

While Saakashvili was leaning toward a revolutionary course, which he knew would give him total control of the country, he was continuing to negotiate with State Minister Jorbenadze. These meetings were largely secret, and it is unclear to this day whether Shevardnadze sanctioned them or the concessions that Jorbenadze was willing to grant Saakashvili. In addition, it is not certain whether Saakashvili truly intended to negotiate, or was simply passing time and showing foreign officials that he was trying his best to find a solution.

On Wednesday, November 12, U.S. Ambassador Miles mentioned one such meeting between Saakashvili and Jorbenadze to the media in a press conference. Whether this was simply a slip of the tongue or a purposeful effort to make the meetings public knowledge is not clear, though either way, Saakashvili refused to negotiate after this announcement. Some U.S. officials have argued to me privately that Miles told the media about the meetings at the urging of the NDI's representative in Georgia, Mark Mullen. NDI Tbilisi, like its Georgian NGO partners, was pushing for a revolutionary course and did not want Saakashvili to possibly reach a deal with Jorbenadze. Telling the public about the secret meetings was the best way of ending these negotiations, and thus of triggering the course of events that increased the chance of a revolutionary change of government.

The NRP was also active during this time since the party had to fight a two-pronged battle in an attempt to ensure that fraud did not take away the party's vote, or the "increase" in the total turnout did not go so far as to leave the party below the 7 percent threshold. The NRP's big problem was that it was not only under attack from the government—specifically Jorbenadze—but also from Saakashvili, who was making the NRP's exclusion from Parliament one of his preconditions for ending the protests. Shevardnadze deserves credit in ensuring that Jorbenadze did not get his way on this issue—as does Nana Devdariani, the chairman of the CEC, who had made numerous mistakes throughout the election, but withstood a great deal of pressure from Jorbenadze during the final tallying and limited the amount of corruption that took place at the very end.[24]

The party's other big goal during this period was to try to find some kind of solution to the crisis. To this end, the party developed a proposal that would have allowed for new elections to be held within six to nine months. On November 2, Georgians had voted in a referendum calling for the reduction of the size of Parliament. Implementing this change required a constitutional amendment, and the plan was to pass it before the next election. Given the opposition demands, the NRP came up with the idea that the new Parliament be allowed to convene, implement this referendum by creating a two-chamber Parliament, and call new elections within six months. Burdjanadze and Zhvania accepted this proposal, since it answered their demand for new elections, as did Shevardnadze—but Gamkrelidze did not have an opportunity to present this idea to Saakashvili until after the first wave of protests ended on November 14. Throughout this time, the proposal was kept private to allow Saakashvili to take ownership of it, should he accept the idea, and announce it as his own compromise.

For the NRP, the biggest problem during the revolutionary period was its inability to deliver a message effectively. The reason was quite simple: the population was too focused on the demonstrations and the three leaders who were leading them, and additional voices had a very hard time breaking through. The party did have three positions that it tried to present on a regular basis. First, notwithstanding the grave irregularities that took place during the election, the vote had to be seen as a move forward, rather than backward, on Georgia's road to democracy, especially if all six parties that had actually received enough votes to surpass 7 percent were recognized as winners in the official count. Second, the official results had to be announced as quickly as possible, to prevent opportunity for manipulation. And third, a revolutionary course would do nothing to advance democracy in Georgia.

As the sit-in continued in front of Parliament, the international media began to cover the events in Georgia with some regularity. The first big piece, which helped drive much of the future coverage, appeared in the *Washington Post* on November 11 under the title "Pressure Mounts on Georgian Leader." "About 15,000 protesters took to the streets after the election and a few of them were injured in sporadic incidents of gunfire," wrote Peter Baker, saying that "about 3,000 to 4,000 demonstrators have remained outside the Parliament building each day." The numbers were exaggerated, which suggested that the media was heavily influenced by the pro-Saakashvili analysts who presented themselves as neutral analysts. One of them, Ghia Nodia, told the *Post* that Saakashvili's "style of speaking is very emotional. This creates the image that he's unbalanced."[25] The implication was that Saakashvili's "unbalanced" appearance was merely a perception, and had little to do with his real state of being.

FAILED ATTEMPT AT REMOVING SHEVARDNADZE:
THE MASSIVE PROTEST ON NOVEMBER 14

The big protest on Friday, November 14, brought about 20,000–25,000 people into the streets. Opposition leaders expected far more people and were surprised by the low turnout. This was the case even though Rustavi 2 spent all day calling on Tbilisi residents to go into the streets to join the protests. Once the demonstration started and the leaders gave speeches, it became apparent that they did not know what to do with those people who came to support them. First, they divided the throng into two groups and asked one group to follow them into Freedom Square on one end of Rustaveli Avenue. Then, they marched another group to the CEC, which was located on the other end. Finally, upon returning, Zhvania called on the mass of people to hold hands and create a live chain around the State Chancellery, located behind the Parliament building.

As the day went by, it became clear that Saakashvili, Burdjanadze, and Zhvania were stuck. They had brought these people into the streets, but they did not have a clear agreement on a goal they wanted to achieve with them, nor did they have a plan for what to do with the masses once the speeches ended. For two days, rumors had been spreading among the political class that the leaders did not have a plan for how to handle the protest, with close associates of the leaders suggesting that they would call on the masses to go home without really accomplishing much. This is exactly what happened after an hour or two, when the leaders declared that the two opposition parties and their allies were going to start a movement of civil disobedience across the country, but that it was time to end the protests in Tbilisi. This announcement sounded too much like what had happened a few months before, in June, when opposition leaders had ended the rally about the CEC composition with a call for a national movement for fair elections.

According to conversations with participants in the months after the revolution, NGO activists and Rustavi 2's Kitsmarishvili pressed Saakashvili all through the protest to march on the State Chancellery, storm the building, and take the reins of government. For unclear reasons, Saakashvili decided against this course of action. It may have been that Burdjanadze and Zhvania were opposed to this, and without Burdjanadze, who as speaker of Parliament would ascend to the acting presidency if Shevardnadze resigned, Saakashvili could never legitimize the president's overthrow.[26] Or it may have been that Saakashvili felt that the numbers in the streets were too small for such a push. Or maybe he was afraid of possible bloodshed, since the State Chancellery was heavily fortified with armed men and Shevardnadze was working there during the demonstrations. Either way, Saakashvili stopped short, and it did not seem as though he had it in him to continue.

As the protests dispersed and the area in front of Parliament cleared of people, all indications suggested that the attempted revolution had failed. Even the sit-in inside the CEC's building that Saakashvili's followers started during the mass rally ended quietly the next day, despite Saakashvili's pledge during the demonstration that it would continue until the final results were announced. As a result, it seemed that Shevardnadze had won the confrontation.[27]

Revolution's Second Wind and Surprising Success

As the weekend progressed, the NRP began to lose its certainty that the protests were going to end. While the widespread civil-disobedience campaign never got off the ground anywhere, Saakashvili's rhetoric and activities began to suggest that he was not planning on stopping the protests. Whether the NGO community and Erosi Kitsmarishvili, Rustavi 2's owner, influenced Saakashvili's thinking after the demonstration on November 14, or whether he himself became convinced that he would succeed with a second push, is unclear. Either way, while things seemed over on Friday, by Sunday all indications were that Saakashvili was going to resume his protests. He was telling his foreign allies as much, as was indicated in an e-mail I received from Zeyno Baran of the Nixon Center on November 17: "As far I can see none of Misha-Zurab demands were met so far—I doubt they will stop. So this whole thing can go on and on, no?"[28]

THE SECOND TURNING POINT: REVIVAL'S PROTESTS IN TBILISI

Monday, November 17, was the day when the balance tipped toward Saakashvili, giving him a second wind that ultimately led him to victory. Out of nowhere, Tbilisi woke up to several thousand people from Adjaria arriving on buses and trains and taking over the area in front of the Parliament on Rustaveli Avenue. The Adjarian protesters blockaded Rustaveli with buses on both sides of the square where they started the demonstration, and started a sit-in that clearly was going to go on into the night and the next day. The protests were being organized by the leadership of the Revival Party, who spent much of the day addressing the crowds about the need to protect the Constitution and stability, while the crowd cheered them on and waved Revival flags.

It was clear from the start that almost all of the protesters were either being paid or were forced to come to Tbilisi by Adjarian police and security services. Most did not have a place to stay in Tbilisi and were forced to sleep on the street or in the buses that were blockading Rustaveli. The appearance of these Adjarian demonstrators had a very negative impact on the ordinary Tbilisi residents, and for many, this development tipped the balance against Shevardnadze and toward the demonstrating opposition. This had to do with both the hatred of Abashidze and the somewhat elitist belief of most who live in Tbilisi (especially those who were born in Tbilisi) that these people "[had] no place here," because they were not locals. When asked about their opinion, the most common response was that they were incensed by the appearance of Adjarian demonstrators, whom people viewed as supporting Shevardnadze. This view was abundantly clear from conversations I was having during those days, even with those Tbilisi residents who had moved to the city from the regions only recently.

Why the Adjarians came never became clear. My view has always been that Abashidze sent them to Tbilisi in order to keep pressure on Shevardnadze, and to make it seem like the president was dependent on Abashidze in maintaining power. Meanwhile, some who spoke with Abashidze about this after the Rose Revolution have told me that Shevardnadze asked Abashidze to send demonstrators to Tbilisi to support the central government. Abashidze even complained that this whole incident cost him money. I have a hard time believing this, because it is difficult to imagine Shevardnadze asking Abashidze for such a favor. However, during those long days in November, the president was not always thinking straight, so the Abashidze version of events could very well be true.

On Monday, not realizing how empowering the appearance of the Adjarians was for the revolutionary cause, Shevardnadze addressed the nation, saying that the Parliament would convene on November 22. Even though the official CEC protocol was not yet approved, it was clear that six parties would have seats in the legislature, and that For New Georgia would finish slightly ahead of Revival (which was slated to come in second), and the National Movement (which was slated to come in third, but only a quarter percent behind Revival). While Jorbenadze was still trying to keep the NRP out of Parliament, this no longer seemed like a viable option (though the state minister continued with his efforts until the day the final CEC protocol was approved).

Given that Saakashvili was still threatening to continue with the protests, on Monday night David Gamkrelidze and Levan Gachechiladze went to see him at the Tbilisi Sakrebulo. Gachechiladze had been Saakashvili's campaign manager in 1999, when the latter was a candidate for Parliament from the Vake district in Tbilisi. Because their personalities and thinking styles were similar, Saakashvili tended to listen to Gachechiladze more than he listened to others. The goal behind the meeting was to try to sell Saakashvili on the NRP compromise proposal, which entailed convening the new Parliament, but only for a brief period, and scheduling new elections within six to nine months.

The next day, when I had a chance to speak to Gamkrelidze about this meeting, he was dumbfounded and very concerned, since Saakashvili came off as being completely unrealistic in his demands and out of control. Gamkrelidze reported that it was impossible to hold a rational conversation with him, because halfway through a discussion of a particular issue—especially when he found himself in a corner, lacking arguments to make his case—he would throw a passionate fit about how this was his unique moment to gain power and that he was the "messiah" who had to save Georgia.

The one issue for which he had a somewhat rational argument was his reason for rejecting the NRP compromise: if he succeeding in bringing down Shevardnadze now, Saakashvili claimed, he would gain all political power in the country, whereas in six or nine months, political dynamics could very well change. When it came to the questions of how he planned on taking over power while still staying within the constitutional framework, or whether it was good for Georgia and its democratic future to have another president removed through extraconstitutional means, Saakashvili had a very simple answer—that he did not care.[29] His goal, Saakashvili told Gamkrelidze and Gachechiladze, was to gain power *now* and to deal with the consequences at a later date.

When Gamkrelidze asked Saakashvili what he planned on doing with Abashidze and if he was willing to go to war with him, Saakashvili declared that he had a plan to have his supporters march into Batumi to remove Abashidze, just like they would march into Tbilisi to bring down Shevardnadze. The idea of ensuring that the demonstrations remain nonviolent was simply not an issue that concerned him. Nor did he care about waiting for over three dozen court cases that were pending before the various courts contesting the election results, and the possibility that the election results would actually be declared invalid, making revolution unnecessary. His focus was on seizing power for himself, and on the idea that he was the "messiah" whose job was to save the country.

Even though Saakashvili, Kitsmarishvili, and the NGO community were in a feisty mood on Monday, nothing happened during the next two days to suggest that a revolution was bound to succeed. Indeed early in the week, narcotics testing facilities were set up in Parliament, because Georgian legislation required newly elected lawmakers to undergo a drug test prior to taking office. If traces of narcotics were found, they could not take their seats. Throughout the week, members of the National Movement's and Burdjanadze-Democrats' electoral lists who were bound to gain seats if CEC results were to be approved, along with soon-to-be elected legislators from other parties, went to take these drug tests. Their appearances at the makeshift facilities in Parliament were reported on television on a regular basis and suggested that the two parties planned on joining the Parliament once it convened.

Official election results were announced on November 20. The night before was very contentious at the CEC, with some of Jorbenadze's allies still pushing for greater manipulation to ensure that the NRP was kept out. Ultimately this did not happen, and the NRP's representative at the CEC voted for the protocol certifying the official results, even though party leaders acknowledged publicly that the official count was full of fraud and manipulation.[30] Meanwhile, representatives of the National Movement, Burdjanadze-Democrats, Labor, and Industry Will Save Georgia voted against the protocols.[31]

Twenty-five seats were redistributed by the discrepancy between the official CEC and the PVT results—17 percent of the proportional seats in Parliament, and 11 percent of the total seats.[32] (See table 8.1.)

The first signs of possible trouble associated with the official opening of Parliament came on Thursday, when Saakashvili traveled to western Georgia, and shooting broke out in the town of Zugdidi. While no one was killed, the event was widely televised and pointed to possible violence on Saturday, November 22, since Saakashvili had called for a large demonstration in Tbilisi to coincide with the Parliament's opening session.

The next signs of trouble came on Friday, November 21. First, Tedo Japaridze, Shevardnadze's national-security advisor and former Georgian ambassador to the United States, gave an impassioned speech, announcing that he could no longer discharge his duties, because the president was isolated and was not listening to arguments about the need to address the brewing crisis. The statement was very critical of Shevardnadze, but reserved its harshest comments for Jorbenadze and other leading figures in the For New Georgia alliance, whom Japaridze accused of withholding information from the president about what was happening inside and outside the country. Japaridze proposed holding

TABLE 8.1 Comparison of CEC and PVT Percentage and Proportional Seat Distribution Results by Party, November 2003

PARTY	CEC RESULT	CEC SEATS	PVT RESULT	PVT SEATS	DIFFERENCE IN SEATS
For New Georgia	21.32	38	18.92	32	+6
Revival	18.84	33	8.13	14	+19
National Movement	18.80	32	26.60	45	–13
Labor Party	12.40	20	17.30	29	–9
Burdjanadze-Dem.	8.79	15	10.15	17	–2
New Rights	7.35	12	7.95	13	–1
TOTAL	87.50	150	89.05	150	

new elections—in effect, he articulated a position that was very similar to the one advocated by Gamkrelidze and the NRP.[33]

Japaridze's announcement, which received a great deal of press coverage, suggested that something very bad was happening inside the president's inner circle—it appeared that Shevardnadze was even more isolated and removed from reality than many realized. However, the focus of everyone's attention was Saakashvili, who in Zugdidi launched a caravan of cars and buses, full of his supporters, moving toward Tbilisi. As the caravan drove across the country, more supporters joined him on the way. Rustavi 2 was operating in an overdrive mode, with continuous updates about the caravan's progress. During his appearances on Rustavi 2 and other channels throughout the day, Saakashvili called on Tbilisi residents to join his mass demonstration on Saturday.

Late on Friday night, it was still unclear what would happen the next day. On the one hand, Revival's demonstration was continuing in front of Parliament, while by early Saturday morning, Saakashvili's caravan was expected to reach Tbilisi. It was not clear how many people had joined this procession from the countryside, nor did anyone know the number of Tbilisi residents who would choose to go into the streets to support Saakashvili. Nonetheless, the opposition demonstration was clearly going to be larger than on November 14, when it had ended without resolving anything. As a result, there was a real possibility that things would end very badly on Saturday, with two demonstrations facing off against each other on Rustaveli Avenue. As a result, Tbilisi was in a very apprehensive and uncertain mood that night, very concerned that a civil confrontation was imminent.

WASHINGTON'S CONFUSED POSITION

While Washington had played a very active role in the preelection period, after November 2 up to the Rose Revolution it did not have a clear position. For days, engagement was limited to pronouncements by U.S. Ambassador Richard Miles about the need to avoid violence. Miles did not think it was his place to be more involved in the country's internal affairs. According to several of his subordinates, in his heart, purely on an emotional level, he felt sympathy for the demonstrators because they reminded him of the civil-rights-era protests of his youth in his native South Carolina in the 1960s. Washington's (and Miles's) continued inaction was extremely harmful to Georgia's democratic process, since its more active involvement could have helped resolve the crisis within the constitutional framework.

Finally on Tuesday, November 18, Lynn Pascoe, the U.S. deputy assistant secretary of state for the Caucasus and Central Asia, came to Georgia on a previously scheduled trip—but understandably, his visit was perceived by the politicians and the media as an attempt by the United States to play a role in defusing the crisis. Pascoe met with leaders of all political parties and with President Shevardnadze. In all the meetings, Pascoe made the U.S. unhappiness with fraud and chaos during the campaign and the vote count very clear, but also left no doubt that the United States wanted to see the constitutional and democratic process move forward.

Pascoe met with Gamkrelidze on November 19.[34] They discussed the NRP's compromise, which Gamkrelidze was now willing to talk about publicly, given that Saakashvili had rejected it. Pascoe viewed the idea quite favorably and expressed a feeling that it was a good solution to the problems that had arisen. The implication was clear that such a compromise solution was acceptable to the United States.

Soon after the meeting, Gamkrelidze drafted a letter to Matt Bryza, who was responsible for the Caucasus and Central Asia at the National Security Council.[35] Given Pascoe's positive take on the compromise, Gamkrelidze hoped to enlist Bryza's support as well, in hopes of getting Saakashvili to reconsider his position.[36] Gamkrelidze also knew that once the official results were announced, the United States would issue a statement that would almost certainly be very critical of the conduct of the elections, but would not go as far in criticizing the government as similar American statements about elections in countries with truly illegitimate and authoritarian rulers had done in the past. He hoped that the statement could speak to the NRP's compromise idea, enabling the United States to have more than just an observer's position during the crisis.

Bryza's response, though extremely thorough, differed significantly from the message that Gamkrelidze had received from Pascoe. Bryza wrote that "peaceful demonstrations are a way to clarify power relations. It is the process of democracy that is most important to my government."[37] This was a view with which no one really disagreed, albeit "demonstrations" do not necessarily mean "democracy." However, then Bryza observed that "we do not and will not urge our Georgian friends simply to compromise for the sake of compromise. . . . [It is essential] to get THIS election right . . . simply 'getting through' this crisis will only postpone the tough decisions for another day, thereby prolonging Georgia's internal weaknesses and deepening its vulnerability."

The views Bryza presented were mutually contradictory. Ultimately, the only way to solve the problem of fraud, while sticking to the Constitution and democratic principles, was to hold new elections. That, in turn, required a compromise. However, Bryza was saying that a compromise was not desirable. This logically left just one option (other than acceptance of fraud)—a revolution, one way or another. Thus, the logical conclusion one had to draw was that Bryza was favoring a revolutionary course, even though it was hard to balance this with the apparent commitment to the "democratic process" or with the notion of "getting THIS election right," since an overthrow of government did neither because it rejected the views of those voters who supported the parties that did not favor the revolution.[38]

Whatever one made of Bryza's e-mail, one thing was clear—Washington did not have a clear policy vis-à-vis Georgia. Pascoe was presenting one point of view—which in this case was more sensible, but sadly involved near total detachment from the process, when in reality its implementation required very active engagement with all the political players on a regular basis. Meanwhile, Bryza was presenting an alternative that was far more engaged than Pascoe's view, but openly put America on the wrong side of the dispute in Georgia.

Absence of a clear policy was also evident in the question-and-answer session during the news briefing at the U.S. Department of State on November 20:

> *Question*: In Georgia, the electoral commission has started to release its final results for the election. Do you find these results credible and fair?
> *Adam Erili, Deputy State Department Spokesman*: We have seen the results released today by the Election Commission on the Georgian parliamentary elections. We will be releasing a formal statement shortly. What I can say now is that we are deeply disappointed in these results, and in Georgia's leadership. The results do not accurately reflect the will of the Georgian people, but instead reflect massive vote fraud in Adjaria and other Georgian regions.
>
> Specifically, the parallel vote tally and exit polling conducted by reputable independent organizations differ significantly from the results released by the Central Election Commission, and these discrepancies, in our view, represent or reveal an extensive manipulation of the vote count. I would say that we are in a regular dialogue on a senior level, both here and in Tbilisi, and we'll be assessing next steps.

Question: Okay. That's pretty strong. But when this happened in Zimbabwe, you came out and said that you didn't consider Mugabe to be a legitimate leader. Will you come to the same . . . will you take the same position in Georgia, that you don't consider the government to be a legitimate government?

Erili: Well, as I said, we're assessing next steps. We'll put out a statement. I don't want to get ahead of ourselves here of what we will and will not do.[39]

Thus, even as late as November 20, Washington was not sure about how to proceed. The question the reporter asked about whether Shevardnadze's government was "legitimate," however, was crucial. If we are to accept the department's formal statement released the next day as representative of the U.S. government's policy, then the answer to this question is that the United States did recognize Shevardnadze's government as legitimate. Indeed, while the statement strongly criticized the election, it did not raise questions about Shevardnadze's status or his future, and certainly did not even imply any support for possible "regime change" or compare him to Mugabe:

The United States is deeply disappointed in the conduct of Georgia's November 2 Parliamentary elections, which failed to meet the commitments made by the Georgian leadership to the OSCE and to the United States. The delay of the vote count and the manipulation of the results revealed an effort by the Central Election Commission and the Georgian government to ignore the will of the people. . . .

The parallel vote tally conducted by the National Democratic Institute and supported by reputable exit polls, which we believe to be the best available gauge of the will of the voters, differs significantly from the results released by the Central Election Commission. These discrepancies reveal an extensive manipulation of the count.[40]

While this was unusual language, the statement did not say anything radical about how developments should move forward. Instead, it made three very sensible recommendations:

▶ That "all sides must now work together to find a way forward that enjoys credibility with Georgia's voters."
▶ That the Georgian government should respect media freedom, the right to demonstrate, and other rights protected in the Constitution.
▶ That the Georgian government should "conduct an independent and transparent investigation immediately and hold accountable those who violated the law."

If this statement is to be taken as a guide for what the United States wanted to see happen, the compromise the NRP had been pushing all along directly addressed the recommendations that Washington was making. Indeed, the NRP's compromise was probably the only solution that could enjoy "credibility with Georgia's voters," assuming that by "voters" the statement meant *all* voters, rather than simply those who had voted for the National Movement and the Burdjanadze-Democrats, including that majority of citizens who had voted for parties other than these two.

Even though this statement could be seen as setting forth a clearer U.S. position, there was still an absence of an active policy of engagement from Washington, despite the United States being probably the most powerful player with influence in Georgia. Beyond constant comments from Ambassador Miles about the need to have peace, there was no effort on part of the United States to help create a "way forward." Rather, the United States was leaving this to Georgians themselves. Sadly, Georgians did not have a real way forward. Because there was such an absence of an active, prescriptive policy, Bryza's ideas ended up being implemented to an extent anyway, even though there was not unanimous support for them.[41]

The story of U.S. involvement would not be complete without discussion of an incident involving James Baker and his repeated attempts to get in touch with Shevardnadze during the crisis. This too probably greatly influenced Washington's position on the events unfolding in Georgia, and on Shevardnadze in particular. This incident is reconstructed based on conversations with several Georgian and American officials who were directly involved in trying to set up the conversation.[42]

Apparently, Baker tried to call Shevardnadze several times on November 19 and was unable to get through.[43] Then, the U.S. government warned Shevardnadze in advance (through both Georgian and American channels) that Baker would try to call again the next day. On this day, Baker was at the White House and he called from there. Again, on November 20, Shevardnadze did not take the call, even though Baker tried several times.[44]

When asked about this incident several months after the Rose Revolution, Baker gave a very diplomatic response: "I did not get through. But you know, I accept this. . . . The difference in time is very difficult for one thing. I accept the fact that he pretty much had his hands full trying to deal with the problem he had in front of him. I don't think he was purposefully stiffing me—I'll never know that of course."[45]

Why Shevardnadze never took the call we will probably never know, since today he is unlikely to give a completely honest answer—and even if he did, the answer would be influenced greatly by the developments that followed this attempted conversation. Shevardnadze could have greatly influenced the course of events had he taken the phone call, since at a minimum, by telling Baker about his willingness to compromise and to hold new elections, he could have taken the wind out of the sails of the protesters. Instead, by refusing to take the phone calls, Shevardnadze left the impression on many that he had lost it, and that Washington could no longer rely on him.

THE STORMING OF PARLIAMENT

The parliamentary session on November 22 was scheduled at 3:00 P.M. Why the president chose to delay it when Parliament usually starts sessions at 11:00 A.M., which was the time originally recommended in the draft decree announcing the session (Shevardnadze changed the time for the final draft), remains a mystery. There was no certainty about what would happen that day, but given the Georgian culture of sleeping in late, chances of Tbilisi residents turning out in the thousands on a Saturday morning at 11:00 was far lower than later in the afternoon at 3:00. Thus the final outcome might have been different had the parliamentary session taken place at its regular time.

Shevardnadze's plan was to hold a brief session, to formally open the new Parliament and recognize its authority, and possibly to elect a new speaker.[46] There was some speculation that he had promised Abashidze that position, though I never saw any real evidence to that effect.[47] Even if such a promise was made, Shevardnadze and Abashidze did not together have enough parliamentarians for such a move—since 118 votes were necessary, but the two parties and their majoritarian supporters had 100 votes at most. Some FNG parliamentarians would have probably voted against Abashidze as well. The position of speaker was crucial, because its holder would become acting president if Shevardnadze were to resign. Burdjanadze's term as speaker would end the minute the new Parliament convened. Were the president to resign without a new speaker being elected, the country would enter a constitutional crisis, because the line of succession of executive power was not delineated any further in the Constitution.

As the first half of Saturday progressed, Saakashvili's supporters gathered at Freedom Square, along with a far smaller group of Burdjanadze's and Zhvania's followers. Meanwhile, Revival's paid demonstrators were still holding ground on Rustaveli Avenue in front of Parliament. Police had been ordered to encircle the Parliament and surrounding buildings, to allow parliamentarians to enter the session later in the afternoon. Shevardnadze's security forces, sensing that something might happen later in the day, moved the president into the Parliament a few hours before the session started.

Only legislators from For New Georgia and Revival were certain to attend the session. This was not a sufficient number for a quorum. The Burdjanadze-Democrats and the National Movement clearly were not going, and a few days before the session, Labor's leader, Shalva Natelashvili, had also announced that his party would not go. Shevardnadze hoped to fill the quorum either with independent majoritarian deputies or with the NRP, which had not announced yet whether it would attend the session or not.

Given the stance that the NRP had taken against the protests and extraconstitutional means, I thought that it made sense to attend the session. This view was shared by some in the party, but many others disagreed. Saakashvili had asked Gamkrelidze not to go, while the president hoped that the party would join the session. NRP's newly elected parliamentarians and other key decision makers gathered a few hours before the session to decide on a course of action.

Everyone agreed that it made no sense to go to the session if Shevardnadze and his supporters in the Parliament did not acknowledge the realities of massive fraud, as well as the mass protests outside, and show some willingness to make the day a real turning point in Georgian democracy. With this in mind, the group formulated a demand: in return for the NRP's participation in the session, Shevardnadze would agree to a parliamentary resolution that would declare no confidence in the November 2 elections, acknowledge massive fraud and irregularities, and call on new elections to be held within the next six to nine months. The NRP's leadership felt that if such a resolution were agreed upon during the session, it would remove the wind from the sails of Saakashvili, Burdjanadze, and Zhvania, and protect the constitutional process in the country while simultaneously moving Georgia toward a more hopeful democratic future.

After a phone conversation with Gamkrelidze, Shevardnadze initially rejected this proposal, and it appeared that the NRP deputies would not go to the session. The party decided to hold a news conference at the its headquarters to announce the demand that had been made and explain why the party was not going to join the session. While waiting for journalists to arrive—just minutes before 3:00 P.M., when the session was scheduled to open—Shevardnadze and his team realized that without the NRP they would not have a quorum, since a few independent majoritarians were refusing to go so long as the NRP was not going, while a few deputies from For New Georgia were in Adjaria negotiating with Abashidze. As a result, Shevardnadze called Gamkrelidze back and agreed to the NRP's proposal; he said that after opening the session, he would call on Gamkrelidze to announce his proposal, would then voice his support for it, and would call on his supporters to vote for it, making the passage likely (while deputies from the Revival were likely to vote against the resolution, it's passage required support of a majority of those in attendance, rather than an absolute majority).

While this discussion was taking place, journalists began to arrive and it was time to hold the news conference. The news that the NRP was not going to attend the session had already leaked to the press and was reported on television, since one of the NRP legislators had spoken with a reporter from Mze TV on the phone about the party's decision. Nonetheless, journalists still wanted to have a confirmation of this leak from Gamkrelidze—but by then, the decision had changed, and it did not seem proper to announce the news of an agreement with Shevardnadze before the session. I was asked to go to the briefing room and tell the journalists that the press conference would no longer take place. The most difficult thing about this task was that I had to say nothing at all, and had to answer their questions about whether the NRP's legislators would or would not go with a simple "I do not know" and "It is unclear."

Not everyone at the NRP agreed with the decision to attend the session, and some of the most prominent public faces of the party (including Levan Gachechiladze) decided to stay behind, but twelve or so deputies crammed into several cars and rushed to the session, which was about to start. Somehow one of the television stations found out about the NRP's final decision and reported it on the air just minutes before Gamkrelidze and other party legislators walked into the Parliament's chamber. With their arrival, Shevardnadze used the gavel to bring the session to order, and constitutionally, the authority of the Parliament elected in 1999 ended and the authority of the new Parliament was technically recognized, since a quorum of newly elected deputies was present. However, an actual quorum call had not yet taken place; this was technically done through registration of deputies prior to them entering the parliamentary chamber.

At that point, Gamkrelidze went to one of the side microphones in the chamber and tried to speak, but Shevardnadze motioned that he would first make an opening statement and then give him the floor. Had Gamkrelidze been Saakashvili, he probably would have started to speak anyway, without giving the president an opportunity to give his speech first. However, Gamkrelidze was too respectful, both personally and with regard to the office of the president, to act that way—though at that moment, I wished he would have his say anyway. Journalists noticed what happened, and at least on Mze TV (whose coverage I was watching at the party headquarters) the commentator, Nino Jijilashvili, described the confusion that had arisen from Gamkrelidze going to the microphone and then sitting down to let the president speak.

Shevardnadze proceeded to give an incomprehensible, out-of-place, and actually rather irresponsible speech, which said nothing, though probably made everyone watching at home very angry. It was reminiscent of speeches given by Soviet leaders during the Community Party congresses, since it seemed that it would never end. The speech said volumes about the extent to which Shevardnadze did not understand, or did not wish to acknowledge, the level of unrest on the streets.

Then suddenly the chamber's main door opened slightly, and it appeared that people were pushing through it from the hallway, while the guards were trying to keep the throng out. The door swung open, and several newly elected MPs from the Burdjanadze-Democrats marched into the chamber, holding roses. They were followed by Saakashvili, who marched into the chamber looking like a maniac, waiving his finger at Shevardnadze (who was standing at the podium on the other end of the chamber and continuing with his speech) and screaming, "Gadadeki, gadadeki, . . . gadadeki" (Georgian for "resign"). In a matter of several seconds, the head of the president's security detail, Sulkhan Papashvili, walked up to Saakashvili and spoke with him, and then almost immediately, security guards grabbed Shevardnadze and whisked him away as a massive crowd of protesters marched into the chamber.

A few minutes later, television stations showed Shevardnadze outside, surrounded by members of Parliament from Revival, addressing the Adjarian demonstrators. This lasted for several minutes, and then he was taken to his residence in Krtsanisi, on the outskirts of Tbilisi. Meanwhile, a chaotic scene developed inside the Parliament's chamber. The legislators quickly cleared out, since the chamber (and the whole building) was full of an angry mob that were running around smashing windows, doors, chairs, and tables. Saakashvili walked to the podium, from where Shevardnadze had been speaking, declared that he would "drink Shevardnadze's tea" (which he then proceeded to drink), and then called on Burdjanadze to "take her place as speaker of Parliament." Burdjanadze then walked to the speaker's chair, where she sat for a few minutes with a red rose planted in front of her in a vase—even though by most interpretations of the Georgian Constitution, she was no longer speaker of Parliament, since a new Parliament had been convened at the beginning of the session.

Meanwhile, outside, the National Movement's supporters took over the State Chancellery, where they also broke everything that got in their way and dragged a white leather chair that Shevardnadze used in his study and burned it outside. Another throng of opposition demonstrators marched from Freedom Square to the area in front of Parliament on Rustaveli Avenue, broke through the way that had been blocked by buses, and kicked out Revival's demonstrators—most of whom simply ran away.

The NRP's parliamentarians returned to the party office, from where everyone went to the apartment of the party's general secretary, David Saganelidze. I had no idea what would happen next. I remember calling Matt Bryza on the phone from Saganelidze's apartment. I encountered a person who was enchanted with what he called "people power," and who marveled with amazement about how wonderful this was for Georgia. While this euphoric reaction was fairly common abroad, I could not understand how such disregard for the constitutional process and the rule of law could be called good or democratic.

In the days that followed, Rustavi 2, which had constant access to his movements, showed what Saakashvili had done in the moments before he marched
into the Parliament's chamber. From these images it appeared that this was a
spontaneous decision, and that he had not planned on taking over the Parliament and preventing the session from taking place. I had an opportunity to
explore this issue with several prominent figures in the National Movement,
and based on their remarks, as well as evidence that I have been able to gather
through other sources, I came to some conclusions about Saakashvili's inside
thinking in those moments, and why he chose this course of action. It appears
that Saakashvili, Burdjanadze, and Zhvania did not have a plan of action in
case the Parliament were to convene—they simply hoped that there would not
be a quorum to hold the session. But Kitsmarishvili and NGO leaders were
pushing Saakashvili to take over government buildings. Saakashvili was confronted with the need to make a quick decision, and had to act on it when
Gamkrelidze and other NRP parliamentarians walked into the chamber.

It is not clear whether Saakashvili knew that Gamkrelidze planned on making a speech, or that Shevardnadze had agreed to publicly back a compromise
resolution; he may very well have known, because ultimately it turned out that
some of the people who were closest to Shevardnadze (such as his chief of
staff, Petre Mamradze)[48] were passing information to Saakashvili and Zhvania
all along. If he knew of the compromise, then he had a much greater reason to
stop the session, because with Gamkrelidze's planned speech, Saakashvili
would lose the initiative. However, preventing the session was crucial under
any circumstances, even if he did not know about the planned speech. Thus,
Saakashvili made a split-second decision to march on the Parliament with a
throng of his supporters.

It appears that Saakashvili told Burdjanadze and Zhvania that he was
going to do this with or without them, making it impossible for them to stop
him, as they may have on November 14. Some in Georgia claim that
Saakashvili had planned his actions all along, though I find little evidence for
this. It seems to me that Saakashvili was constantly going back and forth
between the more moderate and the revolutionary positions, with his mind
constantly shifting according to his mood. On November 14 he did not go
through with the revolutionary option, but on November 22, he pressed all
the way.

The lack of certain commitment to the revolution is evident not only in the
fact that deputies from the National Movement and Burdjanadze-Democrats
all underwent drug testing, but also because in the hours that followed the
storming of Parliament, the trio's actions were generally confused and uncertain, leaving no impression of prior planning. For example, a couple of hours
after the session was stopped, Burdjanadze went on TV and declared herself

acting president, claiming that Shevardnadze could not discharge his duties. However, as time went by and Shevardnadze appeared both physically and mentally fit on television, Burdjanadze changed her tune and no longer referred to herself as acting president. Instead, she spoke about the need to find a compromise with Shevardnadze. This suggests that the trio was making things up as it went along, without a solid agreement on a coordinated plan of action.

The idea of a preplanned march on Parliament is also cast into doubt by some candid remarks from leading National Movement figures in the months that followed the revolution. When the euphoria began to subside and people began to ask serious questions about whether it was really necessary and advantageous for Georgia to have another extraconstitutional transfer of power, several times National Movement spokesmen found themselves in a bind, with no good answers to these questions from journalists. In several such interviews, they declared that it was Gamkrelidze's and the NRP's fault that Saakashvili had to march on Parliament—because had the NRP stayed away, there would not have been a quorum, and things would have turned out differently. Without giving any serious thought to the utterly flawed logic behind this argument, it seems very likely that the decision to storm the Parliament was spontaneous.

By storming the Parliament, Saakashvili succeeded in preventing the session from concluding normally; but the fact of the matter was that it had started, so many experts have argued that legally the new Parliament had convened and Nino Burdjanadze was no longer speaker. There was still a possibility that the Constitutional Court would declare the official November 2 election results void. In that case, Georgia was entering a constitutional crisis, since it would end up with no legislature until new elections took place. Even if one were to argue that the new Parliament had not officially convened, the notion of extending the old Parliament's term was wholly arbitrary and extraconstitutional, since there was no legal or constitutional basis for such action. Hence, either alternative led Georgia into a parliamentary and constitutional crisis, or wholly outside of constitutional space.

SHEVARDNADZE'S UNEXPECTED RESIGNATION

On the evening of November 22, from his residence, Shevardnadze declared that he had introduced a state of emergency and was ready to deal with the protesters by force, if necessary. Privately everyone acknowledged that Shevardnadze would never order troops to clear out the protesters, and even if he did, it was highly unlikely that Georgian troops or police would use force against fellow Georgians, especially on Rustaveli Avenue, given the historic connection of that place to the tragedy of April 9, 1989.[49] Rumors were rampant about the possibility that the new Parliament would convene at a different location on November 23 to elect a speaker, after which Shevardnadze would resign. However, in reality, no one knew what would happen, and neither Shevardnadze nor Saakashvili had a clear plan of action.

Late that evening, Moscow announced that Russian President Vladimir Putin was dispatching Foreign Minister Igor Ivanov to Tbilisi to help resolve the crisis. This was a clever ploy on the Russians' part, since it gave them a large role in Georgia's internal affairs. Ivanov arrived in the early hours of the morning and actually first went to the home of a Georgian businessman, where he ate and drank for several hours. Early in the morning Ivanov went to the Parliament building, where he met with Saakashvili, Burdjanadze, Zhvania, *and* Kitsmarishvili. I am not certain of what was discussed, though probably the most interesting development was Kitsmarishvili's presence at the meeting as a key negotiating partner, even though he was not a political leader and never appeared in public as part of the revolutionary leadership (only the political elite knew about his prominent role). From that moment on, until he was forced to leave Georgia about a year after the Rose Revolution, Kitsmarishvili presented himself as one of the leading players and decision makers in the political process.

After the initial meeting, Ivanov went out to Rustaveli Avenue and addressed the protesters, many of whom (especially those who had been brought in by Saakashvili from outside of Tbilisi) had spent the night in front of the Parliament. Ivanov said nothing of great importance, but the crowed cheered him with the chant, "Sergei, Sergei . . . Sergei."[50]

This was one of those surreal moments that did not quite make sense. Here was a person who used to be despised in Georgia because of his role as the point man for Russia's rhetoric aimed at curtailing Georgian sovereignty and pursuing psychological warfare on issues such as the alleged presence of Chechen "terrorists" in the Pankisi Gorge and separatist conflicts in Abkhazia or South Ossetia. Only a little over a year before, he would regularly appear on TV and threaten to bomb Georgia. Criticizing Ivanov and his boss, Russian President Vladimir Putin, was one of the most popular things to do for a Georgian politician. Yet on the morning of November 23, supporters of two opposition parties were chanting and praising his name, while their leaders stood by and welcomed him with open arms.

As the day progressed, Ivanov shuttled between Shevardnadze's residence and the Parliament, trying to broker a deal. Meanwhile, at one point in the early afternoon, Shevardnadze appeared on TV and seemed to say that he was willing to call for new elections. However, this statement was confusing, and the media did not have an opportunity to focus on it in any serious way. Nonetheless, sometime toward the afternoon, it appeared that Ivanov had brokered a deal. Saakashvili, Burdjanadze, and Zhvania went in front of the demonstrators to announce that Shevardnadze would resign, and that Saakashvili and Zhvania were going to go with Ivanov to the residence to speak to him about this development. Saakashvili then asked a small group of protesters to follow them to the residence.

As these events were unfolding, I went to the NRP headquarters, which is located just a mile or two from the president's residence, trying to collect news about what was going on. There I was able to collect some details from a variety of sources about what the Ivanov agreement involved. I spoke with the American officials in Georgia, who confirmed some of what I had learned from the Georgian sources. According to the deal, Shevardnadze was not going to resign immediately, but rather give Zhvania and Saakashvili a letter of resignation, postdated for sometime in late summer 2004. In the interim period, the old Parliament would convene and schedule new elections for sometime in the early summer. Shevardnadze's letter would have him quit after those elections, triggering a presidential vote within forty-five days.

This deal was quite similar to the compromise the NRP had been advocating, with the only difference being which Parliament (the one elected in 1999, or in 2003) would be in place during the interim period. The agreement to keep the old Parliament in place was a victory for Burdjanadze, because she was speaker of that Parliament, but it was actually worse for the opposition. The NRP had advocated convening the new Parliament, rather than the old one, because in it the strength of the opposition parties was greater.[51]

When Saakashvili, Burdjanadze, and Zhvania referred to Shevardnadze's planned resignation, they were speaking of this postdated letter. According to several sources who were with Shevardnadze immediately before the meeting started, he had not told anyone of his plans to resign that day. Rather, everyone thought that Saakashvili and Zhvania were coming to talk about the agreement Ivanov had reached. When Saakashvili and Zhvania arrived at Shevardnadze's residence, they entered his study for the meeting along with Ivanov, and were joined by Jorbenadze. Ivanov then announced that he had played a role in bringing the two sides together, but it was not proper for him to sit in on the meeting. Then he left for Adjaria, where his mission was to get Abashidze to support the compromise deal.

As soon as Ivanov left, Shevardnadze dropped the bombshell—he announced his decision to resign *immediately*. With that announcement, there was not much to talk about. A few minutes later, Saakashvili walked out of the residence and went to the protest, where he announced Shevardnadze's resignation. In the meantime, Zhvania came out, spoke briefly to the reporters, and also went to the Parliament building. Shevardnadze came out of the building soon thereafter and simply announced that he was going "home."

One of the most striking things about the images shown on television was the dumbfounded confusion that was evident in both Saakashvili and Zhvania as they walked out of the meeting with Shevardnadze. Suddenly, and unexpectedly, all of the nation's problems were their responsibility, and neither had a plan for how to deal with them. It was surprising that the two could not control their feelings, especially Zhvania, who was usually a very stoic politician.

Shevardnadze's immediate resignation caught everyone by surprise. Ivanov found out about it on the way to Adjaria, while the Americans were totally in the dark until after the announcement was made. Indeed, less than half an hour before the meeting between Shevardnadze, Saakashvili, and Zhvania, I received a phone call from one of the political officers at the U.S. Embassy, who was wondering if I knew anything new. The embassy was in the process of putting together talking points for Secretary of State Colin Powell, who was planning on making a phone call to Shevardnadze about what could be done to resolve the crisis. There had been no discussion of possible resignation or change of government.

Another interesting fact with international implications was a report I received later from Germany that throughout the tensest period, there had been a small contingent of German Special Forces present in Georgia, prepared to whisk Shevardnadze out of the country had this become necessary. It appears that Chancellor Gerhard Schroeder kept the promise his predecessor Helmut Kohl had given Shevardnadze to protect him under all possible circumstances, in return for the Georgian president's role in bringing about German unification while serving as Soviet foreign minister.

WHY DID SHEVARDNADZE RESIGN?

Why Shevardnadze decided to resign immediately is still not clear, given that there was a compromise that would have allowed for the constitutional process to continue. Several explanations have emerged. The most popular one is that Shevardnadze came to believe that even with the Ivanov agreement, throughout the period he would be in office he would end up being Saakashvili's hostage. While as president he would be blamed for continuing economic problems (especially ones that were bound to become acute in the winter, such as the electricity shortage), his political maneuvering room would be very limited, and he would not be in a position to influence the political process.

It is true that to an extent, and especially initially, Saakashvili would have the upper hand. However, this explanation assumes that politics in Georgia would stay static—for example, it assumes that the Saakashvili-Burdjanadze-Zhvania alliance would stay in place until after the planned legislative and presidential elections. However, it is easy to envision a scenario where this alliance would fall apart and Shevardnadze would still have had vast political influence. One could see, for example, an alliance between Burdjanadze,

Zhvania, the NRP, the business community, and some of the more acceptable members of Shevardnadze's inner circle (such as Tedo Japaridze). Such an alliance would have been a powerful counterweight to the National Movement, and Shevardnadze would have been in a position to bring this about had he stayed on as president. Saakashvili might have still become the elected president even if such an alliance had existed, but with a serious opposition he would have received a more reasonable percentage of the vote, creating a limit to his power in office and making democratic development in Georgia actually possible.

Another explanation, particularly popular with Shevardnadze's foreign admirers, is that Ivanov asked for far too much in return for playing a role in settling the crisis and in convincing Abashidze to accept the compromise. The price, some have alleged, was agreement from Shevardnadze and the opposition troika to allow for the Russian bases to stay in Georgia indefinitely. Those who advocate this explanation have argued that while Saakashvili and Zhvania were willing to pay this price, Shevardnadze was not, and thus he resigned in order to protect Georgian sovereignty.

It is not too far-fetched to think that Ivanov actually asked for something like this, and it is indeed possible to imagine that Shevardnadze, Saakashvili, and Zhvania indeed all agreed to his demand. However, such an agreement would require legislative approval, and thus it would be impossible to keep secret. Not only does it seem unrealistic that such a proposal would pass in any Georgian legislative body, but Georgia was bound to face great opposition from the United States in implementing such a deal. Thus, such an agreement was unlikely to have stayed in place, especially since Russia did not have a way of enforcing the bargain once the crisis was resolved.

Shevardnadze's detractors, meanwhile, have advanced two other explanations, both of which sound far more plausible. Shevardnadze may have resigned to spite Zhvania, because this way he ensured that all political power in the country would be in Saakashvili's hands. He understood that if he stayed, the Saakashvili-Burdjanadze-Zhvania alliance might fall apart, Burdjanadze-Zhvania might become the focal point of an alternative to Saakashvili, and therefore there was a possibility that Zhvania would come to power through Burdjanadze, as he had envisioned prior to the November elections. Because Shevardnadze believed that Zhvania was largely responsible for the problems that he was facing (caused by the rise of the young reformers and Zhvania's efforts to undermine Shevardnadze's authority throughout the late 1990s), the president may have wanted to limit the gains his former protégé would receive from his resignation.

Another reason why Shevardnadze may have resigned is his vanity: he wanted to leave on his own terms, and to leave his successors in as difficult a situation as possible in order to make it more difficult for them to meet the expectations of the people, so that Georgian citizens would eventually think that they were actually better off when Shevardnadze was in power. Given everything that has happened in Georgia since the Rose Revolution, there is a real likelihood of people actually coming to believe this. Already, an honest observer is bound to acknowledge that Shevardnadze stands alone among Georgian leaders as one who at least allowed for the promotion of political and economic freedom, and under whose rule democratic consolidation was at least *possible*—whereas under his predecessor and successor, society moved toward limitation of political liberty.

No matter what one makes of Shevardnadze and his years in power, and no matter how great an emphasis one puts on his grave political mistakes during his postindependence rule, assuming that the Georgian state survives well into the twenty-first century, Shevardnadze will go down in history as the man who secured Georgian statehood. Indeed, he may very well take his place next to some of the greatest of Georgian rulers. The simple fact is that between 1992 and 1995, Shevardnadze was indispensable, and he brought about success at a time when failure seemed all but certain. In other words, while the National Liberation Movement brought about Georgian independence, it likely would have been lost in 1992 had it not been for the personality of Eduard Shevardnadze. It is hard to predict "what ifs," but the reality is that Georgia was on the verge of perpetual civil war and could have descended into conditions similar to Somalia's. Shevardnadze single-handedly prevented this from happening, and one cannot ignore this achievement in assessing his legacy.

Shevardnadze as a political figure, however, will be judged for things other than his role in protecting Georgian independence and sovereignty. The years that followed—during which he twice failed to take advantage of openings for democracy, gave power to people who were simply not fit to be in positions of power, and ignored the swamp of corruption that developed in Georgia on his watch—will certainly tarnish his reputation. However, ultimately these and other mistakes and failures will be insignificant when compared to his monumental achievement on Georgia's behalf. This will be even more the case if over time, Saakashvili continues along the unfortunate authoritarian path on which he embarked after the Rose Revolution.

SAAKASHVILI IN POWER: THE FIRST REVOLUTIONARY DECISIONS

Upon Shevardnadze's resignation, the Rose Revolution had become a success. What had appeared as delusionary ideas of crazy NGO activists a little over a year before had now become reality. On the night of November 23, the area on Rustaveli Avenue in front of Parliament became an open party, with thousands of Saakashvili's supporters dancing and singing all night. Meanwhile, I spent the night in a depressed mood at home, still not certain how Georgia went from being so close to democratic consolidation to events that destroyed this unique opportunity through total rejection of the Constitution and the rule of law.

Burdjanadze took over as acting president and appointed Zhvania as state minister. Real power, however, was with Saakashvili, though he did not take a formal role during the interim period before the presidential elections in January 2004. Demonstrating his influence, on November 25 Saakashvili, rather than Burdjanadze, announced that all ministers should continue their duties, except for Interior Minister Koba Narchemashvili, who was probably the only minister who had remained loyal to Shevardnadze to the very end.

On November 26, the Supreme Court, with a ruling on a case brought about by the NGO Fair Elections, declared the proportional election results invalid. This decision was questionable, because according to the Electoral Code, disputes over the overall election results had to be adjudicated in the Constitutional Court, rather than the Supreme Court, since they dealt with people's *constitutional* right to vote and elect their representatives. However, at this point, no one in the government cared about the legal or constitutional process. Indeed, no one bothered to dispute claims that the "decision" had little to do with law and was not reached by judges, but rather was a legal presentation of a political decision reached by Saakashvili, Burdjanadze, and Zhvania; Supreme Court judges merely announced the ruling on behalf of the politicians.

This decision said volumes about the real political beliefs of the ruling trio and their commitment to democracy. The basis of the ruling was very broad: because of inaccurate voter lists, fraud, and electoral manipulation during the vote count, the final CEC results did not reflect the will of the people as expressed during the voting. The question was why this only applied to the proportional results and not to the elections of majoritarian deputies, who constituted a third of all members of Parliament. If voter lists were a problem (which they were, because certain people did not get a chance to vote because they were not on the lists), then this certainly was a problem in both the proportional and majoritarian elections. Meanwhile, pressure, fraud, and manipulation during the vote count were far more common in majoritarian elections than in proportional ones and had a greater impact on the result, because in a number of cases the real winner lost because of fraud, while a loser was declared the winner.

The reason for keeping the majoritarian results while invalidating the proportional results was very simple—this suited Saakashvili. In a proportional-election revote, which would be taking place in an environment of revolutionary euphoria, National Movement (as the party in power) was bound to do exceptionally well, while all other parties, which were out of money and were very low in morale, were unlikely to do well. Indeed, the possibility that no other party would get at least 7 percent of the vote to overcome the barrier necessary to enter the Parliament looked very real at the time when the Supreme Court announced its decision about canceling the proportional results from November 2.

Saakashvili also benefited because an electoral revote placed Burdjanadze and Zhvania in a very difficult position. Having gained power together, it was going to be impossible for them to run separately against National Movement, and as a result, they would have to run under Saakashvili's banner. This way, an alternative leader to Saakashvili was unlikely to emerge from the elections. Thus, canceling the proportional results put Saakashvili in the position of king-maker.

Canceling majoritarian results made a lot less sense, because most of these individuals were locally popular, and most would win again even if there were a revote (with the exception of those who had won through electoral manipulation). Thus, invalidating their elections would merely result in angering some of the country's richest and most powerful individuals, who were bound to become Saakashvili's huge supporters in the new Parliament—since majoritarians in Georgia have almost always supported the government, no matter who is in power. So, just as it was politically expedient to cancel the proportional results, it was useful to keep the majoritarian ones.

The meaning of Saakashvili's actions was clear: in the first important decision after the revolution, he put aside values that he had allegedly championed during the protests (such as democracy and fair electoral play) and instead chose a course that was politically beneficial, even though it was undemocratic and made Saakashvili look more authoritarian than Shevardnadze during at least the second half of his period of rule. As a result, the decision sent a clear message about what would happen in the future in Georgia, suggesting the possible rise of new authoritarianism.

The one unresolved issue for the new government was the question of Abashidze, who declared a state of emergency in Adjaria on November 24, posted "officers" on the region's administrative border with the rest of the country, and began to sound separatist themes. Preventing a possible conflict with Adjaria became the principal focus of the Burdjanadze-Zhvania wing of the government, while Saakashvili and the leaders of the revolutionary NGOs were pushing for his forceful and quick removal. Ultimately Abashidze was removed in May 2004, as I examine in the section that follows, but in late November 2003, the new government was fully in control of the country, except for Adjaria.

PART 3

Dangers of New Authoritarianism

9

Revolution's Achievements

A s I have examined, neither Saakashvili nor Zhvania planned on coming to power in November 2003. Even during the days immediately preceding Shevardnadze's resignation, their best-case scenario was to force a repeat parliamentary vote a few months later. As a result, the need to immediately take over the governance of the country was a huge shock for their teams, which were by no means prepared to rule, especially in a state in as dire shape as Georgia.

Saakashvili realized that given the weakness of the Georgian state, keeping the power he had gained was much more difficult than bringing down Shevardnadze. His situation was further complicated by the empty treasury and the challenges of the approaching winter, for which the Shevardnadze government had failed to plan properly. Thus, the new leader's first task was to consolidate his grasp of the state, while strengthening its control over various political and economic elements of society (other branches of government, the business community, the Orthodox Church, the media, etc.) that could challenge his grasp on power in the future. At the same time, Saakashvili's goal was to seek financial resources that would allow him to create an illusion of improvement for the general public by taking care of some of the basic social needs that the previous government had ignored.

These challenges notwithstanding, during its first years in power, Saakashvili's regime had a number of important successes, especially when compared to the Shevardnadze period. However in a number of circumstances, these successes came at the expense of individual rights and liberties, balance among constitutional institutions of government, and decision-making without the consent of the citizens' elected representatives.

The new regime's greatest success was the peaceful removal of Aslan Abashidze as leader of the autonomous province of Adjaria, which he had ruled as his own personal fiefdom since 1992. Because Abashidze's departure allowed Tbilisi to gain full sovereignty over a region that it previously governed largely in name only, this was a significant victory for the consolidation of the Georgian state. This represented the first concrete policy success for Saakashvili. Few believed, myself included, that this risky enterprise would succeed. However, Saakashvili exerted enough pressure to force Abashidze's hand, while pressure from Washington and Moscow was instrumental in convincing the Adjarian leader that it was time to go.

The confrontation over Adjaria started immediately after the Rose Revolution, when the new government made it clear that Abashidze could not continue to act as he had before. In the past, he had refused to pay taxes, had become a flagrant violator of citizens' fundamental rights, and controlled his province with an iron fist. Excessive electoral fraud in Adjaria, before and after the November 2003 elections, played a significant role in bringing about the Rose Revolution. During the fall of 2003 and winter of 2004, Abashidze started to cooperate on a number of fronts with the authorities in Tbilisi: on several occasions, Burdjanadze and Zhvania traveled to Adjaria's capital, Batumi, and extracted concessions from Abashidze. He started to pay taxes, allowed the polls to open for the presidential election in January 2004, and participated in Saakashvili's inauguration, whose first event took place in Batumi. However, every time the relationship improved, Saakashvili would move the goalpost and demand more concessions from Abashidze. To many, this appeared like a clear attempt to start a conflict between Batumi and Tbilisi. This view was reinforced by the fact that several of Saakashvili's advisors regularly pressed him to use military force to remove Abashidze. However, the president's tactic of public pressure and unwillingness to accept a compromise that would keep Abashidze in power ultimately turned out to be a successful strategy.

The conflict reached its ultimate stage in early spring 2004, when on March 14 Adjaria's illegal paramilitary forces prevented Saakashvili from entering the region. Had it not been for the prudent refusal of the U.S.-trained Georgian military officers to participate in a military operation, events could have unfolded very differently, given that Saakashvili repeatedly declared that he would use military force to restore order. Fortunately, as Georgian Ambassador to the United States Levan Mikeladze confirmed to the *Washington Times*, Georgia avoided the dangerous consequences of military action under pressure from the Bush administration, which sent clear signals against the use of force.[1] In response to these threats, Abashidze, who had never declared open secession from Georgia, severed the road link between Adjaria and the rest of Georgia when he blew up the bridges over which the main road led into the region. This was the last straw for the people of Adjaria, who came out into the streets in the thousands to demand his resignation. Moscow was forced to get involved and convinced Abashidze to leave Adjaria for Russia.

Saakashvili's success in removing Abashidze was an important development, not only because it significantly improved Georgian sovereignty, but because it gave the Georgian leadership an impetus to replicate a similar process in Ossetia, a region on the Russian border that Georgia has not controlled since 1992. As I discuss later, Saakashvili was not successful in an effort to regain control over this region, which unlike Adjaria has been in an open secessionist conflict with Georgia for over a decade.

Another important contribution to Georgia's sovereignty was the agreement secured with Moscow in 2005 on the withdrawal of Russian troops from the country by late 2008. Russia had promised to withdraw its troops as part of the renegotiation of the Conventional Armed Forces in Europe Treaty (CFE), which was signed in 1995. However, for a decade Moscow dragged its feet in negotiations with Georgia on how this would happen. In the last two years of Shevardnadze's rule, the Georgian government did not even push the issue. Saakashvili should be credited for putting the issue of troops at the forefront of the Georgian-Russian agenda. Assuming the agreement is implemented, withdrawal of Russian forces will be an important legacy for the Saakashvili administration. On a related note, Saakashvili has made significant advances in pressing Georgia's case for joining NATO in Washington and European capitals. While the Georgian government during Shevardnadze also espoused this goal, it did few concrete things to bring this about. Saakashvili's government has also failed to take any concrete steps necessary to join NATO (such as truly reforming its armed forces), but getting an agreement on the withdrawal of Russian troops out of Georgia was a significant move in the direction of NATO. Furthermore, by keeping this issue on a constant international agenda, Saakashvili has succeeded in moving Georgia to the level of Croatia and Albania as the most likely countries to be next invited into the alliance.

Another significant achievement of the new government was a dramatic increase in state revenue. The national budget went from 1.18 billion Georgian lari in 2003 to 1.77 billion in 2004, an increase in expenditures of almost 600 million lari.[2] In percentage terms, the budget increased by about 50 percent; thus, the often-stated government allegation that the budget tripled between 2003 and 2004, and again between 2004 and 2005, is exaggerated. While this change in the budget was dramatic, a closer look at the underlying numbers raises some concerns. For example, the government was not very successful in increasing what was always the most problematic issue for Georgia: the collection of direct taxes, which increased only by 12 percent to 901 million lari. At the same time, the change in the total budget number was to a large extent due to larger foreign grants (260 percent increase), social-tax income (173 percent increase), and "non-tax income" (338 percent increase). Because of this, the government's ability to continue succeeding in collecting greater revenue in the future remains an open question, because these indirect sources of income are unlikely to continue to increase so dramatically in the future (and are in fact unsustainable).³ Officials hope the new tax code, which went into effect in 2005, will move a greater share of the economy out of the shadows and increase the tax base. However, given that 60 percent of direct taxes are from the value-added tax (VAT), which the new tax code reduced by merely 2 percent, from 20 to 18 percent, it is unlikely to lead to a higher legalization of reported activity.⁴

In addition to increasing revenue collection, the new government had a number of achievements in improving government services. With increased revenue, the government paid many pension arrears that had accumulated over the years, and also doubled the pensions to 28 Georgian lari a month (US $15.3) in 2005 and further increased them to 38 lari in 2006 ($22).⁵ It reduced the number of ministries to a more manageable number. This was followed by a dramatic reduction in the size of the state bureaucracy (an estimated 76,000 to 100,000 jobs were cut), although many have complained that longtime government employees were laid off without any severance pay and with no hope of finding jobs in the private sector. Inside the government apparatus, petty corruption declined; in 2005 it became possible to get basic government services without having to bribe bureaucrats for their services on top of regular fees. However, this resulted in a dramatic increase in the time citizens spent taking care of minor regulatory issues or getting services from the government, because the overall quality of service did not improve, nor was it possible to expedite the process with bribes. The state also failed to establish a tiered payment system leading to faster service for a higher price.

The reform that had the greatest impact on the lives of ordinary citizens involved the police. During Shevardnadze's rule, the police had become the most visible element of decay and corruption of the Georgian state. All over Tbilisi and on all of Georgia's main roads, policemen would stand on every street corner, stopping cars at random, claiming that the driver had violated one or another rule, and demanding small bribes in order to let the driver go. Being a cop was a very profitable job, and by 2000, Georgia had over 70,000 cops—one for every seventy citizens. However, the police were also hated by the people, who had no respect for their work. By 2003, the police no longer even bothered coming up with "reasons" for why a particular car was stopped, while people gave policemen one- or two-dollar bribes not because they feared them, but out of pity.

One of the first acts of the new government was to take the police off the streets, which was viewed very favorably by the population. Then, in the fall of

2004, the government dismissed almost all traffic police in the country and replaced them with new hires. In large cities, traffic cops were replaced by the so-called "Patrol Police," who soon gained the confidence of citizens with their friendliness and good manners. This was probably the most clear-cut reform, and Saakashvili justifiably took a great deal of credit for it.

Another important government reform involved the passage of a constitutional amendment, introduced by Saakashvili, establishing a two-chamber Parliament, with a total of 150 deputies (down from the existing 235).[6] This change was in response to the referendum passed on November 2 that called for the reduction of the legislature's size and will go into effect after the next elections. However, this amendment was passed with little debate. Furthermore, many complained about Saakashvili's failure to fulfill his promise to lower the 7 percent barrier (regarded as artificially high by many democracy activists) that parties must surpass in order to win seats in Parliament during elections.[7]

These successes and the impression of "action" that Saakashvili and his ministers gave the Georgian people and the international community had the effect of strengthening the Georgian state, or at least of creating an illusion of strength. In many respects, strengthening the state was very useful and necessary. Georgia will not develop as a democracy, and indeed may not survive as a country, without a state that has the capacity to enforce its laws, regain sovereignty over the whole territory, and push through the necessary reforms. However, it is unclear that these successes actually led to a truly stronger state. Saakashvili's actions created a regime that moved away from institutional development and became fully dependent on one person. (The constitutional amendments that I examine in the next chapter created the legal basis for such a regime.) Without institutional development, the state may not actually be getting stronger, but rather, *seem* stronger because the person at the top has a great deal of power and energy.

Sadly, there are important parallels and similarities between the regime that existed in Georgia under its first president, Zviad Gamsakhurdia, and the one created by Saakashvili. After the revolution, many people who came into office were also completely inexperienced and incompetent, just like a decade earlier. At the same time, Saakashvili has constantly moved ministers around from one office to another, preventing them from gaining any competence in a given field. Because of this, Saakashvili's government is prone to rush decisions. It also seems to believe that it can do anything it wants, since there is nothing anyone can do to stop them. This too parallels the Gamsakhurdia period. In the pages that follow, I expound on these and other characteristics of Saakashvili's government, and what this has meant for Georgia's democracy.

10

Saakashvili's Constitution and Legal One-Man Rule

otwithstanding the questionable way in which the new Georgian leaders came to power, there was great hope that they would take advantage of the unique opportunity presented by President Shevardnadze's resignation and move Georgia toward consolidation of a representative democracy and the rule of law. For many, this hope was more illusionary than real, since the new leadership's actions immediately called into question its commitment to democratic values and institutions. This became abundantly clear when, in the days immediately after Shevardnadze's resignation, the new leadership forced the Supreme Court to cancel the results of the proportional elections, but keep the results of district first-past-the-post balloting.

Some explained these heavy-handed tactics as being caused by the euphoria and inexperience of the new leaders. Others argued that notwithstanding these problems, the new leaders "meant well." However, any doubts about the intentions of the new leaders disappeared in February 2004, when Saakashvili introduced constitutional amendments that moved the Georgian political system away from republican government and enshrined in the Constitution a system of one-man autocracy.

A constitution is the principal law that shapes the nature of a political regime. When trying to classify a regime, looking at the fundamental law is the place to start. A regime may be a dictatorship even under a "good" or a "just" constitution, but that usually happens when the letter and the spirit of the constitution are not followed by the ruler. By contrast, an "unjust" or an "authoritarian" constitution makes it all but certain that a regime living under it will be authoritarian as well, because such a constitution creates legal justification for dictatorial rule. For this reason, understanding what Saakashvili's amendments did to the Georgian regime is crucial to grasping what sort of a ruler would emerge in the new system.

As I demonstrated in chapter 2, in 1995 Georgia adopted a constitution that was unique among post-Soviet states, particularly because it did not create a superpresidential system of government. Instead, it divided powers between the executive and legislative branches (and to a lesser extent, the judiciary) and allowed the Parliament to function as a check on the president. This was a key reason why authoritarianism never fully developed in Georgia, and why chaotic pluralism was possible between 2001 and 2003.

When President Saakashvili introduced his amendments in February 2004, he alleged that these amendments moved Georgia from the so-called "presidential" system (i.e., a flawed copy of the U.S. model) to a "quasi- parliamentary" (or, put otherwise, "quasi-presidential") system, similar to the one in France.[1] On the surface this seemed true, since the amendments created the post of prime minister, giving Zhvania a place in the political system.[2]

In reality, however, the amendments also altered key elements of the Constitution that differentiated it from other post-Soviet states and served as a guard against autocracy. They weakened the Parliament's oversight and law-making powers. They empowered the president with permanent dominance over every branch of government by giving him the right to disband the legislature and to call early elections at will. They dramatically increased his powers over the judiciary by empowering him to dismiss judges. Furthermore, the newly created post of prime minister was not independent of the president at all. Indeed, its holder could seldom act without the latter's consent.

Thus, using the idea that Georgia needed a prime minister to lead an effective cabinet as a mere pretext, the amendments were a dramatic step backward in Georgia's transition to representative liberal democracy. Saakashvili replaced a flawed, but fundamentally just regime with an unjust order of one-man "dictatorship."[3]

Impact of the Amendments on the Balance of Power

The most damaging aspect of Saakashvili's amendments was that they granted the president the power to dissolve the Parliament, without compensating the legislature with means to counter this new presidential power. The amendments empowered the president to dissolve the Parliament under several circumstances. If the Parliament were to reject the president's nominee for prime minister three times consecutively, the former could dissolve the legislature and appoint his candidate as premier by decree. Moreover, if the Parliament were to vote "no confidence" in the prime minister, the president could choose to either appoint a new prime minister, or dissolve the Parliament and keep the old prime minister. Once new elections were held, the president could again choose to keep the old prime minister, even if he did not have the confidence of the Parliament, for a period of six months.

In this arrangement, the legislative majority was left without the key checks vis-à-vis the executive that exist all over Europe—even in France, the least balanced of European models, which Saakashvili always cited when making the case for his amendments.[4] First, in all European models, the Parliament can dismiss the prime minister with a simple majority vote of no confidence. Presidents (or monarchs) are empowered to call new elections after the government falls (in some cases they are obliged to do so), but they are not in a position to keep the same prime minister in power for months even if that individual does not have support of the people's elected representatives, or to keep the same prime minister in office without parliamentary approval after new elections. Second, nowhere in Europe can a president appoint a prime minister by decree and keep him in office for any reason other than caretaker purposes.

Because of these key differences, the amendments gave the Georgian president great powers over the legislature's fate in disputes between the prime minister and the Parliament, without giving the Parliament ability to counterweigh him. Thus, the Parliament would no longer function as a coequal branch of government, but become subordinate to the president. American University's law professor Herman Schwartz has argued that in such a system, the president has "a Damocles' sword over the Parliament."[5]

Incidentally, the Parliament in Georgia is not even empowered to remove the president through impeachment, should this become necessary. The 1995 Constitution included a theoretical impeachment power—the legislature could introduce an impeachment motion, but the Parliament required a legal finding of a crime by the Supreme Court before it could remove the president from office. For years during Shevardnadze's rule, various political groups and democracy activists had tried to eliminate the judiciary's unnecessary role in the impeachment process. Saakashvili's amendments did not change the impeachment process, thus forever insulating the president from impeachment, especially given his vast powers over the judiciary. In one positive development, the amendments do not allow the president to dissolve the Parliament if and when impeachment proceedings are underway.

BUDGETARY PROCESS

Historically, legislative control over appropriations has been crucial to the success of republican government. The American Founders understood this well, and for this reason, they empowered the Congress with the power of the purse.

This power remains essential for a proper balance between different branches of government in the United States today. No post-Soviet state has had a wholly appropriate balance between the executive and legislative branches on the issue of taxing and spending. This has been a key reason behind the rise of authoritarian regimes in the former Soviet republics. Along with a lack of proper balance, another significant problem is that many transitional states, including those in the former USSR, do not depend on the people for the bulk of their revenue (as is the case in Georgia, where, as I have examined, the VAT and taxation on business are the principal source of state funds).

While the legislature lacked full powers of the purse in Georgia under the 1995 Constitution, it did have an important role. The president was charged with submitting to the Parliament for approval a yearly budget. However, because the Parliament had the authority to approve or reject the budget, it served as a serious check on the executive power—the legislature had the capacity to force a compromise with the president over expenditures. Unlike the U.S. Congress, the Georgian Parliament could not change expenditures set forth in the president's budget.

Under the new system, the legislature's role in the budgetary process was reduced even further. The prime minister was charged with developing the budget, which the president had to approve before it could be submitted to Parliament. While the Parliament could technically reject the budget, it could be resubmitted without changes, and if it were rejected three times, the president would become empowered to dissolve the legislature, call new elections, and approve the budget by decree. Supporters argued that this system would create efficiency by ensuring that the country would never be without a budget. However, by permitting approval of the budget without legislative consent, the system left the Parliament without any real power to control the country's finances. Indeed, it would be suicidal for the parliamentarians to reject a budget, because not only would the budget eventually be approved anyway, but the prime minister could stay in place while the legislators would have to face early elections. In this budgetary area, the new Georgian system has nothing in common with the French model, to which the amendments were most often compared by Saakashvili. There too, the prime minister develops the budget and submits it to Parliament for approval, but the French president cannot dissolve Parliament for rejecting a budget, nor can he approve the budget by decree.

LAWMAKING AND INITIATION OF LEGISLATION

The 1995 Constitution empowered the president and individual members of the Parliament, along with its factions and committees, to initiate legislation. Once bills were passed, they had to be signed by the president to become law.

The president could veto bills, but these vetoes could be overridden by the Parliament, with a three-fifths majority.

The Saakashvili amendments did not touch the veto process and maintained the presidential power of initiating legislation, but also granted the same power to the prime minister. Furthermore, the prime minister was empowered to turn a vote on any bill into a vote of confidence in his cabinet. If the Parliament were to reject such a law, the president became empowered to dissolve it. Furthermore, while parliamentary power to initiate laws was maintained, any bill with impact on financial expenditures required approval from the prime minister before it could become law. Thus, on top of the presidential veto, the prime minister was also granted near-absolute veto over laws, since virtually all legislative initiatives have a financial impact. This was another way of reducing the Parliament's lawmaking powers.

In the area of lawmaking, the French president is much weaker than his Georgian counterpart in either the 1995 system or the one created by Saakashvili's amendments, because he cannot initiate legislation. By contrast, the prime minister in France is more powerful than in Georgia (which is important for the balance of power between the president and the prime minister). He can initiate laws, which can be approved without the support of a parliamentary majority—unless the Parliament censures the prime minister (that is, votes no confidence in him), in which case the premier must resign. Yet to balance this, the French Parliament is also freer in lawmaking than the Georgian one, because it does not require the prime minister's permission before voting on proposed laws with financial impact.

RELATIONSHIP BETWEEN PRESIDENT AND PRIME MINISTER

In addition to weakening the Parliament's powers and increasing those of the president, the amendments failed miserably at what was allegedly their most important task—to create an independent and effective prime minister. The Georgian prime minister is not even permitted to appoint his full cabinet. While he has to seek the president's consent to appoint any minister, the president is permitted to appoint three of the most powerful ministers (security, defense and interior) without the prime minister's approval.[6] Once appointed, the prime minister must reach agreement with the president on the official policies of the cabinet, and the president is empowered to chair cabinet meetings, to give orders to the various ministers, and to revoke government decisions. Thus, the amendments created a prime minister who is "merely the President's creature."[7]

This, too, contrasts with the French system. There, in the constitutional sense, the prime minister is responsible for determining and conducting the policy of the nation (especially domestic policy), without approval from the president. Constitutionally, the prime minister is responsible only to the Parliament, and the president cannot regulate the government's activities and get involved in the appointment of ministers. In practice, France often operates differently. Whenever the French president's party controls the Parliament, he has many of the powers of the Georgian president, and the prime minister is subordinate to the president. However, this is the result of political developments (i.e., victory by the president's party in the legislative elections), rather than constitutional (or institutional) powers. As a result, there are instances when different parties control the executive and legislative branches, in what is called "co-habitation." This difference between the Georgian and French models is crucial, because the French have and Georgians lack an effective and consistent method of regulating the executive's activities. The French can limit the president's powers through parliamentary elections by creating co-habitation, thus ensuring that the prime minister fully exercises his powers. By contrast, Georgians could voice their disapproval of the executive branch through legislative elections, but this would have absolutely no impact on the way the country is governed, because the old prime minister (the one holding office prior to legislative elections) could stay in office, and the president could single-handedly govern through decree, with little regard to the will of the legislature.

JUDICIARY'S INDEPENDENCE

The judiciary in Georgia was the least well-designed branch of government, even though it had gained some independence during the late 1990s. Part of the problem was the division of supreme judicial authority between two bodies (the Supreme Court and the Constitutional Court). This weakened the judiciary's ability to impact governance. Furthermore, Georgia had chosen to follow the system of civil rather than common law, and because of this, the precedent system never developed in the country. However, instead of addressing the real problems within this branch, Saakashvili's amendments had a limited but very damaging impact on the judiciary by permitting the president to remove judges who had been found guilty of violations by Georgia's Judiciary Council, the majority of whose members would be appointed by the president. As a result, the president became empowered to discipline judges almost single-handedly. A truly independent judiciary could never develop in such a system.

Securing the Passage of the Amendments

While the impact of the amendments was obvious, President Saakashvili and his supporters tried to portray them as benign. They argued that the changes actually limited the president's powers, increased the legislature's powers, and most significantly, allowed the prime minister to lead the cabinet independently of the president, ensuring effective governance. Saakashvili, who claimed that the amendments were necessary in order to "create a European model of government,"[8] went so far as to declare that after their passage, Georgia would have the "most powerful Parliament in Europe," while the president would be weaker than he was before.[9]

Saakashvili proposed these amendments soon after his inauguration as president in January 2004, and demanded that they be approved swiftly. In doing so, he violated both the letter and the spirit of the Georgian Constitution, which requires a thirty-day discussion period between the time when constitutional changes are formally introduced in Parliament and when they are voted on by this legislative body. To get around this requirement, Saakashvili and his supporters argued that he was merely "reintroducing" changes that had been proposed by Shevardnadze in 2001 but were never acted upon. The legal validity of this claim was very questionable, given that Georgia had a new president now, and therefore the old president's proposal that had not been enacted upon had "died" with his resignation. Moreover, the moral authority of Saakashvili's claim was even more doubtful, given how he had demonized Shevardnadze and his rule during the Rose Revolution. While the two proposals were indeed quite similar, before the revolution, Saakashvili and members of his political team had been some of the strongest critics of Shevardnadze's proposals, correctly alleging that those changes were undemocratic; once in power, Saakashvili did not have any qualms about supporting the exact same changes for his own benefit, at the expense of democracy.

Saakashvili wanted the Parliament that had been elected in 1999, whose term had been "extended" after the "invalidation" of the November 2, 2003, election results, to adopt the changes. Saakashvili needed the amendments passed before the repeat vote for the Parliament in March, because otherwise they would become a distraction during the forthcoming election campaign. While it remained an open question whether this Parliament had *legal* authority to make laws,[10] this legislature, which was dominated by Shevardnadze's cronies and was elected in a vote that was far more flawed and corrupt than the November 2 balloting, clearly did not have the political legitimacy to so dramatically alter the country's constitutional order.

This issue was raised not only by Saakashvili's opponents, but by many supporters as well. Even Ghia Nodia of the Caucasus Institute for Peace, Democracy, and Development asked, "If this Parliament is so inefficient and worn out, is it legitimate enough to pass laws of such immense importance?"[11] Meanwhile, months after the passage of the amendments, David Usupashvili, a leading Georgian lawyer whose wife, Tinatin Khidasheli, justifiably took credit for "stepping on the Constitution and opening the Parliament's doors"[12] for Saakashvili on November 22, 2003, started to refer to the amendments as a "constitutional coup."[13]

Saakashvili and other leading advocates of the changes never answered the charges from these critics, or from those who took issue with the substance of the amendments. Instead, they argued on behalf of the amendments using the idea of "necessity": "Georgia needs a single energetic government to impose order in all spheres of society and implement needed economic and social reforms,"[14] declared Saakashvili, claiming that his model was "the most effective at this stage."[15] Burdjanadze, who was far less enthusiastic about the changes than Saakashvili and Zhvania, made a similar argument: "I believe this attempt at introducing constitutional amendments should end conclusively, because it is very important that the prime minister and the president have the leverage they demand to meet those obligations they have pledged to the population."[16] If one takes these claims at face value, they have only one logical conclusion—the ends are far more important than the means, even if these means raise irrefutable concerns about commitment to democracy and the rule of law and actually run counter to the very ends they are supposed to help achieve.

Stephen Sestanovich, who was responsible for the former Soviet Union in the Department of State under President Bill Clinton, has also made a similar argument. Writing in the *Wall Street Journal*, he described the similarities between Russian President Vladimir Putin and Saakashvili this way: "Both . . . have a supreme goal of rebuilding the central government's power. . . . [Each] president considers his country especially susceptible to break-up and disorder. . . . [Both] have also focused on making state institutions work. They know that a government that can't collect taxes can't do its many other jobs. And each president has zeroed in on corruption, launching highly publicized campaigns that have included arrests even of members of a predecessor's entourage."[17]

While Sestanovich acknowledges that there has been reasoned criticism of the human-rights policies of both presidents, he admires their actions, because in his view, they show that "there are unavoidable trade-offs between building an effective state and building a real democracy" in the former Soviet Union. Finally, discussing what to him appear as significant differences between the two in terms of commitment to democracy, Sestanovich argues that Putin would be well advised to look to Saakashvili for an example of how this trade-off between democracy and an effective state can work better than it has in Russia.

The main problem with Sestanovich's argument (as well as that of those in Georgia who used "necessity" to justify the constitutional amendments) is that constitutionally concentrating power in the hands of one office, and increasing the powers of the holder of that office through governmental action, does not equal having a stronger or capable state. Recent history, especially in the former Soviet Union, is full of examples where dictators had powers few could match, yet the state was getting less and less effective. After all, who could argue that Soviet dictators Brezhnev, Andropov, and Gorbachev were not powerful?[18] Under each, the Soviet state deteriorated—and eventually collapsed—while the powers of each increased.

In Georgia, the concentration of powers in the president's hands has hardly resulted in what Sestanovich calls Saakashvili's aim of "open[ing] up Georgian politics" and "bringing state institutions under effective legal control." Rather, one could very well argue that the result has been the opposite, as my discussion in the forthcoming chapters suggests. If anything, the differences on the issue of democracy that Sestanovich suggests might exist between Putin and Saakashvili may actually not be so big.

Whatever one makes of Saakashvili's explanations based on necessity, his own allies betrayed far more cynical reasons behind the changes. Levan Ramishvili, one of the leaders of the Liberty Institute and founder of the Kmara Movement, remarked: "Each member of the trio [Saakashvili, Burdjanadze, Zhvania] wanted to formalize his or her post-revolutionary power, but the existing system did not include any division of power. [Changes give Georgia a] weaker parliament than before, a prime minister who duplicates the president on many issues and a president with greater powers than before. This would never have happened if the revolution had had two leaders instead of three. Then the first would have become president and the second speaker. Three do not fit, one of them is surplus to requirements, and unity requires sacrifices. But it was the constitution that was sacrificed."[19]

Unfortunately, even this explanation, which appeared more intellectually honest, did not address the core reason why the amendments were proposed. Given the fact that the amendments consolidated virtually all political power in the hands of the president, the real reason lay in Saakashvili's authoritarian instincts, which led him toward concentrating all authority in his own hands, and in his desire to create a system in which someone else (for instance, the prime minister) could be blamed for lack of economic progress and development, as is the case in places like Russia.

The amendments passed without much political opposition, because the new government used every conceivable means of pressure to secure support for the changes in Parliament. It forced TV stations (Rustavi and Mze) to take off the air their nighttime debate talk shows the day after the changes were announced, in order to limit public discourse on the amendments.[20] It rushed the amendments to a vote with lighting speed: the final vote took place two days after they were officially introduced in Parliament, and the legislature voted on all three readings of the amendments in eighteen minutes. The government threatened formerly pro-Shevardnadze deputies with arrest if they opposed the amendments.[21] The government also silenced opposition from the New Rights Party, the only group in Parliament that had the capacity to mount an effort to defeat the amendments. Through the NRP business allies, Saakashvili sent word to party leaders that if they opposed the amendments, they would have no chance of overcoming the 7 percent barrier in the March 28 repeat parliamentary elections. He threatened to arrest the party's financial backers and to amend the Electoral Code to exclude the NRP representatives from the electoral commissions, in which case the party would have no reason to compete in the elections since it would become impossible to protect the results even if people actually voted for it. As a result, the NRP parliamentarians either abstained or voted for the amendments. This was particularly problematic because on the first reading, the amendments passed with the NRP votes; had the party deputies voted against the amendments, the supporters would have failed to garner the two-thirds majority necessary for passage.[22]

Saakashvili also succeeded in passing the amendments because foreign officials did little to oppose them, even though most grasped the dangers associated with such a concentration of powers in the hands of the president. The U.S. and European representatives in Georgia said little about the actual content of the amendments, and only criticized the secrecy in which they were developed and the speed with which they were being rushed to a vote. Privately, staffers at the U.S. Embassy in Tbilisi and officials in Washington responsible for Georgia appreciated the arguments expressed by opponents of the amendments. Indeed, in private discussions no one disputed that as policy, the amendments were a drastic step backward. However, publicly they failed to oppose the amendments. Some U.S. officials in Tbilisi who wanted to report about the amendments were not allowed to do so, while in Washington, it appears that officials were either forgetting or ignoring, in the middle of their euphoric support for the "democratic" revolution, Lord Acton's famous dictum that "power corrupts, and absolute power corrupts absolutely."[23]

Meanwhile, some U.S. officials demonstrated how little they understood their own democracy and the role of balanced constitutional institutions in securing liberty. For example, one senior administration official who had always been a great friend to Georgia argued that while the amendments were bad, Georgia's new leaders were a "known quantity," and that there was nothing to fear from these changes because Saakashvili would use his powers "wisely." In other words, he was arguing that individuals matter far more than institutions of government in advancing reforms and democratic governance. Through this claim, he was making a mockery out of the beliefs of the American Founders, who created the U.S. political system based on the notion that only stable and balanced constitutional institutions can secure and preserve liberty. Because of such misunderstanding of American (and democratic) government, certain officials gave Saakashvili a free hand, which not only hurt Georgia's transition to democracy, but arguably damaged U.S. interests as well.

Implications of Saakashvili's Changes for Democracy and Georgia's Future

Given the Georgian president's vast powers under the amended Constitution, he became more like an omnipotent sovereign in eighteenth-century England (when His Majesty's Government could continue in office even without the confidence of the Parliament, so long as it had the support of the king) than an executive in a liberal democracy.[24] In Georgia, the only real check on the president's powers is a three-fifths (60 percent) parliamentary supermajority. If the legislature achieves this bar in a special vote of no confidence in the prime minister, then the cabinet must resign and the president cannot dissolve the legislature. This clause was not in the original drafts of Saakashvili's amendments, but was eventually included at the insistence of Nino Burdjanadze, who threatened to vote against the amendments if her demand for this change was not made. However, on the larger scale of checks and balances, this is a very minor means of controlling the president's nearly unlimited powers.

Before the Rose Revolution, Georgia was the only country in the CIS without a hyper-presidential system and with a more or less balanced government. It was very ironic that after the revolution, the Georgian political system became one of the least balanced in the CIS. Sadly, this was all too predictable for anyone who knew what Saakashvili and Zhvania were all about.

In creating such an autocratic regime, the amendments took away citizens' most fundamental political right—to control their government through their elected representatives. Most strikingly, this happened without any consent being sought from the people, even though individuals making the decision had been brought to power through the people, who endured days of demonstrations in the streets in order to ensure their right to elect their government. The result was that Georgia went from a fraudulent election in November 2003, which was 75 percent legitimate and 25 percent illegitimate, to a regime that is wholly illegitimate and unjust, given that it violated the most sacred democratic natural right—the consent of citizens to their system of government.

The Georgian experience with postrevolutionary constitutionalism sharply contrasted with what happened in Ukraine a little less than a year after Saakashvili's amendments were approved. Under President Leonid Kuchma during the 1990s, Ukraine also developed a hyper-presidential system. However, as part of a compromise negotiated between the opposition and Kuchma's supporters during the Orange Revolution, Ukraine implemented dramatic reforms that moved its government system away from such concentration of power in the hands of the president. According to the changes, which went into effect in 2006, the Ukrainian system became similar to most European states—a regime in which the prime minister derives his powers from the consent of the legislature rather than the consent of the president, whose powers in turn are quite limited. Thus, while many tend to find much in common between the "revolutions" in Georgia and Ukraine, in the area of constitutionalism, results differed dramatically. Whereas Georgia backtracked from a system of checks and balances toward an unjust and imbalanced order, Ukraine moved from a superpresidential system toward real reforms and democratic consolidation.

The one argument in favor of Saakashvili's changes that had some validity was the idea that Georgia needed an "effective" government to overcome its political and socioeconomic crisis. Sometimes, especially in the short term, concentration of powers in the hands of one individual does indeed bring about impetus for change; some may argue that Chile under General Augusto Pinochet, or Peru under President Alberto Fujimori exemplify such experiences. However, both of these examples, along with many others, also show that the greatest danger to the sacred value of liberty arises from concentration of power in a single branch of government, and even more so in one person.

The American Founders, as well as the philosopher Montesquieu, from whom James Madison took his lead in drafting the U.S. Constitution, understood that the greatest danger of tyranny arises when different sorts of governmental powers are unable to balance and check each other. This happens when one branch of government is too weak while another is too strong. At the Constitutional Convention in 1788, having had bad experiences with overly powerful legislatures and weak executives in the several states and on the federal level, the American Founders weakened the nation's legislative branch by making it bicameral. They also created a more powerful executive than was the case in the several states, by placing it in the hands of one individual and not defining the meaning of "executive power" that was vested in the president. Coupled with an independent judiciary, these innovations helped create the most successful and effective free government in human history.

Even though the old Georgian Constitution was better than any other in the CIS, it still concentrated too much power in the hands of the president. As a result, unlike America in the late 1700s, Georgian political experience during Shevardnadze's rule had been one of an overly powerful executive and a weak legislature. This constitutional flaw was a significant source of corruption and impediment to reforms. The way to overcome this constitutional flaw was to strengthen the legislative check on the executive and promote a system in which the two branches would direct their "ambitions" (to use Madison's term) against each other, promoting change and good governance. Furthermore, it was necessary to insulate the independence of the judiciary. While many in Georgia urged Saakashvili to do precisely this, he chose to move in the opposite direction—he made the presidency even more powerful than it used to be, while weakening an already weak legislature and judiciary even further.

When Saakashvili's constitutional amendments were passed, many of his supporters, especially those abroad, hoped that the president would use his new-found power prudently. Given that Saakashvili had come into office with a strong mandate for change and expectations of quick reforms, some analysts argued that the president had no choice but to act prudently. Meanwhile, opponents of the expansive executive powers that the amendments created countered that free and balanced constitutions that limit executive powers are necessary in order to protect liberty—not only under just and sensible leaders, which allegedly Saakashvili was, but also under unjust ones, including those who might have bad intentions.

Since the passage of these amendments, experiences of the Saakashvili presidency that I document in following chapters suggest that his government has failed to fulfill the hopes of prudence. Indeed, his rule is an excellent case study for why liberty is endangered in a hyper-presidential, autocratic system of government. For many, this is not unexpected, because the system that Saakashvili's amendments created does not allow for good governance. In other words, it would have been impossible for Saakashvili to rule well in the system that he created, even if he had intended to do so.

Saakashvili's first cabinet, led by Prime Minister Zurab Zhvania, included representatives from Saakashvili's team (usually in the most important positions), from Zhvania's team, and from among those NGO leaders who had supported the revolution. The lack of cohesion in the cabinet created many rivalries, which Zhvania did not have the power to deal with. Because of the way the constitutional system was organized, these rivalries could be managed only by the president. This resulted in numerous reshufflings of the cabinet during Saakashvili's first three years in power.

When Zhvania died in mysterious circumstances in February 2005, Saakashvili appointed Zurab Nogaideli, a longtime Zhvania ally with far less political stature, as prime minister. This cabinet included Georgia's fourth defense minister, third interior minister, third economic minister, and second foreign minister in twelve months; most other positions had seen at least two ministers as well.[25] Such an environment of constant change created a great deal of inefficiency in the government, even though Georgia's democratic future had been sacrificed to create an ostensibly "efficient" government.

Over two centuries ago, Madison remarked that "if men were angels, no government would be necessary, [and if] angels were to govern over men, neither external nor internal controls on government would be necessary."[26] However, neither of these being true, "In framing a government that is to be administered by men over men . . . [it is necessary] to oblige it [the government] to control itself [through] auxiliary precautions." Without these, the regime is "a society under the forms of which the stronger faction can readily unite and oppress the weaker." That is, without proper checks and balances, "liberty is lost" and the government cannot fulfill its core mission of securing "justice" for all.[27] As the discussion that follows demonstrates, Georgia's experiences in 2004–2006 prove that Madison's concerns about the dangers to liberty in an imbalanced system have been far too accurate. Georgian and American interests would have been much better served had U.S. officials, who stood silently by while Georgia's new government pushed forward with these changes, studied the thoughts of the Father of the Constitution with greater care and pressed his advice on the Georgian leadership.

11

The Rule of Law and
the Rule of Men

Once in power, the new government claimed that its most important task
was to fight endemic corruption. It went about this through arrest and
punishment of former government officials and businessmen whom
Saakashvili accused of abusing the system in the past. Allegedly, the anti-
corruption efforts were to be pursued through strict adherence to the rule of law.
Unfortunately, the government's very first steps had very little to do with eliminating corruption, and more to do with shaking down wealthy individuals for
money, or settling political scores. The force of the state was used to illegally
detain prominent former officials and businessmen and extort huge sums of
money from them in return for their freedom, and to scare other wealthy individuals in Georgia, who were not actually detained, to voluntarily give the state
parts of their wealth. As a result, the new government quickly turned the anti-
corruption and pro-rule-of-law rhetoric on its head by corrupting the Georgian
state beyond anything ever seen during the Shevardnadze era.

State Turns into a Mob

For the sake of promoting real rule of law in Georgia, it would have made a lot
of sense to arrest, try in court, and punish Shevardnadze-era officials who
undoubtedly had profited from corruption and illegality under the old government. However, this had to be done in accordance with the rule of law, and
with respect for individual rights and liberties.

By contrast, even the noble goal of advancing the system of rule of law
did not justify going after businessmen, who were nothing but the victims of

corruption during Shevardnadze's regime, just like all other citizens.¹ Most businessmen had no choice but to work outside the legal system and to bribe officials of the old government, because the old regime made it impossible for individuals to engage in free enterprise in a legitimate way. Saakashvili himself acknowledged this when he promised businessmen full amnesty,² as well as quick changes to the tax system and other laws that had a negative impact on the business environment. However, the new government needed money, and this necessity led Saakashvili and his allies to ignore both their promise to leave businessmen alone, and the need to punish criminals *legally* in order to help eradicate corruption. Instead, the state became indistinguishable from a mob—it turned into a regime that abused its power and violated individual freedoms in order to extort money from individuals, while calling this extortion a "fight against corruption."

Saakashvili's close ally and personal friend Irakli Okruashvili oversaw the process of arrests and shakedowns—first from the position of prosecutor general, to which he was appointed immediately after the revolution by Acting President Nino Burdjanadze, and after June 2004 as interior minister.³ It worked something like this:

In the months immediately after the Rose Revolution, every couple of days, Okruashvili would select a high-profile target and dispatch a team of heavily armed, masked Interior Ministry Special Forces to conduct the arrest (the target was usually either an official of the old government or a businessman).

Television stations would be alerted of the planned arrest, and their cameras would join the Special Forces during the arrest, turning the incident into the day's biggest news story; often, the arrests would actually be televised live. Watching this extreme use of force, one was necessarily left with the impression that the detained individual was either a murderer or a terrorist, rather than someone who by no means posed a violent threat to society.

With few exceptions, the detained individual had not been asked to report to the police on his own. In other words, the use of such excessive force was by no means a necessity, but rather a weapon of choice in order to humiliate the individual being arrested, and to scare those who were not yet under arrest into cooperating with the government so that they could avoid a similar fate.

In the vast majority of cases, the arrested individual would be dragged into the courts the next day, with the prosecution alleging that he was guilty of some trumped-up crime (usually improper use of state funds). Many of these individuals were actually guilty of real crimes, but the charges that were presented against them seldom dealt with these real violations. Furthermore, the prosecutor would seldom, if ever, present any evidence to support the allegations, and often chose not to charge the individual with a crime at all. Instead, the government would demand that the detained individual be held in a three-month pretrial detention, pending an investigation. The courts would grant the government's requests in almost every circumstance.⁴ According to human-rights groups, long periods of pretrial detention are one of the most frequent violations of human rights by many governments.⁵ Georgia, where the law permits an unusually long period of pretrial detention, has been a particularly egregious example of this abuse, even though by law, pretrial detention must be used only in very specific, narrowly defined circumstances.

Once in jail, the government would offer the alleged criminal a way out: he could pay a huge sum of money to the state and to senior officials in the new government (in some cases, the detainee was asked to give up property instead of money) and be released, or he could stay in jail (where he would be tortured and abused) indefinitely, since the government had no intention of actually bringing his case to trial. Most agreed to pay and were released a few months later, without ever having to face trial for their alleged crimes or having to agree to a plea bargain by which they accepted guilt and responsibility.

The arcane scheme of three-month pretrial detentions was a leftover from the Soviet days, when it was used to hold any accused person in jail almost indefinitely, without having to present any evidence against him. In the mid-1990s, through legislative reforms, the application of pretrial detentions was limited to only those whose presence out of jail would either endanger the public or complicate the investigation, or for those who were shown to be a flight risk. In all other cases, the accused would either be set free pending a trial, or the courts were allowed to impose other forms of pretrial confinement—such as limiting the individual's ability to leave the country, requiring him to check in with the police on a daily basis, and so forth. While during Shevardnadze's rule, this system was sometimes abused to impose pretrial detentions on people who did not deserve it, under Okruashvili's leadership the abuse of this scheme reached phenomenal proportions, reminiscent of the Soviet era.

In general, the prosecution did not even bother to present in court its arguments for why a detained individual deserved to be in jail. Instead, it would simply demand that he be placed in jail, and the court would agree; virtually every arrest of a former government official during the first year after the revolution resulted in a pretrial jail term. In 2004, the government requested pretrial detention for 1,540 detainees, and the judiciary granted it in 83 percent of the cases.⁶ The vast majority of these cases did not qualify for such confinement under any interpretation of the pretrial detention rules. In some cases, after the initial three months, detention was extended further, until eventually the government was able to reach an agreement with the accused for payment. Thus, numerous Georgian citizens were denied their basic right to due process by government actions that violated human rights and were borderline tyrannical.

While human rights suffered, the state Treasury benefited greatly from funds collected through these tactics. It is impossible to determine the exact amount of money that was extorted, since the government has refused to give out the figures, but estimates vary from 450–500 million Georgian lari, or approximately US $245–273 million. Of this amount, only about 125 million lari were reported in the state budget, while about 325–375 million lari were administered through amorphous and shadowy "funds." These were accounts set up by the government to support various priority projects—such as the Army Development Fund, which was launched shortly after the Rose Revolution but did not become public until 2005.[7] Once the deal was reached about the amount of money, that an arrested individual (or someone else whom the government was threatening with arrest) had to pay, the total was split in two. The smaller, public part of the money would be deposited by that individual (or his family and friends) into the Treasury. The larger amount, meanwhile, would be deposited "voluntarily" by the individuals' relatives to support these various funds.

On top of these "voluntary" extortions, there were numerous allegations in the Georgian media about additional funds being paid by detained individuals to government officials directly, sometimes by giving up stakes in Georgian business. One piece of evidence to support this claim is a 400 percent increase in 2004 (over data from 2003) in the number of changes of ownership of private companies and limited-liability partnerships registered by the Georgian notary public. This huge surge cannot be simply explained as a natural phenomenon. No targeted individual has yet spoken out openly about the funds that he paid to government officials directly, though many have confirmed these allegations in private, including to the author.

While Okruashvili supervised this process, Saakashvili encouraged it through "anti-corruption" rhetoric, which often gave no regard to the rights of citizens, be they criminals or not: "I gave an order to [the interior minister] to start this [anti-crime] operation and, if there is any resistance, to eliminate any such bandit on the spot, eliminate and exterminate them on the spot, and free the people from reign of these bandits,"[8] and "I want criminals both inside and outside prisons to listen to this very carefully . . . [government forces will] use force when dealing with any attempt to stage a prison riot, and to open fire, shoot to kill and destroy any criminal who attempts to cause turmoil. We will not spare bullets against these people."[9]

When confronted about these arrests and abuses of power, Saakashvili usually pointed to the huge sums of money collected by the government using these tactics, and claimed that it was better for these individuals to "return" the money that they had "stolen" rather than have them "rot in jail." He argued that this money benefited the citizens of the country, since his government used it to pay long-overdue pensions and other arrears accumulated under Shevardnadze.

The government did indeed pay many of the arrears, but this in no way addresses the fact that there was no legal basis for the government to accept payments from alleged criminals in return for their freedom. Simply calling these payments "fines" did not legitimize the process, since these fines were not authorized by the law. Saakashvili ignored the fact that you could not build a system of the rule of law if the state itself was willing to set the rule of law aside. He also did not seem to understand that off-the-books exchange of payments from individuals whom the government was accusing of criminal activity actually created an environment of state criminality and the rule of men, instead of law.

Through such actions, the state seemed to be acting like a criminal mob—using tactics that under the most favorable interpretation were legally questionable (though most likely actually illegal), but certainly morally unacceptable. The government was terrorizing its own citizens to force them to pay bribes in order to avoid retribution. This tactic was not very different from a mobster coming to a small storeowner, twisting his arms and putting a gun to his head, and telling him that for a certain payment, his life would be spared, his business would be able to continue in operation, and he could receive protection from the mob. Both are racketeering, though government-sponsored racketeering is far more unacceptable, because it is far more detrimental to the rule of law in a transitional democracy than that of the mob.

Saakashvili's bribery scheme was nothing less than a symptom of corruption, and was just as illegitimate (if not more so) as the actions of the Shevardnadze government, which he was condemning and allegedly fighting through these arrests. The government's actions once again perpetuated an environment, in which not every person was equal before the law, and one's ability to bribe, rather than the merits of the case, determined how the law applied to a given individual.

It was particularly troubling that this "punishment" was very selective: for every former corrupt official that was arrested and forced to pay, many others were never touched, because of their past relations with Saakashvili or Zhvania, or their tacit support for the revolution. As a result, once the government had finished its arrests and extortion of funds about a year after the revolution, the inequality of citizens before the law was a greater problem than it had ever been before; some who were close to the officials in the government were treated favorably, while others were forced to bribe the state.

To this day, Saakashvili is proud of his government's actions. In his 2005 State of the Nation address, he declared that "I have shown the world that I can force them to bring back the money, and I will force even others to bring it back."[10] For Saakashvili and his supporters, these actions were nothing more than their way of fulfilling the promise they had made during the campaign for the November 2003 parliamentary elections to force corrupt government officials to pay for their crimes. It did not matter that the extralegal, off-the-books method of doing this was not only reminiscent of Bolshevism, but was also corrupting the Georgian state and society as a whole to levels never seen before.

The reason the government acted this way is that Saakashvili cares about ends much more than he cares about the means. Some may argue (pointing to Lincoln's suspension of the *habeas corpus* during the Civil War) that this may be less of a problem if one's ends are noble. In some respects this is true, since the Constitution is not a suicide pact, though freedom is worth too much to be sacrificed for even the most noble ends. However, disregard for means is a particular problem when the ends themselves are questionable, as has been the case with Saakashvili. Furthermore, Saakashvili's willingness to set aside the law without any qualms points to his naturally autocratic instincts. These were also obvious in his push for constitutional amendments that consolidated all state power in his hands. These instincts further complicated the very possibility of further democratic development during his rule.

Even if one accepts Saakashvili's line of argument that these detentions and payments were a means of punishing corrupt former government officials, one is left to wonder why the government chose to treat private businesses and entrepreneurs in a similar way, given that Saakashvili had promised them full amnesty. A leading figure in the American Chamber of Commerce in Georgia joked, sixteenth months after the revolution, that the "government simply went down the AmChem list and demanded payments from every single business, with amounts determined by the size of the business,"[11] with the few exceptions being made for those businesses and businessmen who had supported Saakashvili's and Zhvania's campaign in 2003. If the goal was to fight corruption in the higher echelons of the government, why make businesses pay for the sins of the old, corrupt government?

One of the most absurd cases of extortion from the private sector took place in the summer of 2004, during the height of the South Ossetia crisis (described in detail below). In need of money to purchase ammunition for the fighting with the Ossetian separatists, the government demanded a $5 million payment from the Bank of Georgia, one of the most successful financial institutions in the country, whose largest shareholder with a 14 percent stake is the European Bank for Reconstruction and Development (EBRD). The bank paid, knowing that it would end up losing far more money if it decided to challenge the government. While this development was never made public, in private government officials described the payment as "voluntary."

A few weeks later, the Bank of Georgia hosted a reception for the U.S.-Georgia Business Council conference, which was taking place in Tbilisi, where I ran into the bank's director of investor relations and asked her how this incident made her feel about the government. "Well, how do you think it makes me feel?" responded this charismatic woman whom I had known since childhood, who holds an MBA from George Washington University, and who had been an avid supporter of Zhvania and Saakashvili for years. Not sure of how to interpret the response, I then asked her if this incident made her lose hope in the new government. The response was probably more striking than the government's actual treatment of the Bank of Georgia: "Well, only partially." While I could not understand this, since I saw the government's action as a simple robbery, this response spoke volumes about the way most Georgians perceived the new government—they had placed such great hopes in Saakashvili that they were unwilling to let these hopes die easily. That fact in itself placed immense responsibility on Saakashvili to make good on his promises and to avoid actions that so blatantly flew in the face of the rule of law.

International Complacency

One should not be surprised by Saakashvili's unwillingness to see anything wrong with his actions, given much of the world's applause for the "fight against corruption." Many foreign officials, leaders of nongovernmental organizations, and regional scholars acknowledged (mostly in private discussions, though some in public) the problems with Saakashvili's approach, but most argued that ultimately this was the "Georgian people's money" and it was important to get it back.[12] No one disputed the fact that getting back the money could be viewed as a good development; the concern was about the methods that were being used, because they were contrary to everything the West wanted to see in Georgia. Unfortunately, that fact was never considered seriously by any of the foreign apologists for Saakashvili's behavior.

Imagine if the U.S. government publicly alleged that a former federal official was guilty of accepting huge bribes and was responsible for stealing large amounts from the federal budget, and then, as a means of dealing with the accused, the government used Special Forces to arrest him, kept him in jail for months without any real evidence, eventually releasing him after he agreed to pay handsomely into the Treasury, without ever reaching a legal settlement about his alleged crimes—and doing so without any transparency about what amount he actually paid and why. Now imagine the U.S. government doing this not once, but with dozens of individuals who were not only accused of bribery and theft from the state, but whose actions were allegedly at least partly responsible for the collapse of the country's economy.

Undoubtedly, neither the U.S. Congress nor the American people would ever accept such blatant disregard for the law on the part of federal prosecutors, because a regime acting in this way can never lay claim to the values of liberal democracy. Yet this is precisely what Saakashvili's government did repeatedly after he came to power, and nevertheless, U.S. officials and other foreigners applauded his actions as a defeat for corruption.[13] Blaming the senior-most decision makers would be wrong—because they were provided with information by mid-level subordinates, they simply lacked detailed knowledge about what was happening on the ground in Georgia. Real blame lies with these mid-level officials, who refused to look reality in the eye even though most knew very well what was going on. Having tied their fate to Saakashvili, these officials were determined to protect his status as a reformer for as long as possible.[14]

When debating the government's actions, many of Georgia's foreign friends acknowledged that Saakashvili's tactics would never be accepted in the United States or Western Europe, but argued that the same high standards should not be applied to Georgia. This position is troubling for two reasons. First, those making these claims were the same individuals who justified a revolutionary change of government in Georgia because the old regime failed to provide for fully fair and free elections that met Western standards in 2003. Thus, their double standard inevitably begs the question—why was it acceptable to hold the old government accountable on the question of elections using Western standards, but not permissible to apply the same standards to hold the new government (of which much more was expected) accountable on the issue of individual rights and liberties?

Second, while no one expected or even hoped that the Saakashvili government would be as protective of individual rights and the rule of law as, say, the U.S. or British governments, Saakashvili needed to at least try to move in the right direction. This was particularly true if Georgia were to be viewed as a success story of democratic development, and if it ever were to have any hope of becoming a functional, liberal democracy where the rule of law and human rights are sacrosanct. Yet, during Saakashvili's first year and a half in power, the Georgian state was moving far away from these values, not closer to them. Thus, instead of becoming a democratic success story because of the Rose Revolution, the Georgian human-rights record was deteriorating, in order to make it possible for the leaders responsible for the revolution to maintain power. Those foreigners who closed their eyes to these actions because they were supporting the Georgian government were doing a great disservice not only to the Georgian people, but to the very government that they hoped to support—

because no government could ever succeed in Georgia unless it first and foremost secured and protected justice and the rule of law. Furthermore, in many cases, they were also damaging their own national-security interests, which would have benefited from truly democratic developments in Georgia.

One of the most glaring examples of international complacency about the preposterous actions of the Georgian authorities was the "Compact to Promote Transparency and Combat Corruption: A New Partnership between the G8 and Georgia," a document issued by the G8 Summit at Seal Island, Georgia, on July 10, 2004.[15] The document included a statement by the Georgian government and a statement from the G8 governments, who pledged some general steps toward combating corruption not specifically aimed at Georgia, and then a number of small steps specific to Georgia. The trouble with this document was twofold: the Georgian statement was full of claims that had no basis in truth, while the G8 statement failed to even acknowledge the farce that the Georgian government's "anti-corruption" drive had become. Discussing all of the Georgian claims would be impossible, because almost every sentence was either only partly true or completely false. However, I consider some of the key examples below:

The Georgian side claimed that they had conducted "unprecedented arrests of former ministers including Minister of Energy, Minister of Transportation, the Head of the Georgian Customs, the Head of the Georgian Railways, the Deputy Head of the Tax Administration and regional government officials." On its face this was true—these individuals, and many others, had indeed been detained and confined to jail, at least for a short period of time. However, none of these individuals, except for the former minister of energy, had been charged with a real crime—not only as of June 10, 2004, when this statement was issued, but even as late as April 15, 2005. Meanwhile, the due-process rights of each one of the arrested individuals had been violated during their detention. Furthermore, if one assumes (as do most Georgians) that these individuals (or many others who had been arrested) were actually guilty of crimes, everyone except the former minister of energy was let out of jail scot-free, with no criminal record to their names, simply because they paid off the government with large sums.[16]

While the Georgian statement claimed that "in new Georgia accountability means enforcement of laws even if violators are rich and powerful," and that "through our resolute actions, we have demonstrated that no one is above the law," the reality on the ground proved exactly the opposite. Actually, the rich were above the law to an extent never seen in Georgia before, because the new government had sanctioned a scheme to allow known or alleged criminals to pay their way out of jail. Indeed, Georgia had implemented a two-tiered legal system—one for those who could afford to pay off the state, and another for those who could not or did not want to pay. This two-tiered system allowed the government to boast about the increased budget revenue. Instead of promoting the rule of law, the new Georgian scheme undermined the country's legal-justice system and law enforcement at every turn.

In the statement, the Georgians also took credit for passing "anti-corruption legislation that streamlines indictment and prosecution procedures, enables the use of plea bargains, and allows the confiscation of assets gained through criminal activity." Leaving aside the question of the constitutionality of most of these provisions, such legislation indeed passed the Parliament. However, in no circumstance involving the individuals named above, or other former government officials or businessmen who were forced to pay bribes to the government to be released from jail, did the prosecutors actually take advantage of this new legislation. It would have been one thing for the state to accept guilty pleas from the accused individuals and either force them to serve a shorter term in jail than they would have been eligible for in case of conviction, or if convicted, confiscate property and accept a fine from those admitting guilt *within the confines of the law.* The problem was that these individuals were never actually charged with crimes, nor were they ever indicted—let alone forced to plead guilty. Instead, they simply paid the government in return for their freedom.

The Georgians further claimed that "we [the government] will share our financial data with the public and elected representatives in Parliament." Yet in reality, in 2004 alone the executive branch spent over US $200 million of state money through special funds set up and administered directly by the president. The above pledge about disclosure of financing was utterly disingenuous, while the failure to receive parliamentary approval for the executive branch's spending prior to the expenditures being made was a violation of the Georgian Constitution and laws.

Probably the most outrageous of the Georgian claims came at the end of the statement, when the government pledged to work with the Parliament and civil society to "ensure that checks and balances remain vigorous so that executive power is not abused again in our country." This was coming from individuals who had eliminated any semblance of republican-style checks and balances in the Georgian Constitution, and created a government system that formally sanctions one-man rule—and had done this by forcing the Parliament to vote on three readings of constitutional changes in eighteen minutes.

On the G8 side, the claims and pledges were far more modest, with the group promising to assist Georgia in the effort to fight corruption and promote transparency. However, coming nine months into the new government's tenure, when its failure to implement any real anti-corruption reforms was so plainly obvious, one could and should have expected a group that includes the world's leading democracies to speak with a little more moral clarity about what was happening on the ground in Georgia. Instead, the G8 signed on to a statement from the Georgian government that in alleging promotion of transparency, accountability, and integrity sounded too much like the Constitution of the Soviet Union, which on paper protected all rights and liberties one could imagine, yet in practice violated people's most fundamental freedoms on a daily basis. By ignoring the real situation in Georgia and accepting the government's disingenuous claims, the G8 was closing its eyes to dramatic failures on the Georgian road to democracy, and was encouraging the Georgian side to continue on a path that could never result in real, positive change.

Judiciary

During Shevardnadze's tenure, foreign donors, including the USAID, often viewed the judiciary as the most "reformed" of Georgia's political institutions, even though constitutionally it was the least developed. Saakashvili always took credit for creating the exam system for judges in 1999, which allowed for the removal of many of the most corrupt and incompetent judges. It is indeed true that the initial laws reforming the judiciary, passed in May of that year, had an important Saakashvili imprint on them. However, more than anyone, the CEELI program of the American Bar Association (ABA) should claim responsibility for this truly successful testing program, which over the years was cited as an excellent example for how to institute judiciary reforms in transitional countries. Partly because of this program, and partly because Shevardnadze's regime chose not to pressure the judges too often (except for high profile, important cases), in the late 1990s Georgia developed a semblance of an independent judiciary.

This semi-independence was particularly true of the Supreme Court, whose chairman, Lado Chanturia, had a reputation for impartiality and was often mentioned as a possible presidential candidate in 2005. Leading lawyers and human-rights activists, most of whom strongly opposed Shevardnadze's rule, credited the old government with seldom pressuring the Supreme Court to issue particular rulings. They also claimed that when such pressure was exerted, Chanturia was usually successful at rebuffing it.[17]

The Rose Revolution destroyed even the semblance of an independent judiciary, both in form and practice. First, as we have already discussed, Saakashvili's constitutional amendments drastically increased the presidential powers over the judiciary. Second, in July 2004, the Parliament adopted legislation that gave the president additional powers to discipline judges (Supreme Court judges were exempt). Then, in January 2005, Saakashvili proposed even more drastic constitutional amendments aimed at restructuring the entire judiciary; his proposal made FDR's court-packing gamble look mild by comparison. If passed, it would have dismissed the chairman and members of the Constitutional Court and members of the Supreme Court (while keeping the chairman of the latter court, who was the only Saakashvili appointee on that bench). Additionally, the proposal would have empowered the president to appoint all members of the Constitutional Court (previously, three members were appointed by the president, three by the Parliament, and three by a panel of senior judges) and to reappoint them to a second term. The proposal would also have reduced the age of eligibility for the high-court appointments.

Many Georgian NGOs and legal scholars, as well as the international community and even some of Saakashvili's own deputies in Parliament, protested the amendments. They argued that the amendments would destroy the entire judicial system in Georgia, enable the president to appoint inexperienced individuals to the bench, and give him greater influence over judiciary decision-making by permitting reappointment. Embarrassed under this pressure, Saakashvili withdrew the amendments. However, the most interesting fact is that Saakashvili and his allies thought the amendments were a good idea. This speaks volumes about their views of judicial independence. Furthermore, the main point that Saakashvili wanted to make in proposing the amendments was very clear to all judges—they had the choice of either toeing the governmental line, or losing their positions if they acted independently.

The judiciary's actual performance as an independent entity has been less than exemplary since the Rose Revolution, not simply because of government pressure, but also because it chose to be wholly complacent about Saakashvili's disregard for the law. As a result, the judiciary has been a rubber stamp for many of the most dangerous actions of the new government. Initially, the judiciary stood by and sanctioned arrests of questionable legitimacy. Its role was so absurd that when talking about the pretrial detention hearings, defense lawyers would often comment that these "hearings" were reminiscent of Communist-era judicial decision-making, when court hearings were a mere façade and judges simply handed down decisions that were made by Communist officials. During the hearings, judges not only granted nearly every one of the prosecutors' demands for pretrial detention, but also did not question weak and unconvincing evidence often presented to them by the government, such as allegations that anti-tank weapons were discovered in a closet of the arrested individual's child, even though the very same weapon had been used as evidence against some other accused individual the week before.

Judges also ignored clear-cut evidence of torture of prisoners who were paraded in their court rooms, especially in cases when the government was demanding extension of pretrial detentions. Whereas the U.S. State

Department's Report on Human Rights Practices for 2005 states that over 1,000 cases of torture were documented among those who were in pretrial confinement in 2004 in Georgia,[18] there was not a single example of a judge raising an alarm about such incidents involving an individual whose case he was responsible for, nor did a judge ever sanction the state for its failure to provide for the well-being of a prisoner who was under its care. Realizing that many of their decisions about pretrial detention made no sense, judges often closed the hearings to the press and the public. While this was a blatant violation of the Administrative Law, the framework legislation aimed at garnering greater government transparency, it was a better alternative for most judges than being exposed in the media as rubber stamps for the government's improprieties.

THE SULKHAN MOLASHVILI CASE

Some of the worst examples of judicial complacency with government's illegal activity involved those former officials who refused demands to pay for their freedom. The best-publicized and also most brutal case involved Sulkhan Molashvili, the former head of the Chamber of Control who had made many allegations about impropriety by Saakashvili during his tenure as minister of justice and head of the Tbilisi City Council. Molashvili was arrested on April 23, 2004, on allegations that he embezzled state funds and had abused his authority as the head of the chamber. His arrest was almost half a year into the new government's tenure, and rumors of his planned detention had circulated in Georgia for over a month. Furthermore, Molashvili reported to the prosecutor general's office on his own volition. Thus, he was neither a flight risk, since he knew full well that his arrest was imminent and could have chosen to run away prior to that, nor was he unwilling to cooperate with the investigation. Nevertheless, after his detention, the prosecutor demanded, and was granted, a three-month pretrial detention for Molashvili.

In July 2004, Molashvili agreed to hand over some of his property to win his release, though he refused to pay the sum that was demanded of him. His detention was extended three times, and he was not brought to trial until the late summer of 2005. The only formal charge against him was that he moved 10,000 lari within the Chamber of Control's budget from one spending line item to another, without legislative approval. Even if true, such a violation is insignificant in comparison to how the new government often completely refuses to grant the Parliament any say in the appropriations process, virtually managing finances through administrative fiat.

Procedural violations of Molashvili's rights pale in comparison to his treatment in jail after his detention. In June 2004, just two months after his arrest, Molashvili was shown on national television, having lost at least sixteen kilograms, about one-fifth of his weight.[19] He had cigarette burns all over his body, and there was evidence of electric shock. Molashvili looked like someone who had spent several months in a hard-labor camp in Siberia. In some respects, the suffering visible on most Iraqi prisoners in the Abu Ghraib pictures can hardly be compared to the visible suffering Molashvili experienced as a result of torture at the hands of the Georgian authorities. After a national and international outrage that arose following the release of tapes documenting the torture, Molashvili was transferred to a prison hospital. Throughout that period, between April and July, his family was not allowed to visit him. Eventually, family visitation rights were restored at the demand of outraged parliamentarians from the Council of Europe.

Indeed, not only was the family not allowed to visit Molashvili, but initially even members of the Georgian Parliament, who are legally authorized to see prisoners, were not permitted to see him. Only after the absurdity of this decision was raised during the legislative session and became an embarrassment for Speaker Nino Burdjanadze did she demand that the prosecutor general permit David Gamkrelidze, the leader of the opposition, to see Molashvili. While in July 2004 the prosecutor general opened a criminal investigation into Molashvili's torture case, no one was charged with any crimes, and it is unlikely that anyone will ever be.

No one disputes that Molashvili is probably guilty of some crimes—a person who was a government employee for much of his adult life could not have legitimately amassed all the property that Molashvili handed over to the state in July 2004. However, it is clear that the government never cared about Molashvili's guilt or innocence, nor did it care to build a case against him that could lead to his conviction in the court of law. His arrest and torture were a payback for Molashvili's many anti-Saakashvili pronouncements, for his willingness to speak publicly about alleged corruption in the government agencies on Saakashvili's watch prior to the Rose Revolution, and for his unwillingness to pay the state after his arrest. No matter what his crimes may have been, they could never reach the magnitude of the crimes that he suffered at the hands of the state, when his fundamental rights as a citizen were wholly ignored. What is most problematic, however, is the way in which the judiciary refused to investigate Molashvili's torture, even though the courts had placed him into pretrial detention under the state's protection, and proof of his torture was undisputed. Instead, the judge presiding over Molashvili's case simply extended his pretrial detention twice.[20]

Some may argue that while this case may be gruesome, developments in Georgia cannot be compared to the actions of truly authoritarian regimes elsewhere in the former Soviet Union, Africa, the Middle East, and Asia. To an extent, this is indeed true. The Georgian state at its worst does not come close to Mugabe's regime in Zimbabwe, or Karimov's regime in Uzbekistan.[21] However, Georgia must be measured not against the lowest common denominator, but against where it used to be before the allegedly "democratic revolution." In such a comparison, the trend in Georgia is sadly and clearly regressive, rather than progressive.

THE AMERICAN BAR ASSOCIATION'S HONOR FOR SAAKASHVILI

It was in this environment that in the spring of 2004, Carolyn Clark Campbell, the director of the ABA/CEELI program in Georgia, nominated Saakashvili for her organization's Central European and Eurasian Law Initiative Award. In July, Saakashvili was announced as the winner of the award for (in the words of ABA president Dennis Archer) having "embraced the rule of law and steered his country away from a legacy of corruption."[22] Saakashvili himself claimed that the award was for his "contribution to the reform of the legal system."[23] The fact that there was a clear conflict between the rationale for the award and the real picture in Georgia occurred to neither the ABA nor Campbell. Nor did the ABA seem to care about how the blatant denial of due process, evidence of torture, and violation of the most fundamental rights that was taking place on Saakashvili's watch against hundreds of citizens could be billed as an embrace of the rule of law.

Furthermore, it did not seem ironic to Saakashvili that he was being honored for "reforms" that apparently had no impact, since he was now pressing wholly new judicial "reforms." In a conversation about this several weeks after the award was given in August 2004, Campbell explained to me that she saw many problems related to the respect for law under the new government, but she supported giving Saakashvili the award, because as winner of this prize he would be less inclined to act improperly. Meanwhile, she would be in a position to seek his support for the judicial reforms. Whatever one makes of this explanation, there is little doubt that Campbell was also enthusiastic about the fact that having a winner from Georgia made her work in the country look good and shone a positive light on the ABA's ostensive "success" in Georgia. From the perspective of protecting the rule of law in the United States, one can only hope that the ABA will give more honest treatment to future federal judicial nominees than it did to Saakashvili.

12

Elections and Imbalanced Governance

When the Supreme Court canceled the results of the Parliament's proportional elections in late November 2003, it became apparent that Georgia would go through another protracted election campaign. It was up to Acting President Burdjanadze to set the date for the elections. Opposition parties demanded a vote in late spring or early summer to allow for enough time to fix the electoral lists, which were the principal reason for fraud and irregularities during the November vote. Meanwhile, Saakashvili was demanding a quick vote—preferably in late January or early February, soon after his presumptive inauguration as president. Burdjanadze should be credited with withstanding pressure from Saakashvili and setting the election date for March 28, 2004, between the two time frames suggested by the opposing sides.

Burdjanadze showed less independence when it came to establishing the framework for truly democratic and fair elections, when she gave in to Saakashvili's demands for electoral commissions that was stacked with his supporters. Soon after taking over as acting president, Burdjanadze asked the Parliament to amend the Electoral Code to give the president sole authority, with the legislature's consent, to appoint the chairman of the Central Election Commission (CEC)—as opposed to the complex scheme that had been proposed by Baker in the summer involving the Organization for Security and Cooperation in Europe (OSCE) preselecting candidates from whom the president would then choose a CEC chair.

Burdjanadze, Saakashvili, and Zhvania also rejected proposals aimed at making the CEC's composition conform to the real Baker formula, which had been the rallying cry of all opposition parties against Shevardnadze in the summer of 2003. Indeed, in one of the clearest signs that the new government had no plans of actually making good on its democratic rhetoric, the new leaders disavowed their past demands about parity on the CEC. Instead, Burdjanadze appointed five new CEC members to replace Shevardnadze's old presidential appointees, while the National Movement and United Democrats kept their "opposition" seats, even though they now represented the government. As a result, the new government had an eight-person (out of fifteen) voting majority in the CEC as well as district and precinct commissions (the chairman, five presidential appointees, and two "opposition" members). The decision to ignore calls for fairness on the CEC made little sense to anyone who was following the events in Georgia, given that the main justification for the revolution was Shevardnadze's failure to provide for free and fair elections, something that was impossible to achieve because of the stacked CEC.

Presidential Elections, January 2004

The reconfigured CEC's first task under Chairman Zurab Chiaberashvili—who as executive director of the NGO Fair Elections had been responsible, along with the National Democratic Institute for International Affairs (NDI), for the parallel vote tabulations (PVT) in November—was to organize the vote for president in January 2004. This was not so much an election as a coronation, since all potential serious opponents (Burdjanadze, David Gamkrelidze, Shalva Natelashvili, Badri Patarkatsishvili) refused to challenge Saakashvili for the post, because no one thought a fair election was possible in the postrevolutionary environment. While probably only Patarkatsishvili would have had a chance of defeating Saakashvili had he chosen to run,[1] the lack of serious alternative candidates made the Georgian election look more like a "referendum" for the president of Egypt than an exercise in democratic governance.

Nonetheless, the new CEC faced a challenge in needing to make the elections look legitimate. This problem could only be solved with a legally questionable scheme. Because the Constitution required the presidential election to be held within forty-five days of Shevardnadze's resignation, the vote fell in the middle of the Georgian holiday season—January 4, 2005. Yet the Constitution mandated a 50 percent plus one voter turnout to validate the elections. Everyone assumed that getting such a high turnout three days after New Year's Day and three days before Georgian Orthodox Christmas would be almost impossible.

To solve this problem, the CEC decided to make new voter lists from a blank slate, and to count as voters only those individuals who would preregister in advance or register on Election Day, rather than all eligible voters as required by law. This way, meeting the 50 percent mark would no longer be a problem. The trouble was that this scheme was clearly illegal. In the summer of 2003, as part of the reforms to try to prevent fraud, the Parliament passed changes to the Electoral Code mandating the Justice and Interior ministries to prepare a national registry of voters, which was to be used to screen eligible voters at polling places on Election Day. Furthermore, chapter 2 of the Code banned preregistration or addition of voters to the voting lists on Election Day. The reasoning behind this was quite simple: since the right to vote was guaranteed in the Constitution, you could not have preregistration without allowing Election Day registration; yet adding people to the electoral lists on Election Day was dangerous, because Zurab Zhvania had used "additional lists" of people registering on Election Day as a key electoral manipulation tactic in 1995 and 1999 by adding nonexistent "voters" to the rolls.

These clear legal guidelines notwithstanding, CEC chairman Chiaberashvili ordered creation of new lists through preregistration and Election Day registration, explaining that emergency circumstances associated with the need to hold elections so quickly left him no choice. As a result, the CEC placed itself in the position of Parliament by making new law. Much like most others who came to power after the revolution, Chiaberashvili justified disobeying the law by invoking necessity—ends, he claimed, were far more important than the means.

Eight days after the vote on January 4, Chiaberashvili announced that 1,964,556 voters went to the polls, out of 2,231,946 registered voters. If this turnout figure was real,[2] it was actually higher than the 50 percent threshold of all eligible voters (based on the total eligible-voter figure of 3,178,593 from the November 2003 elections). Thus, if this was a real number, the election would have been legitimate even without the manipulation of the election law conceived by Chiaberashvili. However, because the elections were conducted with an illegal registration scheme, the entire process was open to attack, with many alleging that voters who had not actually been to the polls and had not registered were added to the rolls on Election Day in order to increase the turnout rate. The validity of these claims is hard to prove, but detractors' ability to raise them, made possible because a majority in the CEC had ignored the law, was another example of the vulnerability of the "ends justify the means" tactics.

Parliamentary Elections, March 2004

After the presidential vote, all eyes turned to the parliamentary election on March 28, 2004, which National Movement was clearly going to win overwhelmingly. When Burdjanadze set this date in January, the situation looked very bleak for the opposition parties, with all of them nearly dead in the water:

in one private poll, the New Rights Party was at about 3 percent, Labor below 2 percent, and other parties not even registering.[3] However in February, when the revolutionary euphoria began to die down, people's attention turned to the wave of arrests and alterations to the Constitution, creating a small but sizable percentage of citizens that were questioning the government's actions. Furthermore, in the polls, the public expressed a strong preference for an opposition presence in the future Parliament.

In mid-February, the New Rights Party commissioned a poll that suggested it was possible for the party to overcome the 7 percent barrier in the elections in March, but only if the party formed a center-right alliance with the Industry Will Save Georgia party, the only other opposition group that was viewed favorably by the public. The rationale behind an alliance between New Rights and Industry was logical and, as discussed earlier, had been attempted twice before, to no avail. This time around, with both parties realizing that they could only succeed together, the leaders put aside their differences and formed a coalition for the March election, and also promised to work toward unifying the two parties in the future.

The two parties in the government (Saakashvili's National Movement and Zhvania's United Democrats) were also uncertain about how to run in the elections. Saakashvili was legitimately afraid that if the government ran a slate of candidates under the banner of a temporary electoral coalition between these two parties, it would be easier for the Democrats to defect at a future date. For this reason, he demanded that Zhvania fold his party into the National Movement. After some public confrontation between representatives from the two camps over this issue, Saakashvili eventually got his way. Thus, the National Movement's slate was oddly similar to the Citizens Union of Georgia (CUG) slate from the 1999 elections, with one exception—Shevardnadze was no longer in the picture.

The National Movement also faced a crisis over the makeup of its electoral lists. In mid-February, while Saakashvili was on a working visit to the United States, Zhvania and Burdjanadze had a nasty public quarrel over how to divide the 40 percent of the slate that Saakashvili had allotted for their candidates. Eventually the problem was resolved when Saakashvili and Zhvania agreed to marginalize Burdjanadze and only placed about fifteen individuals offered by the speaker on their joint 150-person electoral list.

The election campaign proved particularly grueling and unfair for the opposition. For one thing, no opposition party had any certainty that it could overcome the 7 percent barrier. After taking power, Saakashvili and Zhvania promised the Council of Europe (CoE) to propose a constitutional amendment to reduce the barrier for entry into the Parliament from 7 to 4 percent. However, they refused to do so before the March 28 elections, saying that there was

insufficient time to implement this change. This claim sounded very disingenuous, given that time had been by no means a constraint for the passage of
constitutional amendments in February 2005, which restructured the entire
political regime in Georgia. Opposition parties were also largely out of money,
having spent extensively on the November elections. By contrast, the National
Movement had no trouble securing funding, through both state resources and
business community "donations." Finally, as discussed, the composition of the
election commissions was once again stacked in the government's favor, far
more so than was the case in November 2003.

In addition to money, Saakashvili put all resources of the state, including
active campaigning by regional governors and district *gamgebeli* (heads), to
work on behalf of his party's slate. Several days before the election and on Election Day, Saakashvili campaigned all over the country, with his appearances
paid for by the state. His speeches were either carried live on television, or
dominated the news coverage in the evening. Meanwhile, the media was
largely closed to the opposition. Television coverage of the campaign was often
reminiscent of the Soviet days, with the first thirty minutes of the nightly news
shows devoted to praising the government, especially Saakashvili. By contrast,
of the four main stations, only Patarkatsishvili's Imedi tried to present an opposition point of view in a balanced way on a daily basis.

As voters went the polls on March 28, no one doubted that National Movement would win an overwhelming majority. The issue was whether anyone
else could garner 7 percent of the vote and gain seats in the legislature. After
the counting started that evening, it became apparent that the New
Rights–Industry alliance was running either ahead of or close to the 7 percent
mark. However, soon thereafter, reports started to trickle in from the districts
to the party headquarters about pressure from local-government officials
demanding changes to the results: Saakashvili-appointed local-government
leaders argued that they could offer the alliance a 6.99 percent showing, but
could not allow it to be over 7 percent if they wanted to keep their jobs. Furthermore, to reinforce the idea that only National Movement succeeded in capturing enough votes to enter the Parliament, Rustavi 2 once again announced a
misleading exit poll:

National Movement (Saakashvili) . . . . .78.6 percent

Conservative Opposition: New Rights, Industry . . .4.8

Labor Party 4.4

Revival (Aslan Abashidze's party) 3.7

Political Movement Freedom 3.6

Unity 1.6

National Democratic Party (Traditionalists) 1.4

These numbers were even more inaccurate than the exit-poll results in November, as became evident from the parallel vote tabulations (PVT).[4] The NDI once again conducted the PVT, and their existence was crucial in protecting the authenticity of the election results. According to the staff at the U.S. Embassy in Tbilisi, the night of the vote, the NDI faced pressure from the government to not publicize its findings, but the local staff in Tbilisi showed strong independence and announced the following PVT tally promptly on March 29:

National Movement (Saakashvili)	67.78 percent
Conservative Opposition: New Rights, Industry	7.75
Revival (Aslan Abashidze's party)	6.60
Labor Party	6.14
Political Movement Freedom	4.72
National Democratic Party (Traditionalists)	2.38
Unity	2.19

Given that the PVT had been the Holy Grail of the Rose Revolution, it would become very difficult for Saakashvili and Chiaberashvili to ratify or accept a different official total. Nevertheless, Saakashvili initially pushed a plan to cancel results in certain districts where the New Rights–Industry alliance had done particularly well. Such cancellations would have kept the alliance out of Parliament by reducing its total below 7 percent.[5] Inside the National Movement, there was a split about how to deal with the situation; it appears that Zhvania did not want to manipulate the vote to such an extent, whereas Saakashvili, who publicly argued that New Rights–Industry had "bought" their votes, wanted the National Movement to be the only party in Parliament. Additionally, Rustavi 2's owner Erosi Kitsmarishvili, who at that point still had a great deal of influence over Saakashvili, was afraid of the NRP's relationship with Bardi Patarkatsishvili and was adamant about keeping the coalition out.

Eventually, what may have resolved the situation was active involvement on the part of U.S. Ambassador Richard Miles, who held meetings about this issue with both New Rights leader David Gamkrelidze and Zhvania on the same day in early April.[6] According to several of Zhvania's aides, he apparently pressured the prime minister to stop the process of cancellation of district results, and to keep the final results close to the PVT. According to two sources close to Zhvania, the prime minister used this outside pressure effectively to get Saakashvili to drop his demand for a one-party Parliament. Eventually, the only significant difference between the PVT and the official final results was a reduced total for Abashidze's Revival. This was caused by the CEC's decision to cancel results in two districts in Adjaria, where it alleged electoral manipulation by pro-Abashidze local officials. The final election results were:

National Movement (Saakashvili) . . . . .66.24 percent

Conservative Opposition: New Rights, Industry . .7.56

Labor Party 6.01

Political Movement Freedom 4.39

Revival (Aslan Abashidze's party) 3.86

National Democratic Party (Traditionalists) . . .2.55

Unity 2.19

These elections were without a doubt much better organized than the November vote. In addition, they were judged by international observers as the cleanest elections in Georgian history. In some respects this was true, if one compared the March 28 vote to the fraud presided over by Zhvania in 1995 and 1999, and by Shevardnadze in 2003. However, the parliamentary elections in 1990 (administered by a Communist government) and 1992 (administered by Shevardnadze in the midst of the civil war) were nonetheless the elections with the least government interference.

Lack of fraud can be partly explained by the fact that the National Movement did not require massive manipulation in order to carry the vote—it was going to win an overwhelming majority no matter what happened. However, absence of massive fraud does not mean that the elections were fair, or free of pressure against the opposition. The fact is that National Movement tried to keep all other parties out of Parliament, even though this was probably going to be to its own detriment in the long term. Furthermore, the government exercised greater control over the media than at any point since Soviet days. As a result, the March vote, like the process of the constitutional amendments and the arrests that preceded the election, raised serious questions about the commitment of Georgia's new leaders to the democratic values and principles that they ostensibly were following. In other words, what was happening in Georgia was not the shinning example of democratic success that it was portrayed to be by the Western press.

The possibility of future free and fair elections in Georgia was most called into question in May 2005, when the composition of the new Central Election Commission (CEC) was announced. Saakashvili had pushed for changes to the Electoral Code to make the CEC "nonpartisan." Allegedly, only "professional" election administration specialists were to have seats on this new commission. The law mandated the president to nominate all candidates (a total of seven), who had to be confirmed by the Parliament. Thus, nonpartisan or not, the new law gave the president complete control over the CEC. This was far worse than anything Shevardnadze and Zhvania had done in the 1990s, when the opposition had at least token representation on the commission.

To select his candidates, Saakashvili appointed a committee to screen applicants. It consisted of his chief of staff, his parliamentary secretary, the chief of his administrative office, and two "nongovernmental" representatives, including Ghia Nodia, the head of the Caucasus Institute and one of the leading advocates on behalf of the Rose Revolution.[7] All of the six individuals appointed were said to have ties to National Movement, while two were openly allied with the government: Zurab Pazhava, the deputy governor of Samegrelo, and Zurab Papiashvili, an official in the Ministry of Interior. Meanwhile, the chair of the CEC (and its seventh member) was Gia Kavtaradze, one of the four founders of the legal and financial consulting firm DVNK, whose other founders include Zurab Nogaideli, Saakashvili's second prime minister, and Levan Varshalomidze, chairman of the Adjaria Autonomous Republic's government.[8] So much for nonpartisanship.

Role of Parliament in Governance[9]

The new Parliament convened on April 22, 2004, and quickly elected Nino Burdjanadze as its speaker, completing the division of the three key posts between the revolutionary leaders. The legislature had many young members who had been National Movement activists in the past; many of them were awarded important positions in the new legislature. A number of Zhvania's close allies were elected to prominent positions as well—the deputy speaker and the chairmen of the Rules and Foreign Relations committees came from the United Democrats wing of the majority. Many parliamentarians, especially those who came from the Saakashvili wing of the majority, lacked experience and were very deferential to the National Movement's leadership. During the legislative sessions, almost every majority deputy followed the lead of four parliamentarians—Maia Nadiradze, Giga Bokeria, Giorgi Arveladze, Givi Targamadze—on what to say and how to vote. In this environment, Burdjanadze became a figurehead, while other deputies seemed to never have an independent thought of their own.

While the new Parliament was almost wholly dominated by deputies from National Movement, the majority nonetheless used every tactic imaginable to suppress the ability of the minority to play an active role in the legislature. Specifically, David Gamkrelidze asked for the New Rights–Industry coalition, as the only opposition group inside the legislature, to be recognized as a formal minority. This would have allowed his coalition to lay claim to the positions of deputy speaker and deputy chairman of all committees, which were reserved for the minority by the Parliament's bylaws. Additionally, Gamkrelidze would have become the minority leader, gaining formal privileges on the floor and authority to engage in legislative oversight of the executive. Burdjanadze was in favor of allowing this, but told Gamkrelidze that she could not decide an issue of such magnitude on her own—she could only move forward if she got a green light from the president. That incident in itself demonstrates her dramatically reduced role.

Unlike Burdjanadze, the National Movement's legislative leaders strongly opposed recognition of a formal minority. In order to prevent this, the leaders of the majority created a separate parliamentary group (called "faction" in Georgia) consisting of National Movement deputies who had been elected in the first-past-the-post districts (as compared to proportional lists). These individuals were told not to join the formal National Movement "majority," allowing the Parliament's leadership to allege that the New Rights–Industry group did not qualify for "minority" status because it did not represent more than half of those deputies who were not formally affiliated with the majority. This was a procedural ploy, but indicated the extent to which the National Movement's leadership wanted to control the legislature. Indeed, even when it came to including Gamkrelidze in the "trust group"—a four-person committee of parliamentarians legally entitled to view intelligence materials—the majority refused to ratify his appointment, even though, according to law and precedent, the second-place finisher in the elections was authorized to designate one representative in the group. After the vote, Bokeria declared that any other New Rights–Industry member would be acceptable, but not Gamkrelidze; since the opposition did not put anyone else forward, only three "trust group" positions were filled.

During Saakashvili's first year in office, few decisions with real impact were actually made by the Parliament. Instead, the legislature seemed to have two different functions. First, it played a role akin to a high-school student council, where individuals passionately argue about issues without really having any influence on the decision-making. The only viable opposition in Georgia would voice concern about the government's policies, while the pro-Saakashvili parliamentarians would respond with outrageous rhetorical claims in favor of the government. Instead of arguing issues on their merits, opponents were dubbed as "counterrevolutionaries," "traitors" or "enemies of the state." Usually, pro-Saakashvili deputies would also argue that opposition deputies did not have the right to criticize, because they had not participated in the Rose Revolution and had been "against the people." The implication of this was that those citizens who had voted for the opposition were not actual Georgians and did not have the right to have their representatives voice an opinion.

In this game of name-calling, which was very reminiscent of the Soviet period during Stalin and the two-year rule by Zviad Gamsakhurdia in 1990–91, National Movement deputies were taking their cue from Saakashvili, who also often branded his opponents with the same derogatory terms. For example, the president declared that "anyone who does not see the achievements of my government is simply an idiot, stupid, or blind."[10] He claimed that the opposition's references to the Council of Europe's negative assessment of democracy in Georgia was "provincial and funny drivel."[11] Meanwhile, those who asked for transparency in the Ministry of Defense were "digging in the garbage" and were "blind and foolish."[12] Such remarks became commonplace.

Beyond petty bickering, the Parliament became a rubber stamp for the government's "reform" initiatives—most written by the Liberty Institute, an NGO two of whose leaders had become parliamentarians. There would be a lot of debate in the legislature about various issues—such as the reform of higher education, legislature governing the media, tax policy, and so forth. A few times, the government did actually listen to the proposals coming from the legislature, as was the case with the new tax code. When this happened, it was because of the relationship of a particular deputy to the president or prime minister, rather than because of the institutional influence of the Parliament. As a result, by and large the Parliament was confined to a lot of talk and very little concrete impact on policy.

Often the Parliament did not even play the formal role of approving legislative changes—instead, Saakashvili would order changes (which required legislative action), they would be implemented, and only afterward would the Parliament modify the necessary laws to conform to these changes. This generally happened if it was necessary to appease public outrages. In most cases, this had to do with issues that Saakashvili used for publicity stunts.

For example, in the early spring of 2004, Saakashvili chaired a cabinet meeting in Zhvania's absence. Halfway through the meeting, he proposed that the cabinet go to Pirimze, a center near the State Chancellery in Tbilisi, where various tradesmen (watchmakers, electricians, tailors, etc.) rented space. The whole cabinet, as well as journalists and cameramen from all TV stations, followed the president on this expedition, where Saakashvili spoke with the various tradesmen about job creation and ways to make it easier for these small businessmen to employ more people.

During these discussions, Saakashvili declared that he was ordering an end to taxation of small entrepreneurs—one- or two-person operations no longer had to pay any taxes. This had been a campaign promise in November 2003, and a very popular one, so it made sense for Saakashvili to press forward with this change; those working at Pirimze certainly welcomed this decision. It was quite ironic when a watchmaker pointed out that the president alone could not make this decision, and that a parliamentary vote was necessary first. Saakashvili responded by saying that this did not matter, and that the small businessmen did not have to pay taxes simply because he had said so. Thus, it seemed, a watchmaker knew better than the president that changing the tax code without the Parliament was at best irregular, at worst illegal. The legislature never actually voted on this particular change, though it was in effect for months, until after a more comprehensive reform to the tax code was passed in December 2004.

Another time, in September 2004, Saakashvili visited the headquarters of the Automobile Policy (the Georgian equivalent of the Department of Motor Vehicles), where he declared that cars were no longer required to go through a yearly technical inspection, which was quite expensive and had been very unpopular for years. Saakashvili told the inspectors that this new policy would start right away, even though the technical inspection had been mandated through legislation and thus an alteration in the law was required to change this practice.

STATE FINANCES

Such contempt for the Parliament was not limited to issues that were of more mundane importance. The legislature had virtually no say—nor did it play a significant role—in overseeing the government's actions in the three most important developments during Saakashvili's tenure: state finances, construction of BTC pipeline, and conflict in Ossetia.[13]

I have touched upon the arrests of former government officials and businessmen, the collection of large sums of money from them in return for their freedom, and the failure of the government to report about two-thirds of these funds in the budget. As a result, the Parliament, which is constitutionally charged with oversight of the nation's finances, was kept completely in the dark about huge amounts of revenue and its spending, and it had absolutely no capacity to oversee or control the spending that drew from the special funds. Such spending was illegal, because the executive branch in Georgia is not allowed to spend without budgetary authorization from the legislature. Indeed, Sulkhan Molashvili's year-long confinement in jail has been explained by his alleged use of 10,000 lari for purposes other than those approved in the budget.

When opposition deputies or reporters dared to ask what the money was spent on, government officials generally responded by saying either that the information was secret, or that people should just trust the government with the spending. Eventually the pitfalls of this approach became evident, with the money being either wasted on worthless projects or spent in corrupt ways.

Some funds were used for such important tasks as the purchase of new cars for senior officials and the renovation of their offices. For example, Georgian papers have reported a 180,000 lari authorization from the President's Fund, a discretionary source of money *within* the budget, to purchase a car for the chairman of the Supreme Court, Kote Kemularia.[14] What sort of a car Kemularia planned to buy with a little under $100,000 is unclear, but it turned out that he used part of the money to renovate his office in the Supreme Court building, which had already recently been renovated with foreign assistance.

The discovery of this expenditure was accidental, and it happened only because the money came from budgetary funds. No one knows how many more hundreds of thousands, if not millions, of nonbudgetary dollars were used for similar purposes. For whatever it's worth, since the revolution, most ministers have been observed driving brand new luxury vehicles, and have been accompanied by extensive (at least two-car) motorcades.

It would not be too far-fetched to assume that at least part of the funding for a new presidential residence being built for Saakashvili also came from the secret funds collected through arrests. In Presidential Decree No. 41, which was issued on June 4, 2004, and has since been classified as "Top Secret," Saakashvili ordered the construction of an eight-building residence that will include the following:[15]

- ► The Presidential Palace, consisting of eighteen working and living rooms and five larger halls, plus rooms for security
- ► One building for VIP guests
- ► One building for the National Security Council, housing 80 staffers
- ► Two buildings for the presidential administration, housing 200 staffers
- ► One building for housekeeping and maintenance staff
- ► Ten-car garage
- ► Underground space for "special automobiles"
- ► Open space in front of the president's offices for guest receptions, parades, and a garden
- ► A helicopter landing pad.

The decree also includes an odd clause stating the following: "Accept suggestion from the Parliamentarian Valeri Gelashvili, that prior to the determination of financing sources [for the residence], on his own expense, he be permitted to conduct planning, engineering, and construction work."[16]

When Saakashvili first announced his desire for a new presidential residence on a hilltop overlooking Old Tbilisi, next to the new central Cathedral of the Georgian Orthodox Church, he claimed that it would be located in a slightly remodeled building, which at that time housed the district police. Initially, work on the residence seemed to follow this claim, with construction crews focusing on renovations to the police building. However, since the decree was issued in June 2004, the police building in question has been fully demolished and a new building is being constructed in its place. According to two different owners of construction companies that specialize in building high-end residential apartment buildings (whom I spoke with in Tbilisi), a project based on the specifications spelled out in the decree should cost at least $25–30 million.

Few in Georgia dispute the need for the president to have an appropriate living and work space. However, given that Tbilisi already has spaces that meet most of the specifications outlined in the decree (though they are probably not as posh as what Saakashvili envisions), it remains an open question whether Georgia can afford to spend so much money on such a project. Incidentally, whatever the merits of this project, in most open societies the media would undoubtedly launch an investigation into it and its sources of funding. Yet not a word has been uttered about this subject on Georgian television.

Part of the money collected through detentions also went to procure heavy and light military equipment. This included helicopters, self-propelled artillery, T-72 tanks, and infantry-fighting vehicles—largely from Ukraine and the Czech Republic, but allegedly the black market as well. However, because everything was bought in secret, it is unclear how much of the equipment actually addresses Georgia's military and security needs. NATO military advisors, who visit Georgia regularly as part of the Individual Partnership Action Plan (IPAP) that the organization signed with Georgia in the spring of 2004, were reportedly dumbstruck during their visit in the winter of 2005 by the lack of accountability in military spending and the government's failure to consider Georgia's strategic needs when making these purchases. According to one foreign official involved in the discussions with the NATO experts, "No one in the government even considered checking about the lifecycle of the equipment that the country is buying and how this equipment fits with NATO standards," which Georgia hoped to approach as part of its bid to eventually join the alliance. In the words of another NATO observer, the Ministry of Defense "is just spending. There is no planning. There is no acquisition or procurement process. No feasibility study." "It looks cool. But the hard work is building military institutions—and they have done none of this,"[17] said another.

The National Movement deputies did not care that the legislature's formal and legally mandated role was being wholly ignored in determining military spending. Once, in a TV debate between the legislative majority and the opposition in the fall of 2004, Maia Nadiradze, Parliament's majority leader, praised the defense spending by the government and the improvements that ostensibly had taken place in the armed forces. An opposition deputy then inquired about the funds that were used for these purchases and improvements, since they had not been included in the official budget. Nadiradze's response was mind-boggling: "This was financed through 'other money,'" she said.[18] In other words, the National Movement's parliamentary leader was admitting that there was a shady, nontransparent, off-the-budgetary-books source of funds that the government was using for defense purposes and keeping out of parliamentary oversight.

Nadiradze was probably referring to the aforementioned Army Development Fund, whose name did not become publicly available until 2005. Government officials described this fund as a "non-profit foundation" with contributions from "businessmen living abroad."[19] In reality, according to National Movement parliamentarians, most of the contributions to this fund have come from Georgians who paid to secure their release from detention. How much money has gone through the fund is unclear; estimates range from $12 to $93 million. The latter figure seems closer to the true amount, since the government allegedly collected $200 million of unreported money from various detained individuals in return for their freedom.

There was no way to know if the money in the Army Development Fund was used properly or whether necessary steps had been taken to avoid corruption, since no oversight authority had access to them. When the opposition approached Minister of Defense Irakli Okruashvili on this issue in 2005, he declared that allegations of impropriety were "nonsense" because the spending had been reported to the Parliament's "trust group," all three of whose members are from the National Movement.[20] In his view, the Georgian people had to simply trust that the Ministry of Defense was doing the right thing. This may indeed have been the case, but there was no way to verify this since there was no transparency to the spending. For whatever it's worth, President Saakashvili backed up Okruashvili's comments by stating that "nothing can stop progress in the Georgian army," and that "one would have to be blind and foolish to not see the progress." According to the president, critics are "searching in the garbage and will find good things" if they do not stop.[21]

Such disregard for transparency in defense spending should not be surprising, considering how the executive branch has approached budgetary spending and the Parliament's role in overseeing state finances in general. For example, in the 2004 budget, 10 million lari were appropriated for the President's Fund (the one from which the Supreme Court chairman's car was purchased for $100,000) when the budget was approved by the Parliament. However, it became public in January 2005 that the president had spent 40 million lari instead. As a result, the Parliament voted to amend the budget after the fact, in mid-February, to increase the President's Fund expenditures.[22] The story repeated itself in 2005, when in the first quarter of the year Saakashvili spent 12 million lari, even though only 10 million had been approved in the budget.

Another interesting area of nontransparent expenditures is what appears like lobbying and legal work in Washington, on which the government spent almost half a million dollars in 2005. This comes from a report on the financial monitoring of the Georgian President's and Government's Reserve Funds, called "Georgia's Government under a Very Hot Sun," prepared by the Georgian Young Lawyers' Association (GYLA). On March 16, 2005, the president authorized an expenditure of $377,500 in order to "finance consulting work provided to the Georgian government in connection to Georgia's integration into NATO and other Western organizations."[23] When GYLA contacted his administrative office to inquire about what work was done and how the contractor was selected, it received a response saying, "We [the president's office] do not possess documents regarding the information that you requested," because "funds were authorized from the President's Fund to the Ministry of Finance."

GYLA then contacted the Ministry of Finance, which reported that it had two documents related to this expenditure—two agreements signed between Orion Strategies and Ambassador of Georgia to the United States Levan Mikeladze on March 15, 2005.[24] The documents are identical, except one is for the amount of $120,000 and the other for $240,000. When GYLA contacted the Ministry of Finance to ask why there were two agreements signed with the same firm, on the same day, for the exact same work, but with different amounts, the ministry replied that it "does not have the capacity to answer questions posed in your letter because the Ministry is not the purchasing organization."

A couple of weeks later, on April 5, 2005, the prime minister authorized an expenditure of $80,000 to a "Law Offices [of] Paige E. Reefe," from the Government's Reserve Fund.[25] When GYLA contacted the State Chancellery to inquiry what was purchased for this expenditure, it received a response stating, "Regarding your letter, I [Petre Mamradze, chief of staff to the prime minister] am letting you know that [the] Georgian government does not possess [the] documents you mention." GYLA's report states that "our attempt to find some sort of information about the firm mentioned in the authorization on the Internet . . . proved unsuccessful." I also searched for Paige E. Reefe via Google and could only find only one link: Paige E. Reefe of 3300 Lowell St. NW, in Washington, D.C., was paid a "salary" of $2,088.68 by John Kerry for President, Inc., on August 13, 2004.[26]

These incidents probably speak for themselves. Orion Strategies has done a good job at advancing Georgia's cause in Washington and at NATO—Georgia has a better chance of becoming a NATO member now than ever before. However, as Orion's own hiring process demonstrates, the cause of potential membership in NATO has largely been advanced by presenting a picture of something that the country is not—a nation on the road of reform. Whether a potential NATO member should have a government procurement process that is similar to what one finds is Georgia is an open question.

BTC CONSTRUCTION CRISIS

Beyond state finances, another area in which legislative oversight was nonexistent involves the construction of the Baku-Tbilisi-Ceyhan (BTC) oil pipeline, which was entering a crucial stage in 2004. This project, which had placed Georgia on the international map in the mid-1990s, faced many challenges during the new government's first year in power. The biggest dilemma arose in July 2004, when the government ordered British Petroleum (BP), the leader of the consortium that was building the pipeline, to stop construction work. This was a huge problem, because any significant delay in construction over the summer could set the entire project off schedule by many months, if not years, since work could not be done during the winter. Because the BTC project involves not only Georgia but also Azerbaijan and Turkey, is at least partially financed by international donor organizations, and has backing from the U.S. and British governments, the incident had the potential to become a crisis of significant proportions.

The rationale offered to the public for the work stoppage included environmental concerns in the Borjomi Valley and the fear that oil leaks could damage this national park and source of Georgia's largest foreign export, Borjomi mineral water. However, BP suspected that these "concerns" were merely an excuse, and that the government wanted something else—money—from the company, as became obvious during the discussions between BP and the Georgian government. Under pressure from Washington (the Bush administration dispatched Assistant Secretary of State for Europe Elisabeth Jones to demand the resumption of construction), the Georgian government caved in, but not until it extracted $120 million from BP, both in cash and in development money that the company would spend directly in villages on the pipeline route. Zhvania was credited with preventing the problem from developing into a crisis. After Zhvania's death, Saakashvili's national-security advisor, Gela Bezhuashvili, took credit for forcing BP to pay $120 million, but complained that had Zhvania not intervened on BP's behalf, he might have succeeded in getting $250 million.[27]

This incident is interesting for a number of reasons, not the least being the complete disregard by some officials in the government for Georgia's national-security interests, and their willingness to sacrifice strategically important objectives for short-term personal financial gain. However, another striking fact is that during this entire debate between BP and the government, which lasted for much of July and August, the legislature played absolutely no role. BP did not bother to go to Parliament to seek support from deputies for its cause, because it knew that the legislature could not influence this issue in any way. Meanwhile, the government did not bother informing the legislature about what it was doing, or about funds that it had secured from BP. Indeed, it was never publicly announced that BP had agreed to spend this extra money. Finally, because of the deference with which most legislators treat the executive branch, no one in Parliament expressed an interest in conducting a hearing into what may have gone on and why such a strategic project nearly unraveled. Nor did the legislature care to investigate why the "environmental concerns," which for a while were so important that they justified a two-month work stoppage, suddenly were no longer an issue.

OSSETIA CONflICT

Another important event in which the Parliament played virtually no role was the shooting war that broke out in August 2004 with the Ossetian separatists in an area Georgians call the Tskhinvali region, which the world generally knows as "South Ossetia," the old Soviet-era name. This standoff is one of two frozen conflicts that have caused significant problems to the consolidation of Georgian statehood since the country regained its independence in 1991. The Georgian version of events starts with the alleged attempt, in the late spring and early summer of 2004, to cut off the large contraband (including illegal sale of cars and food products) that went through "South Ossetia" into Georgia proper. This contraband allowed Ossetian leaders to profit greatly and to sustain their separatist movement, and enriched Georgians who participated in it. Cutting it off would have been a strong move on the part of the Georgian authorities, but evidence remains very unclear about whether the government actually did something, or whether it merely talked about cutting off the contraband. Around the same time, Saakashvili and other Georgians issued almost daily statements about their plan to end the conflict with the Ossetians, and the Georgian ability to take back the province by force, if necessary. Privately, individuals in high positions within the National Movement alleged that the government had a plan to march on Tskhinvali, South Ossetia's de facto "capital," and to take the region back.

Whether motivated by a real desire to cut off the contraband, or by a desire to battle it out with the Ossetian rebels, the Georgians deployed forces inside the region of conflict in July 2004, thereby violating the armistice that the two sides had signed in 1992. The Ossetians responded in kind by increasing the presence of their armed forces in the demilitarized area that has been patrolled by a joint Russian, Georgian, and Ossetian peacekeeping force for over a decade.[28] Several nights of shooting and fighting followed in mid-August, and a very bloody conflict nearly broke out. Fortunately, under American pressure the Georgians pulled back, alleging that they had accomplished their objectives, even though it was never clear what these were or how they had been achieved. According to Nick Rurua, the deputy chairman of the Parliament's Committee on Defense and Security, this "was a test, aimed at . . . measuring the [conflict's] temperature."[29]

While it was very difficult to figure out what the government was actually up to in Ossetia, one thing is certain: the president, the defense minister, and the interior minister broke several important constitutional norms and laws during the conflict by ignoring the Parliament's role before and during military action. While the Constitution requires the Parliament to authorize the use of Defense Ministry forces, such permission was never sought by the executive branch, nor was it ever granted. The government alleges that Ministry of Defense forces were not used, and the fighting was done by the Ministry of Interior forces (i.e., heavily armed police), whose use does not require legislative authorization. However, on its face this explanation has no merit, given that at least ten of the soldiers who died were from Ministry of Defense troops trained by the Americans as part of the Georgian Train and Equip Program (GTEP).[30]

Furthermore, even if one accepts the claim that Ministry of Interior forces were used, the Parliament is required to authorize spending for such operations, since they were not included in the annual budget. No such funding request was ever made by the government, and National Movement deputies openly acknowledge in television interviews and discussions that the funding for the military operations came from the "special funds" overseen by the president.

As these examples illustrate, post–Rose Revolution, the Parliament has neither accomplished anything significant, nor has it had any influence on the reform process or any role in the oversight process. Rather than becoming a more active player in national affairs, the legislature developed into a very weak—and in some respects useless—institution. Meanwhile, Saakashvili's refusal to afford the people's elected representatives their proper role in the running of the affairs of the country, and the ease with which he has been willing to break the law to make life easier for himself, speaks volumes about his political values and gives a more accurate picture of his beliefs than the pro-democracy pronouncements that one often hears from the president.

In his book *My Life*, President Clinton explained his reasoning behind his affair with Monica Lewinsky with the words "because I could."[31] This is a perfect analogy for the actions of Saakashvili, who also chooses to disregard the legislature and the rule of law because "he can." Given National Movement's huge majority in Parliament, Saakashvili can get whatever he wants through the legislature, but he ignores it, simply because it is convenient to do so. However, Saakashvili also does not want to set a precedent for the development of institutional governance in Georgia. Instead, he strives to orient the entire decision-making process around himself in order to make himself the indispensable political figure, akin to a monarch in pre-democratic Europe. This development bodes very ill for Georgia's ability to develop institutions of division of power that are necessary for democracy, let alone a functioning representative government.

Local Government

Historically, Georgia is a federalist state—local nobles always enjoyed great autonomy in running their regional enclaves. This tradition was destroyed during Communism. One of Shevardnadze's greatest failures as president was his unwillingness to allow Georgia to develop real local self-government. He opposed giving local communities authority to run their affairs, on the pretext that Georgia was not "ready" for a system that diverted so much power away from the center. Even though Georgia twice held elections for local executive and legislative bodies, these entities were powerless to actually govern these communities. The real power was held by various individuals appointed by the president. He appointed regional "representatives," without the Parliament's consent, who functioned as "governors" and were responsible for running the affairs of the regions.[32] In addition, throughout most of his tenure, Shevardnadze was also authorized to appoint heads (*gamgebeli* in Georgian) of the various districts that constitute each region. Officially, these individuals reported to the president, but in practice they also reported to the president's "representative."

In 2002, before the local-government elections, there was one minor reform in the area of local government, when the opposition (which then included Saakashvili and Zhvania) reached a compromise with Shevardnadze about the procedures for the appointment of *gamgebeli* (heads) of the districts. Whereas in the past the president could appoint any individual of his choice to this position, the new procedure required him to select a *gamgebeli* from among elected chairmen of the *sakrebulos* (local councils) within a given district. The result was that the posts went to individuals who had greater stature and at least partial elected legitimacy in their districts, and because of this, were able to maintain greater independence from the president's "representative."

Saakashvili campaigned in 2003 on the promise of implementing immediate elected leadership on the local level. However, instead of allowing citizens in their communities to elect executive officials and mayors with real authority, Saakashvili implemented a scheme that gave the locally elected officials even less power than they had before, while increasing the powers of centrally appointed officials.

The new government had few allies in the local *sakrebulos*, because neither National Movement nor United Democrats elected many local officials in 2002. Thus, Saakashvili did not have candidates that he could appoint to the positions of *gamgebeli* using the compromise scheme from 2002. In response, the government cooked up a scheme by which the president would appoint a deputy *gamgebeli* (who did not have to come from among the elected *sakrebulo*

chairmen in the district), while keeping the position of *gamgebeli* vacant, allowing the deputy to serve as the "acting *gamgebeli*." This way, the president ran
circles around the law, and since Saakashvili's inauguration (until October
2006), almost all of Georgia's districts were run by individuals in office only
on an "acting" basis.

Incidentally, Saakashvili told the *New York Times* that this system was "too
centralized to be effective. "I have to select 80 heads of local administrations,"
he said. "And I don't know 99 percent of these people."[33] That being the case,
it is unclear why Saakashvili refused to implement more direct control over
local government after coming to power, or why he chose to centralize his powers even more than they had been during the last years of Shevardnadze's rule.
At any rate, this centralized system of "acting *gamgebeli*" continued through
2006, when new local-government elections took place.[34]

Furthermore, while Saakashvili had made direct mayoral elections the rallying cry of his stint as head of Tbilisi's City Council, and was adamant about
holding these elections soon after the parliamentary vote in November 2003,
once he came to power he reneged on this promise as well. Incidentally, the
excuse for this delay has been the same as one offered for years by President
Shevardnadze—that Georgia is not yet ready for such rapid and sudden decen-
tralization. Furthermore, the majority of Saakashvili's supporters in Parliament
seem to favor an indirect election of mayors: instead of voting for individuals
directly, citizens will elect a local council, which will then vote in the mayor.
When asked to explain this, Saakashvili declared, "It is not like I have nothing
better to do but to give control over a 300 million [lari] budget to some
unknown hands."[35] Eventually, in 2006, local government elections came and
went without creation of a directly elected Tbilisi mayor.

ADJARIAN AUTONOMY

In July 2004, Saakashvili proposed and the Parliament approved a new constitutional division of power between Tbilisi and the autonomous republic of
Adjaria. This new system eliminated the idea of "autonomy" for this region in
all but the name, while concentrating all decision-making powers for Adjaria
in the hands of the president. Whether Adjaria should be somehow different
from any other Georgian region in terms of self-government is an open question,[36] but the new autonomous division of power made a mockery of the idea
of self-government. A local village *sakrebulo* (council) member in any district
in Georgia is more independent of the central government than a member of
the legislature in the "autonomy" of Adjaria, because the constitutional
amendments empowered the president to disband the Adjarian legislature,
something he cannot do to a village council. The amendments also gave the
president the power to appoint the head (i.e., "prime minister") of the region's

"cabinet"; he can disband the local legislature for, among other reasons, rejecting his choice.

Thus, the new system created direct presidential rule disguised as autonomy, administered by a president's representative. The only difference between Adjaria and other Georgian regions is that it has a regional legislature, but one that is for all intents and purposes powerless.

After Abashidze was removed, many of those who led the revolt against him became local legislators. In the winter of 2005, they became so fed up with the concentration of power in the hands of "Prime Minister" Levan Vashalomidze that they threatened to resign and to turn to old dissident tactics unless they were given a bigger say in local decision making. Meanwhile, at Adjaria TV, which Abashidze had used as a propaganda machine, the news director and many journalists quit citing pressure from the region's leadership.

Eventually, these problems were resolved, with Saakashvili's direct intervention. However, these incidents demonstrate all too well the problems associated with one-man rule; the lack of proper checks and balances, be it on the local or national level, creates a system that is bound to fail. The situation in Georgia now requires Saakashvili to be directly involved in the decision-making process at every level, on every subject. Such an environment makes strategic planning on a national level impossible and undermines even the *possibility* of transition to institutional governance and democracy, a goal that was ostensibly the reason behind the Rose Revolution.

13

Media Freedom, or Lack Thereof

The media in Georgia can be divided into two categories—the print media, which has a very limited impact on the public and is merely an avenue through which the political elite and the chattering class speak to each other, and the television media, whose grip on the public is dramatic. Because of the Georgian people's huge interest in politics (heightened appreciation for politics is generally the case in the formerly Communist countries), news and political shows generally have the highest ratings and are the most popular programs on all television stations. The television media in Georgia can be further subdivided into two categories: the State TV Channel One, and private stations, three of which (Rustavi 2, Imedi, and Mze) are particularly important.[1]

The press in Georgia under Shevardnadze, especially after 1999, enjoyed an extraordinary degree of freedom. The individuals who came to power after the Rose Revolution knew full well the power of television media. Indeed, it was the existence of three dominant private television channels (one of which openly supported the revolution while the other two were more neutral, but nonetheless anti-Shevardnadze in their coverage) that made November's events possible, by allowing Saakashvili and others to speak directly to the people and mobilize the crowds against the Shevardnadze government. Furthermore, Saakashvili realized that maintaining power after the revolution would be impossible without popularity (since the revolution created a precedent for overthrowing any unpopular regime just as easily as removing Shevardnadze), and that high approval ratings were inherently connected to favorable media coverage. Because of this, new leaders were determined to ensure that the TV stations would serve their interests. Without supportive coverage, the entire revolutionary enterprise was endangered.

Given these realities, the Rose Revolution brought greater changes to the way TV journalists do their job than to any other profession in the country, with reporters experiencing greater censorship and pressure than at any time since the final months of Gamsakhurdia's rule. This environment dramatically altered what kind of information citizens receive on a daily basis, generally reducing the public's access to uncensored, transparent, and honest news. By contrast, because of its limited influence on the public, the print media has not suffered at the hands of the new government.

Independent (Private) TV Stations

Saakashvili's first task was to gain control over the independent television stations. He used three different mechanisms to reach his goal: first, by getting existing owners of television stations to toe the pro-governmental line or by forcing owners to give up control (i.e., to "sell" their stations) to individuals friendly to the government; second, by limiting the press's access to political information involving the government in general; and third, by pressuring TV journalists directly, thus getting them to self-censor their coverage of government's actions. The international community, which has recognized that free media has faced problems in Georgia since the revolution, has largely focused its attention on the third mechanism. The U.S. State Department's Report on Human Rights Practices, for example, states that "criticism of the Government in the media decreased [after the Rose Revolution] due to increased self-censorship."[2] However, pressuring journalists to engage in regular self-censorship was the least important of the government's three main tactics. The most important mechanism of control was the government's influence over owners, who in turned censored the content of the news their stations carried. Those owners who did not cooperate with the government were left with no choice but to shut down (or never actually launch) their stations.

CONTROL THROUGH OWNERS

Of the six private stations with a news service operating from Tbilisi prior to the revolution, only Kavkasia Television remained on the air and continued to resist government pressure a year after the Rose Revolution. However, this channel's audience has always been quite limited, and the station does not have the personnel or the technology to compete with other, wealthier channels. At other stations, dramatic changes took place:

Mze's owner, Vano Chkhartishvili, a prominent banker and former minister of economy who was elected to Parliament in 2003 as an independent deputy, sold a 50 percent stake in the channel to David Bezhuashvili, a member of

Parliament from the National Movement and the brother of the foreign minister (who had served as secretary of the National Security Council prior to his most recent appointment). Georgian newspapers have documented numerous instances when the interests of the two owners were not congruent, making it nearly impossible for the journalists to cover certain events. However, according to journalists, when it came to the coverage of the government, owners were always in agreement—Saakashvili and other officials had to be praised, without deviation.[3]

Rustavi 2's owner, Erosi Kitsmarishvili, was forced to leave the country, even though he had played a vital role in Saakashvili's ascent to power; thus he suffered a fate similar to the one experienced by Vladimir Gusinski and Boris Berezovsky in Russia, who helped bring Putin to power but then was forced out of the country. Rustavi 2 was ostensibly sold to Kibar Khalvashi, who though a successful businessman, did not have the kind of wealth to be able to afford a channel that should have sold for up to $20–30 million. However, Khalvashi is a close friend and former business partner of Defense Minister Irakli Okruashvili. The general working assumption in Georgia has been that Kitsmarishvili was forced to give up the station to Saakashvili and Okruashvili, who in turn installed Khalvashi as its "owner" on paper. Soon after the "sale," Deputy Foreign Minister Nick Tabatadze, a former Rustavi 2 anchor, was made the new general manager at the station, making the channel even more of a mouthpiece for the government.[4]

Bidzina (Boris) Ivanishvili, a Russian oligarch of Georgian origin and Forbes Magazine's 228th wealthiest man in the world, chose to close his station, Channel Nine, in April 2004 rather than be forced to deal with the new government. His decision was particularly striking given that in the summer of 2003, Channel Nine had just moved into spacious new headquarters, had secured a license to transmit nationally (previously it could only transmit in Tbilisi), and had just purchased millions of dollars worth of new equipment.

The news service at Iberia, a minor channel that always had an affinity for Adjarian leader Aslan Abashidze, was closed in the spring of 2004 due to financial difficulties after the government raided the offices of the channel's parent company, Omega, shutting down the firm's vast cigarette import business and local cigarette production plant.

Channel Europe, an all-news service that was being launched by a Moscow-based Georgian entrepreneur, Teimuraz Shengelia (a relative by marriage of the late Prime Minister Zurab Zhvania), was refused a license by the Georgian Communication Commission. According to the individual who was slated to become the channel's news director, Shengelia was told by officials at the commission that he would only receive the license if he reached an understanding with Saakashvili about how the channel would cover the president. Because

Shengelia had made the station's slated leadership a promise of noninterference, he chose not to launch the channel rather than put censored information on the air.

After the ownership changes at Rustavi 2 and Mze, the government gained complete control over what was reported on these stations, how it was reported, and why. With a green light from the new owners, government officials would call the news director at Mze and ask for specific stories and events to be included during the evening newscast, and for other stories to be excluded. In some cases, they would also ask for a particular spin on a given story, demanding that the news director censor the voice-over text. In some very important cases, officials even tried to write the voice-over texts themselves, though the Mze news director generally resisted such direct interference. Meanwhile, at Rustavi 2, parliamentarians and government officials had no trouble getting the anchors and journalists to read prepared texts on the air. Sometimes, narrations would be faxed to Rustavi 2 directly, with journalists not needing to do any reporting at all. These methods allowed the government to have a virtually identical spin on two of the country's three most important TV stations—all too often with the exact same quotes being used on both stations, and with the narratives far too similar for mere coincidence.

Billionaire Badri Patarkatsishvili was the only television station owner who was still fully in control of his channel after the Rose Revolution. Because of his vast fortune and past financial support for Saakashvili and Zhvania, the government had to approach him with more caution than other businessmen. Patarkatsishvili's Imedi TV, Georgia's largest station with nearly 100 percent national availability, became the most-watched network in Tbilisi in 2004, surpassing Rustavi 2, which lost many of its viewers and its hard-earned reputation of neutrality during the revolution.[5]

Initially, Patarkatsishvili did not wish a conflict with Saakashvili, and as a result his channel provided glowing coverage of the president on a daily basis. However, this special treatment did not extend to most other officials. As a result, during much of 2004, Imedi's journalists sensed that they were uniquely positioned to file reports that were closer to the truth than those at other stations, making Imedi far more critical of the government than any other channel. Furthermore, Imedi gave some air time to nongovernmental political parties, providing the opposition with a voice during the crucial weeks prior to the March 2004 elections. Additionally, Imedi hired popular anchors and reporters that had been fired for their independence from other stations, such as Inga Grigolia from Mze and Rezo Sakevarishvili from Rustavi 2, both of whom lost their old jobs because of their unwillingness to abide by the demands of government censors.

From the beginning, journalists were very upset about their predicament and would have preferred to not get involved in the dealings between the government and their bosses. However, most of them followed orders because they feared for their jobs, having seen the experience of Russian journalists who tried to withstand government control at their stations after Vladimir Putin's ascent to the presidency—most of the uncooperative Russian journalists had lost their jobs. Furthermore, journalists had no avenue through which to voice their discontent; their profession was not organized in any association, and the reporters themselves were very competitive and were unwilling to work together. Thus, unable to unite to defend their interests and unaccustomed to censorship, for at least a year most journalists quietly accepted their fate and did nothing to defend themselves other than complain to each other and close friends about the loss of freedom in the media.

LIMITING JOURNALISTS' ACCESS TO NEWS
Working through the owners was not the only tool the government used to control television coverage, though it was the most important one. From the very beginning, the government put a clear limit on the information that it would make available to journalists; senior officials in the new government were far less inclined to give journalists information about ongoing events than in the Shevardnadze government, and were less willing to give comprehensive interviews. Part of this can be explained by the cohesion within the new government; at its start, everyone in power was much more willing to work together than officials during Shevardnadze's last years in power, though this tendency broke down as the months went by. However, limiting journalists' access to information was also part of a concerted strategy to control what went on the air and how news shaped public opinion.

SELF-CENSORSHIP
Finally, Saakashvili and other officials pressured journalists directly, with both carrots and sticks. Journalists who provided favorable coverage were rewarded; for example, station owners were asked to send only those reporters to Saakashvili's foreign trips that were favorably disposed toward the new government. Since this sort of information spread quickly among their peers, some reporters (especially those who were neutral toward the new government) were inclined to provide positive coverage in order to get a chance to travel with the president in the future. Simultaneously, officials would often call those journalists who were responsible for negative coverage, and threaten to tell the owners about the unwillingness of a given journalist to cooperate. All of this helped ensure self-censorship on the part of many journalists, by making reports

either favorable or at least neutral toward the government while providing negative or unfavorable coverage of the opposition groups, also at the government's request.

While self-censorship also became a significant challenge, it would be inaccurate to assume that it was the principal reason for the lack of investigative journalism or critical coverage of the government. A far greater problem lay with the government's control of the owners, and the journalists' inability to protect their freedom and their interests. In the future, securing press freedom in Georgia can only happen if journalists become more willing to reject demands from the government, and develop mechanisms to defend their rights from interference, both from the owners and the government.

Case Examples

The extent to which Saakashvili controlled the media in the aftermath of the Rose Revolution becomes most obvious by considering several case examples. There are far more cases that I could consider here, so I picked some of the most striking ones.

CANCELLATION OF NEWS SHOWS

One direct example of Saakashvili's influence over the private TV stations involves the cancellation of two nighttime debate talk shows on Rustavi 2 and Mze, on February 4 and 5, 2004, respectively.[6] These shows, which aired live at around 11 P.M. and generally lasted 60–90 minutes, were highly popular in Georgia because most people in the country tend to go to bed much later than in Western countries. Generally, the shows focused on one or two of the day's top political stories and consisted of either the anchors' one-on-one interviews with leading officials, or debates between politicians representing various points of view. Both shows were anchored by the biggest stars of Georgian television—Inga Grigolia at Mze, and Eka Khoperia at Rustavi 2. Both shows were cash cows for their respective channels, and politicians of all political persuasions loved to appear on them. Grigolia's show was the highest-rated program on Mze and the only profitable one. Khoperia's show had the third-highest rating on Rustavi 2, behind the channel's 9 P.M. newscast and 10 P.M. David Letterman–like comedy show.

Grigolia, in particular, was very popular in Georgia for her willingness to confront government officials with very tough questions. She refused demands from Mze's owners to tone down her style after the revolution. She was probably the only reporter who openly questioned some of the new government's actions, particularly those related to arrests and confinements. Khoperia was less of a star and had a milder style than Grigolia, but because of the strength of Rustavi 2's other programming, she also generally attracted a very wide audience. Her appeal was also enhanced by her frequent focus on international stories, with live appearances by guests from Washington, Moscow, and London.

In January 2004, under government pressure, Mze's owners considered replacing Grigolia with a different anchor, but chose not to—realizing that they would lose a large share of their viewers, most of whom tuned in to watch Grigolia rather than the show itself. By contrast, Khoperia's position at Rustavi 2 seemed more secure after the revolution, given that she had forcefully supported Saakashvili during the protests, and even severed relationships with a couple of her close friends who objected to her biased reporting during that period. Then, very suddenly and without any warning, Grigolia's and Khoperia's programs both went off the air—Khoperia anchored her last show on February 3, Grigolia on February 4. Neither anchor announced that their show would be ending during what turned out to be their last broadcast. Indeed, neither left even a slight impression that something was wrong; they wished their viewers a good night until the next evening. Thus, the decision to cancel the shows was clearly not planned in advance.

The shows were cancelled right as the debate over the constitutional amendments was heating up, and during their last broadcasts, both anchors created serious problems for the government's effort to present the changes as positive reforms. On what turned out to be her last broadcast, Khoperia hosted a debate between Tina Khidasheli, a major supporter of the revolution but an opponent of the constitutional amendments, and two leading figures from the National Movement—Maia Nadiradze and Kote Kemularia (who later became chairman of the Supreme Court and afterwards minister of justice). In the eyes of virtually every observer, Khidasheli, probably the most flamboyant attorney in Georgia, made both Nadiradze and Kemularia look ridiculous as they tried to argue that the changes actually increased legislative powers and decreased the president's authority. It was obvious that if similar debate continued on television for several more days, the general public would become quite negatively disposed toward the proposed changes. According to sources in the National Movement, the threat posed by such debate talk shows to the prospect of the passage of the constitutional amendments was one of the main impetuses for canceling the shows.

Meanwhile, on her second-to-last broadcast, two days before her show was cancelled, Grigolia hosted Zurab Zhvania, whom she chastised and attacked over the proposed constitutional amendments. According to one of Mze's owners, the debate became so heated that Zhvania was prepared to walk off the air, and demanded during a commercial break that Grigolia stop attacking him.

(Incidentally, Grigolia's best friend, also the sister of her producer, was Zhvania's press secretary at the time. However, Grigolia was long known to have animosity toward Zhvania because of his role in getting her fired from Rustavi 2 in the late 1990s.) This interview also played a role in convincing Saakashvili that he needed to do something about the nighttime television shows, which were becoming uncontrollable.

After the shows went off the air, Mze's and Rustavi 2's management explained that the cancellations were planned and both channels had taken the shows off the air for "reformatting," but did this simultaneously to avoid viewers from one channel going to another. However, this explanation made little sense, given that neither anchor made any suggestions that her show would be ending. Khoperia's show had gone through reformatting in August 2003, when it was moved to a new studio. This and other past experience suggested that in the case of daily programs, shows were usually taken off the air for reformatting at the end of the week. Furthermore, in private discussions, reporters and management representatives at both stations stated that both shows were cancelled because of direct demands from Saakashvili, who was incensed by the very negative spin that the constitutional changes had received. Saakashvili apparently did not want the shows on the air during the forthcoming parliamentary elections, because they would inevitably give the opposition a forum for electioneering.

After the cancellations, Grigolia moved to Imedi, where she hosts a weekly taped interview program and a weekly live talk show. Meanwhile, Khoperia continued to work for Rustavi 2 as news director, though she has not been seen on the air, and her role at the station was minimal.[7] In October 2004, after the ownership change, the reigns of Rustavi 2 were given to former Deputy Foreign Minister Nick Tabatadze. There was an attempt to start a new nighttime debate show on Rustavi 2 in the spring of 2004, but the program quickly folded because it no longer had the appeal of the old show.

GLOWING COVERAGE OF THE GOVERNMENT

Ever since the revolution, on a weekly basis Georgian television stations have interrupted regular programming to bring live coverage of the president's, and sometimes the prime minister's, statements, press conferences, and public meetings. At least twice a month, Saakashvili had a lengthy live appearance on television, covered by all networks simultaneously. As a result, for those in Georgia without cable (which is the vast majority of the population), on days when Saakashvili chooses to address the country, nothing was available but Saakashvili's self-congratulation.

It would be one thing if such appearances happened infrequently and involved certain important announcements. However, by and large, these

appearances serve as a means for Saakashvili to comment positively on the various political developments in the country, to praise his actions and achievements, to give out orders to various ministers, and to reject any criticism that
may have been voiced against him. According to various senior reporters and
news producers at all three of Georgia's main private channels, at various times
each station has attempted not to air these primetime remarks live, since they
are not regarded as newsworthy and are damaging to ratings. The owners would
generally decree that this was not an option, even though they too would have
chosen not to air the remarks if they had a choice. Indeed, when Imedi TV
refused to provide live coverage of the National Movement's party convention in
November 2004, the party's senior leadership was furious and blamed the station's news director, who is regarded as being unsympathetic to the president.

Furthermore, even though privately most reporters said that they found the
arrests and extortion of citizens troubling, and thought it was crucial to inform
the public about what the government was actually doing, unlike their print-
media colleagues (who generally told the full story of the hypocrisy behind
these extortion schemes), television journalists did not dare to criticize the government's actions. The leaders of the National Movement in charge of public
relations often demanded that journalists present the arrests in a positive light,
though most of the time anchors reported in a very stoic manner that yet
another individual had been arrested because he had been accused of some
crime, and then, a few weeks later, would report that the individual had been
released because he had agreed to pay for his freedom. During the reports,
there was no discussion of any evidence that the government might have had
against those who were arrested (because in most cases, there never was much
evidence). Most importantly, TV journalists did not dare to probe where the
money paid by these individuals went, even though the print media had extensive investigative reports about lack of transparency and corruption associated
with the payment of these funds.

COVERAGE OF THE MARCH 2004 ELECTIONS

TV stations showed only slightly more independence during the coverage of
the March 2004 parliamentary revote, though this was generally because by
this time journalists were so fed up with so much control that they used the
elections as an excuse to try to cover news outside of the shell created for them
by the government and their owners. During the campaign, TV stations usually started their newscasts with glowing reports about campaign stops by
Saakashvili or National Movement leaders. However afterwards, they countered this one-sided coverage with reports about the opposition's campaign
activities, even when other parties were doing nothing special. At Imedi, journalists competed with each other over who would get to cover the New

Rights–Industry campaign, knowing that the presence of Mzia Totladze (the sister of the channel's owner, Badri Patarkatsishvili) high on the party's list ensured that their stories were less likely to be censored.

Such small acts of courage notwithstanding, the analysis of the coverage of the March elections clearly showed distinct bias toward the government. According to data compiled by the Organization for Security and Cooperation in Europe (OSCE), the media's "coverage of [President Saakashvili's] almost daily press conferences [during the campaign] . . . went beyond the need and the duty to inform the public on government's activities."[8] Specifically, during the election period (February 16–March 28, 2004), State TV allocated 46 percent of its political news to the president, 20 percent to other government officials, and 14 percent to the National Movement. Thus a total of 80 percent of its coverage was pro-Saakashvili. Revival, the party of Adjarian leader Aslan Abashidze, received 9 percent, and all other parties received 11 percent.

The situation was not much better at the two private channels that the OSCE monitored. On Rustavi 2, the president received 38 percent of the coverage, other government officials received 19 percent, and National Movement received 14 percent, for a total of 71 percent pro-Saakashvili coverage. Imedi was slightly more balanced, with pro-Saakashvili coverage totaling 63 percent, and opposition parties receiving 27 percent.

Such bias was not accidental, nor was it simply self-censorship, which could explain limited negative coverage but not extreme positive bias. Rather, these statistics are probably one of the clearest signs of the dramatic change Georgian TV media experienced after the Rose Revolution, as the comparison to the November 2, 2003, preelection period suggests. During the period between September 9 and November 2, 2003, State TV allotted 71 percent of its airtime to the president, the government, and Shevardnadze's Block for New Georgia, while the rest of the time focused on the opposition. At Imedi, 27 percent of the coverage focused on Shevardnadze and Block for New Georgia, 17 percent on Burdjanadze-Democrats, and 11 percent on the New Rights Party. While OSCE did not monitor Rustavi 2 in percentage terms, the coverage on this channel "clearly favored opposition parties and gave critical assessment of the president, the Government, Revival, and in particular [Block for New Georgia]."[9]

COVERAGE OF THE SOUTH OSSETIA CONFLICT

Notwithstanding this background, not a single subject was more censored than the coverage of the Ossetian separatists in the summer of 2004. Stories on this subject were not allowed to go on the air until they had been formally approved by the press services of the Security, Interior, or Defense ministries. Journalists who were located in the region were so shocked by what was happening that many admitted in the weeks after the conflict dissipated that they had blatantly lied to the public about developments. One prominent journalist, who was in the separatist region during the entire conflict, put it this way: "I knew that people were dying, both military and civilian, yet I was not allowed to say this. I had to report that nothing was wrong, and that no one was dying. It was disgusting and probably the hardest thing I have ever had to do. Georgia almost got embroiled in another civil war and I was merely contributing to this."[10]

This journalist also described one concrete instance that caused a great deal of tension between reporters and their handlers. Several days into the most intense period of the conflict, residents of several villages close to the separatist lines held a small protest, complaining about the lack of water and other basic supplies, and what they perceived as the unwillingness of Georgian authorities to protect them from Ossetian infiltrations and attacks. Several channels sent reporters to cover the protests. However, before the story went on the air, the Georgian authorities sent Special Forces to break up the protests with force. While this was captured on tape, the authorities not only prevented the video from being shown on the air, but also confiscated the footage, citing national-security concerns.[11] Another journalist from a different television station confirmed this, but no public evidence about it is available.

GOVERNMENT'S RESPONSE TO CRITICISM

The National Movement leaders generally declared that there was no censorship on Georgian TV, though in some respects they couched their pronouncements in novel understandings of the meaning of freedom of speech. In an interview with *Rezonansi*, parliamentarian David Zurabishvili, formerly a pro-democracy activist with the Liberty Institute, claimed that "censorship is not government's policy. . . . If I were told that someone called and in the name of the government interests planned on conducting censorship, my reaction would be very strict. But if this remains merely a rumor, nothing will happen."[12] When asked about this, newsmen showed no interest in following Zurabishvili's advice to publicly name those who were censoring them, since in their view all this would lead to is reporters losing their jobs.

Such a reaction should not be surprising, given what another prominent National Movement parliamentarian seems to understand as freedom of speech. According to Giga Bokeria, the fact that a show on Imedi was removed "is not intervention. If Badri [Patarkatsishvili] wants a good relationship with the government, that is his choice and freedom of speech has nothing to do with this, because freedom of speech means that the owner can have the kind of television that he wants."[13] Thus, if a businessman decides to censor news on his channel for the sake of good relations with the government, then freedom of speech is not violated. This is the sort of interpretation of freedom of speech that would be favorably viewed by Russian President Vladimir Putin, who made clear during his February 2005 press conference with President Bush that he saw little difference between the firing of Russian journalists from government-controlled channels on his orders, and the decision by CBS News to replace Dan Rather as its Evening News anchor.[14]

Journalists did not deny the reality that in times of conflict, the authorities certainly had a greater interest in protecting some information from getting on the air, in order to defend Georgian interests, prevent public panic, and so forth. However, even Saakashvili's most ardent supporters in the media were incensed by the heavy-handed tactics used by the authorities during the period of the conflict in South Ossetia. Indeed, this experience led many, especially reporters at Rustavi 2, to change their minds about the new government. As a result, the Ossetian conflict was probably the breaking point for most journalists, who were ready to take the first opportunity available to try to break out of such extreme censorship, at least to the extent that they could. Such an opportunity presented itself several months later, with the death of Prime Minister Zurab Zhvania in February 2005. Unfortunately, the response from the government created even more censorship.

Zurab Zhvania's Death: A Small Opening for Media Freedom before Greater Censorship

The circumstances surrounding Zhvania's death were strange from the start. According to the official version of the story, he died on February 3, 2005, at around 4 A.M., from carbon-monoxide poisoning in the apartment of a young "friend," Raul Usupov, who was also found dead. Furthermore, Zhvania and Usupov were allegedly playing backgammon, and the prime minister was found dead in front of the game board, while Usupov was discovered in the kitchen. Almost no one in Georgia believed this official version, because its timeline made little sense and it left many questions unanswered. For example, why was the country's prime minister visiting, in the middle of the night, someone of no political standing, with whom he was not known to have any sort of a personal relationship or friendship, playing a game he was known to dislike? Or, why did the prime minister's security officers not raise concerns sooner, after Zhvania did not answer calls from them to his cell phone for two hours? Or, if the two men were both awake when they died, as the authorities claimed, how was it that whoever died first was not noticed by the other, who then did not try to report the death to the security guards who were ostensibly standing outside the apartment? Or, why did the authorities initially claim, and later recant, that Usupov was a deputy governor of the Kvemo Kartli region?

Because of these questions, many in Georgia thought that Zhvania was murdered, though there was very little evidence to support this claim.

According to several members of the Georgian leadership, Zhvania and Usupov were actually lovers, and they both died asleep in bed. According to this "unofficial" version, the night of his death Zhvania was driven to his home in his motorcade, where he switched to his wife's car and drove it, with just one security officer, to Usupov's apartment. There, he told his security guard to not bother him until about 4 A.M. According to these sources, the authorities hatched the "official" version when they discovered the two in bed, in order to ensure that the truth about the prime minister's sexual orientation would not be made public. If this indeed was the case, many of the most obvious questions raised about the official version are no longer relevant or applicable. The explanation that the two died from carbon-monoxide poisoning seems far more realistic if one accepts the unofficial version, since it is much more likely that two individuals would be poisoned to death simultaneously while asleep. Furthermore, given Georgian views of homosexuality, it is not at all unreasonable to assume that the authorities did not want to make information about Zhvania's sexuality public. Rumors about this had long been heard in Georgia, lending further credence to this version of events.

Whatever the real story may be, the government's version clearly made little sense, and some journalists at private stations jumped on it. The day of Zhvania's death, Mze TV invited Maia Nikolaishvili, a prominent forensic expert, to its nighttime talk show *Archevanis Zgvarze* ("On the Edge of Choice"). During the appearance, Nikolaishvili raised many of the aforementioned questions and argued, quite persuasively, that the government's story simply did not add up. However, Nikolaishvili and the journalists who were interviewing her during the program did not offer the more realistic explanation of what may have actually happened. Even though most reporters knew about this version, they did not wish to speak about it out of deference to Zhvania's wife and children. One of the journalists who participated in the show stated that while s/he believed the "unofficial" version, a person's sexuality was simply not a subject that s/he or anyone else at Mze felt comfortable discussing on national television. As a result, Nikolaishvili's interview only fueled the rumor mill in Tbilisi about the possibility that Zhvania was murdered. Most people became so convinced that the government was lying about the circumstances of his death that anyone who tried to argue otherwise had no credibility.

Understandably, Nikolaishvili's appearance and claims infuriated Saakashvili and other authorities, who demanded explanations from Mze's owners (two members of Parliament, one of whom is both a brother of the president's national-security advisor at the time and a member of National Movement). In turn, the owners demanded that the journalists who participated

in the program go on the air the next day and retract claims made by Nikolaishvili. Furthermore, the owners ordered Mze's management to not re-air the
show the next morning, as is usually the case. In an amazingly courageous
move, Irakli Imnaishvili, the show's lead anchor, as well as other journalists
involved in the program jointly stood their ground, rejected this demand, and
refused to go on the air under duress.

Not repeating the show in the morning created a huge backlash, both
among ordinary citizens, most of whom assumed that the show was being cancelled the way Grigolia's program had been taken off the air for challenging the
government, as well as among nongovernmental organizations and foreigners
working in Georgia, who saw in this incident a clear-cut case of government
censorship of the media. According to several sources at Mze, the phones did
not stop ringing at the channel all day on Friday, with viewers demanding that
the program be permitted to go back on the air. Apparently even Saakashvili got
involved, calling one of the two owners and demanding that the show be put
back on the air immediately, in order to prevent any claims about his involvement in the show's alleged "cancellation."

Faced with an unwinnable situation, and realizing that this incident was
doing huge damage to the channel and its standing with the viewers, Mze's
owners capitulated and took back their demands. The show went back on the
air and suddenly became far more popular than it had ever been. For several
months after the incident, the journalists at Mze enjoyed far greater freedom
in their coverage of politics. One journalist at the station joked to me at the
time that "we have become like uncontrolled children—compared to what we
had endured since the revolution, we are saying almost anything that we
want." The new "rules" allow journalists to say almost anything, except attack
the president directly.

This freedom had its limits, of course. For example, on March 7, 2005,
Mze's second story on its 8 P.M. evening newscast dealt with popular standings
of the various political parties, and the visible fall in Saakashvili's and the
National Movement's approval ratings. The report included interviews with
two of the country's leading pollsters, Gocha Tskitishvili and Merab Pachulia,
about plans both had to conduct national polling during the month of March.
Both argued that they expected their surveys to show a significant change in
the public-opinion picture compared to the fall, with Saakashvili and his party
experiencing a significant loss in popularity, and with opposition parties probably gaining some support. Furthermore, Tskitishvili went so far as to suggest
that he expected the Parliament's only opposition party, New Rights, to be
building itself into a viable alternative to National Movement.

This report incensed the National Movement's leadership, which blamed
the station's owner, parliamentarian Bezhuashvili, for failing to pay sufficient

attention to what was happening at his station given this and past problems. Bezhuashvili, meanwhile, took his anger out on the leadership of the station's news division, for failing to check with him about a story of such political importance. However, whereas before the changed atmosphere created by the coverage of Zhvania's death, such an incident would have led to the severe reprimanding, if not the firing, of the journalist who reported the story—for failing to self-censor the story—this time around, nothing happened.

Just days after the incident, I ran into the head of the Mze's news division and commented to her about the station's new-found independence. "Compared to what?" she said. "Things are much better than they have been for the last year and a half, but if you think of before . . . now I know what real democracy was all about," she said, referring to the Shevardnadze era.[15] Such praise of Shevardnadze's willingness to accept media scrutiny was not unique—many journalists have been regularly making similar comments.

Censorship continued at other stations as well. For example, in April 2005, *Droeba*, a weekly Sunday-night news magazine anchored by Imedi's news director, Giorgi Targamadze, was forced to shelve a story about illegal transactions by leading officials in the Financial Police (the government entity responsible for tax collection from large businesses). According to the previews to the April 3 show, the story was based on taped conversations between the chief of the Financial Police, David Kezerashvili, and his friend Zurab Tseoradze, who had recently been dismissed from a position with the police on drug sale and addiction charges. The two were recorded discussing how the Financial Police had illegally transferred a confiscated vehicle to the Finance Minister without recouping any financial benefit for the state coffers from the transfer. Kezerashvili also mentioned how officials in the Financial Police had taken ownership of other confiscated vehicles without purchasing them in an open tender. The charges would have been explosive under any circumstance, but were particularly so given Saakashvili's emphasis on fighting corruption.

At the start of his broadcast on April 3, Targamadze announced that the story would not be aired, because he "was asked by the owner of Imedi television, Mr. Badri Patarkatsishvili, to not show it."[16] Patarkatsishvili himself explained the next day that he did not want his television to be "a battlefield of compromising evidence. I do not need to speak with the authorities through compromising evidence. If I want to tell something to the government, I can do so personally and directly."[17]

The tapes were made public on Monday, April 14, 2005, by Koba Davitashvili. Formerly one of Saakashvili's most prominent and closest allies, he had declared his opposition to the government, largely because the National Movement agreed to merge with Zhvania's United Democrats. Davitashvili, who had given the tapes to Imedi in the first place, charged that senior members of the government had personally intervened to stop the airing of the story on Imedi. The president's spokesman Gela Charkviani called the accusation "groundless," but according to several sources at Imedi, Saakashvili himself had intervened to stop the story from being aired.[18] Apparently, the president saw the story as a means to further tensions between Minister of Defense Irakli Okruashvili, who is a godfather to one of Davitashvili's sons, and Minister of Public Order and Security Vano Merabashvili, one of Kezerashvili's leading patrons. Though this was a clear example of owner-induced censorship caused by the need to please the government, the fact that the channel admitted what had actually happened was a significant move forward for the Georgian media.

What appeared like a greater level of media freedom lasted through late June. Then, on June 28, 2005, the police arrested the president of Georgia's Wrestling Federation, Aleko Davitashvili, and world silver-medalist Giorgi Revazishvili on charges of extortion. This began a series of events that ultimately ended very badly for the media.

Circumstances surrounding Davitashvili's and Revazishvili's arrest were questionable, as with almost all arrests of prominent individuals that had taken place since the Rose Revolution. The questions were less about their guilt or innocence, but about the individual whom they allegedly threatened, since he had been accused by several families of being an active trafficker of women. In response to Davitashvili and Revazishvili getting three months pretrial detention on June 30, several wrestlers trashed the court chamber. For this, they too were arrested. This resulted in a fairly large group of wrestlers and their supporters taking over the territory in front of Parliament on Rustaveli Avenue (where the demonstrating revolutionaries had held their own protests in November 2003) and blockading the street from traffic.

After several hours of Rustaveli being closed by these protesters, Special Forces from the Ministry of Interior came out with heavy weapons and broke up the demonstration. Understandably, this caused a great deal of unease among many who were not at all supportive of the protesters' cause, and much interest from the media. Mze, Imedi, and even Rustavi 2 and State Channel One had several hours of continuous broadcasts from the scene. After Rustaveli was opened by Special Forces, the protesters continued to linger in front of Parliament, and they were soon joined by opposition politicians, some of whom only came because they saw other opposition politicians on TV commenting about the event.

Throughout the night, the police, with many officers dressed in civilian clothes, went out of their way to prevent journalists from being able to report from the scene and interview the politicians who had assembled there. Initially the journalists were simply told that they were not permitted to report live. When most refused to listen, every time a journalist was seen interviewing a politician, a small band of "civilians" would suddenly close around the reporter, eventually pushing the journalist and the cameraman to the ground. After this happened several times, most reporters began to lose their neutrality and started to criticize the government. The situation was quite remarkable, with reporters from various stations going around to policemen, asking into the microphone, "Who ordered you to prevent me from doing my job?" These questions were generally met with glaring silence. Irakli Imnaishvili, the anchor of Mze's show "On the Edge of Choice," probably made the most noise.

Whatever one made of the protests or of the way opposition politicians reacted to the police action against them, journalists were indeed only trying to do their job. In a democratic society, their bravery for being willing to report from the scene would have been applauded. However, the reaction from Georgian officials was mind-boggling. For example, the next day, Giga Bokeria, an old NGO hand who had become a leading National Movement parliamentarian, went on Mze and Imedi and got into a screaming match with journalists interviewing him. He told Imnaishvili that "the time for journalists like you has passed in Georgia," and that there was a need for reporters who "know their place."[19] While declaring that the government could do nothing about this, Bokeria cautioned journalists that their superiors could. Reaction from other officials was just as vicious.

Developments over the next several weeks proved that Bokeria was not kidding. First, Imnaishvili's show was cancelled in late July 2005. No excuse was given publicly, but Imnaishvili was told by the executives at Mze that senior government officials were demanding his removal because of his actions during the protests. A week later, Mze's entire news division was shut down, allegedly just for the month of August. However, many journalists never came back to work. Mze's news director Inga Dadiani was fired on September 9, 2005, while twelve of its most prominent on-air personalities and reporters resigned the next day to protest Dadiani's firing.

After Zurab Zhvania's death, many reporters began to push the envelope of censorship, and at least sometimes they got the news out. However, with Mze's leading journalists now unemployed, most of the reporters at other stations who may have pushed the envelope prior to Mze's closure became too frightened to say even a word more than allowed by their censors.[20]

State, or "Public," Television

Beyond his influence at private stations, once in power, Saakashvili gained total and direct control of State TV. As if to signify the change of government, this station, which had supported Shevardnadze until his last day in office, suddenly became Saakashvili's most ardent fan. In one of the most bizarre appointments after Shevardnadze's resignation, acting president Nino Burdjanadze reappointed Zaza Shengelia as the general director of the State Broadcasting Company—which operated Channel One, particularly popular among older viewers, and Channel Two, which was like a Georgian version of C-SPAN. Shengelia, who had resigned this position several days before Saakashvili stormed the Parliament on November 22, had over the years turned State TV into the mouthpiece of the old government.

Ostensibly, Shengelia's task was to turn State TV into public television in order to give the station independence. His first move was to fire journalists and anchors that were known to be unsympathetic to the leadership of the new government. Since then, Channel One has continued to report the news by simply reading government press releases and propaganda, while chastising anyone who dares to criticize the government. The only difference between the station before and after the revolution is that before, it at least pretended to report news about the opposition—albeit in a slanted fashion—whereas after, its reporting has been reminiscent of television coverage during the Soviet era.

During several parliamentary debates about bias at Channel One, National Movement deputies never tried to rebut charges that the station had not changed under their rule. Instead, they argued that this was precisely the reason why legislation was necessary to convert the State Broadcasting Company into an independent *public* broadcasting network, akin to the British Broadcasting Company (BBC). The idea that somehow, through structural change, the reporting at Channel One would become unbiased did not quite add up. Furthermore, this argument did not respond to the question of why Saakashvili, had he wanted a truly independent station, could not demand unbiased coverage from Shengelia while these changes were being considered, instead of the one-sided reporting that had become the norm.

On December 23, 2004, the Parliament passed the Law on Broadcasting, which mandated the creation of public television and set forth regulations for private television stations and radio channels. Backers of the law claimed that the mechanism of managing public television through a nine-person board of directors, whose members would be appointed by Parliament from among a group of nominees submitted by the president, would ensure that it would be independent of political and business pressure. In addition, the law created the Broadcasting Commission to oversee the entire television sphere, whose members would be appointed by the president with Parliament's approval. However, no provision was set forth to give the minority factions in Parliament say in the appointments of either public television's board of directors or the Broadcasting Commission. In other words, even though the backers claimed to provide for structures that would be free of political pressure, in reality the legislation gave the president full control over both public television's board of directors and the Broadcasting Commission. As such, the law continued consolidation of all political power in Georgia in the hands of the president.

The Law on Broadcasting was written by the Liberty Institute, and in its initial version might have destroyed private television in Georgia, because it required the Broadcasting Commission to conduct, once every ten years, an open competition over every private channel's licenses. As a result, after securing a license and spending ten years investing in its business and growing, a private channel could suddenly see itself without a license based on the whims of a politically stacked commission. This provision was eventually changed, providing for automatic renewal of the private channels' licenses if they meet certain requirements set forth by the Broadcasting Commission. However, the commission was given a great deal of freedom in deciding what these requirements will be, and they may include mandates that certain views and opinions should not (or should) be aired. Because of this, private TV channel owners have expressed fears that the Broadcast Commission will become a new vehicle for censorship of political views.

The law left the public television station's financing in a state of flux. Initially, Liberty Institute proposed that 1.5 percent of all income-tax revenue received by the state in a given year be directed to public television to ensure that state agencies would not be involved in determining the station's budget. This provision was rejected, due to pressure from the chairman of Parliament's Economic Committee. As passed, the legislation directs the state to finance public television through income-tax revenue, but does not specify how much money the station should receive. As a result, the new corporation will be just as dependent on the government as State Television was in the past. Additionally, over objections from private broadcasters, the law permits the public television station to run commercials. Private channels argued that public television could undercut the price of advertisements because it would be receiving some funding from the state, thus creating an imbalance in the advertising market.

Members of the opposition fought the Law on Broadcasting and argued that State TV should be privatized. The Liberty Institute came out strongly against this idea, even though Saakashvili had made privatization of all other state assets one of the key goals of his presidency. Supporters of public television argued that privatization would hand business interests control of a vital national asset.

In November 2004, even before the proposed Law on Broadcasting was passed by Parliament, Channel One suddenly went off the air for several weeks, only to reappear in mid-December as "reformed" Channel One, called "Public Channel." Thus, even before the proposed legal changes necessary to create the new station were put into effect, Shengelia claimed to have converted his station into public television. However, this move did more to discredit the idea behind public television and its possible impartiality than any opponent of public television could have ever hoped. The new station had changed everything—it had a new logo, new studios, new programs, and new anchors. The only thing that had *not* changed was the bias on behalf of the government in its news coverage: the one-sided reports lionizing Saakashvili and other government officials and policy, while belittling or ignoring those who have a different point of view, continued in full force. Thus, the new "public station" discredited the main reason behind the proposed Law on Broadcasting. Public television, in the minds of most, turned out not to be impartial at all.

14

Civil Society, Illusionary and Real

Thus far in Part Three, I have examined the impact of Saakashvili's authoritarian instincts and governance style on the political institutions within the constitutional framework of the Georgian regime. Furthermore, I discussed a number of case examples of his regime's limited successes and distinct failures in promoting reforms, implementing democratic and good governance, and protecting human rights. I also touched upon how Saakashvili has dealt with a key nonconstitutional institution within the body politic, what one may also call the extraconstitutional check on state power—the media.

In this chapter, I examine another extraconstitutional element of democracy—the civil society. My goal is not merely to analyze what impact Saakashvili's government has had on civil society, but above all to understand what is understood by "civil society" in Georgia, and what it should mean if it is to begin to make a real contribution to democratic governance.

Georgia's NGO Class

One encounters in Georgia a group of NGOs that style themselves as the only civil society, while rejecting the elements of the real civil society that so impressed Alexis de Tocqueville in nineteenth-century America. These groups demand to be classified as "civil society," even though they have little to do with what actually is a civil society. The question is whether the real civil society will have an opportunity to play its proper role in sustaining Georgian democracy.

Most American and other Western activists who are at the forefront of advancing democracy in transitional or closed societies believe that developing a civil society is essential for political change. Civil society, in their view, must become a cornerstone in the development of political institutions that make freedom and rule of law viable. This notion dates back to Montesquieu, but more importantly, to Hegel and Tocqueville. Tocqueville convincingly demonstrated in his monumental work *Democracy in America* how the success of American democracy was tied to the country's vibrant civil society—what he understood as membership-based associations and organizations. "Among the laws that rule human societies there is one that seems more precise and clearer than all the others. In order that men remain civilized or become so, the art of associating must be developed and perfected among them in the same ratio as equality of conditions increases," wrote Tocqueville.[1] Modern American civil society includes a wide range, such as places of worship, labor unions and business groups, interest groups like the ACLU and the Family Research Council, think tanks, private universities, and even groups like the Rotary Club and soup kitchens.[2]

Given the predominance of the view that civil society is crucial for democracy—a view I generally share—some readers may have been taken aback by my criticism of the NGOs in Part Two. One key reason for my criticism is that these groups have little, if anything at all, to do with the Tocquevillian civil society that is so important for self-government, especially because they are hostile to what any reasonable human being would consider to be essential (though certainly not exclusive) elements of civil society—namely, the independent business community, and faith-based or religious associations.

It would be fabulous if, as a result of Western efforts to promote civil society, transitional countries developed groups like those described by Tocqueville—groups that actually represented given elements and factions within the body politic. Such a development would truly contribute to the effort to advance democracy abroad. Indeed, in some cases, Western efforts have actually worked quite successfully—Poland's Solidarity Movement is but one important example.

More often than not, however, attempts to foster a civil society in transitional democracies result in the emergence of a small group of "intellectuals" and "activists" who are English-speaking and very young, and who often find themselves and their ideas wholly out of touch with the positions of the body politic in which they operate. Instead of nurturing democracy, often these groups operate like parasitic growths on the body politic. Sadly, they are financed almost exclusively with Western money. This has been particularly true in Georgia. Rather than being voluntary associations representing interests in the body politic, these NGOs and their leaders represent themselves;

they are a "self-defined NGO class."[3] This class—unlike the business class, for example—is not self-sustaining and is completely dependent on support from foreign donors. As a result, the views and policies advanced by it usually parallel the wishes of its foreign supporters.

Leaders of this "class" are adamant about being called "civil society," and reject any other group's claim to be a part of it. Nothing shows this better than a paper by Ghia Nodia called "Civil Society Development in Georgia: Achievements and Challenges," written as part of a USAID project called Citizens Advocate.[4]

Nodia is the most respected political thinker in Georgia and the best-known scholar outside of the country. Indeed, internationally many prominent political scientists regard him as one of the most interesting thinkers on the subject of democratic governance; he even serves on the editorial board of the most respected publication in this field, the *Journal of Democracy*. Nodia is to the Georgian NGO class what Irving Kristol and Norman Podhoretz are to American neoconservatism—he is the founding father of the NGO movement in Georgia. Nodia was the first person to articulate the notions of "civil society" that are popular with the NGO class, and as such he is its intellectual father.

His role with the NGO community goes beyond laying its intellectual foundations. Many of the leaders of the NGO groups are either his former students or served as younger colleagues in his think tank, the Caucasus Institute for Peace, Democracy, and Development. At the same time, for many years Nodia chaired the board of directors of the Soros Foundation in Georgia, and through this position was able to influence which NGOs would receive vital financing from one of the largest donor groups in the country. Furthermore, because of the respect he wields in the international scholarly community, for many years his views helped shape funding decisions at governmental donor groups (such as USAID). Thus, he was able to direct funding to the NGOs that shared his vision. For all these reasons, Nodia has wielded tremendous influence over other activists in the Georgian NGO class.

Another reason why Nodia's views represent a good way of considering the NGO class as a whole is that Georgian NGO activists share a trait that Owen Harries has identified in Western intellectuals. Quoting the art critic Harold Rosenburg, Harries has written that intellectuals are like "a herd of independent minds. . . . Intellectuals are generally prone to run together. Beneath their often savage surface differences and scorn for orthodoxy, there is usually a surprising degree of uncritical acceptance of erroneous views concerning the way things are, and in particular, the way things are going."[5] This applies perfectly to the representatives of the NGO class in Georgia, except that their "acceptance of erroneous views" goes beyond the issues of how things are at any given time, to their vision of how things *should* be. In part because they share this trait with Western intellectuals, I analyze the Georgian NGO class through a focus on Nodia's writings, since his thought creates the impetus for the rest of the NGO leaders. Finally, an important reason why it is worth to focus on Nodia is that most Georgian NGO activists do not write documents worth analyzing—Nodia is one of the few whose writings one can engage and analyze with care.[6] Thus, his writings can be taken as a representative view of the Georgian civil society.

In the introduction to this essay on civil society, Nodia writes that "at present, the term civil society more often refers to those forms of social relations and activities that are *beyond* the spheres of family, business, and the State."[7] In Georgia, he says that this largely means "NGOs, business associations, and community-based organizations."[8] The term he uses to describe these groups is "civil society organizations (CSOs)," because as far as Nodia is concerned, these groups are the only groups that constitute civil society.[9]

Functioning and active community-based organizations are virtually nonexistent in Georgia. For this reason, they are justifiably not a serious part of Nodia's analysis. Meanwhile, Georgia has about two dozen active business associations, of which about five have real dues-paying members and real influence over public policy. As such, they are truly Tocquevillesque associations. It took years of arguing on their behalf before these groups were accepted by Nodia, and his allies in the NGO class, into "civil society." Even now, this acceptance is only partial.[10] Thus, not counting these very few business associations, what Nodia classifies as "civil society" actually boils down to political nongovernmental organizations. These are groups in Tbilisi that claim to be political interest groups, but in reality, they do not represent anyone. They are not voluntary associations that came together to defend a preexisting interest. Rather, they are groups created from the top that aim to establish interests within the body politic from the outside. They defend and advance not the interests of constituents, but rather the ideological views of their founders, even when these views have virtually no real support from the people. This is why in my view, the NGOs are a "class" all to themselves.

Anyone familiar with Hegel or Tocqueville would find Nodia's definition of civil society unsatisfying and incomplete, given that it excludes what have always been viewed as key elements of civil society—in particular, religion and business.[11] The issue of religion is complex, and it is at least possible to argue that it should not be included in civil society. However, business should be less of a concern, given that few would exclude it.

Indeed, the philosopher who coined the term "civil society" saw property and market economy as essential for liberal democracy. According to Louis Hunt, "Hegel places the discussion about the appropriate place of the market in the modern social and political order in a broader historical and philosophical account of the nature of human freedom. He argues that private property and the market are necessary but not sufficient conditions for the realization of such freedom." Furthermore, Hunt believes that "the affinity between Hegel's conception of civil society and the idea of the market in classical political economy does not, however, imply either that he uncritically endorsed the market economy or that he thought civil society could be reduced to its economic basis. In Hegel's account, civil society encompasses not only the market narrowly conceived but also the legal, social, and (in part) political framework within which, and through which, the market operates. Under the rubric of civil society, Hegel includes a range of institutions that serve both to foster the operations of the market economy and to check its excesses."[12]

Nodia is aware of this and knows that some readers may wonder why business is not part of his definition.[13] As a result, he tries to explain his decision to exclude business by saying that entrepreneurship is where "individuals come together in order to gain a profit,"[14] which ostensibly makes such associations ineligible for membership in the civil society. This statement, however, does not prove very much, because no explanation or reason is given for why profit-seeking should be viewed as not belonging in civil society. Furthermore, the reality in Georgia is that leaders of the largest and most active NGOs earn far more money than the vast majority of the entrepreneurs—indeed, having a senior position in a local branch of a Western NGO is probably the highest-paid job for the overwhelming majority of citizens.[15] Nodia acknowledges as much when he writes later in his analysis that "against the background of a general lack of economic development, western grants provide an opportunity for a relatively high income to their recipients."[16] Thus, the notion that the Georgian NGOs are somehow not "profitable" for those who are active participants in them, as compared to businesses in which individuals earn a "profit," is at best misleading.

This forces us to consider what may be Nodia's real reason for excluding business from the civil society. I would venture to suggest that in Nodia's philosophic universe, business is not a good phenomenon. Rather, business is something that must be limited, and against which civil society, in conjunction with government, must act. So, while "trade unions have a special place in the civil society . . . [because they] act as opponents to business," "corporations" have to be excluded.[17] The logical assumption underlying these statements—which Nodia does not write about here, but has expressed to me in private discussions—is that business, and profit from business activity (especially in Georgia), is troublesome for the society as a whole, while the civil society is good, and thus the two cannot be intermixed.

Another element absent from Nodia's definition of civil society is religion—or rather, religious organizations. This omission is actually far more important than that of business, because opposition to religion is probably the most fundamental and unifying characteristic of the Georgian NGO class (although there would probably be more support among secularists in the West for excluding religion from civil society than for exclusion of business). Nonetheless, Nodia is aware that many would place the religious realm in civil society, so he writes that although "faith-based, confessional organizations and churches" may "fall formally under [a] wider understanding of civil society," they "may not be particularly happy to be included"[18] in this category. The reason is that "civil society takes its roots in the liberal tradition—but some religious organizations may have an ambivalent and negative stance toward it."[19]

Some Georgian religious organizations may indeed not wish to be included in Nodia's analysis of "civil society." However, what about those who would not object? It makes little sense to go from the potential objections of "some" to the absolute exclusion of all. The reality is that religious organizations in America at the time when Tocqueville wrote *Democracy in America* were not rooted in the liberal tradition either, and they also might have objected to being included in his analysis of civil society. However, the American regime was the first attempt to bring into action the theoretical views of modern liberal political philosophers. And even if they were not liberal, Tocqueville correctly noted that religious groups were at the core of American mores and characteristics that made democracy and the preservation of liberty possible. Given this background, analyzing religious groups as part of civil society in Georgia is not only beneficial, but may actually be absolutely necessary. This reality undermines Nodia's explanation even further, and points us to examine Nodia's thought about religion a little more deeply in order to understand what actually may be at work.

In telling us that civil society is "rooted in the liberal tradition," Nodia suggests that he is using the term "liberal" as in "liberal democracy," and not as "left-of-center."[20] However, Nodia has written elsewhere that "liberal democracy requires complete separation of the religious and socio-political spheres, that is to say, making the religion a matter of private life."[21] Certainly that is an argument that is very open to debate, since at a minimum, thinkers, politicians, and, most importantly, millions of voters in the most developed of Western democracies would take a contrary view. But for Nodia, it turns out that liberal democracy is synonymous with and limited exclusively to a society of secularism that views religion from a perspective that one would fairly describe as a radical viewpoint from the very Left.

The interpretation that Nodia uses the term liberal democratic to describe what is generally known as leftist secularism is supported by the fact that he juxtaposes his vision of the "liberal tradition" (from which civil society originates) with a tradition from which an uncivil society originates. This uncivil society, Nodia tells us, includes "religious fundamentalism."[22] But by religious fundamentalism, Nodia does not merely mean something akin to Ayatollah Khomeini, to the Taliban, or to Wahhabism. Rather, for him, anyone who is religious is actually a fundamentalist. He told me as much, once, when he defined me as a fundamentalist because I told him that I consider it appropriate for religion to play an active role in the public sphere.

Nodia has written as much in "Is Georgia Threatened by Religious Fundamentalism?" Nodia's understanding of fundamentalism means "giving up on the separation of religion and socio-political life and submitting the latter to religion as much as possible."[23] Nodia believes that according to "international sociological practice," one way to determine if someone is a religious fundamentalist or not is to ask him or her if "faith and religious values should determine all aspects of the life of society and the state."[24] When support for this view is high in a given polity, this apparently means that support for religious fundamentalism is also high in that society. In Georgia, according to a survey conducted by Nodia's think tank, 65 percent of Georgians agreed with this view. For this reason, Nodia concludes that "according to this survey, Georgia is ready for religious fundamentalism."[25]

If this question were really the measure of religious fundamentalism, then certainly Pope Benedict XVI is a religious fundamentalist, as is his predecessor Pope John Paul II, as well as probably any serious religious leader. Not only that: any person who takes religion and religious worship seriously would then be described as a religious fundamentalist as well. Indeed by this definition, Israel is probably a fundamentalist state, given the extent to which it is defined by Judaism.

While probably only a tiny minority in most traditional Western democracies share Nodia's view of religious fundamentalism, this vision is extremely representative of the view of the NGO class in Georgia, which defines itself to a large degree by rebelling against religion. Its members take pride in having liberated themselves from religion, tradition, and "old" moral values in favor of secularism and "progress," and wish to effect a similar liberation on their fellow countrymen. In the words of Zurab Kiknadze, "We must challenge our past."[26] Individuals in the NGO class believe that it is their job to create a "new" morality on which to found the new political regime. This new morality is necessary because in the NGO class's view, the old religion-based morality is incompatible with what they like to call democracy and freedom.

DEMOCRATIC RHETORIC AND THE NIHILISTIC VISION OF THE HUMAN CONDITION

The NGO class claims to be advancing liberal democracy, as Nodia's focus on the "liberal tradition" is meant to imply. However, its views about the people who are supposed to engage in self-government in a democracy call this proposition into question. To explain how, I once again turn to Ghia Nodia.

In October 2004, shortly after the government's endeavor in South Osse-tia,[27] Nodia published a lengthy article titled "How to End the Revolution" in the Georgian daily *24 Hours*.[28] The crux of the piece is quite sensible—Nodia claims that Saakashvili and the new government must end the revolutionary crusade and start "governing the country." If things do not change, he writes, the impression seems to be that "the government may find itself in front of a crisis." In the piece, Nodia also recommends a number of concrete steps Saakashvili must take in order to start governing. Among other things, he makes another sensible suggestion, urging Saakashvili to stop pretending and claiming that he has absolutely nothing in common with Shevardnadze.

Nodia's article is most interesting, however, not for its comments about Georgian politics, but for two philosophic views it advances about the nature of men and of government within the framework of analyzing the Georgian polit-ical situation. These two ideas illustrate the relativist, illiberal, and somewhat Nietzschean foundations of Nodia's political thought. They are also founda-tions that the NGO class shares. Nodia comes off as a proponent of democ-racy—he declares that it is time for Georgia to have "normal government," and in "today's universe [that] means democratic" government. Looking deeper into his thinking, however, questions are born about whether Nodia's reasons for favoring democracy are the same as the traditional basis for liberal self-gov-ernment, or whether his argument actually undermines the very foundations of liberal democracy, both in thought and in action.

Nodia begins his article by pointing out that Saakashvili's "honeymoon is over," and that "the government's rating is not . . . what it used to be several months ago." He attributes this rising discontent partly to the South Ossetia debacle, and partly to the absence of a strategic plan; the government "impro-vises and acts in a chaotic and inconsistent manner," he writes. While people are unhappy, "society does not know what it wants because it does not know what to demand from the government."[29] In other words, the people are con-fused because they do not have a "concrete political program," and "if you ask [people] what the government must do, you will hear numerous, often contra-dictory, thoughts." Therein is the first of his two important theoretical observa-tions: citizens are ignorant and do not know what they want, and therefore cannot give the government a clear set of demands. One has to wonder—does this mean that such citizens can never be satisfied by any government?

Nodia's other important theoretical observation is that in governance, one "seldom has a choice between good and evil," but rather, "the law of life" is that "the choice is between bad and worse."[30] In Georgia's case, this results in the presidency of Mikheil Saakashvili, which may be essentially bad, but if it is indeed bad, the reason is that this "it the best government Georgian peo-ple's current [political] condition" can yield. So, "like it or not," Saakashvili's government "is the best that we can have in the present circumstance," just like Shevardnadze's government "was the best during history's concrete period."

Accordingly, when the Georgian people favored Saakashvili over Shevardnadze during the Rose Revolution, they were merely picking the lesser of two evils, for according to Nodia, they do not have the capacity for a fundamentally good government. However, Nodia states that revolutionaries in general, including the Georgian revolutionaries, do not understand this reality. Instead, they believe that they are in a struggle between good and evil. Since they view themselves on the side of good, they often justify questionable actions as necessary in order to achieve their good ends. So, the Georgian revolutionaries are saying that "now, when there is such an emergency, we may put aside the necessity to abide by the law and procedures of governance, conduct the necessary reforms by force and then, in the bright European future . . . everything will be done normally."

To his credit, Nodia claims that he does not agree with the revolutionaries that abiding by the law is not necessary so long as there is a simple emergency. However, the reasoning that leads him to this disagreement is fascinating. Since "law of life [mandates choice] between bad and worse," Nodia recommends that to end this revolutionary ends-justify-the-means environment, the government "must explain to the society and to itself what is achievable [and what is not] and [to admit] that it requires far more time and resources [to reach the achievable]." In other words, instead of striving for the absolute good, to end the revolution the Georgian government must live by the law of nature, and be willing to accept the least bad of many bad options—even if this option is not the ideal.

Nodia's first observations inevitably make one wonder—how can modern liberal democracy, founded on the notion that it is just for citizens to make an informed judgment about the fundamental issues facing them, function if citizens do not know what they want and do not have the capacity to make decisions? In other words, how can a view that citizens "do not know" square with the principle of self-government? Some may view this as evidence of contempt for the Georgian public, which many in the NGO sector appear to have.

The combination of Nodia's two central points could be seen as pointing to a nihilistic view of human life and the condition of men. Nodia's statements suggest that men should submit themselves to the rule of fate and accept their government, regardless of how corrupt and unjust it may be, because it is "the best that we can have." At the same time, Nodia believes that all choices are choices between evils, and therefore no government, not even representative democracy, is fundamentally just. According to this view, since even a democracy is subject to the law of nature that dictates the choice of the lesser evil, it cannot claim to embody the principles of political justice and prudence. But one has to wonder whether this view is compatible with liberal democracy's claim to rule.

Liberal democracy claims to be the *best* regime because it is based on the *true* understanding of human nature and is dependent on the will of the people. Liberalism is based on a viewpoint that considers citizens to be capable of governing themselves wisely, partly by empowering representatives that will secure and serve their true interests and liberties. A representative liberal democracy claims to be just, precisely because it is responsive to the interests of the population from which it derives its legitimacy. Nodia's view that men are incapable of ruling themselves wisely deprives such a government of its higher claim to justice. For this reason, Nodia appears to be not a democrat, but rather an anti-democrat. This view is shared by an overwhelming majority of Nodia's colleagues in the Georgian NGO class, and for this reason makes it virtually impossible for this group to actively participate in promoting a democratic, free way of life in Georgia.

The vision of liberal democracy articulated here was originally conceived by thinkers such as Locke and Montesquieu, among other modern political philosophers, and first put into practice by the American Founders. These philosophers and lawgivers believed that there is indeed a common good and a just political order, and that men institute government among themselves in order to secure these principles. The view of America's role abroad which places advancement of freedom at the forefront simply builds on the liberal democratic truths regarding the human condition, truths on which the American regime is founded.

By contrast, if people do not know what they want in life, and their existence forces them to always choose between "bad and worse," the idea of *good* government becomes virtually impossible, as does the notion that the political regime should strive to promote the common good. In this moral universe, all regimes seem deficient, even those that are founded on the sanctity of the rule of law. Nodia's understanding of politics and of the human condition is fundamentally incompatible with the notion that there are any immutable principles of justice, and therefore it is irreconcilable with the principles of justice that underpin liberalism.

In making this argument, Nodia may be following in the footsteps of postmodernity, which continues to shape Europe's intellectual and political life today. Instead of condemning Saakashvili's ends-justify-the-means logic, Nodia's argument, perhaps inadvertently but not without reason, comes close to supplying it with a moral justification. Indeed, if all regimes are deficient and the only measure of justice is the choice of the lesser evil, then on what grounds can Nodia condemn extraconstitutional and extralegal actions that are employed by the government because they are conducive to any given political goal?

If one takes Nodia's view that the choice is always between "bad and worse" to its logical conclusion, it becomes obvious that democracy is good only because *it is the least bad of the various alternative systems of government.*[31] With this view, the aforementioned contradiction between his belief that people do not know what they want and his support for democracy disappears. However, if democracy and the sanctity of natural human rights are good only because the alternatives are worse, then logic would dictate that government can violate individual rights by simply offering a sufficiently strong justification for why such a violation is better than other alternatives.[32] Since Saakashvili thinks that the current Georgian emergency justifies actions documented in this narrative, Nodia's argument, which he wants to use against Saakashvili's "ends justify the means" approach to governance, actually becomes a vindication of that very approach.

To provide the reader with a taste of the extent to which Nodia's views about human nature are shared by other activists in the NGO class, I point to these examples: Ramaz Sakvarelidze, who often represents the NGO class in TV appearances and newspaper interviews, commented (when asked about the Saakashvili government) that Georgians are "lazy and that is why [they] do not think about alternatives."[33] This is a very prominent view in the NGO class, and is largely based on the view expressed by Gaga Nizharadze that "the Georgian culture is hysterical."[34] Giorgi Margvelashvili has offered a more radical expression of this view, writing that the "diagnosis is indisputable—mentally weak, at the level of soft idiotism. In other words, [Georgian people are] in a condition when the person's psychological development stops at a certain level and does not reach completion. Such an individual has the body of a fully developed human being, but an intellect appropriate for a younger age. This is the present condition of the Georgian population, of the Georgian nation. . . . The diagnosis is—mental retardation."[35]

POLITICAL NGO CLASS IN GOVERNMENT

Such a political philosophy would not be a matter of such great concern if it were merely an academic view of an intellectual sitting somewhere in a think tank or university. After all, many academics around the world may very well share some of the views held by Nodia and others in Georgia. However, the problem is that these views are actually the key elements of the ideology of the Georgian government—if not the whole government, then at least a key part of it.

As examined earlier, the Rose Revolution brought three distinct groups to power—Saakashvili's group, Zhvania's group, and the NGO class. Each of these three groups sought power for very different reasons. Saakashvili's team wanted power for power's sake, while Zhvania's team looked at power as a business enterprise. By contrast, the NGO class sought power to advance its vision of Georgia through "reforms." These "reforms" entail fighting corruption through bureaucratization and greater regulation of citizens' everyday lives by the state, introducing "new values" and reducing the influence of the Orthodox Church, imposing control on private enterprise, altering the curricula at institutions of secondary and higher education, and gaining control over State Television in order to educate Georgians in its vision of human nature.

During the first year after the revolution, the civil-society team within the new government experienced a mild split, with some members moving into the "opposition." Specifically, the Republican Party, which had been part of the National Movement coalition for three years, along with certain NGOs that had previously supported Saakashvili, began to confront the president.[36] Meanwhile, other activists from the NGO class became very active in the government on the side of Saakashvili. For example, Giga Bokeria and Givi Targamadze from the Liberty Institute became leading parliamentarians; Soros Foundation's former executive director Kakha Lomaia became minister of education; Ghia Nodia and several others have become directors of Public Television; while Nodia served on the four-person committee that stacked the Central Election Commission with the president's supporters.

This apparent split notwithstanding, the NGO class has been united in advancing its "reform" agenda. Its representatives have actually sometimes promoted an agenda that members of Saakashvili's and Zhvania's teams would have preferred to avoid; at times, the latter two succeeded in scuttling the agenda, as was the case with the failed attempt in the fall of 2004 to try to reduced the influence of the Georgian Orthodox Church through an internal conflict. Most of the time, however, the NGO class has successfully pushed through proposals that even President Saakashvili and his supporters realize may harm them politically in the future—as was the case with the Higher Education Law—but were obliged to support in order to avoid a deeper split in their coalition.

The Higher Education Law, which the NGOs have championed vigorously against vehement opposition from students, university faculty, and the public at large, is a key example of their success.[37] The law was enacted in the fall of 2004 and came into force in the summer of 2005, when the application process to Georgian universities (both public and private ones) took place through a new set of complex regulations imposed by the law. The legislation originates in a laudable desire to remove the corruption endemic in higher education—especially at state institutions, where acceptance to some of the most popular programs (such as law, international relations, business, etc.) used to require a bribe of $10,000 to $30,000. However, the mechanisms that it created are overly authoritarian and unwise for a weak state like Georgia, because they overtax the institutional capabilities of the state.

For example, the law centralized all undergraduate admissions in the Ministry of Education, which administers nationwide examinations and assigns students to universities, programs, and departments based on the scores they achieve on these examinations. Students who score the highest on the exam are awarded a State Education Grant, which can be used at public and private institutions. However, the law prohibits public institutions from charging higher tuition than the grant. This, in turn, is a problem, given the fact that state funds are by no means enough to create quality university education. Thus, state schools are suffering a serious lack of funds and resources.

The law also reduced the number of first-year openings at universities, including at private ones, by over a half—without considering what will happen to those graduating high-school students who, cannot attend universities. Because of the economic stagnation in Georgia, many parents have used the option of placing high-school graduates at an institution of higher education as a means of preventing their children from turning to alcohol, drugs, and crime. This option is no longer available to thousands, and a possible result is a generation of dissatisfied, unemployed youngsters.

The Real Civil Society

One may find the NGO class's positions mistaken, but few democrats would dispute that these views have the right to exist in the marketplace of ideas, where others can disagree with them and make their argument against them. However, the Georgian NGO class does not wish to argue and defend its views. Rather, its preference is to exclude, demonize, and chastise as "uneducated" anyone who does not agree with them. Therefore, it often works to prevent the emergence of real civil-society elements in the body politic that could rival it (such as membership-based interest groups, the business community, religious groups, political parties with different philosophic points of view, etc.). When such elements either develop, as was the case with the Georgian business community during the late 1990s, or already exist, such as the Georgian Orthodox Church, the NGO class tries to put them down by arguing that they are not "real," or that they are backward, corrupt, and anti-democratic.

Unfortunately, Western efforts often inadvertently foster the NGO class, while ignoring those groups that constitute the more Tocquevillian civil society. This is particularly true of USAID, which for years has supported the NGO class in Georgia, even as it has promoted values that are utterly incompatible with the founding principles of American government. That said, President

Ronald Reagan's magnificent achievement of semiprivate institutional vehicles created to support real democratic activism—the National Endowment for Democracy and its affiliated institutes, such as the Center for International Private Enterprise (CIPE)—are notable exceptions in their work around the world in support of real civil society organizations.

NONGOVERNMENTAL ORGANIZATIONS

Notwithstanding my criticism of the NGO class, it would be unwise to reject the NGOs themselves as a key element of the real civil society. For this reason, I include them in my discussion of the real civil society.

Among the two dozen NGOs that have influence over public policy, organizations can be divided into several categories. One such group can be classified as defenders of human rights. Two of these, Liberty Institute and the Georgian Young Lawyers' Association (GYLA), play a very active role in lawmaking. Indeed, they are responsible for the vast majority of the Parliament's legislative output, since National Movement deputies have not shown much interest in writing legislation. Liberty, which has limited its pronouncements about human rights since the Rose Revolution, has been particularly influential, because three of its leaders (Giga Bokeria, David Zurabishvili, and Givi Targamadze) are members of Parliament. GYLA, meanwhile, is aligned with the Republican Party and, to its credit, is far more active in raising its concerns about the government's abysmal human-rights record than Liberty Institute.

On the other side of the spectrum of human-rights NGOs are Former Political Prisoners for Human Rights and the Georgian Human Rights Documentation Center, both of which have been very critical of the government's actions and continue to show a great deal of vigilance about human-rights abuses. Unlike GYLA and Liberty, these two do not enjoy the government's favor.

Among think tanks, Nodia's CIPDD along with the Georgian Foundation for Strategic and International Studies (GFSIS) and Partnership for Social Initiatives (PSI) deserve mention. Each is more scholarly oriented than the aforementioned organizations. CIPDD probably has the most pro-government stance, while PSI has the most critical one, though it has succeeded in working with the government in a number of economic-reform areas such as welfare and social-protection reform.[38] GFSIS's leaders, meanwhile, have become critical of the government and of the ability of the Georgian people to ever succeed in overcoming their problems, *but only in private.*

Unfortunately, most other NGOs of influence are biding their time as they watch how the political situation develops in Georgia. Many foreigners who are concerned about the political trends in Georgia under Saakashvili hope that the NGO community will serve as a serious check on the government and will help protect democracy and human rights in the country. However, right now this is unlikely, given that some of the most active elements of the NGO community are the driving force behind some of the most controversial initiatives facing Georgia.

POLITICAL PARTIES

Political parties were one of the seeds of democracy in prerevolutionary Georgia. The problem for each of the political parties in the past (and even more so today) was that they were built around a political personality rather than a political philosophy. Thus, while there was a great deal of political pluralism in Georgia, political parties were not institutional entities that could grow and develop on their own. Most would cease to exist if and when the leader around whom they were created left the political scene.[39] As a result, the ability of these political parties to contribute to democratic consolidation was limited then, and is even more so now. However, even though pluralism today is very limited, opposition does exist and it needs to be cultivated further. Indeed, there is even an opportunity for the emergence of a new political force that could play a pivotal role in moving Georgia forward.

Whatever one makes of the Rose Revolution, the fact is that it was possible to build a multiparty pluralistic system in Georgia after the events of November 2003. However, this would have required Saakashvili and others in government to help nurture such a pluralistic environment, something that they failed to do, as my examination of the March elections, Saakashvili's refusal to lower the barrier for entry into Parliament, and the government's treatment of the media demonstrate.

Nonetheless, because two parties overcame the 7 percent barrier and gained seats in Parliament, even after the March elections it was still possible to sow the seeds of party pluralism in the country. Unfortunately, Saakashvili and his allies in the legislature chose to disparage and put down the parliamentary opposition, rather than try to strengthen it for the sake of Georgian democracy. One can understand their reasoning—it is much easier to limit the opposition's ability to engage in political discourse than to try to defeat the opposition's argument in a vigorous political debate. Limiting the opposition, however, can be very harmful, and has certainly been in Georgia's case.

Some Georgian analysts claim that the country's political culture today is not capable of supporting more than one political party and political elite.[40] Fortunately, this sort of claim ignores facts, because there is nothing in the Georgian political culture that prevents the development of the opposition. Rather, the opposition in Georgia is indeed weak—but because it is being put down by the regime, not because there is no capacity in the body politic to support a differing opinion. This is not to suggest that the opposition parties are not responsible for their problems. However, in a closing political society such as Georgia, pluralism is very difficult to sustain, with opposition parties spending all their energy trying to survive rather than on efforts to try to expand their base of supporters.

One of the biggest problems facing party-building in Georgia has to do with the National Movement and the role that Saakashvili sees for his party in the body politic. Instead of moving in the direction of a traditional, Western political party, in building a long-term political union around a certain ideology and values, the National Movement has developed into another "state party," which exists only because of its leader and is wholly dependent on the support of the state administrative resources. Political scientists sometimes call parties such as India's Congress Party, Japan's Liberal Democrats, and Italy's now defunct Christian Democrats, which do not have an ideology but exist as unions of seemingly incompatible constituencies, each of which is unified only by the desire for power, "brokerage" parties. Once a democracy matures, such parties either convert into more traditional, philosophic unions (for example, Japan's Liberal Democrats are undergoing this change now) or disappear (as happened with Italy's Christian Democrats). Brokerage parties can exist without one unifying leader, and have the capacity to continue after its leading political figure leaves the scene. Because of this, the National Movement is not even a brokerage party, but an even less developed entity—a union of diverse political groups around one person while that person is in power. Without that person or state power, these groups would have nothing in common, not even a cohesive quest for power. Thus, National Movement is a "state" party.

Unfortunately, such "state" parties have become the norm in Georgia, and indeed in the former Soviet Union. Both Shevardnadze-Zhvania's Citizens Union of Georgia (CUG) and Adjarian leader Aslan Abashidze's Revival Party functioned as "state" parties—one on a national and another on a regional level. Like the CUG (which disappeared when Shevardnadze resigned), the National Movement would fall apart if Saakashvili chose to move away from it, or if he were to leave the political scene. Because it is not a traditional political party, the National Movement's political tactics tend to suck away too much political oxygen and make it very difficult for other, more traditional parties to develop. This is also what was happening in the mid-to-late 1990s, when Shevardnadze-Zhvania's CUG helped destroy any vibrant democratic opposition until the CUG began to fall apart.

Unlike the CUG, the National Movement has shown very little interest in building a vast regional political structure. Zhvania, who was the general secretary of the CUG, followed the old Communist Party model and devoted enormous effort to taking care of the CUG's regional leaders. By contrast, the National Movement does not seem to care what regional people may be up to. Indeed, when the International Republican Institute (IRI) organized a meeting for the National Movement's leadership with their district chairmen in February 2005, during which these district officials complained about the lack of progress and expressed fears about the National Movement's future popularity, senior national party officials decided to walk out of the meeting to show their displeasure with the complaining chairmen. National Movement leaders in Tbilisi make no effort to understand the concerns of regional officials, because they believe that the strength of the party is entirely connected to Saakashvili and his national popularity. When activists or party officials voice concerns, they are dubbed as being "Leiboristebi," the Georgian term for members of the Labor party, another group that advocates populist ideas akin to National Movement's.

The situation is not much better on the opposition front, where three groups deserve mention. Each one of these, to a varied degree, is also built around individuals, though they all are slightly more "ideological" than the National Movement. The Labor Party is the most personality-driven group in Georgia today, but it is actually ideological and is proud of being a leftist party—unlike the National Movement, which does not like to be classified as such. Labor's leader Shalva Natelashvili has always been viewed with contempt by much of the media, the "chattering class," and by most of the foreigners who interact with this group. He lost a great deal of his popularity immediately after the November 2, 2003, elections, even before the revolution, by referring to the Georgians as "stupid" for voting for National Movement in such large numbers (even though Labor's vote was also quite high—12.4 percent in the official results, 17.3 percent in the parallel vote tabulations).[41]

In the aftermath of the Rose Revolution, Natelashvili lost the support of more voters than anyone else, since his poverty-stricken supporters were the most obvious proponents of a revolutionary change. Nonetheless, it is possible that Natelashvili will regain some of his past popularity, especially if the government continues to fail in pressing reforms that have a significant impact on people's lives. Natelashvili is a great populist, and his rhetoric is bound to appeal to some. However, his resurgence would by no means be an improvement for the democratic environment, given Natelashvili's personal views and the Bolshevik ideas of those who surround him. If ever thrust into power, Saakashvili's failures with respect to good governance and the rule of law would pale in comparison to what the country would be likely to face under Natelashvili.

On the other side of the spectrum, one finds the only opposition group that succeeded in entering the legislature in the March elections—the New Rights Party (NRP) and its smaller ally, Industry Will Save Georgia. From the start, the NRP envisioned becoming a traditional political party—an organization that would continue to exist after its founding generation of leaders stepped away from political life and handed leadership over to a new generation. The party also hoped that its unifying political ideas (which it undoubtedly holds), rather than political personalities, would be the basis of its popular support. Unlike Natelashvili, few would accuse the NRP's leader, David Gamkrelidze, and his inner circle of being incompetent to rule, should the party ever come to power. On the contrary, the NRP probably has the best cadre of potential government leaders in Georgia. However, the party still suffers from the problem that is all too common in Georgia: notwithstanding its philosophic foundations, it is too centered on one individual, and has not yet developed into a political institution; if anything were to happen to Gamkrelidze today, the party would almost certainly lose much of its core.

There is a view, especially among analysts in Washington, that the NRP weakened itself by not siding with the revolutionaries in November 2003. I believe that this view is mistaken. The NRP is in a far more powerful position today, as the only viable opposition in Georgia, than it would have been had the 2003 legislative election results stayed in place, because in that case, it would have been one of four opposition parties with a viable future. Gamkrelidze is the only real opposition alternative to Saakashvili, whereas he would have been one of at least four potential alternatives to Shevardnadze. Unfortunately, Georgian analysts, most of whom are heavily influenced by the NGO class's distaste for pro-business ideology, are unwilling to give the NRP its due.[42]

It remains to be seen if the NRP has the capacity to grow enough to make Georgia a real two-party state. Of course, much of this depends on Saakashvili and his government, since without an open media and access to finances needed to engage in political activity, the NRP will have a hard time succeeding. Given the way Saakashvili's government has been treating entrepreneurs since coming into office, most are scared to support the opposition in any way, even if it is led by an old friend and colleague.

Ultimately, the key to the NRP's future is its leader and how his personality grows. Without a doubt, Gamkrelidze could manage the affairs of the country better than anyone else in Georgian politics today. His character has many qualities that a strong leader requires. However, judging by his actions thus far, he has not fully grasped the main political lesson of the Rose Revolution—that ultimately, democratic politics is dependent not on decisions made in the halls of power, but on the support of the people. Whereas Saakashvili suffers from an inability to manage the affairs of state, he excels, more so than any politician in the former Soviet Union and maybe even in Eastern Europe, at public politicking and mass communication. By contrast, Gamkrelidze does not yet know how to appeal directly to the people, and spends too much time considering what he might do if he ever were to be *entrusted* with power, rather than with the public politics necessary to *gain* that power. Instead of aiming to gain absolute victory, or to gain power on its own or as part of some coalition in the next legislative election, the NRP should follow its strategy of slow growth toward becoming a real party. In this regard, doubling its votes from 2004 would be an excellent showing.

Since the Rose Revolution, Georgia has seen the reemergence of an old political group that nearly disappeared in the late 1990s—the Republican Party. This party affiliated itself with Saakashvili in 2001, and several of its leaders were elected to Parliament through the National Movement's list in March 2004. Though the Republicans would deny this, their ideology closely parallels that of European socialists. This party core comes from Tbilisi's "intellectual elite" and has never had broad public support—even its own leaders often call their organization "a debating club."

The party has many allies inside the government and the NGO class. Indeed, it is led by one of the leaders of this class, David Usupashvili. It has some strong contacts in the West. In its membership, the party also has a wide range of individuals capable of making public remarks and appearing on television—a rarity in Georgian politics. For all these reasons, Saakashvili is not willing to give up so quickly on members of the government who would march over to the Republican side if they were removed from office. However, as Saakashvili's popularity continues to fall—which it is certain to do, even if the government improves and stops making the monumental governance mistakes that it has been making thus far—the Republican Party could emerge as an important force in Georgia. Its cause will be strengthened should George Soros choose to continue to finance the activities of its leaders and their NGOs, as he has in the past.[43]

Georgia's current political environment also creates an opportunity for the emergence of a new opposition group, led by the first generation of citizens who did not come of age under Communism, unlike all of the current political leaders in the country. These are individuals who were born in the decade between 1973 and 1983, and were at most in their early-to-mid teens when, on April 9, 1989, the Soviet troops violently crushed, on Tbilisi's Rustaveli Avenue, peaceful pro-independence demonstrators—largely university students and young adults. At least symbolically, Georgia became independent on this day, with the Communist government losing even the semblance of legitimacy after the death of nineteen young Georgians at the hands of Russian soldiers. For almost anyone older than the age of ten, April 9, 1989, remains the defining moment of their coming of age and the core of Georgian present-day patriotism. As a result, those who became intellectually curious and grew up after April 9 constitute the first generation of truly independent Georgians.

The mentality and natural instincts of this generation are far more democratic and liberal than those of older generations. For a variety of complex reasons, these Georgians are devotedly religious, in contradistinction to the secularist relativists in Tbilisi, who are generally a generation or two older than this group. Many from this generation currently live abroad and excel in a variety of fields, especially business. Others are small- and medium-level entrepreneurs in Georgia. A large majority of this generation saw great hope in the Rose Revolution, though most did not actively participate in it and, like a majority of Georgians, have since lost hope in the new government's ability to fulfill the promises of the revolution. A small group of leaders from this generation could easily coalesce into a powerful political force. Such a development is bound to happen at some point in the future. Whether this will develop in the current electoral cycle remains to be seen.

Thus, notwithstanding great difficulties, the rise of political pluralism is possible in Georgia. However, this will only happen if the country's foreign friends commit to the development of a real multiparty system of governance, including by ensuring that elections in 2008 are free and fair (not only on election day but in the period prior to the vote, including in the area of media coverage). Unfortunately, there already are some signs to the contrary. For example, the leadership of USAID in Tbilisi has declared that building political parties in Georgia is not a priority for now, and that the focus must be on supporting the "democratic government."[44] Even if one ignores the obvious question of whether Saakashvili's government is actually democratic or not, it is mind-boggling that USAID cannot see the need to assist the party-building process, especially given President George W. Bush's pro-democracy policies. How can one envision the development of real democratic institutions and civil society in Georgia without strong, institutional, and philosophically grounded political parties?

BUSINESS COMMUNITY

During the second part of the 1990s, in spite of economic stagnation, Georgia developed a strong and vibrant business community, albeit one that was disorganized and largely operated in the shadow economy. However, as I have already examined in chapter 3, uniquely among the post-Soviet states, the businessmen were not under state control. The most successful private enterprises were not launched through shadowy privatization schemes, and as a result, their owners were minimally beholden to the government. It is true that some businesses had benefited either from special legal environments created on their behalf (often on the initiative of Citizens Union of Georgia parliamentarians, including Zurab Zhvania) or from their association with Shevardnadze and members of his family. For example, MagtiCom, one of the two main mobile-phone providers in Georgia, probably would not have grown as much as it did had its main shareholder not been Shevardnadze's son-in-law. Others in the Shevardnadze family also "succeed" beyond their natural capabilities. Yet, unlike Ukraine under Vladimir Kuchma, or Russia under Boris Yeltsin (whose families included some of the largest oligarchs in their respective countries), Georgia did not have a "presidential clan" whose members controlled a large share of the economy.

These diverse factors allowed the business community to play a very favorable role in nurturing the seeds of democracy in Georgia in the last years of Shevardnadze's rule. As discussed in Part I, business leaders and their political allies were most responsible for the collapse of Shevardnadze-Zhvania's CUG, which opened up political space for opposition parties. Additionally, the business groups played a crucial role in helping finance the opposition-party campaigns for the November 2003 elections, not only for the pro-business New Rights Party but also for National Movement and United Democrats.

Most importantly, business leaders helped create a pluralistic media environment by supporting several national television stations—which could never have succeeded merely on revenue from commercials, because of Georgia's small advertising market. Though media moguls usually funded these stations first and foremost to protect their own interests, without this pluralistic environment in the media, opposition parties would never have done as well as they did in the November 2003 elections, NGO activists would not have gained prominence, and revolutionary leaders would not have been able to bring the masses into the streets. Nonetheless, despite this positive role in Georgia's democratic development, the Georgian "intellectual elite" generally disparaged the business community, and alleged that it was corrupt and one of the biggest stumbling blocks for reforms. Because of this, two elements within the body politic that should have been allies in promoting the rule of law and democracy were bitter enemies.

Had the political process in Georgia continued on the constitutional path, with presidential elections in April of 2005, the business community could have become an even more active and favorable player in the consolidation of democracy through the constitutional transition of power from Shevardnadze to a new president. After November 2003, the business community would have probably unified behind one opposition presidential candidate—like Nino Burdjanadze, David Gamkrelidze, Badri Patarkatsishvili, or some other person not on the political scene at that point. (Saakashvili was unlikely to unify the business community in an ordinary election, because his rhetoric, beliefs, and political inner circle by and large did not appeal to the business leaders.) Through such an alliance, the business community could have played an instrumental role in preventing Shevardnadze from handing power to a chosen successor—as happened in Russia and Azerbaijan, and almost happened in Ukraine.

Instead of growing to become an even more positive influence on public life, the business community was probably the single biggest loser after the Rose Revolution. A very large percentage of the 500 million lari that the government received in "voluntary donations" and extortion in 2003-5 came from large businesses, as some of the aforementioned analysis suggests. As a result, after the Rose Revolution the businesses were under huge financial strain. Furthermore, fearful of an environment in which the rule of law is completely ignored and there is no guarantee that the government will not once again resort to extortion tactics in the future, prominent businessmen either left Georgia completely, closed their business ventures, or, in the best of circumstances, took their capital out of the country, refusing to engage in any new investment. This was the case with both entrepreneurs who had made their fortunes in Georgia, and Georgians who had made their fortunes elsewhere—like Bidzina Ivanishvili, one of the wealthiest men in Russia, who announced in April 2005 that he would be pulling virtually all of his investments out of Georgia.[45]

Additionally, the government's policies vis-à-vis private enterprise forced many entrepreneurs to reach a deal with the government on an individual basis, destroying the semblance of camaraderie and unity that is crucial if entrepreneurs are to have a significant civil-society role in policymaking. In forcing every large businessman to fend for himself in hopes of protecting his property, the government succeeded in eliminating much of the business community's political influence.

In short, 2004 and 2005 were very damaging years for the business community. Government tactics notwithstanding, things could have improved if Saakashvili's promise of a truly reformed tax code had been implemented. While there were some members of the cabinet who pushed strongly for fundamental changes in the way the state treats taxpayers and collects revenue (especially Minister of State for Economic Reform Kakha Bendukidze), ultimately the new tax code merely reduced some taxes without changing the actual revenue collection system. This way, it maintained the imbalance between the taxpayer and the state, but dramatically increased the powers of the state vis-à-vis the allegedly delinquent taxpayer. The new law even allowed the government to stop business operations by freezing the funds in private accounts, if the state believes that the company owes back taxes. It is up to the taxpayer to prove his innocence, and should he do so, the government must merely unfreeze the frozen accounts, without paying any compensation for the damages caused. Such action can easily lead to the collapse of the business, because an enterprise will not be capable of actually doing its work while it tries to prove its innocence.

On April 21, 2005, the Parliament approved a proposal from Prime Minister Zurab Nogaideli and National Movement parliamentarian Giga Bokeria to eliminate the most popular and taxpayer-friendly component of the new tax code—the arbitration scheme, which allows a three-judge panel (with the Ministry of Finance, the taxpayer, and the judiciary each appointing one of the members) to adjudicate disputes between the state and the taxpayer. Arbitration was described by the minister of state for economic reform as a "revolutionary idea,"[46] and was hailed as a major step to help improve the relationship between business and government. Since January 1, 2005, when the new tax law went into effect, only two cases were adjudicated through arbitration. The government lost both—3,000 lari to Coca-Cola Bottling, and 10 million lari to Telasi, the electricity distributor in Tbilisi. The latter case was the driving force behind the government's decision to eliminate the scheme. Instead of special panels, adjudication of disputes over taxes is again in the hands of the judiciary, which the executive branch controls. This way, the government can avoid cases, such as the two that were adjudicated thus far, where even minimal amount of fairness would lead to a victory for the taxpayers.

Government officials offered some striking commentary about why this change was necessary. "Some think that there is no need to pay taxes. [Arbitration] was the government's mistake and now the government must correct it," declared Saakashvili.[47] Prime Minister Nogaideli stated that the charge by the entrepreneur Badri Patarkatsishvili that "the government unilaterally violated the agreement between the authorities and business" was "absurd."[48] In Parliament, Majority Leader Nadiradze told opposition New Rights Party leader David Gamkrelidze immediately before the vote that "when you come to power, do that, whatever you'd like."[49] Her comment spoke volumes about the National Movement's perception of governance—once in power, it can do whatever it wants.

Nonetheless, with such disappointments comes a unique opportunity—the possibility that the business community will truly come together and form a united front to advance its interests through policy advocacy. Such a development would be very beneficial for the future of democracy and pluralism in Georgia, and could help improve the conditions of the private media and of the political parties. Whether the business community will be capable of engaging in the political process without triggering retaliation from Saakashvili is unclear, but after failed promises from the revolutionary leaders, private entrepreneurs may be prepared to chart a new course.

ORTHODOX CHURCH

Another crucial, yet often ignored and ostracized component of Georgian civil society is the Orthodox Church. During the Soviet period, most Georgians practiced their faith in secret. As a result, the country has seen a dramatic increase in openly religious believers since the mid-1980s, and even more so

since 1991, when Georgia regained its independence. An overwhelming majority of Georgian citizens are Orthodox, and according to some surveys, over two-
thirds practice their faith regularly. The most recent data I have seen on this
comes from a poll conducted by the International Republican Institute (IRI) in
June 2005. Eighty-six percent of those questioned said they were Orthodox,
and of all Georgian citizens, 40 percent attend religious services at least once
a month. This is a strikingly high number, since Orthodoxy is practiced very
differently from Catholicism and Protestantism, where weekly church attendance is the norm. More importantly, attendance is particularly high among
the youth compared to middle-aged people and pensioners, who are still heavily influenced by the Communism in which they were raised.

Thus, compared to Western Europe, where the influence of churches has
been waning over the past decades, the Georgian Orthodox Church has a great
deal of influence over the public, much as churches have in America. This
gives the Orthodox Church an opportunity to play an important role in promoting political change and democratic transition. Indeed, it may be that without
giving the Church a prominent role, achieving such a transition will be impossible, because the Church is the only national institution that people truly trust.
However, the NGO class believes that such a religious influence is very dangerous, because the Church is theologically too doctrinaire and insufficiently "progressive."[50] Because of this, the NGO class wants to reduce the influence of the
Orthodox Church, replacing its teachings with new, secular values.

The truth is that it is Georgia's good fortune that the current leader of the
Church, Catholicos Patriarch Ilia II, as well as most of the Church hierarchy that
surrounds him, are nothing but robust advocates of democratic reform and of a
strong alliance with the United States. Indeed, the patriarch once remarked to
me that in his view, Georgia should become as close an ally to the United States
in its region as Israel is in the Middle East. Furthermore, the patriarch has been
a strong advocate of promoting a tolerant and respectful society.

Nonetheless, there are two groups inside the Church who do not share the
patriarch's vision. First, the so-called "traditionalist" elements, whose members
are not tolerant of other faiths, and some of whom want to force radically "conservative" views on the public. Second, the so-called "reformers" or "progressives," who are secularists and believe that the Church should not be involved
in public life at all. Neither of these groups command even close to a majority
inside the Church's hierarchy or among lay people, though the "traditionalist"
group is much larger than the "progressive" one. Moreover, neither group has
a strong theological case for their arguments. The Orthodox Church's role in
Georgian society should be viewed from its historical perspective. It has served
as a moral compass for Georgia for over 1,500 years—a role that it is destined
to continue to play in the future. In addition, for centuries the Georgian

Church has been nothing but tolerant of other religions and ethnic groups. Because of this, the "traditionalists" have very little to do with the tradition of the Church, while the "reformers" are trying to impose views that have no basis in Orthodox theology.

These two groups endanger the Church, not because they are influential or have massive public support, but because they are loud. The "reformers" are universally unpopular among the lay people and exist only because they are supported by the self-styled civil society, which looks at religion as a whole with a great deal of contempt and believes that the Church is a huge stumbling block on Georgia's road to progressive reform.[51] Advocacy of this secularist perspective empowers the "traditionalists," who can count on support from probably 15–25 percent of the practicing believers (largely in the regions). Secularist attacks on Orthodox theology drive more worshipers, who are incensed about outside interference in the Church, toward the "traditionalist" view, as a counterpoise to secularism.[52] "Traditionalists" use the outside attacks on the Church as evidence that the Orthodox faith is under attack, and that it should stop being tolerant of nonbelievers and demand to be declared the state religion. They also back the patriarch and the vast majority of the Church's leadership into a corner by trying to force them to pick the "traditionalist" side over the "progressives."

The Church's "reformist" detractors would be perfectly content if church attendance in Georgia dropped, or if the people became as secularist as they are in continental Europe. This view comes from the postmodern notion of democracy, which fails to understand that for centuries, religious people have actually helped promulgate the values of liberty, and are not a problem so long as they do not try to limit the ability of others to practice their own faith or enjoy their civil liberties. However, even if one accepts the secularist view of democracy and indeed sees religion as a problem, limiting religion in Georgia conflicts sharply with the overly religious nature of the Georgian people, who connect the Orthodox Church to their nationalism and their values, culture, and history.

In the fall of 2004, the Liberty Institute and its parliamentary allies tried to ferment a broad conflict between the "progressives," the "traditionalists," and the vast majority of the Church hierarchy, using an alleged lack of pluralism in the Church's official seminary as an excuse. Specifically, with Liberty's support, several seminarians wrote a public letter criticizing the Church's doctrine. For this, the Church's doctrinal watchdogs removed them from the seminary, because the seminary's regulations do not allow its students to openly criticize the Church. Secularists outside the Church used this decision to attack the Church as being too dogmatic and anti-democratic, and saved particularly striking rhetoric for Patriarch Ilia II.

This nearly turned into a major conflict, but Saakashvili and Zhvania forced Liberty and its allies to retreat, knowing that even the perception that the government was attacking the Church and its beloved leader, who is probably even more popular among Georgians than Pope John Paul II was among the Catholics, would do nothing but harm to the government's public standing. So long as Ilia II continues to serve as patriarch, these two groups, along with the vast majority of the worshippers who agree with neither of them and want to continue with the moderate tradition of the Georgian Church, will continue to coexist together. However, a conflict may arise when it is time to elect a new Church leader.

This conflict between the secularist views of the NGO class and the religious nature of the general public is bound to come to a head eventually, and may become a serious political problem. It could easily become a way for a nationalist leader to gain popularity very quickly, should one emerge to rally the faithful against the secularists through populism and demagogy. If conservative religious ideas and figures are pushed out of the regular public discourse and the "mainstream" by Tbilisi's intellectual and NGO elite, a conflict is likely to arise. By contrast, if democracy activists were to engage the Church and channel the energies of the overwhelming majority of its leaders toward advancing democracy and tolerance, the Orthodox Church could become a vital medium in helping consolidate democracy in Georgia.

Civil Society and Future of Democracy in Georgia

Advocates of democratic change are correct in believing that modern liberal democracy requires an active civil society. Representative government functions properly only when citizens are engaged in their self-government not only through the voting booth, but by promoting their interests with the government through associations and organizations, and by governing themselves outside the sphere of the state. Therefore, democracy will only be possible in Georgia if its civil-society institutions become stronger and act as a channel for citizens to become active participants in the governance of the body politic.

For this to happen, however, the civil society must be real rather than illusionary. It must speak on behalf of real political interests, and it must have real members among the citizenry. NGOs that speak for no one but their very limited membership, or entities that are funded purely from abroad and that would disappear without this foreign backing, are not the be-all and end-all of civil society. These organizations should be regarded as part of civil society, but merely a part. They should not be permitted to define the meaning of the term "civil society" by limiting it purely to themselves and excluding groups that actually speak on behalf of interest groups and citizens.

Georgia is fortunate to have a very strong foundation for the growth and development of a real civil society. The question is whether these foundations will be allowed to prosper, or whether they will continue to be ignored or ostracized by both the "civil society" activists inside the NGO class and their foreign backers. In many respects, determining whether democracy will be possible in Georgia in the future depends on the answer to this question.

Conclusion

The history of Georgia's postindependence politics is a tragic story, because it is full of missed opportunities. Three times Georgians had a chance to move toward real democratic governance, and each time, the opportunity closed because national leaders made the wrong choices.

It is true that throughout Shevardnadze's rule, and even under Saakashvili, Georgia has been far more open and democratic than most other post-Soviet states. However, Georgia never transitioned to real democracy, notwithstanding unique opportunities that made such democratic consolidation possible. Existence of greater openness than in other states of the former Soviet Union, coupled with the failure to bring about a full transition, is what makes Georgia's story particularly tragic. Nonetheless, precisely because Georgia looked better than other states in the former USSR, and because its chances to create a real democracy were far more tangible, one is left with the impression that Georgians are capable of coming very close to democracy, but not capable of living in democracy.

Leaders of the Rose Revolution came to power promising to govern based on the values of liberal democracy. However, as was expected among many who opposed their quest for power, they have done exactly the opposite. They have led a government that regularly violates individual human rights and civil liberties through illegal imprisonment, financial extortion, disrespect for property rights, censorship of the media, and massive concentration of power in the hands of the president. By any measure, when it comes to governance, the Rose Revolution has been a huge step backward, when compared to Georgia prior to November 2003.

Under President Saakashvili, Georgia has not yet become a tyranny on the model of Turkmenistan under Saparmurat Atayevich Niyazov. But it is developing into an autocratic state, which one could classify as a closing society.[1] This term describes what is somewhat of a new phenomenon in political science and is particularly applicable to states in the former Soviet Union—states that a short while ago were tyrannies, but then had a brief period of political openness and greater freedom, and afterwards started to move backwards toward less freedom. Saakashvili inherited a Georgia that was a very open society—chaotically so, but open nonetheless. In three years, it has rapidly moved toward closure, and the daily political struggle in Georgia today is not about making the country more open and democratic, but about trying to prevent even greater loss of freedom. The constant question is not whether freedom will be lost under the Saakashvili government, but how much will be taken away, how quickly. In this environment, no consideration is given to how to institutionalize a free society, because of the pressure of trying to limit the damage government's actions cause every day.

Given this dangerous environment, certain key questions still have to be asked about the Rose Revolution. Answering these questions is particularly incumbent on all those intellectuals and policymakers who supported the revolution and refused to acknowledge even the possibility that things could go wrong. Did things have to end this way? Was the Rose Revolution inevitably going to be a failure, or did something go wrong after what appeared to the outside world as a magnificent expression of popular support for democracy in the streets of Tbilisi? How could conventional wisdom be so wrong? How could almost everyone expect a success that the new Georgian government has not even come close to achieving? Finally, what are the Georgian people to do now, since they really do not have an avenue that will lead them out of the abyss of the postrevolutionary crisis?

Meaning of the Rose Revolution

The world became enchanted with demonstrations in the streets in November 2003 because the media covering the event simply assumed that 25,000–30,000 protesters spoke for all Georgians. The media ignored the history of those who were leading the protests. It also assumed that those voters who did not vote for the revolutionaries simply did not matter. This suggests that those who fell in love with the revolution—the media, and through them the intellectuals, scholars, and political leaders—understood democracy more in terms of mob rule and one's ability to make noise in the streets, rather than as a system of government that respects constitutionalism and the rule of law, the very basic institutions that make free government work. The trouble is that deciding issues through street protests, especially when the street is not the avenue of last resort, brings the polity awfully close to the state of nature, in which individual rights are under a great deal of threat. The Georgian example shows the pitfalls of this approach.

The only major American paper to raise questions about the Rose Revolution was the *Wall Street Journal*, which wrote in an editorial: "The opposition was right to protest against the results of the parliamentary poll. Only Mr. Saakashvili and his supporters, who at best can count on the support of a third of Georgians, quickly rejected any compromise and focused their efforts on deposing the president. It would be tempting, even reassuring, to conclude the thousands of protesters who stormed parliament were exercising 'people power.' But what happened in Tbilisi over the weekend looks disturbingly like a coup against a president with strong democratic credentials, certainly by the standards of the region." For this reason, the *Journal* called events in Georgia a "popular coup" and accurately concluded that "circumstances surrounding [Shevardnadze's] overthrow give cause for pessimism" for Georgia's democracy.[2]

In those few words, the *Journal* captured much of what was wrong with the Rose Revolution. In this analysis, it also pointed to the reason why the aftermath of the revolution has become such a disaster. The problem was, and remains now, the simple truth that the Rose Revolution had nothing to do with democracy or majority rule. The revolution gave leaders of political parties that together had received just 37 percent of the popular vote all the political power, as if they represented all of the electorate. In reality, the majority had actually voted for parties that opposed the revolution. As a result, the revolution was nothing more than an avenue for its three leaders to gain power, through undemocratic and extralegal tactics, that was beyond their reach through the democratic process.

Liberal democracy stands for majority rule. In most well-functioning democracies, checks are also in place to ensure that the majority does not tyrannize the minority. However, as a whole, in a democratic society, the citizens' majority is sovereign. This does not mean mob rule. People's sovereignty is expressed through the ballot box—through their elected representatives. For such a system to function, procedures, rules, and laws must be respected. When one side or another violates the procedures or laws (as Shevardnadze's government did in 2003), a just democratic system must have a means for self-correction. Such means usually are the courts, though the political process can also play a part. Both of these checks were available in Georgia in 2003, but unfortunately, neither the courts nor the constitutional political process were given a chance to work.

There are times when procedures and rules fail, or when they are merely a façade for a tyrannical form of rule. In those circumstances, it would be point-less to appeal to them in hopes of redressing grievances and securing justice. However, no one could argue with a straight face that Shevardnadze was a tyrant, or even a truly authoritarian leader. As Vladimir Socor, an astute Amer-ican analyst of Georgian politics, has written, "A 'regime' that must struggle to obtain a mere 20 percent of the vote—as the pro-presidential block did in these elections on party lists [in November 2003]—is hardly 'authoritarian.'"[3] Rather, Shevardnadze's regime was corrupt and weak, with a very chaotic but open and pluralistic political system in which democracy was possible.

As discussed in chapter 8, Saakashvili had other options short of revolution that he chose not to pursue. For example, he never waited for the court rulings on the elections, nor was he willing to accept (until the last minute, when Ivanov got involved) a compromise mandating new elections. For him, the rev-olution was the choice of the first resort because it benefited his political ambi-tions most, at the expense of Georgia's democratic future.[4]

On November 13, even before the first massive demonstration, I had an e-mail discussion about what was happening in Tbilisi with Charles Fairbanks, a mentor and friend who over the years had done a great deal to advance Geor-gia's cause in Washington. Fairbanks, who understands the politics of the for-mer USSR as well as any American political scientist, looked at the protests favorably. He believed that "the pattern throughout the NIS [Newly Independ-ent States] . . . is that popular participation is ebbing AWAY, allowing the steady drift everywhere toward neo-Communist authoritarianism. Don't the Georgian people deserve some credit for being the only people who resisted a fraudulent election?" he asked. Many other analysts in Washington shared this assess-ment. In my view, it was based on a very flawed understanding of what hap-pened in Georgian politics between 1999 and 2003, and helps explain why so many scholars misunderstood what the Rose Revolution was going to do to the possibility of democracy in Georgia.

Fairbanks wrote those words before events in Ukraine and Kyrgyzstan in 2004 and 2005, where popular protests also brought about change in govern-ment toward what appeared as greater openness. In November 2003 it was indeed true that in the former Soviet Union the general trend was away from democracy, with popular participation in governance decreasing virtually everywhere. However, Georgia was the exception to this trend throughout the 1990s, starting with the cleanest elections anywhere in the post-Soviet space in 1992. Even in the aftermath of the flawed elections in 1999, Georgia was more democratic than most other former Soviet republics. More importantly, popu-lar participation actually *increased* dramatically between 1999 and 2003; this was especially true in daily governance of the country, starting especially after

2001 with the rise of political pluralism and more diverse and independent media, and in elections, if one compares the 1999 legislative vote to 2003.

As a result, in November 2003, Georgia did not fit into the pattern of drift toward neo-Communism authoritarianism that Fairbanks correctly identified in other post-Soviet states. This only becomes obvious, however, when Georgia is judged on its own terms. Doing this requires looking at elections in November 2003 in the context of past elections, and in terms of their implication for the future of the country's open, yet chaotic, political society, rather than comparing Georgia to other post-Soviet states.

Testifying before the U.S. Senate Armed Services Committee on September 22, 2004, Secretary of Defense Donald Rumsfeld had this insightful comment (about elections in Iraq): "Let's say you tried to have an election and you could have it in three-quarters or four-fifths of the country. But in some places you couldn't because the violence was too great. Well, so be it. Nothing's perfect in life, so you have an election that's not quite perfect. Is it better than not having an election? You bet." This comment was in more ways than one applicable to Georgia. In November 2003, Georgia had parliamentary elections that were far from perfect. However, they were an improvement, because they were more free and fair than either the votes in 1999 or 1995, and because they fostered an environment that would allow for even better presidential elections in 2005.

To achieve even better elections in the future, Georgia required institutionalization and formalization of its open, pluralistic, but chaotic political environment. This could have been achieved with two developments. First, a constitutional transition of power, which would have helped strengthen the already nascent democratic institutions. Second (though connected to the first), a "soft landing" for Shevardnadze after 2005. Accomplishing both was not only plausible but actually quite realistic in the year and a half in which the new Parliament would have to function between November 2003 and the expected presidential elections in March 2005.

In Georgia's postindependence history, the country has never experienced a constitutional transition of power within the legal framework. Its first president, Zviad Gamsakhurdia, was removed by force before the end of his term in office. So was Shevardnadze—without bullets, but nonetheless violently and unconstitutionally. Thus, political transition has never taken place with respect for constitutional elected terms and for legally set political processes. Without a wave of constitutional political change, democracy is impossible. The Rose Revolution not only continued the pattern of preventing a leader from finishing his constitutional term in office, but actually advanced the notion that it is perfectly permissible and acceptable for a *minority* to rise up, go into the streets, and remove a leader if that leader is unpopular. If Georgian people took anything away from the Rose Revolution, it is that once their next leader becomes unpopular, there is nothing wrong with using some issue as a pretext to go into the streets and remove him from office, ignoring all of the constitutional rules and procedures. This can be done without any justification for why that leader deserves to be removed, and without any consideration of the implications of revolutionary change of power for fledgling political institutions.

What made the least sense in the Western reaction to the Rose Revolution is that scholars and politicians classified an event as "democratic" even though it set off a chain of events that have endangered the very foundations of a government by, for, and of the people in Georgia. By advancing the point of view that it is perfectly acceptable to remove a leader, the Rose Revolution promoted lawlessness, further damaging prospects for a society based on the rule of law, since disregard for the law is already all too common in Georgia among ordinary citizens. During the revolutionary protests, these citizens were told that disregard for the law was actually good and democratic. Not only did the Georgian leaders advocate this point of view, but foreign heads of state and legislators actually praised Georgians for ignoring the law, while in the next breath constantly repeated that Georgia needed to institute the rule of law. How both of these could be true simultaneously was never made clear.

Events in Georgia post–November 2003 would have developed very differently had the Parliament elected that month convened, and had Shevardnadze been able to finish his term. After the November vote, all of the political parties that had a serious level of support among the electorate had access to the legislative platform. Without ignoring the grave problems of electoral fraud in the November elections, the reality also was that the CEC's official results gave six parties seats in Parliament—all of the same parties that gained seats in reality, as the PVT showed. It is true that the four opposition parties had a total of about twenty-five fewer seats (11 percent of the total seats) than they would have had if the official count had been brought closer to the PVT count. However, these twenty-five seats did not change the fact that with six parties in Parliament, Georgia was entering a period of exceptional political pluralism, had the legislature elected in November continued to function for the year and a half before the April 2005 presidential elections. Nor did fraud change the fact that the four opposition parties were in the majority. Furthermore, because Shevardnadze's For New Georgia was bound to fall apart, pluralism in the legislature was all but certain to increase even further.

At the same time, had the constitutional process continued, and had Shevardnadze stayed in power for the reminder of his term, the media, especially television, was bound to remain independent and pluralistic, because under Shevardnadze the state simply did not have the capacity to control the private media. Because of this, there was an exceptional foundation for a civil, dignified, and pluralistic political debate leading up to the April 2005 vote for president.

After the initial protests during the early days after the November vote, a soft landing for Shevardnadze was virtually assured. Any notion (however remote) that Shevardnadze was going to try to stay in office past 2005 had disappeared, both nationally and in the minds of the president's most loyal supporters. Even if Shevardnadze himself wanted to stay, no one around him, especially his family, would have allowed him to try. Meanwhile, at least four opposition politicians were viable candidates to succeed him. It is possible that a new candidate would have emerged, maybe from the business community (some pointed to Badri Patarkatsishvili). All of these candidates would have competed for the hearts and minds of the Georgian electorate, making it likely that the people would go to the polls to make a choice for president that would be informed by the ideological views of the candidates. This way, the new president would have been able to point to majority support for his platform. Yet the person elected would probably have had a strong opposition as a check on his or her actions.

It is all but certain that the new president elected in 2005 was going to be a member of the opposition. Because of this, drift toward "neo-Communist authoritarianism," though certainly a huge problem in all other post-Soviet republics, was not a threat to Georgia. To the contrary—the country stood a real chance of consolidation of democracy.

Instead of this course, Georgia ended up with a leader who has faced virtually no opposition, and has no limits on his power. He was brought to power not because a majority of the people supported Saakashvili's ideology or policies, but because he was the revolutionary hero and the only viable candidate.[5] Meanwhile, with Saakashvili in power, the real possibility of "neo-Communist authoritarianism" was born in Georgia for the first time since the collapse of the Soviet Union. Shevardnadze's overthrow and the rejection of the constitutional process not only destroyed pluralism, but brought to power individuals who have little respect for democracy. After all, they had demonstrated what they thought of the values of freedom and liberal democracy during the time when they were in power (between 1995 and 2001). During that period, their maneuvering room was limited by the Shevardnadze presidency. Now that they had full power with no viable check from the opposition, there would be no constraints on their actions. This could easily result in an authoritarian regime. As my analysis suggests, Georgia developed elements of such authoritarianism in 2004–2006.

Given what the Rose Revolution did to pluralism and who came to power in its aftermath, the notion that November's protests resulted in greater democracy in Georgia is simply a grand illusion. Nonetheless, the view that the

Rose Revolution was democratic is still a predominant scholarly position. In the introduction, I cited a number of scholars who have specifically made this argument about the Georgian revolution. Another example comes from Ghia Nodia, who has written that democracy "require[s] participation of the 'masses,' for practical reasons as well as for the sake of legitimacy. . . . [This] implies that revolutions need to have something to do with democracy."[6] For this reason, in Nodia's view the Rose Revolution was democratic. The point Nodia and many others quoted earlier miss is that in a democracy, people's participation must happen through the political process and democratic institutions, not the street.

Even if one were to ignore the intricacies of the Georgian revolution, historical evidence suggests that thinking of a revolution in democratic terms is extremely inaccurate. Except for the American Revolution, for much of modern history "revolutions" seldom resulted in advances for democracy—the Russian, the Chinese, the Iranian revolutions, to name just a few, all led either to political systems that violated individual freedoms and liberties, or to civil wars. Even the French Revolution, which was motivated by democratic principles, ultimately resulted in certain decidedly undemocratic, and quite possibly tyrannical, outcomes. Indeed, in the twentieth century, advancing socialism, and by extension tyranny rather than democracy, is by far the most common thread in all of the world's revolutions.

This is not to suggest that revolutions are always bad or unnecessary. At times, revolutions are not only justified, but may indeed be necessary. However, when considering the question of what methods to use to promote democratic change and whether to use revolutionary tactics, it is crucial to appreciate the difference between just and unjust, or tyrannical, regimes. That, in turn, requires us to turn away from Weberian social science to the kind of political inquiry that is capable of making value judgments.

A just political regime may be significantly deficient, but its fundamental, constitutional principles may nonetheless be sound, because they are capable of resolving, over time, the regime's deficiencies. The United States is probably the best example of how a fundamentally just regime was able to grapple with its deficiencies—such as slavery, racial discrimination, inequality of men and women before the law—*through the Constitution*. Each of these problems can be dealt within the constitutional framework and through constitutional principles, rather than through steps that might have shaken the foundation of the American political regime. Indeed, the greatest injustice in U.S. history—slavery—was brought to an end with the Civil War, which was fought to *defend* the Constitution and the Union.[7]

For this reason, when confronted with the question of extra-legal means to affect change in American law, Herbert J. Storing, one of the greatest students of the U.S. system of government, raised cautionary flags. Storing believed that extra-legal activity was in effect a rejection of the principles of the American regime. Even when aspiring to produce a dramatic and positive reform in American law, activity outside of the law discards the legitimate instruments of the political process, such as those afforded by the legislative and the judiciary branches, and replaces them with "an unsuccessful attempt to combine, on the level of principle, revolution and conventional political action."[8] Accordingly, insofar as extra-legal means in their essence challenge the very idea that laws are the ultimate arbiter, they obscure the crucial "distinction . . . between the reform of a political system that is fundamentally sound, although unjust in some very important particulars, and the overturning of one that is corrupt at heart."[9]

I believe that Storing's argument can be particularly applied to Georgia, since the political regime there under Shevardnadze was fundamentally just, but seriously deficient (though nowhere near as deficient as the American regime was before the end of slavery). The Georgian regime was deficient because it was capable of pushing through a twenty-five-seat shift in the official results from the actual vote, but it was just because it was not authoritarian, and because it created a framework in which core problems could be corrected *within* the constitutional process. This is the reason why the revolution was not necessary.

Unlike Georgia before the Rose Revolution, a truly authoritarian regime, such as a Communist government, enslaves and tyrannizes people. As such, it is so fundamentally unjust that striving to "improve" it by appealing to higher moral and constitutional principles is impossible. Such a regime must simply be "ended" and replaced. A revolution, or some other form of a rebellion, may be the only means of changing this sort of a regime. People who choose such a course should be applauded, because they may very well be endangering their "lives, fortunes, and sacred honor"—just as the American Founders did when they revolted—for the sake of bringing about a more just political regime. However, even in such a case, making an argument, a case, against the regime and justifying a revolution would probably be a sound choice. Why else, after all, did the greatest of democratic revolutionaries—the delegates to the Continental Congress in 1776—endorse the Declaration of Independence, which is perhaps the most popular and persuasive of all revolutionary declarations?

Understanding what tactics are best at which point is crucial, because while some methods may be appropriate for an unjust regime, using them in a just regime may have very counterproductive results, as the Georgian example shows. When under tyranny, it is not only permissible and probably necessary, but also, to paraphrase Thomas Jefferson, *obligatory* for citizens to revolt and overthrow the chains of tyranny. Meanwhile, revolting in a deficient but just regime is not only questionable philosophically, but can have dangerous consequences, because the underpinnings of a good system may be destroyed and ultimately result in a bad system, even if the revolt was driven by the noble desire to create a more just society.

Therein lay the fundamental difference between Georgia's Rose Revolution, on the one hand, and Kyrgyzstan's Tulip and Ukraine's Orange revolutions, on the other. The Rose Revolution rejected a fundamentally just regime totally, and did not even try to apply available constitutional tools to address the grievances that brought people into the streets, resulting in the destruction of a fundamentally just system of government and its replacement with a fundamentally unjust political order. By contrast, in Kyrgyzstan, people rebelled against a regime that was completely unjust, repressive, and authoritarian, and rebelling may have been the only course of action. Thus, while the Tulip Revolution was justified and made sense, the Rose Revolution was unjust, pointless, and quite possibly counterproductive.

Meanwhile, the Orange Revolution was actually not a rebellion. Its leaders worked through the procedures of the rule of law set forth in the system, resulting in positive change brought forth by respect for political institutions and the constitution. Incidentally, this was done in a regime that was far more authoritarian than the one found in Georgia. Eventually, through the application of constitutional norms, Ukraine was able to replace its unbalanced political scheme with a fundamentally just order of more balanced division of powers, while Georgia created a far more unbalanced and unjust system.[10]

While Ukraine has seen an improvement in its constitutionalism, and Kyrgyzstan may see such a development, since the Rose Revolution, Georgia has seen the rise of a political regime in which the people's ability to influence their lives through the political process and to voice their grievances through their elected representatives is more limited than it was in the past.[11] As such, Georgia is a poster child for how counterproductive the rejection of the rule of law by popular leaders can be in a system that is fundamentally sound. Lack of dependence on the people in Georgia's new hyper-presidential system, and the inability of the people to play a role in self-government may not seem to be an immediate practical problem, while Saakashvili remains popular. However, what is to happen if one day he is no longer so well liked? The president's popularity is bound to fall, if the history of Eastern Europe serves as a guide.[12]

Additionally, making the Georgian president far more powerful than he was before, weakening the other political institutions (especially the Parliament), and running a state that has little respect for the individual rights and liberties of its citizens creates a fertile soil for a situation in which people will once again feel obliged and justified to resort to extraconstitutional means of having their voice heard. After all, in the current environment, what can the people do if the president decides to ignore their will again? The case that

Georgia has a fundamentally just regime is far more difficult to argue, in light of the first two years of Saakashvili's rule, than it was after a decade of Shevardnadze. Hence the popular temptation for a revolutionary change is far more likely to develop under Saakashvili than it was under Shevardnadze.

In November 2003, Saakashvili, Burdjanadze, and Zhvania told the people (inaccurately) that the Georgian political system did not give them an opportunity to bring about change through constitutional means. They alleged that the president, with his administrative resources, was far too powerful to be influenced through electoral and legislative channels. It was said that the president could ignore the will of the people, unless he was forced to go through a popular uprising. As my narrative shows, this was not exactly true. After all, the revolutionary leaders made no effort to use the constitutional process to seek a redress for their grievances. But given the perception of a system that could not be controlled, the revolutionaries succeeded in resorting to extraconstitutional means to take power.

Saakasvhili's Opportunities

While the Georgian political system has undoubtedly been far less responsive to the people since the Rose Revolution than before, the worst possible outcome for Georgia would be another extraconstitutional transition of power, because it would only serve to strengthen the revolutionary precedent that the Rose Revolution already established: that it is both normal and justified for people to overthrow their elected leaders when those leaders become unpopular. If the Saakashvili government continues on its current autocratic path, people may feel that they do not have another choice. However, another extraconstitutional transition will certainly bring more long-term problems than solutions.

If Saakashvili's government is removed before it loses all of its legitimacy (similarly to what happened with Gamsakhurdia), then the Georgian political environment will likely revert to that of the early 1990s, when a very large percentage of the population lost hope and faith in the country. The pattern is bound to repeat itself, because for better or worse, a lot of people still associate the possibility of a good life with Saakashvili, like many did with Gamsakhurdia in 1991–92. By contrast, if Saakashvili were to be removed after his ratings plummet and once he loses his legitimacy, it is likely that Georgia will witness a repeat of the post–Rose Revolution scenario, with one leader gaining so much popularity that he will never be able to fulfill expectations.

Neither of these would lead Georgia toward becoming a real democracy, while both have the potential to move it closer to being a failed state—a desperate condition it barely escaped from in 1992–1994, only thanks to Shevardnadze's leadership role. Instead, what Georgia needs more than anything is a constitutional transition of power from one leader to another. This can only happen if Saakashvili quickly moves to change his tactics and starts governing the country in a wholly new style.

Saakashvili must begin his transformation with first principles—the Constitution. Georgia requires a complete constitutional refounding, focused on three key areas. First, powers of the government in general: there is a need for a judicious discussion of what the government should be empowered to do and what should be left to the people. Today, due to the expansiveness of the powers enumerated in the Constitution, the government feels empowered to do whatever it likes, and this endangers liberty. Second, separation of powers: it is crucial to restore some balance to the relationship between the president, the legislature, and the judiciary branches. This would inevitably mean Saakashvili giving up a great deal of power, though the details of how to distribute powers between the branches should be an issue for a constitutional dialogue between all political parties and all citizens. Third, division of power between the central and local authorities: in my view Georgia requires an American- or a German-style federal arrangement. Many dispute this view, but at the very least, the issue of how to divide power between the central authority and local government must be an issue considered by the people.

After this constitutional refounding, Georgia should have new legislative elections. If they are free and fair, they will result in a Parliament that is more representative of the diverse points of view of the people. This will help improve pluralism, and will allow the legislature to better function as a check on executive power. This election must take place in a free and fair environment, with National Movement not receiving support from the administrative resources of the government simply because Saakashvili is president.

Moreover, in order to ensure that Georgia can get back on a democratic path, Saakashvili must rid himself of all those advisors and ministers who not only believe in but practice the "ends justify the means" theory of governance. Constitutional changes are vital, but alone they will not restore pluralism and respect for liberty. People with authoritarian, indeed even tyrannical, instincts simply should not be allowed to stay in office, because during the fledgling period of transition, they can do far too much damage. Removing them from power is the only way to ensure that the government stops terrorizing business, ends extrajudicial detentions and arrests, and stops pressuring the free media. The danger, of course, is that Saakashvili himself has extreme authoritarian instincts, and containing them will be very difficult under any and all circumstances.

Finally, Saakashvili must bring together a government that actually wants to govern Georgia and does not see its period in office as simply a time for personal aggrandizement. Georgia has real economic problems, but there are policies that can help spur economic growth, create jobs, and give citizens an opportunity to live better lives. By and large, these policies can be described as having the government "get out of the way." However, this can only be brought about with a strategic and painful reform process, something that requires a government full of individuals truly committed to change.

Implications for U.S. Foreign Policy

It is highly unlikely, of course, that Saakashvili will follow these recommendations, though I am convinced that these steps are the only ones that can give Georgia the chance to become the democratic success story that so many in the West, especially the Bush administration, would like to see. Given its vast influence in Georgia, the United States can actually play a very active role in getting Saakashvili to change his direction. However, given what the history of U.S. policymaking in Georgia has been over the years, it is not clear that the United States will be capable of using its influence to actually achieve any of its policy goals.

Early in 2003, President Bush set forth a very clear policy of supporting free and fair elections in Georgia. This was expressed through letters to Shevardnadze and visits by U.S. emissaries to the country. The ultimate step in this effort was the visit by former Secretary of State James Baker, who came as the president's special envoy. Baker had a particular agenda and left crystal-clear instructions for the U.S. ambassador. One could not expect anything more from Washington in terms of clarifying what the policy was, and how the president expected it to be implemented.

Unfortunately, when left to the bureaucracy, this policy was only partially implemented, if at all. Ambassador Richard Miles, and presumably his superiors at the Department of State, did not pursue logical actions that would have advanced the Bush policy. This was most visible in Miles's refusal to get involved in the debate over the Baker formula for the Central Elections Commission. However, in a number of other areas, policy implementation also failed to support the president's goal of free and fair elections. For example, the USAID did nothing to prevent the failure by its contractor, the IFES, in typing the voter lists, nor did it do anything to stop the NDI, another contractor, from supporting a revolutionary course, even though a revolution was contrary to the president's policy.

What is particularly striking, however, is not just that the president's policy was ignored, but that the implementers would then actually claim that they had pursued the policy in good faith, even though all the evidence pointed to their mismanagement. So, Ambassador Miles regularly claimed, all the way to the end of his tenure in Georgia, that the Baker plan was followed, even though anyone with even a basic sense of what happened in Georgia knew that this was not the case. He also demanded that the new Georgian government not investigate the problems with electoral lists, knowing all too well that an investigation would point to devastating failures by the USAID and IFES.

The events in Georgia, particularly during the summer and fall of 2003, point to the problem that has long been identified as a challenge for all administrations, but particularly difficult for Republican ones—the foreign-policy establishment's refusal to follow and implement the president's policy, and often actively campaign against it. This has been a constant issue since George W. Bush has been president, especially during his first term—and not only with regard to policy toward Georgia, but on issues and areas that are far more crucial, such as the democracy agenda in the Middle East.

In many respects, "hiding" the truth from policymakers about events unfolding in Georgia has been a regular pattern on the part of the U.S. Embassy in Tbilisi and the USAID since the early 1990s. This has been particularly true on the issues of "reform" and "democracy." Through the 1990s, the USAID reported to Washington that Georgia was reforming, and that U.S. support for "democratic reforms" was having a dramatic impact. Shevardnadze, meanwhile, was "for more than a dozen years invariably described . . . as a stalwart friend of democracy and a liberal, honest fellow."[13] This was being done, of course, to justify spending more and more money in Georgia, allegedly by building on reforms that were already in place.

Then, towards late 2001 and early 2002, the bureaucracy began to sense that support for Shevardnadze had wavered in Washington, and that it was beginning to be too difficult to hide the truth about Georgia and what had happened in the 1990s. However, the bureaucracy could not permit the real culprits to be made known, since these very culprits were the ones that the USAID had trumpeted as great reformers throughout the 1990s. As a result, a new picture was presented to Washington—that Georgia had suddenly become an authoritarian state, that it did not have democracy at all, that there was pressure on the civil society and the media, and that Shevardnadze was the cause of all the ills in the country. In these discussions, all the alleged success from the 1990s was suddenly forgotten, since the very same reforms that had been pursued throughout that decade needed to be implemented all over again.

The truth was that in the 1990s, the bureaucracy painted a picture that was far too positive, while after 2001, it painted a picture that was far too negative. In reality, Georgia had indeed made huge strides in the 1990s. Often, however, the very "reformers" that the USAID, the U.S. Embassy, the EU representatives, the IMF, and the World Bank promoted had stood in the way of these moves forward, or pushed policies that made it harder for Georgia to truly reform. Nonetheless, at the beginning of the new decade, Georgia was much better off than many post-Soviet states. Indeed, by the lead-up to the November 2003 elections, Georgia was politically a chaotic country, but one in which a vigorous political debate was taking place about the future.

When Shevardnadze was removed, there was an opportunity for the foreign-policy establishment to present a new face as the great leader of democracy. Saakashvili got the "same lavish treatment from the State Department and the media [that Shevardnadze had in the past. Saakashvili was painted] as honest, liberal, and democratic."[14] Meanwhile, Shevardnadze suddenly became not just authoritarian, but a Milosevic-like tyrant. In all the praise lavished on Saakashvili, there was no mention, of course, of what he had done during the 1990s, or of just how questionable his democratic credentials really were.

It would be unfair to say that everyone in the foreign-policy bureaucracy thought or operated like this. For example, at the U.S. Embassy in Tbilisi, there were very honest and hardworking career officials who tried their best to tell the truth about the Rose Revolution in their reporting. However, they were often prevented from doing this by their superiors. In early 2004, things got so bad that the State Department sent a senior office "minder" to the political and economic section of the embassy in order to stop the staff there from reporting about what was happening in Georgia in the aftermath of the revolution. The minder regularly reprimanded the section's officers because the section's reporting "did not reflect Washington's policies" and had contradicted the conventional wisdom about the "democratic revolution" that the State Department and the foreign-policy establishment were pushing. The minder argued that Washington needed to hear "what it wants."[15] One officer was even allegedly removed from the embassy for refusing to distort the truth about what was happening in Georgia.

This was an astonishing way to defend and promote U.S. interests. Was it not the job of the U.S. Embassy to monitor what was happening in Georgia and report the truth to policymakers, so that they could decide on what actions to take based on the best available information? One had to wonder—if Washington was forcing its staff in Tbilisi to ignore the truth, what was happening in Iraq, where the stakes were (and remain) far greater?

Bureaucracy could not be so complacent, though, if the political appointees in the administration were more willing to look reality in the eye. Often, when policy toward Georgia has been criticized, the response from the supporters of the Bush administration has been to argue that few senior people pay much attention to it, and that one cannot expect much more than what is already being done. Unfortunately, this excuse is insufficient, even to someone who may admire the president's goals. For all of its sound strategic-policy judgments in a number of key foreign policy areas, the Bush administration's greatest faults have been its unwillingness to admit mistakes, and its inability to follow good strategy with sound tactical implementation.[16] This has been actually true in both foreign and domestic policy, and could become a huge stain on the president's legacy in the long term. Sadly, these traits have had a very negative impact on Georgia.

Once the administration declared that the Rose Revolution was a democratic success, it was clear that it would be very difficult, it not impossible, to make a case to the contrary, no matter how strong the evidence. Even though the case is overwhelming that the Rose Revolution has been a disaster, the administration refuses to consider that maybe things were going wrong. Take, for example, the president's response to criticism of the Georgian government during his visit to Georgia in May. Bush had a meeting with representatives of ethnic-minority organizations in Georgia, during which one of the participants voiced concern about claims that Georgia was a democracy, pointing to many authoritarian tendencies in the Saakashvili government. President Bush's only response was that "Saakashvili is my friend."

After September 11, President Bush articulated a new framework for America's place in the world. In the president's own words, "The survival of liberty in our land increasingly depends on the success of liberty in other lands [and therefore it] is the policy of the United States to seek and support the growth of democratic movements and institutions in every nation and culture, with the ultimate goal of ending tyranny in our world."[17] By placing democracy at the forefront of U.S. foreign policy, this "Bush Doctrine" provides the only viable strategy for a stable global order in the post–Cold War era.[18]

In a very practical sense, the administration has gone beyond a policy change and has implemented concrete actions that have advanced the cause of freedom around the world. For example, through programs such as the Millennium Challenge Account (MCA), the Bush administration has made good governance a key component in determining who receives substantial U.S. financial assistance. As another example, in the aftermath of the wars in Afghanistan and Iraq, the administration has pressured countries in the Middle East to open their societies. There, it has achieved substantial progress, especially in Lebanon and Kuwait, not to mention the fact that even in the midst of bombings and kidnappings, Iraq became the first Arab country to hold truly free elections, ever. There have been successes elsewhere as well, with Ukraine and Liberia being but two very prominent examples. The one prominent example that stands counter to this trend is Russia, where on the

Bush administration's watch, democracy and political liberty has been dramatically all but stifled.

Given that democratic change takes years, if not decades, it is far too early to judge the Bush foreign policy merely on the basis of where democracy has taken hold on its watch. By placing democracy on the agenda, President Bush has given hope to those fighting on behalf of freedom the world over that America and its political might will be on their side in their struggles on behalf of justice and good government. It is for this that the president deserves the strongest applause.

In light of its actions, the administration's policies toward Georgia after the Rose Revolution are particularly mind-boggling. It simply makes no rational sense how the Bush administration, with everything that it has at stake when it comes to democracy and freedom abroad, could approve of a president giving a speech in which he called Georgia a "beacon of liberty." By turning postrevolutionary Georgia into a core example of the success of its democratic project, the president has in some respects made a mockery of the ideas of democracy and free government.

The logic of President Bush's speech in Georgia in May 2005 is that the world should judge his democracy project at least in part by looking at Georgia. Yet any impartial look at Georgia raises, at the very least, substantial questions about what is happening there. Any honest analysis makes it impossible to call the country's post–Rose Revolution "transition" a success. This inevitably begs the question—if Georgia is to be judged a success in the administration's view, should the same parameters be used to judge "success" in Iraq and Afghanistan?

If so, then President Bush's vision has completely failed, and this new framework for America's relations with the world is nothing but rhetoric that damages rather than promotes U.S. security. The truth, however, is that the Bush vision is not merely rhetoric, and that the reorientation of U.S. foreign policy represents a strategic and fundamental shift of America's place in the world. Policy differences and arguments notwithstanding, history will likely give the Bush administration substantial credit for his work on behalf of freedom, somewhat akin to how history has judged the actions of the Truman administration.[19] Sadly, given its record in Georgia, the Bush administration's action there will be a stain on this courageous legacy.

Whatever the faults of the Bush administration's policies vis-à-vis Georgia, making democracy work there is ultimately the responsibility of Georgians. This is especially true of the younger generation, which was raised post-Communism and thus has a far greater appreciation for the value of freedom. It is incumbent upon them to help nurture a political process that will allow Georgia to transition to an environment in which the people's voice is heard through elections and political institutions, rather than through the streets. Having worked in the trenches of Georgian politics and experienced the natural dignity of the Georgian people, I am confident that they can, even if it was not possible to succeed in 2003.

Notes

Preface

1. For example, President Mikheil Saakashvili and some of his Washington-based supporters were furious by an op-ed entitled "Four Questions for Mikheil Saakashvili," which I published in the *Washington Post* during the president's visit to the United States in February 2004, though even ardent supporters of the Georgian government agreed that my observations were fair and balanced. Also, when I published "Bush and Georgia's Faded Rose" in the *Christian Science Monitor* about President Bush's trip to Georgia in May 2005 and what he could do to advance democracy there, a lobbyist for Georgia, a respected Washington Republican with whom I probably agree on many foreign policy issues (though clearly not developments in Georgia), accused me of spreading "Russian sponsored bull——."

2. This has already started, as I examine in chapter 14.

Introduction

1. CIS is a union of the republics of the former Soviet Union (totaling 12), excluding Estonia, Lithuania, and Latvia. Throughout the book, the terms "post-Soviet space," "Newly Independent States," and the "NIS" all refer to only those countries that are members of the CIS.

2. The official results had a discrepancy of 25 seats in favor of the two governmental parties at the expense of the opposition parties when compared to the results of the more accurate parallel vote tabulations (PVT). This amounted to 17 percent of the proportional seats in the 235-person Parliament, and 11 percent of the total seats.

3. Indeed, no viable pro-Shevardnadze candidate was even on the horizon in November 2003. The weak Georgian state did not have the capacity to build up a possible candidate from scratch, unlike the state in Russia, which did just that with Vladimir Putin. This was particularly true after the disastrous results of the pro-Shevardnadze party in the November legislative elections. For this reason, it was quite likely that the presidential race in 2005 would involve only opposition candidates, along with a possible pro-business candidate who might have emerged later.

4. Georgia's first post-Soviet president, Zviad Gamsakhurdia, was removed in a bloody coup.

5. Richard Carlson, "Georgia on His Mind—George Soros's Potemkin Revolution," *Weekly Standard*, May 24, 2004.

6. Editorial page, *Wall Street Journal*, November 24, 2003.

7. Zeyno Baran, "Georgia's Rose Revolution," November 24, 2003, http://www.nixoncenter.org/index.cfm?action=showpage&page=Georgia's.

8. David Phillips, "Corruption Next in Georgian Cleanup," *Christian Science Monitor*, February 5, 2004.

9. Stephen Blank, "Georgia's Revolution, America's Opportunity," *In the National Interest* 2, no. 47 (December 3, 2003). http://www.inthenationalinterest.com/Articles/Vol2Issue47/Vol2Issue47Blank.html.

10. Ariel Cohen, "Our Challenge in Georgia," *Washington Times*, January 15, 2004.

11. Charles H. Fairbanks, "Georgia's Rose Revolution," *Journal of Democracy* 15, no. 2 (April 2004).

12. Charles King, "A Rose among Thorns: Georgia Makes Good," *Foreign Affairs* (March–April 2004), http://www.foreignaffairs.org/20040301facomment83203/charles-king/a-rose-among-thorns-georgia-makes-good.html?mode=print.

13. Bruce Jackson, testimony, U.S. Senate Subcommittee on European Affairs of the Committee on Foreign Relations, March 8, 2005, foreign.senate.gov/testimony/2005/JacksonTestimony050308.pdf.

14. Saakashvili fired Zurabishvili in October 2005.

15. See Remarks by Secretary of State Condoleezza Rice at the Institut d'Etudes Politiques de Paris, February 8, 2005, http://www.state.gov/secretary/rm/2005/41973.htm. See also Address by President Bush to the International Republican Institute (IRI), May 18, 2005, http://www.whitehouse.gov/news/releases/2005/05/20050518-2.html.

16. http://www.whitehouse.gov/news/releases/2004/02/20040225-1.html.

17. http://www.whitehouse.gov/news/releases/2005/05/20050510-2.html.

18. Some may argue that demonstrations were evidence enough for a pro-revolutionary mood in Georgia. However, as I show in chapter 8, most of these demonstrations were far from spontaneous. They were not organized by ordinary citizens who went into the streets to support Shevardnadze's overthrow. Rather, the protests were largely sustained by activists from the National Movement and Burdjanadze-Democrats. The size of the demonstrations was quite small when compared both to past protests in Georgia (such

as during the pro-independence movement) and, in relative terms, to other popular protests in recent years (such as Ukraine and Serbia).

19. While it is true that the official results were manipulated, as I show in chapter 8, this fraud did not fundamentally alter the balance of power in the Parliament when compared to the more accurate PVT count.

20. Charles King, "A Rose among Thorns: Georgia Makes Good," *Foreign Affairs* (March–April 2004), http://www.foreignaffairs.org/20040301facomment83203/charles-king/a-rose-among-thorns-georgia-makes-good.html?mode=print.

21. The only country to which it was similar (in limited ways) was Ukraine.

Chapter 1. Independence and the Failure of Gamsakhurdia's Rule

1. Website of the Georgian Orthodox Church, http://www.patriarchate.ge/istoria/1e.htm.

2. Some have argued that Shevardnadze himself engineered these protests in order to have a strong argument to present against the proposed Constitution to the Soviet leadership.

3. The weakness of the state was a phenomenon that outlasted the Communist period, and was a significant impediment·to effective rule for all Georgian leaders in the years that followed.

4. The South Ossetian autonomous district ("oblast") was created in 1922.

5. Charles H. Fairbanks has argued that the problem was more deeply rooted. "All the autonomous nationalities had looked to Moscow during Soviet times, as their patrons against the 'titular' nationalities ruling the Union republics, and had built strong ties there." As an example, he points to the relationship between the KGB and the family of Vladislav Ardzinba, who would lead the Abkhaz separatist rebellion against Georgia.

6. My research team was not able to find specific statistics for the number of dead in the Ossetian conflict. Paata Zakareishvili, a political scientist who has studied that period, estimates that about 3,000 people died on both sides. Others have suggested that this figure is far too large and that the real number is closer to under 1,000.

7. While some believe that Gamsakhurdia's ability to overcome a possible conflict in Abkhazia should be a credit to the period of his rule, I do not think that this modus vivendi would have lasted in the long run had Gamsakhurdia stayed in power.

8. Referred to in Georgian as "kanonieri kurdi," and in Russian as "vor v zakone." Through the book, unless otherwise noted, all translations from Georgian are mine.

9. Comments from Charles H. Fairbanks, September 10, 2005.

10. Ninety-three percent of voters supported independence.

11. May 26 was the day the Georgian government declared independence in 1918, after the fall of the Russian tsar.

12. This group was led by the other wing of the pro-independence movement, and also included the Soviet-era nomenklatura, the academic intelligentsia, Mkhedrioni, the National Guard, and some former supporters of the president, like Sigua.

13. Carolyn McGiffert Ekedahl, and Melvin A. Goodman, *The Wars of Eduard Shevardnadze* (University Park, Penn.: University of Pennsylvania Press, 1997).

14. With the exception of Estonia, Latvia, and Lithuania.

15. Based on data provided to me by Charles H. Fairbanks, according to the Soviet census, Georgians constituted 43 percent of the population, while the Abkhazians amounted to less than 17 percent. The rest were other minority groups, including Russians and Armenians.

16. There were many instances of torture and extrajudicial executions, and this was not limited just to the Abkhaz side. While the Georgian forces also were responsible for their share of crimes, ethnic Georgians who lived in Abkhazia suffered the greatest ethnic cleansing, death, and destruction at the hands of the Abkhaz and Russian fighters. The death toll on both sides was very high among the fighters as well—9,000 Georgian soldiers and 4,500 Abkhaz separatist fighters died.

17. One has to wonder if things would have turned out differently had George Bush been reelected as U.S. president in 1992, and had Shevardnadze's friend Jim Baker continued to hold a leadership position in the U.S. government throughout the 1990s.

18. An American official who worked in Georgia during Shevardnadze's tenure reported to me that the president and several of his advisors told him that Shevardnadze did not know.

19. The late 1980s and early 1990s were a monumental time for a person to come of age, especially for someone like me who was addicted to politics from a very early age. My observations about Gamsakhurdia are undoubtedly influenced by these personal experiences. I was too young to be a part of the pro-independence movement. Indeed, I often got depressed about my youth—I was seeing history in the making, with thousands of Georgians fighting for their own freedom, yet because of my age I could not be a part of it. I was not old enough to have a role later, when the opposition took a stance against Gamsakhurdia, but I vividly remember the difficulty of falling asleep while hundreds of men only four or five years older than I were shooting at each other just a mile or two away.

20. An agreement to this effect was signed in February 1994, during Russian President Boris Yeltsin's visit to Tbilisi.

21. I include myself in this group.

Chapter 2. Shevardnadze's Constitutional Founding and the Rise of Zhvania's "Young Reformers"

1. CUG held an informal party congress in November 1993, while its first formal congress took place in March 1994.

2. Carolyn McGiffert Ekedahl and Melvin A. Goodman, *The Wars of Eduard Shevardnadze* (University Park: University of Pennsylvania Press, 1997), 275–77.

3. Zbigniew Brzezinski, "The Premature Partnership," *Foreign Affairs* 73 (March–April 1994): 70.

4. In my conversations about this period with opinion makers in Washington, some even argued that the Clinton administration in effect granted Russian President Boris Yeltsin a free hand in the republics of the former Soviet Union in return for Moscow's support for U.S. policy in Haiti in 1993 and 1994. I was not able to obtain concrete evidence to back up this view.

5. While the European system is generally seen as securing liberty and representative government, if one were to follow Montesquieu (as I do), the so-called "parliamentary system" suffers from a great flaw—it unites much of the executive and legislative powers in one set of hands, that of the prime minister. This alone has been reason enough for me to steadfastly oppose calls to make Georgia a "parliamentary" system, and I have instead called for a proper system of checks and balances. In my view, however, "parliamentary" systems have numerous other flaws when compared to a properly organized separation-of-powers model.

6. Incidentally, even after Shevardnadze introduced a compromise, some of his supporters were still pushing for a far more hyper-presidential model. Zhvania, for example, advocated having a referendum to determine if people supported the hyper-presidential powers or not, knowing all too well that such a referendum would probably pass.

7. One third of parliamentarians were elected in so-called majoritarian districts.

8. Many Georgian politicians and political analysts have long opposed fully district-based elections, both out of the belief that this creates too much dependence on the people, and out of fear that wealthy people (i.e., "oligarchs") could "buy" elections by spending huge sums of money in majoritarian (district) constituencies. Dependence on the people is indeed bound to arise from district-based elections, but that is precisely the reason to favor such a model, since dependence on the people is the principle control on tyranny in a representative democracy. Meanwhile, the fear of candidates trying to buy their way into Parliament is also a real possibility, especially given that there is some historical precedence for this in Georgia. Throughout the 1990s and in 2003, many people in the one-third of Parliament elected through district-based elections have been wealthy men who care less about their local constituencies and more about using the parliamentary seat to advance their personal interests. However, this would certainly change if the size of the Parliament were reduced to a more manageable size, and if the only seats available were majoritarian ones, since prominent national politicians would have to seek these seats rather than depend on party lists to gain election. At the same time, requiring several years of residency in the community that one hopes to represent would be another way of preventing the wealthy from moving to districts purely to run for office, since most of these alleged "oligarchic" candidates would not want to give up comfortable lives in Tbilisi and move to their districts. Finally, a far better proportional alternative to fully district-based elections would be to have parties submit electoral lists not for the whole country, but separately for each region of the country. This way, individuals elected would

be closer to the people and would be serving specific constituencies, while maintaining the alleged benefits of the proportional system. This model was followed in 1992.

9. Steven Levitsky, "The Rise of Competitive Authoritarianism," *Journal of Democracy* 13, no. 2 (April 2002).

10. See, for example, Yuri Zarakhovich, "Future Favors the Brave: Shevardnadze Survives Another Assassination Attempt, But How Long Can His Luck Hold?" *Time* magazine 146, no. 11 (September 11, 1995).

11. Saakashvili was educated in Ukraine, served in the Soviet Border Guard, and then won a U.S. government fellowship to attend Columbia University for an LL.M. He was pursuing another law degree at George Washington University when Zhvania invited him to return to Georgia and join the Parliament in 1995. Burdjanadze, daughter of the longtime and close Shevardnadze confidant Anzor Burdjanadze, was educated as a lawyer in Moscow and then spent several years teaching at Tbilisi State University prior to entering politics.

12. Zhvania was godfather to óne of Mamaladze's children. In the theology and tradition of Georgia's Orthodox Christianity, the godparent-godchild relationship is regarded as more sacred than the parent-child relationship. For this reason, politically Zhvania and Mamaladze were viewed as closer than brothers.

13. I obtained these statistics from the Tbilisi office of the World Bank, by phone.

14. See, for example, "Meeting Report" from July 19, 2000, on a lecture Zhvania delivered at the Carnegie Endowment for International Peace, Washington, D.C., July 20, 2000. At http://www.ceip.org/files/events/meetingzhvania.asp?pr=2&EventID=193.

15. http://www.ceip.org/files/events/meetingzhvania.asp?pr=2&EventID=193.

16. Lance Fletcher was instrumental in helping me understanding the Georgian VAT system.

·17. I obtained these statistics from the Tbilisi office of the World Bank, by phone. Some observers of Georgian politics have attributed this at least partly to Russia's economic crisis. Certainly the Russian crisis had an impact on the Georgian economy. But that alone is not sufficient to explain what happened.

18. VAT has been popular with the political elite in Europe, but not in the United States. This is not to suggest that everyone in Europe supports the welfare model; indeed, many prominent intellectuals, public-policy scholars, and political leaders have come to believe that the welfare model is unsustainable and needs to be reformed. However, among Georgian "reformers" (and among many foreign "advisors" who worked in Georgia in the 1990s helping the government in the "reform" process), copying the European social-welfare model was a key political driver.

19. USAID, Request for Applications (RFA) No. 114-02-018, *Citizens Advocate! Program for Georgia*, February 8, 2002. The internal quote comes from "Focus Group Analysis of Local Democracy in Georgia," National Democratic Institute, March 2001.

20. This was an area (along with domestic-security issues) that Shevardnadze controlled fully—unlike domestic politics, in which he let the "young reformers" take the lead.

21. The pipeline was originally known as Baku-Ceyhan, but later was renamed Baku-Tbilisi-

Ceyhan (BTC). According to several American policymakers who were involved in these discussions during the 1990s, the situation with BTC was very complex, because initially, while the oil companies claimed to favor the pipeline and argued that it was financially viable, in reality this was not the case. Only gradually, after the wars in Chechnya and the rise in oil prices, did the oil firms find the financial resources necessary to build the BTC.

22. The country had seen a surge in emigration in the mid-to-late 1990s, especially to Russia.

23. This last report is from Pikria Chikhradze, who met with the president and urged him to stop Zhvania's manipulations, which he did.

24. Some may wonder about this argument and ask, "What about corruption?" and "What about Georgia's weak state?" Fundamentally, as I have argued, the "reformers" were responsible for a large share of "corruption." I would even argue that they were in part responsible for the weakness of the state, because these "reforms" estranged the citizens from the government by pushing people into the shadow economy. Thus, in my view, the reforms were the root cause of many of the problems that have generally been regarded as explaining Georgia's greatest difficulties. It is true that other factors, such as Russian meddling in Georgian affairs, were also significant (and separate) problems. However, these were things over which the Georgian government had far less control. By contrast, the "reforms" originated in the Georgian government, and thus the government was promulgating efforts that ultimately hurt the state itself.

Chapter 3. Gamkrelidze and the Collapse of the CUG

1. "Faction" is the name for political groups inside the Georgian Parliament that consist of ten or more members. Traditionally, each party with more than ten deputies in Parliament would be a faction, though sometimes parties have split their representation into more than one faction to allow them to have extra benefits, such as a car provided by the Parliament, a larger office, and most importantly, a seat on the Parliament's Bureau and greater access to the microphone during legislative debates. Different factions come together to form a majority and a minority.

2. Private party polling done for the New Faction and the New Rights Party in 2000 and 2001. While I did not have access to these polls at the time of the writing, because the data was no longer available, I had an opportunity to review these polls in November 2001.

3. Georgia did not start privatizing state-owned factories and businesses in any significant way until 2004, under the government of President Saakashvili. The few privatization deals that went through under Shevardnadze—Borjomi Mineral Waters being the most prominent example—actually led to businessmen taking over enterprises that had collapsed and saving them from total destruction.

4. This party was first known in English as the "New Rights Party," with "NRP" as its abbreviation. After April 2004, it has often been referred to as the "New Conservative Party,"

with "NCP" as its abbreviation. I have decided to use "New Rights Party" and "NRP" throughout the book. The reason for this double name is that there is no exact translation of the party's name from Georgian into English. In Georgian, the name is "axali memar-jveneebi—axlebi." These three terms literally translate as "new," "believers in right" (used here to imply conservative), and "new people." The use of "new" and "new people" stems from the fact that the party was organized around the New Faction of Parliament.

5. At the time, I was living in Washington, D.C., working as a business consultant, but I had spent the previous summer in Georgia and had a chance to learn many details about Georgian politics. What I discovered, especially about the so-called "reformers," their "achievements," and their political views, made me very depressed about the possibility of democratic change in Georgia. I was particularly incensed by the claims of the "young reformers'" that they were democrats, given that their actions had nothing in common with democracy. Therefore, as I watched from afar the formation of the first "philosophically driven" political party in Georgia's recent history, I began to see a ray of hope. This was the reason why I decided to contact Gamkrelidze soon after the formation of the New Rights Party and ask whether I could be of any assistance to him, even though I was in the United States. It was this e-mail that led to a long professional relationship and friendship that continues to this day.

6. I do not mean to suggest that other opposition parties never had popularity. The Revival Party and the National Democratic Party, for example, were both popular at different times. The difference in my view—as well as of several analysts with whom I discussed this issue—was that the New Faction was seen as being *better* than CUG, whereas almost all other opposition groups that had a share of popularity in the past were supported by those who were simply too disillusioned by Shevardnadze and his team.

7. Private party polling done for the New Faction and the New Rights Party in 2000 and 2001.

8. http://www.mosnews.com/mn-files/georgia.shtml; and Erin Arvedlund, "Rose Revolution," in *Columbia Magazine* (Winter 2005), http://www.columbia.edu/cu/alumni/Magazine/Winter2005/saakashvili.html.

9. Constitutionally, the speaker of Parliament becomes acting president, and elections take place within forty-five days.

10. *Washington Post*, April 13, 2001, A12.

11. *The National Interest*, no. 58 (Spring 2001).

12. I had an opportunity to meet King in Washington after the article was published and discuss it with him in detail, including his sources.

13. A Soviet-era term for the Ministries of Defense, Interior, and Security (which replaced the KGB), and the General Prosecutor's Office.

14. My principal source for this is David Gamkrelidze. However, I also had an opportunity to confirm this with Kakha Targamadze when I sat in on an interview, conducted by an American colleague in August 2003, about the war in Abkhazia.

15. These were the three individuals who would come to dominate Georgian politics after the

Rose Revolution—as president, leader of the opposition, and speaker of Parliament.

16. I should note here that from the very beginning of my work on Georgian politics, it was clear in my mind that I was not going to hide my views and allegiances. Indeed, in American domestic politics, which I had been following closely for years, I did not greatly appreciate the so-called "neutral" analysts who were actually quite partisan and ideological. My intention, therefore, was to be as honest about my allegiances as possible.

17. NDI's counterpart on the other side of the political spectrum is the International Republican Institute (IRI), the affiliate of the GOP.

18. Zhvania's speech at NDI, February 2002. These and other quotes from this speech are based on the notes I took during his address.

Chapter 4. 2002 Local-Government Elections and Zhvania's Political Rebirth

1. By seat, I mean a variety of elected positions in the *sakrebulos* (councils). There were village councils, town/city councils, and district councils.

2. While adding up the results that the two parties received separately would leave them about six points behind Labor, I believe that the Industry-NRP combination was an alliance that would have garnered additional votes, particularly from those in the electorate who were disenchanted with all the parties and did not come out to vote. I examine the wisdom behind this argument in chapter 5.

3. Every parliamentary faction leader was usually given an opportunity to speak to the Parliament after a presidential State of the Nation address.

4. Three Sakrebulo members from the Labor party quit the party soon after the election and were not supporting Saakashvili.

Chapter 5. Parties Prepare for the Parliamentary Elections While the NGO Community and Rustavi 2 Prepare for the Revolution

1. Gamkrelidze's initial idea was that I would return in late spring or early summer for the most important part of the race. For me, this was the most incredible opportunity, but also a huge challenge. I was extremely committed to Georgia and to using my knowledge to help the country secure a democratic future. I also strongly believed that Gamkrelidze offered the best opportunity to help secure that future, because I saw in him, unlike most other members of the Georgian political class, a committed democrat and a believer in the free market who had a clear idea of what government in Georgia should be like. For these reasons, I accepted the offer and in the winter of 2003, I made plans to go to Tbilisi by the early spring to help plan the campaign.

2. I was actually quite insistent on this point because I did not feel comfortable making this choice without him.

3. I do not have first-hand information about what happened at NDI's Tbilisi office internally. From the outside and from second-hand recollections, it appears that many of the NDI activities that I criticize originated with Mullen. Mitchell may have even been opposed to some, with the exception of the idea of an opposition alliance. For this last issue, Mitchell was actually the point man.

4. Zhvania's United Democrats do not appear on the map because at the time of the poll, their support was so low that the party was basically not registering with voters. The percent supporting them was so low that subdividing it made no sense. The same was true of the two governmental parties, For New Georgia and Revival, which did not register much popular support but would end up having a significant result nonetheless because of fraud and other manipulations. At the same time, the core support for these groups was in Adjaria, Kvemo Kartli, and Javakheti, where the poll was not conducted. Their results would have been higher had the poll taken place in these regions as well. It is also important to note that Shevardnadze's new group, For New Georgia, had not yet been formally formed when the poll was conducted.

5. The most ironic thing was that the negative commentary was having little impact on average voters, since newspapers did not have mass circulation.

6. At the time, this was approximately US $7.

7. Natelashvili explained to U.S. officials that he did not have the money to respond to Saakashvili. I have my doubts about this explanation, given that several businessmen hedged their bets and funded all political parties, including Labor. Furthermore, Natelashvili's second-in-command was Pridon Injia, former minister of telecommunications, who was one of Georgia's wealthiest men and a key financial backer of the Labor Party.

8. Starting in September, Rustavi 2 was most extreme in its attacks against For New Georgia. However, other television stations were not far behind.

9. I was told by a U.S. official working in Georgia at the time that the steps at the Ministry of Interior were painted after the activists were not arrested for some of their actions the day before. However, neither he nor I were certain about what they had done then.

10. Radio Free Europe/Radio Liberty Caucasus Report, vol. 15, no. 34, October 11, 2004.

11. I was once asked if I would have objected had the International Republican Institute (IRI), the NDI's counterpart, done the same for the NRP (since ideologically NRP and the GOP were closer). My response then was vehement—yes, I would have objected. For example, the IRI sided with Russian President Boris Yeltsin throughout the 1990s, including the 1999 presidential election in Russia. That was just as inappropriate as the NDI's decision to side with the "young reformers" in Georgia. The issue is not whether you like whom the IRI or the NDI sides with, but whether these organizations should follow their mandate (as the IRI had done in Georgia over the years) by working with all *democratic* political parties on behalf of democracy and freedom.

12. It is often argued that the Founders opposed political parties. However, given that the first of the two parties in American history were formed by the Founders (John Adams and Alexander Hamilton on the one hand, and Thomas Jefferson and James Madison on the

other), this view is not necessarily representative of history.

13. "Misha" was the way most people referred to Mikheil Saakashvili. This is a paraphrased quote.

14. The decision to sell the "ORT frequency" to Rustavi 2 had to be officially made by the Georgian Communication Commission, which Shevardnadze controlled informally but whose chairman was said to be Kitsmarishvili's partner in Georgia Online, an Internet provider that was Rustavi's side business.

15. In Georgian, this sentence reads: "Shevardnadze, shen xar seni, dagvekhseni." It was used because it rhymes.

Chapter 6. Failure of the United Opposition and Failure of the Baker Formula

1. Letter of Senator John McCain to President Eduard Shevardnadze, June 6, 2003. I had always been a great admirer of the senator because of his courageous military service and his steadfast support for distinctly American internationalism, especially after September 11. When I read the letter, I became even more convinced that his brand of conservatism was vital to the success of American foreign policy. In many respects, McCain's words came true in the end, and to this very day I do not quite understand why Shevardnadze, for all of his skills as an international diplomat, never grasped their full meaning. (In addition to Mike Murphy, Dan Twining, Senator McCain's foreign policy advisor at the time, was also instrumental in making the letter possible.)

2. http://www.whitehouse.gov/news/releases/2003/07/20030703-15.html.

3. Aslan Abashidze's Revival Party was technically considered an opposition party. It was probably the only one that did not like the Baker proposal, because it would have reduced, if not completely prevented fraud in Adjaria, the Black Sea region Abashidze ruled and where the party expected to get almost all of its votes.

4. Statement by Senator John McCain on the Situation in Georgia, July 31, 2005.

5. While Baker was no longer secretary of state, he was visiting Georgia as the presidential envoy, thus speaking on the president's behalf.

6. OSCE was somewhat upset by having to be involved—apparently not because it did not want to be, but because there was a failure to clear with OSCE the idea of its involvement *before* the proposal was made public. Elizabeth Jones had to make a special stop on the way back from Georgia in Europe to meet with OSCE officials to smooth the way to their participation.

7. Usupashvili was close to the Republican Party, which was part of Saakashvili's National Movement (Usupashvili would become chairman of the Republican Party in 2005). However, he was also a lawyer who was very committed to his image of neutrality, and thus would probably have acted in a fair manner had he been chosen as chairman. Khmaladze was nominated for the post by the NRP, but was extremely neutral and was probably the best candidate for the post.

Chapter 7. The Fall Campaign

1. Interview with Inga Grigolia on Mze TV, November 2, 2003.
2. I discuss the New Rights Party's activities last because this is the campaign that I know best, since I was one of the people who had designed and was implementing its strategy. As a result, my observations are bound to be more detailed than those about other parties. However, I think that these observations are interesting, because they shed a light not only on the NRP but also on all other political groups and on a number of key issues of democratic transition in general.
3. These were not the specific words that Saakashvili used, but express his idea.
4. I owe this example to David Kochel.
5. These include, but are not limited to, Pikria Chikhradze, David Saganelidze, Irakli Iashvili, Valeri Kvaratskhelia, Mzia Totladze, Mamuka Katsitadze, and a few others.
6. When I say "did not exist," I am quite literal—there was no written program one could read. While NRP had its "900 Days" plan and Burdjanadze-Democrats had their economic plan, which was written by former Economics Minister Lado Papava, National Movement's "program" was simply not available.
7. There were numerous reports about this in virtually all British newspapers in the lead-up to the British election in 2005. See, for example, Nick Wood, "The Insider," *Guardian*, April 18, 2005, where he writes, "Going back to the 1992 election, the polls have consistently underestimated the strength of Conservative support and overestimated backing for Labour."
8. In 2005, the final election results for the UK were as follows: Labour 36 percent, Conservatives 33 percent, Liberal Democrats 22 percent, with Labour's victory margin in the national aggregate total over Conservatives being 3 percent. Of the final polls, taken a couple of days before the election, only NOP/Independent predicted this margin. All other polls gave Labour a far larger lead over the Conservatives. Communicate Research/IoS had an eight-point lead for Labour, ICM/Guardian and Populus/Times had a six-point lead for Labour, and YouGov/Telegraph and MORI/FT had a five-point lead for Labour. These numbers were taken from www.bbcnews.com.
9. I myself favored an American-style self-registration, with the electoral registry developed through citizens going to the proper agency to register, either by party or as independents, and with only those who were registered in advance being allowed to vote. While I knew that this would reduce the turnout, in my view democratic citizenship was about more than simply showing up to vote on Election Day; rather, democracy needed the active participation of individuals who knew that self-government was a matter of daily life. Furthermore, I felt that allowing citizens to register party affiliation would help strengthen the party system—at least those parties with enough organizational capacity to mobilize their supporters to register. Almost everyone in Georgia—pro- or anti-governmental politicians, experts, foreigners, and NGO activists alike—argued that such a pro-

posal was anti-democratic and contrary to the Georgian Constitution, which guarantees the right to vote. I mention this here because it is important in light of the system that was adopted for registration after the Rose Revolution, as I examine in chapter 11.

10. Http://www.civil.ge/eng/article_elections.php?id=5361.

11. According to the Rustavi 2 exit poll, whose data should be taken with a grain of salt for reasons discussion in the upcoming chapter, 4.2 percent of voters were unable to find themselves on electoral lists.

12. Rob Parsons, "Unrest Rises in Georgia," *Sunday Herald*, November 14, 2003, http://www .sundayherald.com/38065.

Chapter 8. The Rose Revolution

1. Kitsmarishvili had used the exit poll as leverage against Jorbenadze to try to convince the government to give him the ORT frequency.

2. I base this belief on my conversations with several Rustavi 2 journalists, including those who were very close to Kitsmarishvili.

3. Even in the United States, where political polling is probably more advanced and more widely used than in any other country in the world, the exit polls failed both in the 2000 and 2004 presidential election. In 2000, the exit polls led the networks to call Florida inaccurately. Meanwhile, in 2004, the exit polls suggested that John Kerry would win the presidency, even though George W. Bush eventually got more votes than any other presidential candidate in history.

4. While statistical sampling is generally supposed to fix such problems, sampling was one of the reasons why the 2004 exit polls in the United States were so inaccurate.

5. The exit polls were conducted by Georgian pollsters, whose work was supervised by a representative of Global Strategy Group, an American Democratic political consulting and polling firm.

6. In my research, I was unable to get the data for how Imedi's poll distributed the results, but like the PVT, it showed six parties overcoming the 7 percent threshold to gain seats in Parliament. However, the victor in the poll was For New Georgia.

7. *24 Hours*, November 4, 2005.

8. Ibid.

9. Ibid.

10. Protesting was a fundamental right protected by the Georgian Constitution, and during the revolutionary period, citizens were never prevented from demonstrating. Those of us, including Gamkrelidze, who opposed the protests were not questioning the right of the people to protest, but rather questioned whether it made sense to engage in protests that would lead to a revolution.

11. *24 Hours*, November 4, 2005. "Papa" is the Georgian word for porridge. In Georgian, this is an expression similar to the English expression "eating pie."

12. *24 Hours*, November 5, 2005. "Bloody votes" was referring to votes from Adjaria, which Saakashvili's supporters alleged the NRP would receive because, according to them, Abashidze favored the NRP.

13. Or at the very least, the government would have been willing to compromise earlier.

14. *24 Hours*, November 6, 2005.

15. Giga Chikhladze and Irakli Chikhladze, "The Rose Revolution: A Chronicle," in *"Enough!" The Rose Revolution in the Republic of Georgia 2003*, ed. Zurab Karumindze and James V. Wertsch (New York: Nova Science Publishers, Inc., 2005), 9.

16. *24 Hours*, November 10, 2005. I have heard from a variety of sources, both Georgian and American, that Shevardnadze's impression of Saakashvili was extremely negative. After the incident at this residence, he told American officials, for example, that he would never meet with Saakashvili again, though he was happy to meet with Burdjanadze and Zhvania.

17. Ibid.

18. By saying that Shevardnadze accepted Revival's results, I mean that he would not stand in the way of them being certified by the CEC. Shevardnadze, through FNG's five CEC representatives, could have blocked the certification of these results, since opposition parties would have supported such a motion.

19. Shevardnadze often spoke about his fear of "another Abkhazia" in his conversations with foreign ambassadors, including American officials.

20. I base my comments on Abashidze's network in Moscow on information obtained from Charles H. Fairbanks.

21. *24 Hours*, November 11, 2005.

22. The NRP was invited to join this, but it refused, with Gamkrelidze declaring that he would not participate in anything that included Revival.

23. Miles was meeting with Shevardnadze to deliver a message from Washington that the official results (which at this stage were not yet available) had to be "adjusted" in order to bring them closer to the PVT.

24. I do not mean to suggest that she did not allow for a great deal of fraud. However, Jorbenadze wanted far more fraud, and Devdariani was not willing to go that far.

25. Peter Baker, "Pressure Mounts on Georgian Leader," *Washington Post*, November 11, 2003, 14A.

26. Burdjanadze continued as speaker until the newly elected Parliament convened.

27. I was quite disturbed by this. As I wrote Zeyno Baran at the Nixon Center, the outcome was most unfortunate, because "after the elections, by looking at the results, you were left with the impression that Shevardnadze for the first time 'lost' an election because he would not be in a majority [and] because [the] opposition as a whole received more votes than the government. [However, after] the collapse of these protests, [Shevardnadze] once again comes out as a major victor, with the leaders who had brought people to the streets looking very idiotic. . . . They had to stop, even though none of their goals were accomplished. In some ways, all of this echoes back to what happened in June, when there was a huge demonstration calling for a democratic electoral commission. We achieved noth-

ing at that point, looked very silly. The demands were far more radical this time around." (Irakly Areshidze, e-mail to Zeyno Baran, Friday, November 14, 2003.)

28. Zeyno Baran, e-mail to Irakly Areshidze, Monday, November 17, 2003.

29. I am paraphrasing here, since I am restating Gamkrelidze's report on his conversation with Saakashvili.

30. The NRP's representative voted for the protocol because it was the best possible one could have gotten from the election, given the chaos and manipulation that had taken place. Furthermore, even with these problems, the protocol was still far closer to the real votes of the people than the 1999 election protocol. Some argued that the NRP supported the protocol in order to be "given" a showing of over 7 percent in return for legitimizing the election results. However, as the PVT results make clear, the NRP had gotten more than 7 percent, and its efforts in the CEC after November 2 were simply aimed at protecting the votes that it had received. If there was a quid quo pro (though I am not aware of one), the NRP voted for the protocol in order to ensure that its results would not be manipulated.

31. Industry's representatives voted against the protocol because its leaders were upset with Jorbenadze for not keeping his promise to them from the period when he had urged them to not join the NRP in an alliance—and said that he would use his administrative resources to get them into the Parliament, even if they did not receive 7 percent on their own (which they clearly did not).

32. This chart was prepared by Matt Christ of the U.S. Embassy in Tbilisi.

33. I was so impressed by his remarks that I sent him a thank you e-mail, even though the two of us had butted heads in the past.

34. I had an opportunity to sit in on the meeting.

35. In all fairness, it should be noted that I was largely responsible for drafting this letter.

36. E-mail from David Gamkrelidze to Matthew J. Bryza, November 19, 2003.

37. E-mail from Matthew J. Bryza to David Gamkrelidze, November 19, 2003. Please note that I have not received permission from either David Gamkrelidze or Matt Bryza to quote from this e-mail exchange. Indeed, I have refrained from showing this section of the manuscript to Gamkrelidze because I did not want him to stop me from quoting from the e-mails, since he may value their confidentiality. I believe that this information is so instructive that making it public is instrumental to understanding exactly what happened.

38. I was told by individuals who were working closely with Saakashvili during the revolutionary period, as well as by an official from the U.S. Embassy in Tbilisi, that Bryza was in constant communication with Saakashvili during this time as well.

39. Press Briefing, U.S. Department of State, Washington, D.C., November 20, 2003, at http://www.state.gov/r/pa/prs/dpb/2003/26502.htm. Anyone who is familiar with the responses that the spokesman usually gives during these briefings is aware that most of them are prepared comments, already cleared with various officials at the department. The first two paragraphs of Erili's response seem particularly like a previously prepared response that he simply read.

40. "Presidential Election in Georgia," U.S. Department of State press statement, Washington, D.C., November 21, 2003, at http://www.state.gov/r/pa/prs/ps/2003/26539.htm.

41. Some opinion makers in Washington have suggested to me, with good reason, that the Pentagon and the Office of the Vice President were closer to Bryza's view than was the State Department. In addition, the Pentagon, it appears, instructed Georgian military officials (including those who were U.S.-trained) that the army should not get involved in the dispute. There are a variety of views about whether Shevardnadze was willing to consider the use of force, though all the real evidence I have been able to gather suggests that this was never the case. If that is true, than military-to-military caution against the use of force probably did not have a great deal of impact. The CIA also must have been important, but I was unable to determine its position.

42. I cannot be certain that the details I describe here are absolutely accurate or fully present a picture of what happened.

43. This could have been on November 18.

44. I have an unconfirmed report that Shevardnadze and Baker actually did connect one time, but then the line went dead. If this indeed happened, it is not too far-fetched to imagine that someone sabotaged Shevardnadze.

45. Interview with James A. Baker by James V. Wertsch in *"Enough!" The Rose Revolution in the Republic of Georgia 2003*, ed. Zurab Karumidze and James V. Wertsch (New York: Nova Science Publishers, Inc., 2005), 82.

46. Electing the speaker was not necessary for legitimizing the election results. Constitutionally, the new Parliament's authority was recognized once more than half of the deputies registered before the opening of the first session and a quorum was reached.

47. In 2006 the Georgian media also advanced the notion that Shevardnadze offered Abashidze the post of State Minister rather than Prime Minister. However, the likelihood of either seems small.

48. Mamradze became Prime Minister Zhvania's chief of staff after the Rose Revolution.

49. The threat of violence was still very real, however, because a small armed band (possibly from Adjaria) could easily trigger an armed confrontation.

50. I have heard reports from those who were close to Ivanov during the appearance that he was drunk. This was certainly plausible, given that he had spent the night drinking.

51. The real loser from keeping the old Parliament rather than the new one was the Labor Party, which had done exceptionally well in the November 2003 elections. It had been kept out of the 1999 Parliament by Zhvania, as I have already indicated.

Chapter 9. Revolution's Achievements

1. http://washingtontimes.com/op-ed/20040509-103915-5701r.htm.

2. During much of 2003, US $1 equaled approximately 2.10 lari, but the exchange rate changed dramatically in 2004, with US $1 equaling about $1.80 lari. The value of the lari

fell further in 2005 and 2006. As a result of this rise in the value of the lari, in U.S. dollars the increase in the budget was far more pronounced than in the Georgian lari.

3. For me, even if we ignore the sustainability argument, a key question is whether it is good to have a government whose spending is continually becoming a larger part of the national economy. As someone who believes that government should only take care of those things that citizens cannot do for themselves, I find the Saakashvili administration's focus on bigger and bigger government disturbing. However, this is a policy difference, unlike many of the more fundamental differences over citizens' rights that I examine below.

4. I examined the problems associated with the VAT for an economy such as Georgia's in chapter 2.

5. Pensions were further increased to 38 lari in 2006.

6. This amendment was passed in the summer of 2005 by the Parliament elected in March 2004. It is not connected to amendments discussed in chapter 10.

7. Higher than in many countries in Europe, the 7 percent barrier prevents small parties, with minimal public support, from gaining seats in Parliament. As a result, I believe that such a high barrier could assist in the development of a two- or three-party system in the country. For this reason, I do not share this criticism of the government.

Chapter 10. Saakashvili's Constitution and Legal One-Man Rule

1. Saakashvili's supporters understood by the "presidential" system one in which the president functions as both the head of state and the head of government (as is the case in the United States), whereas by the "parliamentary" system they understood a regime in which the president (or the monarch) serves as the ceremonial head of state while the prime minister runs the affairs of the country as the head of government (as is the case in the United Kingdom, Italy, and so forth). Accordingly, the idea behind the "quasi-presidential" or "quasi-parliamentary" model is a scheme that seeks to combine elements from both systems. In Europe, only France, and to a lesser degree Poland (where presidential powers are weaker than in France) have such a form of government.

2. The full text of the Georgian Constitution, including all of the recent amendments, is available at http://www.parliament.ge/LEGAL_ACTS/CONSTITUTION/consten.html.

3. Interviews with Vakhtang Khmaladze, former member of Parliament, October–November, 2004.

4. In Europe, with the exception of France, and to a lesser degree Poland, the president is generally merely a figurehead, which is not the case in Georgia.

5. Herman Schwartz wrote an analysis for the Parliament's Judiciary Committee of constitutional amendments that were proposed by Shevardnadze in 2001. I obtained this letter from David Usupashvili. Shevardnadze's 2001 amendments were nearly identical to the ones that passed the Parliament in 2004. Supporters of Saakashvili's amendments

argued that because these two sets of changes were so similar, there was no need for debate now, since discussions had been ongoing for three years.

6. In the Soviet Union, while most ministers reported to the chairman of the Council of Minister (i.e., the prime minister), the ministers of interior, defense, and foreign affairs and the head of the KGB reported directly to the general secretary of the Communist Party. The superpresidential constitutions, like the one in Georgia, follow this model.

7. Herman Schwartz letter.

8. http://www.rferl.org/featuresarticle/2004/02/8a6494b7-c89c-4a33-b1f0-b284eaebf705.html

9. Imedi TV News, February 7, 2004.

10. Because the Parliament that was elected on November 2, 2003, had convened its first session before the Supreme Court invalidated the proportional results, constitutionally the term of the 1999 legislature had ended. Furthermore, even if one accepts the validity of the Supreme Court decision, at least one-third of the deputies in the 1999 Parliament, who had been voted into office directly in first-past-the-post districts, were clearly illegitimate and no longer empowered to continue in office, given that their replacements had been elected and duly certified, and their election had not been invalidated by the courts.

11. http://www.eurasianet.org/departments/insight/articles/eav030104.shtml.

12. Appearance on Imedi Television, February 19, 2005.

13. Discussion between David Usupashvili and Devi Khechinashvili, March 2004.

14. http://www.rferl.org/featuresarticle/2004/02/8a6494b7-c89c-4a33-b1f0-b284eaebf705.html.

15. http://www.eurasianet.org/departments/insight/articles/eav030104.shtml.

16. http://www.rferl.org/featuresarticle/2004/02/8a6494b7-c89c-4a33-b1f0-b284eaebf705.html.

17. Sestanovich, Stephen, "A Tale of Two Post-Soviet Presidents," Wall Street Journal, July 20, 2004.

18. I owe this observation to Charles Fairbanks.

19. http://www.iwpr.net/index.pl?archive/cau/cau_200402_218_1_eng.txt.

20. In chapter 12, I provide a full discussion of what happened with the shows.

21. Interview with Zakaria Kutsnashvili, November 2004. Interview with David Gamkrelidze, February 2004.

22. During the vote on the amendments, I was in the process of planning the NRP's electoral strategy for the March elections, and believed that the vote for the amendments was not only morally reprehensible but also damaging politically, because it opened the party to attack from other opposition groups who would allege that the NRP had made a deal with Saakashvili. This was probably the only time I publicly broke with the party leaders during the time when I served as their consultant, by openly speaking against the amendments both in Georgia and abroad. This caused serious internal problems because many of the NRP's financial backers demanded that party leaders silence me, since they were feeling the heat from Saakashvili—especially after I published an op-ed in the Washing-

ton Post on this subject during the president's trip to the United States in February 2004.

23. These observations are based on my discussions with staffers from U.S. and European embassies in Tbilisi.

24. William Pitt the Younger, the legendary prime minister of the United Kingdom, stayed in office for several months after having lost the confidence of Parliament in 1784. He was able to do this because he still had the confidence of the king. This period allowed him to gain popularity and win the next election. However, this was an exceptional case; even in eighteenth-century England, the prime minister (unlike his twenty-first-century Georgian counterpart) eventually had to resign if he lost a no-confidence vote.

25. By late 2006, many of the cabinet posts had gone through one or two additional changes in ministers.

26. James Madison, "Federalist Paper No. 51," in *The Federalist Papers*, ed. Clinton Rossiter (New York: A Mentor Book, 1961), 322.

27. Ibid., 324.

Chapter 11. The Rule of Law and the Rule of Men

1. This is not to suggest that there were not truly corrupt "businessmen" in Georgia. However, these were a tiny minority of the business sector.

2. Though I was not able to get a date for this, Saakashvili made the promise of amnesty during a speech to businessmen at an event organized by the chairman of the Georgian Federation of Businessmen, Badri Patarkatsishvili, soon after his inauguration as president in February 2004. The new government worked on an amnesty proposal for over a year after Saakashvili's inauguration, but the eventual proposal that passed did not provide for real amnesty.

3. Okruashvili became defense minister in December 2004. Okroashvili was removed as defense minister on November 10, 2006, and appointed minister for economic development, a post he resigned on November 17.

4. I say "almost" because there may have been a case when the courts did not grant a government request. However, my research team and I could not find such a case.

5. See reports by Human Rights Watch at www.hrw.org.

6. Interview with Nana Kakabadze, March 2005.

7. One of the first to report on the Army Development Fund was Teresa Freese, in an article titled "Defense Reform Poses Crucial Civil Society Test for Georgia" for EurasiaNet, an Internet news site which covers the Caucasus and Central Asia. http://eurasianet.org/departments/insight/articles/eav040705.shtml.

8. Interview with Rustavi 2 Television, February 3, 2004.

9. Interview with Rustavi 2 Television, January 12, 2004.

10. Address to Parliament of Georgia, February 8, 2005, reported live by Imedi TV and other television stations.

11. Conversation with Amy Denman, executive director of AmChem, February 27, 2005. AmChem refers to the American Chamber of Commerce in Georgia. Its members are not only companies with American investors, but also most of the prominent businesses in Georgia.

12. This particular quote comes from a former U.S. legislative staffer who has served his country with distinction. Because our conversation was off the record, I have chosen to withhold this person's name. However, I had similar conversations with numerous foreign-policy and opinion makers, where variations of similar explanations were used to explain why it was okay for the government to act in this manner.

13. See, for example, analysis of the "Compact to Promote Transparency and Combat Corruption: A New Partnership between the G8 and Georgia," below.

14. Whatever the reason behind America's praise of these "reforms," such a response reminded some older Georgians of Shevardnadze's Communist-era fight against corruption (when he was minister of public order and security). Then, too, nothing actually changed, but the future Georgian president was able to build for himself a reformist's reputation in Moscow.

15. http://www.whitehouse.gov/news/releases/2004/06/20040610-33.html.

16. The former head of the Anti-Terrorism Center has also been charged, prosecuted, and convicted, but he was not included in the list above.

17. I personally have heard numerous foreigners involved in judicial reform issues praise Chanturia repeatedly during my years of active involvement in Georgian politics.

18. http://www.state.gov/g/drl/rls/hrrpt/2004/41682.htm.

19. Sixteen kilograms is about thirty-five pounds.

20. Molashvili was finally tried in August 2005, convicted, and sentenced to nine years in prison for misappropriating 10,000 lari.

21. Although some in the revolutionary NGOs did try to compare Shevardnadze's Georgia to Karimov's Uzbekistan.

22. http://www.abanet.org/media/releases/news072804.html.

23. http://www.keepmedia.com/ShowItemDetails.do?itemID=520305&extID=10030&oliID=226.

Chapter 12. Elections and Imbalanced Governance

1. Patarkatsishvili's candidacy would have dramatically altered the media landscape in Georgia, discussed later, by forcing at least two stations (Imedi, which he owned, and Mze, which at the time was fully owned by his close business associate) to support his candidacy openly. Patarkatsishvili was extremely popular—since mid-2003 he has had one of the highest favorability ratings of any public figure in Georgia.

2. I have my doubts about whether so many people actually went to vote.

3. Private poll by Paata Chakhnashvili.

4. Mark Mullen resigned from NDI soon after the November elections, resulting in the organization regaining some of its credibility with the opposition and nongovernmental groups.

5. According to the Election Code, if the results were cancelled in a given district, all parties lost the votes that they received in that district, but the total voter turnout, from which the 7 percent was calculated, did not change.

6. The meeting took place during the first seven days in April, though the exact date is not certain.

7. Presidential Decree No. 401, May 25, 2005.

8. www.civil.ge, June 2, 2005.

9. One topic that I have chosen not to discuss, even though it is a key example of the characteristics of the post–Rose Revolution government I describe below, is privatization. I made this decision because I lacked evidence and information to properly assess this issue.

10. *Human Rights in Post-Revolutionary Georgia*, report by Former Political Prisoners for Human Rights, Tbilisi, 2004.

11. *24 Hours*, January 18, 2005. The word "drivel" is used here as an approximation of the Georgian word "gniasi," which does not have an exact equivalent in English.

12. April 11, 2005, www.civil.ge.

13. I could examine numerous other issues, but picked these three as case examples because they differ from each other and present different ways in which the executive avoided legislative oversight.

14. *Akhali Versia*, January 21, 2005. This fund, which is part of the budget, must be distinguished from the totally secret funds, which are not part of the budget, discussed below.

15. Decree No. 41, dated January 4, 2004, was obtained prior to it being made secret.

16. In July 2005, Gelashvili was attacked while driving in his car in Tbilisi and severally injured. He blamed government officials for the attack, returned to Vilnius, Lithuania (where he made his fortune) for treatment, and stopped financing the construction of the residence. While construction continued through much of 2005 and 2006, little progress has been made, because the government has been short on funds to pay for the completion of the residence.

17. Ibid.

18. "Reaction with Inga Grigolia," Imedi TV.

19. http://eurasianet.org/departments/insight/articles/eavo40705.shtml.

20. www.civil.ge, April 8, 2005.

21. Imedi TV, April 11, 2005.

22. *Akhali Versia*, February 14, 2005.

23. Georgian Young Lawyers' Association (GYLA), *Georgian Government under a Very Hot Sun*, August 2005, 14–15.

24. Orion Strategies is a firm operated by Randy Scheunemann, a former foreign-policy advisor to Senators Bob Dole and John McCain. I have always admired the work that he has

done in advocating for the liberation of Iraq and in advancing NATO membership for East European countries. My intention is by no means to raise any questions about the work that he is doing on Georgia's behalf. Rather, in presenting this case, my intention is to raise questions about how the Georgian government operates, and how it pays for its contracts.

25. Georgian Young Lawyers' Association (GYLA), *Georgian Government under a Very Hot Sun*, August 2005, 20.

26. U.S. Federal Election Commission, John Kerry for President, Inc., Schedule C Itemized Distributions, line 23. At http://herndon2.sdrdc.com/cgi-bin/dcdev/forms/C00383653/135870/sb/23/3.

27. A report of a conversation between Bezhuashvili and a senior National Movement parliamentarian, as detailed by the latter.

28. The Georgians allege that the opposite was true, and that they were merely responding to the aggressive moves by the Ossetians.

29. Interview with Nick Rurua, in *Rezonansi*, September 9, 2004.

30. The Georgian government claims that only sixteen soldiers died in all, though some reports put the number at seventeen. However, many analysts allege that the death toll had to be higher, given the fighting that took place. Journalists who were covering events also make similar allegations in private. This is reinforced by the government's refusal to release the names of even those soldiers whose death it actually acknowledges.

31. Bill Clinton, *My Life* (New York: Vintage Books, 2005).

32. There are a total of eleven regions in Georgia, two of which are autonomous republics and have different systems of governance; thus, a total of nine governors were appointed by the president.

33. C. J. Chivers, "With Bush Coming, Georgia Spruces Up," *New York Times*, May 7, 2005.

34. Saakashvili's State of the Nation address, February 10, 2005. No real changes to the system of local government took place in 2006. The local officials who were elected in the fall of 2006 do not have the sort of power that they require to actually run local affairs. Thus, their dependence on the central government continues. Saakashvili also kept in place the position of "governor" appointed by the President.

35. Saakashvili's comments on November 16, 2004, during a public appearance at Tbilisi Technical University, in response to a question from one of the attending students about direct elections of the Tbilisi mayor. The Tbilisi municipal budget is actually closer to 450 million lari.

36. Some would argue that it should not be any different from other regions, since a special status for Adjaria is not a historic development, but rather an artificial creation left over from Russian empire/Soviet days. When talking about "other regions," Abkhazia is not included, because virtually everyone agrees that the only resolution to the conflict there is by granting the region greater autonomy.

Chapter 13. Media Freedom, or Lack Thereof

1. Of these three, only Imedi is available everywhere nationally all the time, while Rustavi transmits nationally through its affiliated local stations only during select periods in the day, generally when it runs news and political shows; Mze's national availability is more limited. State TV became Public Broadcasting after the Rose Revolution.

2. Country Reports on Human Rights Practices, U.S. Department of State, February 28, 2004.

3. In September 2005, several Georgian newspapers reported that Chkhartishvili left the network altogether and abandon it to Bezhuashvili. I was able to confirm this in 2006.

4. In November 20, 2006, just days after Okruashvili left the government, Civil.ge reported that Khalvashi sold Rustavi 2 to Georgian Industrial Group (GIG), a company controlled by Bezhuashvili. This way, Rustavi 2 and Mze both became part of a holding company controlled by the brother of the foreign minister. The change may have been a coincidence, or simply another sign that Okruashvili, on whose behalf Khilvashi controlled Rustavi, had lost his influence and was stripped of Rustavi 2 (http://www.civil.ge/eng/article.php?id=14136)

5. Outside of Tbilisi, Imedi has been the most-watched network since mid-2003, according to polling.

6. Imedi TV never had such a show, while Channel One cancelled a similar program immediately after the revolution. However, Imedi closed a weekly live talk show in the winter of 2004, after the anchor and several participants challenged then Prosecutor General Irakli Okruashvili over some of the arrests and mistreatment of prisoners.

7. Khoperia quit Rustavi on July 7, 2006, after complaining on the air of "unacceptable" censorship. (http://www.civil.ge/eng/article.php?id=12983)

8. OSCE/ODIHR Election Observation Mission, Georgia Repeat Parliamentary Elections, Report Part II, Warsaw, June 22, 2004, p. 15.

9. OSCE/ODIHR Election Observation Mission, Georgia Repeat Parliamentary Elections, Report Part I, Warsaw, January 28, 2004, p. 13.

10. Interview by Irakly Areshidze, September 2004.

11. This incident was confirmed by sources at all three of the main private stations.

12. *Rezonansi*, February 24, 2005. Zurabishvili left the parliamentary majority on August 29, 2005, declaring that there was too much compliance among the National Movement parliamentarians vis-à-vis the executive branch. See http://www.rustavi2.com.ge/view.php?id=12033.

13. http://www.humanrights.ge/stat15.shtml. This comment was in reference to the live talk show Imedi cancelled in the winter of 2004.

14. Press conference by President George W. Bush and President Vladimir Putin, Constitution Hall, Bratislava Castle, Bratislava, Slovakia. At http://www.whitehouse.gov/news/releases/2005/02/20050224-9.html.

15. Conversation with Inga Dadiani, March 10, 2005.

16. Imedi Television, *Droeba*, April 3, 2005.

17. Imedi Television News, April 4, 2005.

18. Then again, if one follows Giga Bokeria's aforementioned understanding of freedom of speech, Patarkatsishvili choosing to remove a story from the airing in order to maintain a "good relationship" with the government does not constitute censorship at all.

19. Mze TV, *On the Edge of Choice*, July 1, 2005.

20. The Georgian media reported on April 29, 2006, on a major development in the Georgian news media that could dramatically increase press freedom. According to the agency Prime News, Rupert Murdoch's "News Corporation bought shareholdings of the Georgian Imedi TV, [according to] Giorgi Kvitashvili, press secretary of Badri Patarkatsishvili, founder of the TV company. Kvitashvili did not specify the exact volume of the purchase, but according to RTVI 30% of shares were sold." (http://eng.primenewsonline.com/?c=122&a=7785.) (RTVI is a Russian language Israeli satellite network owned by several Russian oligarchs of Jewish heritage.) Other news sources also reported on this development, including Imedi TV. By bringing Murdoch in as a partner, Patarkatsishvili secured the backing of probably the most powerful media corporation in the world, which has vast holdings in the United States, UK, Australia, and several other Western countries. For obvious reasons, it will become much more difficult for the Georgian government to put pressure on a TV network a third of which is owned by the News Corporation. (In November 2006, Imedi appointed an American Chief Executive who had previously worked for the News Corporation.) Even one free TV channel will have a huge opportunity to finally start reporting the full truth about government action (for the first time since the Rose Revolution), dramatically increasing the possibilities of positive democratic development. While a free media channel alone will be far from sufficient to make democracy possible again in Georgia, without such a station, a democratic possibility is unlikely to come about.

Chapter 14. Civil Society, Illusionary and Real

1. Alexis de Tocqueville, *Democracy in America*, trans. Harvey C. Mansfield and Delba Winthrop (Chicago: University of Chicago Press, 2000), 492.

2. This is a far from exhaustive list.

3. Daria Vaisman, "Tbilisi Dispatch: Agree to Disagree," *The New Republic Online*, May 10, 2005.

4. Ghia Nodia, *Civil Society Development in Georgia: Achievements and Challenges* (Tbilisi, Georgia: CIPDD, 2005). Unless otherwise noted, all references from this volume are on pages 6–8.

5. Owen Harries, "Suffer the Intellectuals," *The American Interest* 1, no. 1 (Autumn 2005): 80.

6. In my analysis, I am almost exclusively using Nodia's writings in Georgian or those published only in Georgia, because he seldom makes his real views known as openly and directly in writings published abroad.

7. Nodia, *Civil Society Development in Georgia*, 7.

8. Ibid., 8.

9. Ibid.

10. I worked actively with several of these business associations over the years and was one of the individuals making a point on their behalf to "civil society."

11. See, for example, Louis D. Hunt, "Civil Society and the Idea of a Commercial Republic," in Michael Schechter, ed., *The Revival of Civil Society: Global and Comparative Perspectives* (New York: St. Martin's, 1999). See also Louis D. Hunt, "Hegel's Institutionalist Liberalism: Political Economy and Civil Society in the Philosophy of Right," in Norman A. Graham and Folke Lindahl, eds., *The Politifcal Economy of Transition in Eurasia* (East Lansing, MI: Michigan State University Press, 2006).

12. Louis D. Hunt, "Hegel's Institutionalist Liberalism: Political Economy and Civil Society in the Philosophy of Right."

13. To restate, Nodia's definition of civil society is "those forms of social relations and activities that are *beyond* the spheres of family, business, and the State." Thus, even though business associations were included in the definitions, business as such was not.

14. Nodia, *Civil Society Development in Georgia*, 6.

15. Until the Rose Revolution, the only exceptions were about 200 businessmen owning successful companies, and several hundred corrupt government officials from both the Shevardnadze and Saakashvili periods. This list of corrupt officials who have enriched themselves through state funds has grown dramatically since November 2003.

16. Nodia, *Civil Society Development in Georgia*, 13.

17. Ibid., 8.

18. Ibid., 7.

19. Ibid.

20. Ibid., 8.

21. Ghia Nodia, "Is Georgia Threatened by Religious Fundamentalism?" *Church, Government and Religious Minorities in Georgia* (Tbilisi, Georgia: CIPDD, 2000). I quote from an English translation of this essay that I obtained from Ghia Nodia as a Microsoft Word document. For this reason, page numbers are not available.

22. Nodia, *Civil Society Development in Georgia*, 8.

23. Nodia, "Is Georgia Threatened by Religious Fundamentalism?" In the essay, Nodia also notes that "it is noteworthy that approximately 70 percent of students appeared to be among the supporters of fundamentalism, which hints at the growing prospects for this trend." In my view, this is further support for the claim I make below that young people are far more supportive of religion than their parents, and especially grandparents.

24. Ibid.

25. Ibid.

26. Zurab Kiknadze, "Discussion," in *Church, Government and Religious Minorities in Georgia* (Tbilisi, Georgia: CIPDD, 2000).

27. Examined in chapter 11.

28. Ghia Nodia, "How to End the Revolution," *24 Hours*, October 18, 2004.

29. In Georgian, the primary connotation of the remark "does not know" is that someone is ignorant or unaware of his needs, rather than conflicted between multiple directions or unsure.

30. David Losaberidze, Nodia's colleague at the Caucasus Institute, has offered a slight alternative on this law of life, writing that "there is no such thing as good and bad government. There exists a government you can stand and a government you cannot stand." *24 Hours*, September 3, 2005. Meanwhile, according to Irakli Shavishvili, a member of the NGO class who used to be an important player in the pro-independence movement in the 1980s, "In human history, there has never been, there is not now, and probably never will be in the future good government. One government may be better than the second, but good government does not exist." Irakli Shavishvili, interview in *Full Week*, September 5, 2005.

31. Some may argue that this is similar to the argument found in Book VII of Plato's *Republic*, and to views about democracy articulated by Aristotle. However, the ancient political philosophy of Plato and Aristotle was not shaped by the nihilistic vision that shapes Nodia's viewpoint, nor did Plato and Aristotle claim to be democrats or proponents of democracy, as Nodia does.

32. Though it is unclear who is to judge whether a sufficiently strong case was made. Presumably, the representatives of the NGO class.

33. Interview with Ramaz Sakvarelidze, *Full Week*, September 5, 2005.

34. Gaga Nizharadze, "Georgian Supra in Cultural Context," in *Georgian Supra and Civil Society* (Tbilisi, Georgia: CIPDD, 2000), 24.

35. Giorgi Margvelashvili, "Nechurta!—I am Georgian," in *Peace Times* (Tbilisi, Georgia: ICCN, 2001), 73–74.

36. Georgian Young Lawyers' Association (GYLA), for example, has been a strong watchdog in a number of areas. Indeed, I have cited their work to back up some of my claims in earlier chapters.

37. My analysis of the Higher Education Law is based heavily on informal discussion of this issue with a respected American academic who would prefer to remain anonymous.

38. The reform of the social-security, health-financing, and welfare systems could become one of Saakashvili's government's great successes. The late Tinatin Danelia of PSI was largely responsible for the Ministry of Health, Labor, and Social Policy accepting a very free-market approach to these issues. As an advisor to the ministry, she convinced the ministry to pursue legislation to provide for market-based solutions to pensions and health financing, and to create a means-tested welfare scheme. These ideas, which were originally developed by PSI—a think tank with which I have worked since its founding— have been endorsed by Lado Chipashvili, the minister of health, and received support from the president and the prime minister.

39. The disappearance of the Citizens Union of Georgia (CUG) and Revival Party after the revolution exemplifies this.

40. Ghia Nodia, "How to End the Revolution," *24 Hours*, October 18, 2004.

41. Interview with Inga Grigolia on Mze TV, November 2, 2003.

42. See, for example, Ghia Nodia, "Is Georgia Heading for a New Revolution?" *Radio Free Europe/Radio Liberty Caucasus Report* 8, no. 31 (September 10, 2005). In the article, Nodia examines the opposition, which he criticizes and characterizes as "weak, irresponsible, and immature." However, while Nodia devotes a great deal of time to discussing the standing of various opposition leaders (largely from the Republican Party, which is aligned with the NGO class), he makes no mention of the New Rights Party, the only party that has a representative group in Parliament and that overcame the 7 percent barrier in the March 2004 elections. This is quite typical of how Nodia treats the NRP.

43. In late August 2005, Usupashvili had a car accident in which two people died. While the accident was not his fault, given Georgian realities, this incident has damaged his ability to be the public face for his party. He has been often absent from the public scene since.

44. I was told this by the American head of one of the USAID contractor organizations in Georgia, who has asked to remain anonymous, given his employment.

45. Interview with *Venomously*, April 7, 2005. "I am selling all of these [firms]. . . . I have no political ambition. . . . The younger generation has come into power in Georgia. I am neither for, nor against them, that's all I can say."

46. www.civil.ge, April 20, 2005.

47. Rustavi 2 News, April 21, 2005.

48. Imedi TV News, April 21, 2005.

49. Rustavi 2 News, April 20, 2005.

50. In some respects, claims made against the Georgian Orthodox Church parallel claims made by European intellectuals against the Catholic Church under John Paul II and Benedict XVI, arguments that were so often heard in 2005 after John Paul's passing.

51. Recently a number of church leaders have joined the "reformist" camp, less because they agree with its positions and more because they wish to advance their own careers.

52. Remarks that are particularly poorly received by worshipers are similar to comments that came in April 2005 from Tea Tutberidze, a prominent civil-society activist who played an instrumental role in the Rose Revolution as head of the Kmara (Enough) Movement, who told Imedi TV in an interview that she "does not believe in God," but will be prepared to "stand in front of the Patriarch's Office and yell enough unless the Church reforms." (*Droeba*, Sunday, April 5, 2005).

Conclusion

1. I did not invent the term "closing society," but I am not certain to whom I should attribute it. Specifically in reference to Georgia, it grew out of extensive conversations with colleagues and round-table meetings about post–Rose Revolution events that I was part of in Tbilisi. A Lexis-Nexis search for this term yielded minimal results and no scholarly piece that could be cited. Meanwhile, a Google search for the term yielded many results

that refer to post–9/11 America as a "closing society," especially on a website called Open-Democracy.net. While there are a number of serious arguments against some of the domestic "anti-terror" policies of the U.S. government, it is hard to take seriously the view that political space is closing in what probably is the freest and most vibrant political environment in the world.

2. Editorial, *Wall Street Journal*, November 24, 2003.

3. Vladimir Socor, "Georgia's Elections and Aftermath: Chaotic Pluralism in a Weak State," *IASPS Policy Briefings: Geostrategic Perspectives on Eurasia*, no. 38, November 19, 2003.

4. In fairness to Saakashvili, he was not fully committed to the revolution until the very end, since his mind seemed to constantly move between a revolutionary perspective and something more moderate, probably because he was uncertain about the possibility of success.

5. Indeed, we know that only 26.6 percent of the voters actually supported Saakashvili's policies, as was evident from the November 2003 parliamentary election results.

6. Ghia Nodia, "Breaking the Mold of Powerlessness: The Meaning of Georgia's Latest Revolution," in *Enough!*, ed. Karumidze and Wertsch, 97.

7. One could argue that the Emancipation Proclamation was extraconstitutional. Without taking a position on either side of that debate, what matters most is that President Lincoln constitutionalized the end to slavery through constitutional amendments.

8. Herbert J. Storing, "The Case Against Civil Disobedience," in *Toward a More Perfect Union*, ed. Joseph M. Bessette (Washington: AEI Press, 1995), 237.

9. Ibid., 241.

10. The difference between the constitutional changes approved in Georgia and Ukraine in the aftermath of the revolutions is also noteworthy, as I discussed earlier.

11. I do not know Ukrainian politics suffiently well to comprehensively assess the impact of the Orange Revolution on the political, economic, and social challenges facing the country. My goal here is to merely assess Ukraine's constitutional order in the aftermath of the Orange Revolution, which is significantly more open, balanced, and responsive to the will of the people than the constitutional order that arose in Georgia after the Rose Revolution.

12. According to a nation-wide poll conducted by GORBI April 2005 Saakashvili's approval ratings had fallen to below 40 percent.

13. Richard Carlson, "Georgia on His Mind—George Soros's Potemkin Revolution," *Weekly Standard*, May 24, 2004.

14. Ibid.

15. These are remarks from a U.S. official who worked at the embassy at the time.

16. President Bush's willingness to admit mistakes and take responsibility for the problems associated with the federal government's response to Hurricane Katrina is unfortunately an exception that proves the rule.

17. George W. Bush, Second Inaugural Address, http://www.whitehouse.gov/news/releases/2005/01/20050120-1.html.

18. Engaging in a detailed argument on behalf of the Bush national-security vision is beyond

the purview of this work. For a comprehensive case on behalf of democracy as a core element of American foreign policy, see Charles Krauthammer, "Democratic Realism: An American Foreign Policy for a Unipolar World," the American Enterprise Institute's 2004 Irving Kristol Lecture, February 2004, http://www.aei.org/publications/pubID .19912,filter.all/pub_detail.asp.

19. For a comprehensive argument examining the similarities between the Bush and the Truman administrations, see David Gelemter, "Truman Beats Dewey! Again!!" *Weekly Standard*, November 15, 2004.

Bibliography

Published Works

Baker, Peter. "Pressure Mounts on Georgian Leader." *Washington Post*, November 11, 2003, 14A.

Brzezinski, Zbigniew. "The Premature Partnership." *Foreign Affairs* 73 (March–April 1994).

Bush, George W. Second Inaugural Address. Washington, D.C., January 20, 2005. Http://www.whitehouse.gov/news/releases/2005/01/20050120–1.html.

Carlson, Richard. "Georgia on His Mind—George Soros's Potemkin Revolution." *Weekly Standard*, May 24, 2004.

Chikhladze, Giga, and Irakli Chikhladze. "The Rose Revolution: A Chronicle." In *Enough! The Rose Revolution in the Republic of Georgia 2003*, ed. Zurab Karumindze and James V. Wertsch. New York: Nova Science Publishers, Inc., 2005.

Chivers, C. J. "With Bush Coming, Georgia Spruces Up," *New York Times*, May 7, 2005.

Clinton, Bill. *My Life*. New York: Vintage Books, 2005.

de Tocqueville, Alexis. *Democracy in America*. Translated by Harvey C. Mansfield and Delba Winthrop. Chicago: University of Chicago Press, 2000.

Ekedahl, Carolyn McGiffert, and Melvin A. Goodman. *The Wars of Eduard Shevardnadze*. University Park: University of Pennsylvania Press, 1997.

Fairbanks, Charles H. "Georgia's Rose Revolution." *Journal of Deomcracy* (April 2004).

"Focus Group Analysis of Local Democracy in Georgia." Washington, D.C.: National Democratic Institute, March 2001.

Former Political Prisoners for Human Rights. *Human Rights in Post-Revolutionary Georgia*. Tbilisi, 2004.

Gaga Nizharadze. "Georgian Supra in Cultural Context." In *Georgian Supra and Civil Society*. Tbilisi, Georgia: CIPDD, 2000.

Georgian Young Lawyers' Association (GYLA). *Georgian Government under a Very Hot Sun*, August 2005, 14–15.

Harries, Owen. "Suffer the Intellectuals." *The American Interest* 1, no.1 (Autumn 2005).

Hunt, Louis D. "Civil Society and the Idea of a Commercial Republic." In *The Revival of Civil Society: Global and Comparative Perspectives*, ed. Michael Schechter. New York: St. Martin's, 1999.

Hunt, Louis D. "Hegel's Institutionalist Liberalism: Political Economy and Civil Society in the Philosophy of Right." In *The Politifcal Economy of Transition in Eurasia*, ed. Norman A. Graham and Folke Lindahl. East Lansing, Mich.: Michigan State University Press, 2006.

Kaplan, Laurence, and William Kristol. *The War over Iraq: Saddam's Tyranny and America's Mission*. San Francisco: Encounter Books, 2003.

Karumidze, Zurab, and James V. Wertsch, eds. Interview with James A. Baker by James V. Wertsch. In *Enough! The Rose Revolution in the Republic of Georgia 2003*, p. 82. New York: Nova Science Publishers, Inc., 2005.

Kiknadze, Zurab. "Discussion." In *Church, Government and Religious Minorities in Georgia*, ed. Ghia Nodia. Tbilisi: CIPDD, 2000.

King, Charles. "A Rose Among Thorns: Georgia Makes Good," *Foreign Affairs* (March–April 2004).

Krauthammer, Charles. "Democratic Realism: An American Foreign Policy for a Unipolar World." The American Enterprise Institute's 2004 Irving Kristol Lecture, February 2004. http://www.aei.org/publications/pubID.19912,filter.all/pub_detail.asp.

Levitsky, Steven. "The Rise of Competitive Authoritarianism." *Journal of Democracy* 13, no. 2 (April 2002).

Madison, James. "Federalist Paper No. 51." In *The Federalist Papers*, ed. Clinton Rossiter. New York: A Mentor Book, 1961.

Margvelashvili, Giorgi. "Nechurta!—I am Georgian." In *Peace Times*. Tbilisi: ICCN, 2001.

Nodia, Ghia. "Breaking the Mold of Powerlessness: The Meaning of Georgia's Latest Revolution." In *Enough! The Rose Revolution in the Republic of Georgia 2003*, ed. Zurab Karumindze and James V. Wertsch. New York: Nova Science Publishers, Inc., 2005.

Nodia, Ghia. *Civil Society Development in Georgia: Achievements and Challenges*. Tbilisi: CIPDD, 2005.

Nodia, Ghia. "How to End the Revolution." *24 Hours*, October 18, 2004.

Nodia, Ghia. "Is Georgia Threatened by Religious Fundamentalism?" In *Church, Government and Religious Minorities in Georgia*, ed. Ghia Nodia. Tbilisi: CIPDD, 2000.

OSCE/ODIHR Election Observation Mission, *Georgia Repeat Parliamentary Elections*, Report Part 1. Warsaw, January 28, 2004, p. 13.

OSCE/ODIHR Election Observation Mission, *Georgia Repeat Parliamentary Elections*, Report Part 2. Warsaw, June 22, 2004.

Parsons, Rob. "Unrest Rises in Georgia." *Sunday Herald*, November 14, 2003. http://www.sundayherald.com/38065.

"Presidential Election in Georgia." U.S. Department of State press statement, Washington, D.C., November 21, 2003.

Radio Free Europe/Radio Liberty Caucasus Report. Vol. 15, no. 34 (October 11, 2004).

"Russian and Eurasian Program Issue Brief." Vol. 2, No. 4, Carnegie Endowment for International Peace, Washington, D.C., July 20, 2000, based on a lecture delivered by Zhvania on July 19, 2002. www.carnegieendowment.orgpublications/index.cfm? fa=view&id=403.

Saakashvili, Mikheil. State of the Nation address, February 10, 2005.

Sestanovitch, Stephen. "A Tale of Two Post-Soviet Presidents." *Wall Street Journal*, July 20, 2004.

Socor, Vladimir. "Georgia's Elections and Aftermath: Chaotic Pluralism in a Weak State." *IASPS Policy Briefings: Geostrategic Perspectives on Eurasia*. No. 38 (November 19, 2003).

USAID, Request for Applications (RFA) No. 114-02-018. *Citizens Advocate! Program for Georgia*, February 8, 2002.

Vaisman, Daria. "Tbilisi Dispatch: Agree to Disagree." *The New Republic Online*, May 10, 2005.

Wood, Nick. "The Insider." *Guardian*, April 18, 2005.

Zarakhovich, Yuri. "Future Favors the Brave: Shevardnadze Survives Another Assassination Attempt, But How Long Can His Luck Hold?" *Time* 146, no. 11 (September 11, 1995).

Interviews Conducted by and Conversations with the Author

Below is a selected list of sources that were used for in my research. Many of these individuals were formally interviewed by me or a member of my research team. In some cases, discussions of issues were informal, but I drew on the information that they provided in my writing.

- Merab Adeishvili, former Minister of Transport and Communications (not on record)
- David Akubardia, Director and Owner, TV company Kavkasia
- Giorgi Arveladze, General Secretary, National Movement; Member of Parliament; in 2006 appointed Minister of Economics (not on record)
- Fady Asly, Chairman, American Chamber of Commerce, Georgia
- Gia Bazgadze, Partner, Earnest & Young CIS
- Kakha Bendukidze, Minister of State for Economic Reform
- Bishop Abraam, Georgian Orthodox Church
- Bishop Iob, Georgian Orthodox Church
- Bishop Zenon, Georgian Orthodox Church
- Zviad Bokuchava, People United for Traditional Values
- Elisabeth Brocking, US Embassy
- Carolyn Clark Campbell, Georgia Office Director, ABA/CEELI (not on record)

- Giorgi Chakhnashvili, former member, Central Election Commission
- Lado Chanturia, former Chairman, Supreme Court of Georgia
- Pikria Chikhradze, Member of Parliament, New Rights Party
- Paata Chakhnshvili, Pollster
- Matt Christ, US Embassy
- Inga Dadjani, former News Director, Mze TV (not on record)
- Amy Denman, Executive Director, American Chamber of Commerce, Georgia (not on record)
- Anna Dolidze, Acting Chairman, Georgian Young Lawyers Association
- Luba Eliashvili, former News Director, Iberia TV
- Maka Ekizashvili, Director of Investment Relations, Bank of Georgia (not on record)
- Charles Fairbanks, School for Advanced International Studies (SAIS), Johns Hopkins University
- David Gamkrelidze, Chairman, New Rights Party; Member of Parliament
- Djemal Inaishvili, Chairman, Georgian Chamber of Commerce and Industry
- Giorgi Isakadze, Executive Director, Georgian Federation of Businessmen
- Gia Jandieri, Vice President, New Economic School
- Charita Jashi, President, Gender for Economic and Political Development
- Gia Jorjoliani, Professor, Tbilisi State University
- Tamar Jvania, Chair, International Institute for Democracy and Fair Elections
- Nana Kakabadze, President, Former Political Prisoners for Human Rights
- Alto Kakhniashvili, Political Scientist
- George Kapanadze, Editor in Chief, Newspaper *Georgian Times*
- Ivliane Khaindrava, Member of Parliament, Republican Party
- Mamuka Khazaradze, Chairman, TBC Group (not on record)
- Tinatin Khidasheli, Chairman, Georgian Young Lawyers Association
- Dimitry Khitoshvili, former Chairman, Central Election Commission (CEC) (during March 2004 elections), and later, Chairman, National Communication/Broadcasting Commission
- Vakhtang Khmaladze, former Member of Parliament (1992-2004) (opposition)
- Zakaria Kutsnashvili, Political Scientist, former pro-Shevardnadze Member of Parliament
- Mark Lenzi, Georgia Office Director, IRI
- Gogi Loladze, Chairman, Georgian Stock Exchange
- Georgia Margvelashvili, Rector, Georgian Institute of Public Affairs
- Mariam Megvinet-Ukhutsesi, EBRD Georgia
- Nodar Meladze, News Producer, Channel One Television
- Marina Muskelishvili, Political Scientist; Director, Center for Social Studies
- Vano Nakaidze, Chairman, GeorgianOil (Saknavtobi)
- Ucha Nanuashvili, Executive Director, Human Rights Information & Documentation Center
- NATO Defense Policy Experts (visited Georgia in 2004 and 2005)

- David Natroshvili, Ministry of Economics
- Gela Nikolaishvili, Former Political Prisoners for Human Rights
- Maia Nikolaishvili, Forensics Expert
- Gia Nodia, Chairman, Caucasian Institute for Peace, Democracy and Development
- Niko Orvelashvili, Economist, President, Georgian Economic Development
- Levan Ramishvili, Liberty Institute
- Alex Rondeli, Georgian Foundation for Strategic and International Studies
- Levan Sebiskveradze, Newspaper *Axali Versia*
- David Tarkhan-Mouravi, Owner and President, Amaltea LTD
- Giorgi Tavadze, President, GMT Group
- Elene Tevdoradze, Chairman, Parliament's Committee on Human Rights and Rule of Law; National Movement
- Tamar Tsagareishvili, former News Anchor and Reporter, Channel One Television
- Tea Tutberidze, Chief Organizer, Kmara Movement; Liberty Institute
- Daniel Twining, former foreign policy advisor, Senator John McCain (not on record)
- David Usupashvili, Law Expert, IRIS Georgia, and later, Chairman, The Republican Party
- Natia Zambaxidze, Anchor and report, Rustavi 2 Television

At the same time, I spoke with over three dozen news reporters, producers, and anchors at all of Georgia's leading television stations (Imedi, Mze, Rustavi, State Channel One/Public Television). These individuals are not named in order to protect their careers and job prospects.

My research team made numerous attempts to interview Giga Bokeria and Maia Nadiradze, who are two leading National Movement leaders in Parliament in addition to Arveladze, to no avail.

I also drew on additional sources, with whom I had conversations before I began the process of writing this book. Some of these individuals include:

- Catholicos Patriarch Ilia II, Georgian Orthodox Church
- Zeyno Baran, Nixon Center
- Giga Bokeria, Member of Parliament, Majority Leader
- Matthew J. Bryza, Director, Caucasus and Central Asia, National Security Council
- Gia Chanturia, former President, Georgian International Oil Corporation (GIOC)
- Vano Chkhartishvili, Co-Owner, Mze TV
- Anton Ingorokva, Banker
- Bruce Jackson, President, US Committee for NATO
- Tedo Japaridze, former Ambassador of Georgia to the US
- Ed Johnson, General Director, British Petroleum Georgia
- Maia Nadiradze, Member of Parliament, Majority Leader
- Merab Pachulia, Pollster
- Patricia Shearing, former Budgetary Advisor, Ministry of Defense of Georgia
- Gocha Tskitishvili, Pollster

Newspaper and TV Interviews and Appearances, and Other Correspondence

- Matthew J. Bryza and David Gamkrelidze correspondence, November 19–21, 2006
- Senator John McCain to President Eduard Shevardnadze, letter, June 6, 2003.
- Interview with Nick Rurua, in *Rezonansi*, September 9, 2004.
- Interview with Ramaz Sakvarelidze, *Full Week*, September 5, 2005.
- Interview with Bidzina Ivanishvili in *Venomously*, April 7, 2005.
- Interview with Irakli Shavishvili in *Full Week*, September 5, 2005.
- Interview by an American colleague with Kakha Targamadze, August 2003.
- David Usupashvili and Devi Khechinashvili, discussion, March 2004.
- Numerous Georgian TV news reports (Rustavi 2, Imedi TV, Mze TV, Channel One TV)

Index